D0896920

POMPEII

DATE DUE

APR 2 2 1998	
JUN 0 9 1998	
DEC 0 7 1998	
APR ~~· 8~~ 1	
OCT 2 5 2005	
APR 2 0 2005	

POMPEII

An Architectural History

L. Richardson, jr

The Johns Hopkins University Press

BALTIMORE AND LONDON

© 1988 The Johns Hopkins University Press
All rights reserved
Printed in the United States of America on acid-free paper

Johns Hopkins Paperbacks edition, 1997
06 05 04 03 02 01 00 99 98 97   5 4 3 2 1

The Johns Hopkins University Press
2715 North Charles Street
Baltimore, Maryland 21218-4319
The Johns Hopkins Press Ltd., London

LIBRARY OF CONGRESS CATALOGING-IN-PUBLICATION DATA

Richardson, Lawrence.
  Pompeii : an architectural history.

  Bibliography: p.
  Includes index.
    1. Architecture—Italy—Pompeii (Ancient City)
2. Pompeii (Ancient City)—Buildings, structures, etc.
I. Title.
NA327.P6R53   1988   722´.7´09377   87-17299
ISBN 0-8018-3533- x (alk. paper)

ISBN 0-8018-5661-2 (pbk.)

CONTENTS

ILLUSTRATIONS

PREFACE

This book is the product of forty years of thinking about Pompeii. Its general shape was decided on, and the actual composition begun, in 1972–73, when I was able to spend a year in Italy, most of it in or near the excavations of Pompeii. It has advanced irregularly since then. The body of the manuscript was completed in 1979–81, when again I was in Italy for an extended stay. Final checking of the descriptions and details was accomplished in the summer of 1985.

Over the years my work has been supported by fellowships granted by the John Simon Guggenheim Memorial Foundation, the American Council of Learned Societies, and the National Endowment for the Humanities. Grants in aid for assistance in the typing of the manuscript and the checking of notes have been provided by the Research Council of Duke University. For this help I am profoundly grateful.

I have also been helped in ways too numerous to count by the staffs of the excavations of Pompeii and the other Campanian cities, the Museo Nazionale Archeologico in Naples, and the library of the American Academy in Rome. I have discussed problems with, and drawn on the wisdom and experience of, a great many friends and colleagues on both sides of the Atlantic. To all of these I owe a debt that goes beyond definition, and to all I offer my heartfelt thanks.

In the book that follows the code of the excavations of Pompeii is used for the identification of buildings. The upper-case Roman numeral represents the regio of the city, one of nine, eight being disposed in a ring around the central ninth. The lower-case Roman numeral identifies the city block within the regio, and the Arabic numeral the street door, or doors, of the building within its block. The names of the buildings in Latin are the names found on the comprehensive map of Pompeii, first published in the *Corpus Inscriptionum Latinarum*, volume 4, supplement 2 (1909), from which all subsequent maps of any complexity derive. This in turn is based on a master survey begun by Giacomo Tascone under Giuseppe Fiorelli a half-century earlier. The names in Italian, especially those of houses, are the names by which these buildings are most commonly known. Many of them are arbitrary, but they are still the best means of keeping the buildings distinct. A concordance of the names and code numbers follows the glossary. According to the convention observed by almost all Pompeianists, it is assumed that the main streets of the city, the Via di Nola and the Via dell'Abbondanza, are oriented east and west and that buildings square with the cardinal points of the compass. In fact, of course, the axis of the city lies rather southwest/northeast.

INTRODUCTION

Pompeii is the oldest archaeological site still under more or less continuous excavation, and discoveries there produce new and startling information about its ancient life at least every few years. We have learned to look to it more than to any other source for illumination of the world of the great writers of classical Latin. Cicero had a Pompeianum, and Seneca probably owned property there also; Martial was familiar with the city, and it is very likely that there was an imperial estate in the near neighborhood. It was not a fashionable resort like Baiae, but it was a prosperous seaport with thriving agriculture and fishing, as well as a complement of small industries, to bolster its economy. It always had its aristocracy, some members of which made a name for themselves in Rome, and the pride its inhabitants took in their city emerges in many of the inscriptions with which they adorned and defaced the walls along the busier streets. It is no wonder that for the interpretation of puzzling details of life in Petronius and Juvenal we look first to the evidence of Pompeii. It is so rich that we are apt to be more surprised when it does not offer help than when it does. And over the years it has been called upon for information of every sort imaginable.

It is therefore surprising that one of its greatest funds of information should continue to be poorly appreciated, neglected, and largely misunderstood. It should be one of the keystones in the architectural history of antiquity. Our richest concentration of municipal buildings, of houses and villas of every size and representative of every income, and of tombs, it is still written off as atypical, provincial, or too hybrid a combination of Greek and Roman elements to be of importance in the history of architecture, either Greek or Roman. If its amphitheatre is repeatedly cited in handbooks, it is because it is the oldest amphitheatre known and an oddity. Its houses are included as examples of an older and more expansive approach to domestic architecture than one would have been able to find in Rome after the time of Augustus and very likely were a peculiarly Campanian sort of house from their earliest beginnings. Among its public buildings only the basilica regularly figures, and that is largely because of its early date and puzzling upper storey. Its temples, the Aedificium Eumachiae and the macellum, the baths and gymnasia, are rarely mentioned and almost never discussed, the fortifications or water system still less. Yet there is abundant evidence that Pompeii not only was in constant contact with Rome and responsive to Roman changes in style and developments in engineering and the uses of space but also received ships and news from all over the Mediterranean world and had tentacles in Alexandria and the East as well as in Spain and Africa.

The explanation of this neglect and general misunderstanding of so rich a resource lies in part in the extraordinary circumstances of the city's destruction and in part in a serious distortion of the history of the city in antiquity. Because Pompeii was overwhelmed by the eruption of Vesuvius on the twenty-fourth and twenty-fifth of August A.D. 79, in which drifts of lapilli and ash buried everything up to the second storey, the lower parts of buildings, and much that they contained, have survived the centuries in between in an extraordinary state of preservation. Wall paintings appear almost as fresh as when they were painted; tables set for meals, cupboards full of tableware, shops with their tools and their stock, if it was not perishable, even loaves of bread carbonized in the ovens, have come down to us miraculously preserved. Even when a perishable body has decayed and disappeared, the volcanic debris enclosing it has often formed a matrix that, with meticulous care on the part of the excavators, can be opened and filled with plaster to make an accurate cast. By this process have been recovered the forms of wooden objects and fittings, things as complicated as a high-wheeled farm cart and as intricate as inlaid furniture, not to speak of numerous victims of the tragedy, animal as well as human, some contorted in agony, others seemingly in dignified composure. In these circumstances it has seemed imperative to recover as much as possible while disturbing what was recovered as little as possible, to try to recapture the moment of destruction as completely as possible and to preserve it for study and for posterity. It has seemed unwise to probe under floors and pavements of the city of A.D. 79 in the hope of discovering evidence of earlier times and buildings, lest we destroy something of great value in pursuit of a Fata Morgana. Consequently, while at other sites stratigraphic excavation is not only regular procedure but pursued with great enthusiasm and brilliant results, so that whole millennia of life on a site lie revealed in successive strata, at Pompeii practically no stratigraphic excavation at all was undertaken until

Amedeo Maiuri began a series of explorations, first in the Casa del Chirurgo in 1926, then in the basilica in 1929–30 and in the Thermae Stabianae and the Aedes Apollinis in 1931, and finally at a series of points in and around the forum from 1935 to 1941, with a return to further work in the basilica in 1950–51. These excavations shed brilliant new light on the history of the buildings in which they were conducted. The Temple of Jupiter (Capitolium) at the north end of the forum emerged as having had originally a very different and original design, and the series of great buildings along the east side of the forum were revealed as successors to a line of unpretentious shops. But the excavations had to be strictly limited to soundings and trenches so as not to destroy or damage the buildings of the last period, and much that Maiuri found he was unable to explain without enlarging his area beyond what was permissible. Consequently, reconstruction of any considerable part of the city that preceded the one we see today proved impossible. Since then, further stratigraphic explorations have been conducted with various aims in mind at a variety of points scattered all over the site, but nothing very much has ever come of them. The work has not been coordinated, and often the excavators have been in complete ignorance of the trenches and the discoveries of their predecessors; the result has been at best disappointing, at worst baffling confusion. Pre-Roman Pompeii continues to be elusive.

Actually there is good reason for this. If we read the historical record correctly, down to the First Punic War Pompeii was not much of a place, and even down to the end of the third century B.C. its architectural legacy would have been unimpressive. We have been misled by the splendid remains of the archaic Doric temple in the Forum Triangulare and the archaic material from the precinct of the Aedes Apollinis into supposing that there was a Greek or Greco-Etruscan city here in the sixth century that then underwent metamorphosis into a Samnite metropolis, that somewhere beneath the surface of Pompeii there lurked a sister city to Paestum on a somewhat smaller scale. In fact, there was nothing of the sort, and what turned up in the trenches of the stratigraphers repeatedly bore this out. But the trenches were always too limited in their sample to be used as evidence for the whole site. More recently, however, two important excavations have confirmed the thesis that no earlier city lies under the Pompeii that we see today. In the early years of the present decade the British archaeologist Paul Arthur supervised the excavation of a deep trench for the laying of electric cable from the offices of the Direzione degli Scavi on the Via del Foro to the edge of the site, a trench running down the whole length of the forum, along the precinct of Apollo, along the Via Marina, and out through the precinct of Venus.

The archaeological evidence of every sort recovered in the course of this operation was scrupulously saved and meticulously tested and analyzed (P. Arthur, "Problems of the Urbanization of Pompeii," *Antiquaries Journal* 66 [1986] 29–44). It showed that there was no monumental construction of early date under the area of the forum; that the sacrifices offered in the temples had been poor, for the most part only small animals, down to a late date; and that the pottery recovered indicated that down to the third century Pompeii was a poor place and sparsely populated. A little earlier, from 1976 to 1979, excavations by the Istituto di Archeologia of the Università degli Studi di Milano under the direction of Maria Bonghi Iovino were carried out in regio VI, block v, doors 17–20. Here, in the Casa della Colonna Etrusca, where an unfluted Doric column of tufa with extraordinarily strong entasis and an apparently archaic capital had been built into a wall, it seemed likely that substantial remains of early buildings might be discovered. The location was not far from the forum, in the northwest quarter of the city, where traces of a city plan older than that of the Roman city were believed to remain. And in the last period the area was occupied by housing of poor architecture and insignificant decorations. An extensive series of trenches and soundings was carried down to hardpan with essentially negative results. Although material dating from the last quarter of the seventh century through to the early fifth century was found in some quantity and in an apparently continuous stratum otherwise marked by abundant traces of burning, no remains of architecture of any sort could be associated with it (M. Bonghi Iovino, *Ricerche a Pompei* 1 [Rome 1984] 357–71). The evidence suggests that the area was a beech grove down to the fifth century and that the column was a votive column, standing in isolation, of uncertain date. The earliest architectural remains in the area are of the Hellenistic period and recognizable as a small house with a traverse atrium of the type discussed in appendix II.

We now know that as a city Pompeii grew and blossomed with phenomenal rapidity in the third century. Down to the time of the First Punic War it was little more than a large village, a marketplace alongside an important sanctuary surrounded by farms clustered along winding lanes with fields adjacent or nearby. The lanes connected centres of activity on the site, and roads ran off along the coast and up the Sarno Valley to connect Pompeii with other settlements. The Samnites who had taken over the site at the end of the fifth century were not builders; Samnium is famous for having been a territory in which there were very few cities, the people preferring to live in small hamlets and townships. And while it may be presumed that those who had migrated to the coastal plain of Campania had taken on at least some color of the civilization they dispossessed in the process, it did not go so far as to incline them to organize urban commonwealths. Pompeii as a village would have been more to their liking than Pompeii as a port, with its potential for far-flung commerce.

But the First Punic War changed that. The desperate need of the Romans for ships to fight that war and the rich natural resources of southern Campania, together with ideal conditions for shipyards along the Sarno River, must have drawn people and money to Pompeii. Shipbuilding must have boomed throughout that war, and at its end Pompeii found itself with a population several times the size of its prewar population and a new prosperity. Rome was reaching out, flexing its muscles, and looking to new things, and Pompeii went along with Rome in thinking big. Probably most of the new population was Samnite stock drawn out of the mountainous hinterland, but by this time it was a population that was urban- and civic-minded, perhaps because of the experience of the long war. The walls of Pompeii, an extended circuit that shows a curious combination of simplicity and sophistication, seem to belong to the period between the first and second Punic wars, the years 241–218 B.C.

Before the Pompeians could enjoy the prosperity the change in their economy had brought, they had to endure the long, hard years of the Hannibalic War. But throughout these years Pompeii remained faithful to Rome, and as soon as the war was over the Pompeians launched on a building program that was to last for the best part of a century. This was the golden age of Pompeii. Populous and prosperous, it became one of the great cities of Italy. Its sea traffic gave it vital ties to the other great cities of the Mediterranean, east as well as west, and made it the export/import hub for part of central Italy. Its agriculture, especially viticulture and winemaking, burgeoned under the warm Campanian sun and with improved commerce. Its fisheries and small special industries expanded with the economic boom. And together with this impetus came civic pride and private ostentation as well as the availability of luxuries and a general improvement in the quality of life. The second century was a time of optimism and rapid development for Pompeii, and this is reflected in the architecture and planning. Handsome mansions rose to line the more important streets; luxurious bath complexes catered to self-indulgence; and elegant temples and a splendidly innovative basilica bear witness to a continuing interest in whatever was new and stylish. It is small wonder that in the Social War Pompeii should have chosen to side with the Samnites and their allies and should have been proud of the role it played in that war, despite its bitter consequences.

The humiliation of Samnite Pompeii in the years after the Social War is more a matter of inference than of record. Certain old family names disappear, and the more active and important Samnite leaders were probably proscribed. The real humiliation was the settlement of a veteran colony in Pompeii about 80 B.C., with a reform of the constitution to make it conform with that of other colonies and the disenfranchisement of all the old aristocracy. But the Roman colonists brought new wealth with them, some of it destined to benefit the city significantly, and they brought new ideas about architecture, both public and private. If the Theatrum Tectum has some awkwardnesses in its arrangements for moving the spectators in and out, its trussed roof, unsupported by columns for its whole span, was a brilliant accomplishment in engineering. The Temple of Jupiter was a singularly successful design that gave the forum dramatic focus as well as new meaning. Such houses as the Casa delle Nozze d'Argento, with its Rhodian portico on the peristyle, its stately tetrastyle oecus, its elegantly appointed bath suite, and its splendid decorations, pointed the way to new refinements in domestic architecture. And about the middle of the first century spacious villas first began to appear, villas out from the city, set among vineyards and orchards, but planned as places of luxury and pleasure, set to command expansive views over mountains and sea, framed by gardens and opening to the landscape with porticoes and windows. The years 80–30 B.C. were the silver age of Pompeian architecture.

Toward the end of the republican period one sees a decline in Pompeii that continued into the early years of the principate. New houses are rare, and those there are appear unpretentious and utilitarian, often a patchwork of parts of older houses or else built almost without out a design. Perhaps the civil wars of the forties took a heavy toll of the young leaders of Pompeii, as they did of those of Rome itself, and the domination of the sea by Sextus Pompey may have cut deeply into the sea trade of Pompeii. Be that as it may, the city finally got an aqueduct, probably in the twenties, thanks to Agrippa and the construction of the Portus Iulius beyond Baiae, and a little later things took a turn for the better. The selection of the island of Capri as an imperial retreat and preserve may also have had something to do with it. New temples to the Genius Augusti and Fortuna Augusta were built by public benefactors; the spacious and stylish Aedificium Eumachiae rose to balance the basilica on the opposite side of the forum; the vast Palestra Grande was created adjacent to the amphitheatre; and the venerable Theatrum Maius was overhauled and given a new stage building. Although most of these works were accomplished on individual initiative, it seems clear that there was at this time a great need for new public buildings on a scale that suggests that the city was again growing and enjoying a healthy and expanding economy. This new surge of activity continues beyond the Augustan period with only slightly diminished vigor. The macellum may be of Tiberian date, and the rebuilding of the Temple of Venus in marble, undertaken about this time, was on so magnificent a scale that work was still in full swing when the earthquake of A.D. 62 struck. Scarcely a public building in the city does not show alteration or redecoration in the Julio-Claudian years, much of it paid for by freedmen and their descendants, who appear increasingly in control of great capital wealth, though a comforting share was still the responsibility of such representatives of old families as Marcus Holconius Rufus. But in contrast to this, private housing in this period is small in quantity and disappointing in quality. Probably that is in large part because private builders now preferred to expend their efforts on villas out beyond the city, where there was abundant space and their fields and vineyards were adjacent, of which only the splendid suburban Villa di Cicerone and the Villa di Agrippa Postumo at Boscotrecase have come to light so far. Still it is surprising that there are so few Third Style houses, when there is so much public building.

The earthquake of A.D. 62 was a cataclysm. We see its havoc all over the city—in the mountains of debris, in the buildings cleared of fallen masonry but still unrepaired when the eruption came seventeen years later, in the buildings hurriedly put back in working shape because they were vitally necessary but could not be more than thrown together. Most of all we see it in the houses, some of them surrendered to squatters and the interests of small industry, some left largely shattered wrecks, few, if any, with rebuilding completed in 79. The death toll must have been appalling. The toll in property damage must have ruined many. The forum was a shambles; the aqueduct was out of commission. Probably not a house was habitable.

But the Pompeians who survived rose to the occasion. Thereafter they were determined to build a new Pompeii far more splendid than the one they had lost. With this goal, they laid out a master plan for the reconstruction and a schedule of priorities. First the debris had to be cleared away and the vital necessities provided, the aqueduct repaired and the food supply organized, buildings patched and shored up and parts of buildings that were not too badly damaged made serviceable, even if not always for their original purposes. Then they turned to executing a grand scheme for the reconstruction of the forum and the Temple of Venus. The forum was to be magnificent. Several buildings that had been the pride of the city were to be restored more or less to their original design, with here and there a touch of improvement. The Temple of the Genius Augusti was one, the Aedificium Eumachiae another. The venerable Temple of Apollo was apparently among the buildings that had suffered least, but it was now considered antiquated and drab, so its fabric was repaired and given a heavy sheath of stucco throughout, its architectural decoration reshaped to the new taste and painted in bright colors. Among the completely, or almost completely, new buildings added to enhance the elegance of the square were a new curia and housing for the municipal government at the south end and the great shell of ambitious engineering known as the Sacellum Larum Publicorum. But more important was a new colonnade of white limestone in two storeys that was to run the whole length of the west side of the forum, pulling the whole together visually and providing place for the spectators at municipal ceremonies. This and the program of statuary for which bases were installed around the forum were to change its appearance radically and bring it into line with the new architecture of the capital.

Moreover, the Temple of Venus was to be rebuilt and framed on three sides with magnificent Corinthian colonnades in two storeys; a grand new bath complex of the latest design in thermal engineering was to be added to the public amenities; and the amphitheatre was to be refurbished with a new superstructure. There were probably important projects for the port and the road system as well. But it is clear that the Capitolium and the basilica on the forum were left in ruin for the time being, the macellum and Palestra Grande patched up in a form that was intended to be only temporary, and the Villa Imperiale at Porta Marina simply abandoned. We cannot recover the master plan for the new city in its entirety, but we can see its outline.

At the same time, work on private houses and villas was going forward as best it could. For some this meant extensive rebuilding, sometimes almost a whole new house. For more it was a question of fixing up a part, sometimes only a few rooms, enough to make do, to keep life alive and business functioning until labor could be drawn off from more important projects than housing. And for many it was entirely makeshift, squalid shelter and the conversion of the damaged remains of once fine houses into tenements, factories, and workshops. Side by side with fine new housing of advanced and inventive architecture brilliantly decorated we see contrasting poverty and deprivation. At the time of the eruption of Vesuvius in A.D. 79 Pompeii was a patchwork of the newest in architectural forms and engineering interwoven with layers, often ruined, of past grandeur and juxtaposed with the ramshackle domestic arrangements of those less well-off, poor but determined to overcome an almost unbelievable catastrophe.

This book attempts to tell the story of Pompeii through its buildings. More than that, it attempts to put Pompeii into its proper place in the history of Roman architecture, to rescue it from being a curiosity, a provincial town of small importance where the architecture was the creation of local contractors and autodidacts, and to see it as a place of real importance with a sound economy and a citizenry that had strong cosmopolitan elements, people who got to Rome, and to Athens, Antioch, and Alexandria as well, and were interested in, and alert to, what was going on in art and architecture. After introductory chapters on geography and general considerations, it is divided into four sections, according to the four major building periods of the city. For each period there is a section on public buildings, arranged according to location and type of building; one on private buildings; and one on tombs. Each building is described and placed according to its relative date and importance in the development of that particular architectural form. The work is intended for everyone seriously interested in Pompeii and in Roman architecture, and while it assumes a basic knowledge of architectural forms and building techniques, it is not highly technical and should give any well-informed layman little difficulty.

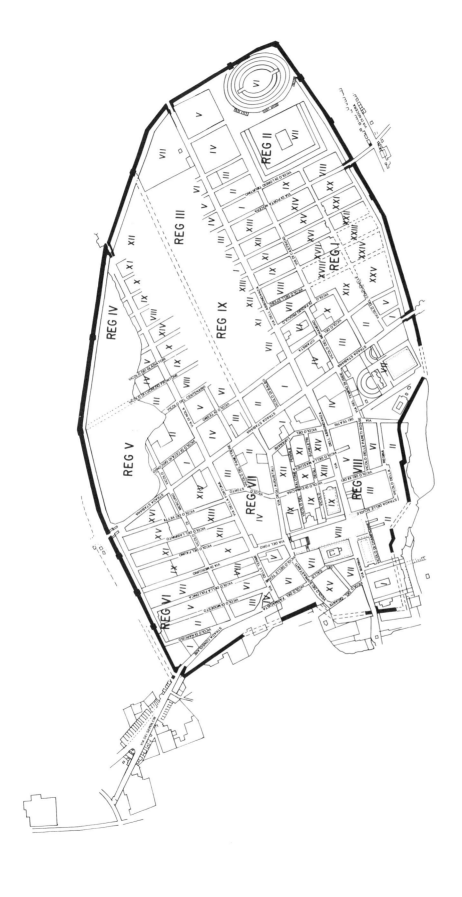

Simplified plan of the excavations of Pompeii showing the regiones, block numbers, and modern Italian names that have been given to the streets of the ancient city. They have been adapted from a number of sources, but especially from the plans of M. Della Corte, *Case ed abitanti di Pompei* (Naples 1965) and H. B. VanderPoel et al., *Corpus Topographicum Pompeianum* (Rome 1977–).

ABBREVIATIONS

AUTHORS

Andreae and   Andreae, B., and H. Kyrieleis, eds. *Neue For-*
Kyrieleis   *schungen in Pompeji.* Recklinghausen 1975.

Boethius and   Boethius, A., and J. B. Ward-Perkins. *Etruscan and*
Ward-Perkins   *Roman Architecture.* The Pelican History of Art.
                     Harmondsworth 1970.

Boyce   Boyce, G. K. *Corpus of the Lararia of Pompeii.*
                     MAAR 14. Rome 1937.

Castrén   Castrén, P. *Ordo Populusque Pompeianus: Polity and*
                     Society in Roman Pompeii. Acta Instituti Romani
                     Finlandiae 8. Rome 1975.

Conway   Conway, R. S. *The Italic Dialects.* Cambridge 1897.
                     Reprint. Hildesheim 1967.

Crema   Crema, L. *L'architettura romana.* Enciclopedia
                     Classica 3, vol. 12, 1. Turin 1959.

Della Corte[3]   Della Corte, M. *Case ed abitanti di Pompei.* 3d ed.
                     Naples 1965.

de Vos and de   de Vos, A., and M. de Vos. *Pompei Ercolano Stabia.*
Vos   Guide Archeologiche Laterza. Rome and Bari
                     1982.

Eschebach 1970   Eschebach, H. *Die städtebauliche Entwicklung des*
                     antiken Pompeji. *RömMitt* Supp. 17. Heidelberg
                     1970.

Eschebach 1978   Eschebach, H. *Pompeji: Erlebte antike Welt.* Leipzig
                     1978.

Eschebach 1979   Eschebach, H., et al. *Die Stabianer Thermen in Pom-*
                     peji. Denkmäler antiker Architektur 13. Berlin
                     1979.

Fiorelli 1873   Fiorelli, G. *Gli scavi di Pompei dal 1861 al 1872.* Na-
                     ples 1873.

Fiorelli 1875 Fiorelli, G. *Descrizione di Pompei.* Naples 1875.

Grant Grant, M. *Eros in Pompeii: The Secret Rooms of the National Museum of Naples.* New York 1975.

Helbig Helbig, W. *Wandgemälde der von Vesuv verschütteten Städte Campaniens.* Leipzig 1868.

Herrmann and Bruckmann Herrmann, P. Continued by R. Herbig. *Denkmäler der Malerei des Altertums.* Munich 1904–50.

Jashemski Jashemski, W. *The Gardens of Pompeii, Herculaneum and the Villas Destroyed by Vesuvius.* New Rochelle, N.Y., 1979.

Kockel Kockel, V. *Die Grabbauten vor dem Herkulaner Tor in Pompeji.* Mainz 1983.

Kraus and von Matt Kraus, T., and L. von Matt. *Lebendiges Pompeji: Pompeji und Herculaneum: Antlitz und Schicksal zweier antiker Städte.* Cologne 1973.

Laidlaw Laidlaw, A. *The First Style in Pompeii: Painting and Architecture.* Rome 1985.

La Rocca, de Vos, and de Vos La Rocca, E.; M. de Vos; and A. de Vos. *Guida archeologica di Pompei.* Verona 1976.

Maiuri 1931 Maiuri, A. *La Villa dei Misteri.* Rome 1931. Reprint, abbreviated. Rome 1947.

Maiuri 1933 Maiuri, A. *La Casa del Menandro e il suo tesoro di argenteria.* Rome 1933.

Maiuri 1942 Maiuri, A. *L'ultima fase edilizia di Pompei.* Rome 1942.

Maiuri 1953 Maiuri, A. *Roman Painting.* Lausanne 1953.

Maiuri 1973 Maiuri, A. *Alla ricerca di Pompei preromana (Saggi stratigrafici).* Naples 1973.

Mau 1882 Mau, A. *Geschichte der dekorativen Wandmalerei in Pompeji.* Leipzig 1882.

Mau 1908 Mau, A. *Pompeji in Leben und Kunst.* 2d ed. Leipzig 1908.

Mazois Mazois, F. *Les Ruines de Pompéi.* 4 vols. Paris 1824–38.

Mercklin Mercklin, E. von. *Antike Figuralkapitelle.* Berlin 1962.

Nash Nash, E. *Pictorial Dictionary of Ancient Rome.* 2 vols. 2d ed. London 1968.

Neuerburg Neuerburg, N. *L'architettura delle fontane e dei ninfei nell'Italia antica.* Naples 1965.

Nissen Nissen, H. *Pompejanische Studien zur Städtekunde des Altertums.* Leipzig 1877.

Noack and Lehmann	Noack, F., and K. Lehmann-Hartleben. *Baugeschichtliche Untersuchungen am Stadtrand von Pompeji*. Berlin 1936.
Overbeck and Mau	Overbeck, J., and A. Mau. *Pompeji in seinen Gebäuden, Alterthümern und Kunstwerken*. 4th ed. Leipzig 1884.
Pernice 1932	Pernice, E. *Hellenistische Tische, Zisternmündungen, Beckenuntersätze, Altäre und Truhen*. Die hellenistische Kunst in Pompeji 5. Berlin and Leipzig 1932.
Pernice 1938	Pernice, E. *Pavimente und figürliche Mosaiken*. Die hellenistische Kunst in Pompeji 6. Berlin 1938.
Platner and Ashby	Platner, S. B., and T. Ashby. *A Topographical Dictionary of Ancient Rome*. London 1929. Reprint. London 1950.
Robertson[2]	Robertson, D. S. *Greek and Roman Architecture*. 2d ed. Cambridge 1969.
Rostovtzeff SEHRE[2]	Rostovtzeff, M. I. *Social and Economic History of the Roman Empire*. 2d ed. Oxford 1957.
Ruesch	Ruesch, A. *Guida del Museo Nazionale di Napoli*. Naples 1911.
Salmon	Salmon, E. T. *Roman Colonization under the Republic*. London 1969.
Schefold	Schefold, K. *Die Wände Pompejis*. Berlin 1957.
Sogliano	Sogliano, A. *Pompei nel suo sviluppo storico: Pompei preromana*. Rome 1937.
Spinazzola 1928	Spinazzola, V. *Le arti decorative in Pompei e nel Museo Nazionale di Napoli*. Milan and Rome 1928.
Spinazzola 1953	Spinazzola, V. *Pompei alla luce degli scavi nuovi di Via dell'Abbondanza*. 3 vols. Rome 1953.
Vetter	Vetter, E. *Handbuch der italische Dialekte*. Heidelberg 1953.
von Rohden	von Rohden, H. *Die Terracotten von Pompeji*. Stuttgart 1880.
Ward-Perkins	Ward-Perkins, J. B. *Cities of Ancient Greece and Italy: Planning in Classical Antiquity*. New York 1974.

JOURNALS AND REFERENCE WORKS

AntCl	*Antiquité classique*
ArchCl	*Archeologia classica*
ArtB	*The Art Bulletin*
BdA	*Bollettino d'arte*
BdI	*Bollettino dell'Istituto di Correspondenza Archeologica*

BPI	*Bollettino di paletnologia italiana*
CAH	*Cambridge Ancient History*
CIL	*Corpus Inscriptionum Latinarum*
CronPomp	*Cronache pompeiane*
EAA	*Enciclopedia dell'arte antica*
JRS	*Journal of Roman Studies*
MAAR	*Memoirs of the American Academy in Rome*
MélRome	*Mélanges d'archéologie et d'histoire de l'École Française de Rome*
MemLinc	*Memorie. Atti della Accademia Nazionale dei Lincei, Classe di scienze morali, storiche e filologiche*
MonAnt	*Monumenti antichi*
Museo Borbonico	*Real Museo di Napoli*. 16 vols. Naples 1823–68.
NSc	*Notizie degli scavi di antichità*
PAH	Fiorelli, G., ed. *Pompeianarum Antiquitatum Historia*. 3 vols. Naples 1860–64.
PECS	Stillwell, R., et al., eds. *The Princeton Encyclopedia of Classical Sites*. Princeton 1976.
PP	*La parola del passato*
RE	Pauly-Wissowa. *Real-Encyclopädie der klassischen Altertumswissenschaft*
RendNap	*Rendiconti dell'Accademia di Archeologia, Lettere e Belle Arti, Napoli*
RömMitt	*Mitteilungen des Deutschen Archäologischen Instituts, Römische Abteilung*
StEtr	*Studi etruschi*
YCS	*Yale Classical Studies*

PART I

Preliminary and General Considerations

1 · THE HISTORICAL RECORD

The rare appearances of Pompeii in the annals of Roman history are unsatisfying but still instructive. A Campanian port town on the less fashionable part of the Bay of Naples, we might expect it to have had a quiet, prosperous existence, its economy too dependent on Rome in the late republican period for its citizenry to have had much independence in either politics or cultural taste, and under the empire it might have been little more than a small supplier of mills and food to the capital and of services to the great villas in its neighborhood. Without the charm of situation of its near neighbors on the bay, without the geographical advantages of Puteoli, it might have had little initiative or character of its own. But this was not quite the case.

There was some sort of settlement on the site at least as early as the sixth century B.C. This is attested by the finds of architectural terracottas and black-figure Attic pottery in the precincts of the Forum Triangulare and the Aedes Apollinis. The size of the four Doric capitals in Sarno limestone still to be seen in the former suggests that there was once a large archaic temple here, though its ground plan cannot be recovered. The terracottas show stylistic affinities with terracottas of Capua and Cumae, and not with those of Paestum.[1] There is no archaic architecture associated with the Aedes Apollinis except possibly a column base in yellowish tufa composed of a thick disc under a deep torus, with a profile not unlike that of an archaic echinus, the date of which is doubtful.[2] There is no ground around the Forum Triangulare suitable for development as an agora or forum, so it must always have been an isolated sanctuary. The Aedes Apollinis may well have been a temenos adjacent to a market that eventually became the forum of Pompeii.

[1] See, e.g., Sogliano 98–99 and pl. 10, fig. 26. Compare these with H. Koch, *Dachterrakotten aus Campanien* (Berlin 1912) pls. 1, 3–5; and M. Napoli, *Paestum* (I documentari visioni d'Italia 27, Novara 1967) figs. 22–25.
[2] It is wrongly identified as a capital in Sogliano 92 and fig. 28.

The amount and character of the Greek goods from the site need not mean that the original settlers were Greeks. The site is naturally attractive, and there was probably an Oscan (Ausonian) settlement there before the Greeks arrived. The whole of the Bay of Naples got at least a veneer of Greek culture, and in some cases a profoundly Greek character, in the seventh and sixth centuries B.C. The inland road behind Vesuvius to which Pompeii's life was tied seems never to have been Greek. It was heavily traveled by the early Iron Age at least and very likely much earlier. It became thoroughly Etruscan in the sixth century and seems to have continued to be down to the time of the Samnite conquest of Campania in the late fifth century.[3] At San Marzano sul Sarno and San Valentino, up the river from Pompeii, have been found necropoleis containing significant quantities of Campanian bucchero,[4] and among the sherds from the votive deposits of the Aedes Apollinis are some of bucchero inscribed in Etruscan.[5] While it is hardly likely that a purely Etruscan settlement would have built a temple with Greek capitals, probably the sixth-century population of Pompeii was a racial mixture of Greeks from the neighboring cities who appreciated the excellence of the river port, Etruscans there because of the commerce on the road, and an indigenous substratum of Ausonians who had farmed the valley, pastured flocks on the uplands, and fished the waters of the bay from time immemorial. They got along because they benefited and depended on one another, and while the inland road must have been the chief reason for the presence of the Greeks and the Etruscans, Pompeii's protection of the road against raids from the sea gave the city a place in the larger world and assured its permanence. It is probably no

[3]Consult *StEtr* 3 (1929) 91–101 (A. Maiuri); and *PECS* s.vv. Capua (A. De Franciscis), Nola (L. Richardson, Jr.), Nuceria Alfaterna (L. Richardson, Jr.), Salernum (V. Panebianco), and Picentia (E. H. Richardson).

[4]*BPI* 27 (1901) 41–56 (G. Patroni); *NSc* 1949, 178–182 (P. C. Sestieri).

[5]Sogliano 91; A. Maiuri, "Greci ed etruschi a Pompei," *MemLinc* ser. 7, 4 (1944) 121–49, esp. 123–31. Maiuri sees the early history of Pompeii as having three important phases, the first from ca. 600 to ca. 530, when an original Oscan village was taken over by Greeks from Cumae and Naples and built into a city (the Doric temple and foundation of the cult of Apollo belong to this period); the second from ca. 530 to 474, when Etruscan expansion in Campania brought Pompeii into the Etruscan sphere; the third from 474 to 425/420, when the Greeks, after crushing the Etruscans in the great naval battle off Cumae, repossessed Pompeii, laid out the city plan of the northwest quarter, and built the original fortifications on the line of the existing walls. This was the city the Samnites took over toward the end of the fifth century. Maiuri supposes Pompeii to have been an important settlement from at least the middle of the sixth century and points to the Doric temple as evidence. But we do not know enough about that temple to assess its importance, and Maiuri is certainly wrong in assigning an early date to the walls and the city plan. While Pompeii may have passed back and forth between Greek and Etruscan domination, it is more logical to see its fate as tied to that of Nocera, which did not.

accident that Pompeii seems to have felt closer in spirit to Capua than to many nearer towns.

The name Pompeii, like so many place names, is mysterious.[6] Since the site was a conspicuous natural landmark, the name may go back very far. If it is Oscan, it may be connected with the root meaning "five," but there is no way to tell whether five roads or five trees were responsible for the name. Since the name Pompeius is well attested not only in the annals of history but also in the prosopography of Pompeii, it may possibly have been derived from that.[7] Speculation is entirely fruitless; we shall never know the truth. The Romans treated the name as a plural.

In the sixth century, then, Pompeii was already cosmopolitan and commercial, albeit in a very limited way. Still, it was receiving goods from Athens and Etruria, and it built a Doric temple, possibly on a grand scale. The distance from the Doric temple to the Aedes Apollinis shows that Pompeii's extent was considerable, but it was probably not all built-up. There is no sign of fortifications, and the population must have been small enough to retire to some stronghold when danger threatened, perhaps a palisaded temenos or a naturally strong point higher on the slopes of Vesuvius, since Nuceria seems too distant to have served as a refuge. The Pompeians do not seem to have been much afraid of violent assault, and probably each house was something of a fortress in itself, as many of the houses of the last period still were. These must have stood along roads that had the character of village lanes, laid out with an eye to linking places to one another rather than in conformance with any sort of plan, radiating from the marketplace and the religious centre, the houses clustered together for companionship and protection, their façades aligned on the road, their backs giving out into gardens with fields beyond, while other fields ringed the settlement with a broad belt of agriculture.

For many years Pompeii's existence was marginal. It grew little, if at all, and it followed perforce the lead of its more important neighbors. Toward the end of the fifth century the Samnites, already Hellenized by more than three centuries of contact and commerce with the Greeks of Magna Graecia, broke out of their Apennine fastnesses and swarmed down on the rich cities of the coast. Capua fell to them in 424/423 B.C., Cumae in 421/420 (Livy 4.37.1, 4.44.12; Diodorus 12.76.4). We have no date for the loss of others, but if such important and powerful places went so quickly, we can presume that lesser cities were not far behind. Within a decade or so the only Greek city

[6]See, e.g., Sogliano 34–37.
[7]But see Castrén 205–6.

surviving on the bay was Naples itself, and the only other considerable Greek cities in Italy were Elea (Velia) and Tarentum. These Samnites did not come to plunder and withdraw, as they might have a century earlier; they came to take over the existing cities and fields. Capua, Livy tells us (4.37.2), endured a blood bath, yet it was Capua that appealed to Rome for help against her Samnite cousins a hundred years later and so provoked the First Samnite War. Whatever violence this wave of invaders was capable of, their prime objective was to make themselves masters of the Greek cities, to move in and enjoy the Greeks' higher standard of living. In Poseidonia (Paestum), for example, although there is no identifiable Lucanian architecture or style of decoration, and there are elements of the provincial and the barbarous in all the products of this period, contact with the more civilized world was by no means broken off. Coins continued to be minted with the characteristic figure of Poseidon and inscriptions in Greek, and a local school of pottery painters, including such masters as Assteas and Python, prospered and flourished in the fourth century. The Lucanians, close cousins of the Samnites of Campania, made themselves masters of the city. They did not destroy, or apparently even plunder, the Greek temples, and they seem to have learned from the Greek craftsmen and artists, as we see in the numerous Lucanian tombs of the fourth century.[8] Presumably things will have been much the same in Pompeii. The Samnites were not an uncivilized people and were probably cousins of the Oscans,[9] who were perhaps the strongest element in the old Pompeian amalgam. They were a tough mountain people, shrewdly intelligent and hungry for the luxury of the life of the coastal cities. They would have readily appreciated the necessity of keeping the roads open and the sea lanes active. Pompeii was not in itself a great prize, though the Sarno Valley was good land, but it was a vital station where the road was vulnerable to piratical raids, so the Samnites will have had the same reasons as their predecessors for holding Pompeii and keeping a guard and a lookout there.

The first mention of Pompeii in history comes in the long Second Samnite War. According to Livy (9.38.2–3), in 310 B.C. a Roman fleet under the command of P. Cornelius put in at Pompeii. The landfall, he implies, was almost accidental. The *socii nauales* then left ship to proceed to the devastation of the territory of Nuceria. Evidently, at this time Pompeii was not a town in its own right but a dependency of Nuceria. Since the coastal area was soon pillaged and the plunderers met no opposition, they proceeded inland, too far from the ships

[8]On Paestum in the fourth century see Napoli (supra n. 1) 60–63; and *EAA* s.v. Paestum 5.838–40 with bibliography (P. Zancani Montuoro).

[9]Consult *RE* s.v. Osci 1545–49 (E. Vetter).

to be able to return safely. This must mean that in Pompeii there was little or nothing, too little to satisfy the greed of the marines; they therefore wandered through the countryside pillaging such farms as they happened upon. Quite clearly they did not get near enough to Nuceria to bring out the local militia, for it was the countrymen themselves (*agrestes*) who mustered strength and caught the marines on their return, weighed down with loot, not far from the ships. The booty had to be abandoned, some were killed, and the rest were driven in rout back to the ships. The whole episode is of the greatest interest, for it shows that Pompeii was dependent on Nuceria for protection as well as in politics and that it was still essentially nothing but an agricultural community. It was part of the *ager Nucerinus*. Had it been walled and populous, the plunderers would never have dared to go off into the Sarno Valley, or even to start on a campaign of devastation, without first making sure that there would be no retaliation from that quarter. In 310 B.C. Pompeii was obviously a very inconsiderable place.

How and when did Pompeii come into being as a place in its own right? At the end of the fourth century it was negligible; by the middle of the second century it was a town important enough to boast mansion-lined streets and a forum that rivaled in size that of Rome itself. It had a city plan with ample provision for expansion as a metropolis and a busy port that was probably under strict municipal control. Its government seems to have been efficient, and its economy thriving. It had a theatre and public baths. When and why did all this come about? No one tells us, so we can only conjecture. There must have been a sudden change in Pompeii's fortunes, a sudden growth of industry and population that is most likely to have accompanied the growth of Rome itself. In the First Punic War the Romans had to learn all the technology and strategy necessary to conduct a naval war successfully. Fleet after fleet, hundreds of ships, were built and lost, the great majority to the treacherous vicissitudes of the Mediterranean weather, in a quarter of a century. The first of these consisted of a hundred quinquiremes and twenty triremes and was built in a remarkably short time (Polybius 1.20.9–21.3). The cities with the yards that built these ships must have drawn labor to them and grown rich on their construction; and offshoot industries must have been almost as important as shipbuilding itself. The Bay of Naples offered many advantages for shipbuilding, as it does today; under Augustus, Misenum and Portus Iulius became the headquarters of the imperial fleet. In the first intense burst of such work probably all the ports on the bay had a share, Naples and Pompeii as well as Baiae and Puteoli. As part of the best location for such industry south of Rome, with the training ground of the bay at its doorstep, it would be strange if Pompeii did not become deeply involved in shipbuilding at this time and draw to itself workmen from the mountains and valleys of Samnium, as well as from Nola and Nuceria. Only a phenomenon of this sort seems adequate to explain such a sudden influx of great wealth and a great increase in population.

Throughout most of the Samnite period there is no historical record for Pompeii, only an archaeological record. It seems to have continued to be in some sense a dependency of Nuceria, for it never coined its own money, though in the second century it seems to have elected its own magistrates and managed its own affairs. Livy (23.15.1–6) records a curious incident for 216 B.C., one of the blackest years of the Hannibalic War. Hannibal, wishing to secure his grip on Campania after the capitulation of Capua, tried first to take Nola; then, when Nola was strengthened by the arrival of Claudius Marcellus with his army, Naples; and finally, when he found Naples in the charge of a Roman prefect, M. Junius Silanus, Nuceria. Livy says that Hannibal's chief motivation was the need for a port to which ships could come from Africa in safety, and it is easy to see that with Capua in his hands his first choice would be Naples, Cumae's beach-and-lagoon port having evidently become increasingly unusable with the passage of time since the Samnite conquest, thanks to their neglect of port installations,[10] and Puteoli being well defended by nature as well as walls but vulnerable unless Naples could also be secured. When Hannibal was balked in his move against Naples, he turned to Nuceria and laid siege to it, eventually starving the city into surrender. The terms of the surrender were mild, however, and the citizens were allowed to disperse. They found shelter among the neighboring cities, after which Nuceria was sacked and burnt. Hannibal then led his army against Nola.

What, one asks, was the fate of Pompeii at this time? The campaign against Nuceria was intended not only to reduce one of the strongest cities in the region but to open the way between Capua and the sea at Pompeii and Salernum, both ports of considerable importance. Ultimately this attempt failed, thanks to the dogged resistance of Nola, a vital station astride that road, but one would have thought that the natural sequel to the surrender of Nuceria might have been a siege of Pompeii, were Pompeii prepared to stand siege, as it was later in the Social War. That this is not mentioned at this time and that none of the Nucerian refugees is explicitly said to have found shelter at Pompeii might be taken to indicate that it fell with Nuceria, that it had no fortifications and was unable to contemplate opposing

[10]R. F. Paget, "The Ancient Ports of Cumae," *JRS* 58 (1968) 152–69, esp. 158. Even though the harbor of Cumae had deteriorated, it was still of interest to Hannibal (Livy 23.36.6).

the Carthaginians' advance. On the other hand, without Nola in his possession, Pompeii would be useless to Hannibal, whereas if Nola fell, Pompeii might be expected to capitulate. That might have been part of Hannibal's object in the great leniency shown to Nuceria. Our whole decision in this matter must ultimately depend on the date we assign to the walls of Pompeii. Since the Romans seem to have known for many years that war with Carthage was inevitable and to have armed themselves for it in advance, we may incline to a date between the first and second Punic wars, when the population of Pompeii, now greatly enlarged, could turn its attention from ship-building to housing and municipal development and defense.

There seem to have been many willing hands and no lack of money for this, another indication that it was the work of boom years. This was also the time when Pompeii got its complete city plan. To the second century B.C. belongs the great flowering of the city. The finest temples (the rebuilding of the Forum Triangulare and the Temples of Apollo and Zeus Meilichios), the basilica, the grandest mansions (the Casa di Sallustio, the Casa del Fauno, the Casa della Fontana Grande, the Casa dell'Argenteria, the Casa del Torello di Bronzo, the Casa di Pansa, and the Casa dei Capitelli Colorati, to name only a few in the northwest quarter of the city), all belong to this century. Pompeii's economy was expanding in every direction; its civic spirit seems to have been exuberant, and the leading citizens vigorous rivals of one another. It will have begun to attract investment from Rome in its enormously productive agriculture and commerce, for one finds that Scipio Africanus already had a villa at Liternum to which he retired in 185 B.C. (Seneca *Ep.* 86), and we can be sure that he was not the first. If Pompeii found the spirit and the wherewithal to build on a scale and in a style that would have been unthinkable up to this time, there is really nothing to be surprised at in this.

At the same time, Pompeii's new prosperity seems to have drawn it into closer league with its neighbors, and probably sometimes into friction as well in the struggle for ascendency. Pompeii was tied to Nuceria by common interests and tradition, and these ties extended to Nola and a network of inland communities. Stabiae was probably too close for comfort, and Pompeii and Stabiae would probably have had rival interests in the same fishing grounds. The towns on the far side of Vesuvius probably posed no threat to Pompeii's well-being at this time and may rather have promoted Pompeii's prosperity by their own, as may have been true of Surrentum, out on the peninsula. But it was the towns in the Sarno Valley that most commanded Pompeii's interest and attention.

According to Appian (*Bell.Ciu.* 1.39), when the Social War broke out in 91 B.C., the Pompeians were among the first of the Italians to raise the standard of revolt, and the only Campanians in the first wave, if we exclude the Picentini, who lived south of the Sorrentine Peninsula. The first surge of insurrection took hold chiefly among the mountain peoples of the central and southern Apennines. If Appian is right about this, we must presume that the other Campanian towns were too softened by a century of prosperity, and too loyal to a Rome that looked upon Campania with special affection, to see that their one hope for the future lay in solidarity with the Italians, and we must applaud the Pompeians for their enterprise and farsightedness. It was probably, then, at the instigation of the Pompeians and to relieve them of a threat at their backs that in one of the first actions of the war the great Samnite general C. Papius Mutilus led an army into Campania to win over or subjugate the other Campanian towns. He immediately took Nola by treachery, then Stabiae, Surrentum, and Salernum by storm, and plundered the territory of Nuceria until all this part of Campania capitulated and agreed to supply him with men and materiel (Appian *Bell.Ciu.* 1.42). He then proceeded north against Acerrae. We can see pretty clearly that Pompeii was looking to its own advantage as well as to the prosecution of the war.

Ultimately the Italians failed, thanks to Roman concessions and a lack of leadership and a coordinated strategy. There were many heroes, and there was much suffering. Early in 89 the Romans took the offensive and once again proceeded to make Campania one of the principal theatres of the war. In the course of the winter Pompeii was laid under siege, the Roman forces being under A. Postumius Albinus. When his men suspected him of treachery and lynched him, Sulla himself took charge (Livy, *per.* 75; Valerius Maximus 9.8.3; Orosius 5.18.22–23). Pompeii's fortifications were strong, and he set about reducing the town by starvation while harassing it with bombardment from the high ground to the north along its most vulnerable front. A Samnite army under Lucius Cluentius, the south Campanian leader, or meddix, attempted to relieve Pompeii but was defeated in battle and driven to take refuge in Nola after terrible losses, including Cluentius himself (Appian *Bell.Ciu.* 1.50). Stabiae was taken by storm and utterly destroyed on 29 April, after which it ceased to exist as a town (Pliny *HN* 3.70). Herculaneum was also taken but seems to have suffered a milder fate (Velleius Paterculus 2.16.2). But Pompeii seems to have held out, as did Nola, and when summer came Sulla seems to have decided on a bold advance into the country of the Hirpini (*CAH* 9.199–200). Here he was able to do great damage to the rebels' cause and to break their hold on the central mountains. With the fall of Asculum to Pompeius Strabo late in the year, the worst of the war was over, and what remained was chiefly to mop up pockets of resistance.

It is not clear whether Pompeii ever fell. Nola did not and had to face siege the next year, when again it survived. By the end of 87, Roman citizenship had been extended to all the Samnites (Salmon 375–76), and the Social War was formally over. Nola did not surrender to Sulla until 80, and then only under threat of a siege (Livy, *per.* 89; Granius Licinianus 36.9–10), yet it was situated astride an important highway. Pompeii, well fortified and easily bypassed in the important operations of these years, probably was ignored after the first efforts to take it and submitted only when it saw that its isolation was complete. Had it been taken by storm after an extended siege, it surely would have been put to the torch and sword, yet there is no sign of this. The fine mansions continued to stand unscathed; the temples show no scars of pillage. Pompeii was proud of her record in the war and kept the painted inscriptions that were wartime emergency measures bright on the streets a century and a half later. The stone ballista balls with which the city had been bombarded became prized garden ornaments. Probably at the time of its surrender its military leaders were proscribed (as Papius Mutilus was at Nola [see Livy, *per.* 89]). Certain of the names from the Eituns inscriptions directing troops during this siege later disappear from Pompeii, but at least some of these probably contrived to escape abroad. The real punishment of Pompeii was the settlement on it of a colony of Sulla's veterans under the leadership of P. Sulla, probably the dictator's nephew (Cicero *pro Sulla* 62).

We do not know the size of this veteran colony, but it took the name Colonia Cornelia Veneria Pompeianorum, which shows that it regarded Sulla with affection. Land for such colonists was regularly taken from the *ager publicus,* plus a certain percentage of the holdings of the larger landlords of the place, until the requisite amount had been obtained. Cicero (*pro Sulla* 62) says that Sulla performed his work as *tresuir coloniae deducendae* so well that he seemed not to have dispossessed the Pompeians but rather to have firmly settled both Pompeians and colonists. The goal of any program of colonization seems always to have been to break up the great estates and to reestablish the yeoman farmer in Italy, but it seems to have been accomplished in only a very small proportion of any such effort, and there must always have been injustices and abuses in confiscations and allotments, accompanied by hardship and, one must suppose, bribery. If Sulla was only moderately successful, then he did a great deal.

Together with the confiscation of land and its redistribution to the new colonists went a new constitution and changes in the municipal organization.[11] Latin now became the official language for all records and public documents, and the administration was put in the hands of four magistrates, two *duouiri iure dicundo* and two aediles, with the duovirs of every fifth year known as *duouiri quinquennales* and given censorial powers. The magistrates presided over, and were advised by, the *ordo,* or *decuriones,* of the city, a body of ex-magistrates and men of the greatest wealth, probably limited in number to a hundred. It was also possible to convene an assembly of the whole citizenry when that might be needed. The real work of running the city was in the hands of the magistrates and a corps of *serui publici;* at least some of the latter were probably slaves in name only, since they could execute contracts and witness documents. These were the bureaucracy of Pompeii, and probably most municipal business had to go through their hands before it got any higher. Whether there were also committees of the decuriones with special commissions that reported to the magistrates—a committee on the port facilities, for example, or the public markets—is not known, but it seems likely.

One notes in the inscriptions of Pompeii that most of the magistrates of the late republican period do not have Oscan names, that Oscan names are exceptional, and we can infer that the colonists clung tenaciously to their control of the city as long as they could. This was done in large part by disenfranchisement of the descendants of the proscribed; they were not reinstated until 49, by Julius Caesar.

P. Sulla in due course became *patronus coloniae* and candidate for the consulship in Rome. He was elected but then charged with *ambitus* (bribery), convicted, and disqualified. There are signs that certain others of the leading men of the colonia had ambitions beyond Pompeii: M. Porcius and C. Quinctius Valgus, who as duovirs let the contract for the Theatrum Tectum and as quinquennial duovirs gave the amphitheatre at their own expense. In an inscription from Aeclanum (*CIL* 1^2.1722), Quinctius appears as patronus of another town as well. Their names suggest a Roman origin, and the emphasis on the words *coloniai* and *coloneis* in the amphitheatre inscription (*CIL* 10.852), as well as the letter forms, shows that they were early magistrates. Cicero (*pro Sulla* 61) tells us that the native Pompeians had a quarrel with the colonists *de ambulatione ac de suffragiis suis,* which suggests that their voting in municipal matters was not on a parity with that of the colonists, possibly being deferred until after the colonists had voted. But these seem to have been temporary inequities, eliminated in the course of the next generation.

The colonists seem to have brought to Pompeii not only a new

[11]On the constitution and magistracies of the colony of Pompeii see Castrén 55–67.

constitution and new blood but a good bit of new money and energy as well. If they were a burden on the Pompeians, they did not come merely to plunder them; many of them came to stay. There are a number of fine houses that should belong mainly to the early colony, houses like the Casa delle Nozze d'Argento and the Casa di Obellio Firmo, and at least one big public building as well, the Terme del Foro. If they packed the *ordo decurionum* with, first, those who had been military officers and, then, past magistrates, and manipulated elections to ensure that their men won all the offices, they were doing no more than any such privileged group would have done. As they intermarried with the older population and found among them men with whom they could do business and whom they could trust, these will have been gradually admitted back into the circles of privilege and power. The Pompeians knew their land and how best to farm it for maximum profit; few of the colonists did, and their allotments of about twenty jugera (ca. 13.2 acres) per colonist were made more for market gardening than for viticulture (Cato *Agr.* 1.7, 11.1; Varro *Rust.* 1.18.5), which apparently was the mainstay of Pompeian agriculture. Many of them probably sold their allotments within a short time after receiving them. Cicero's allusion in a letter (*ad fam.* 7.1.3) to Oscan theatricals in the senate of Pompeii may mean that the older population had regained a foothold in the ordo by 55 B.C., but it is clear that in the years of the civil war, if not before, the older families made a surprising comeback. These were years of turmoil and of opportunity, and at least some Pompeians seem to have made the most of them.

The only record we have of Pompeii itself in this period is a letter from Cicero to Atticus (10.16.4; see also *ad fam.* 7.3.1), where he tells us that in the course of his journey south to join Pompey in May of 49 he stopped at his Pompeianum and received information from Ninnius that the centurions of the three cohorts stationed there wished to deliver custody of the town over to him. He pondered this offer and discussed it with a friend who also had a house there, M. Marius, and then decided to leave very early the next morning to avoid the meeting, since three cohorts was a very small force and he feared a trap. But as Sulla's heir, Pompey probably had a very strong following in Pompeii, and Cicero's conference with Marius is confirmation of this. Adherence to Pompey's cause probably cost some Pompeians their lives and others property.

There can be no doubt that the new regime, first of Julius Caesar, then of Augustus, brought wide-ranging changes in Pompeii.[12] Those

---

[12] On the general effects of the new regime in Pompeii see Castrén 92–103. Some of the details he offers are open to question (e.g., there is nothing to suggest that the remodeling of the theatre of Pompeii was in imitation of the theatre of Marcellus in Rome), but the overall picture seems correct.

who endorsed the revolution or who leapt on the bandwagon stood to profit and flourish, and in Pompeii these seem to have been a mixture of the old Samnite families and new families that arrived during the years of turmoil with money to spend and ambition to establish themselves respectably in the aristocracy of the city. Some of these were probably Caesar's soldiers, either those he settled as veterans in Campania (Suetonius *Diu.Iul.* 38; Appian *Bell.Ciu.* 3.40) or those who retired with their pockets well filled, such as the *praefectus fabrum*, M. Lucretius Decidianus Rufus. One notes especially that the non-Campanian names that appear in this period seem to belong in central Italy: Clodius, Egnatius, Sallustius, Tillius, Tullius, Valerius Flaccus. But there are as many old Campanian names: Alfidius, Audius, Istacidius, Melissaeus, Veius, Vibius. The pattern here, then, seems to reflect what was going on all over the Roman world: the displacement of those reluctant to accept the new order by those who were eager for change and willing to lend their efforts to it and the growing realization by the conservative established families that they would have to accept the Augustan reform if they were to survive and that this was not necessarily a bad thing. At all events, we find the Pompeians taking up the cult of Augustanism with enthusiasm. The public priestess Mamia built a temple to Augustus on the forum (*CIL* 10.816); the magistrate M. Tullius built a temple to Fortuna Augusta (*CIL* 10.820–22); and the public priestess Eumachia built a porticus dedicated to Concordia Augusta and Pietas in imitation of the Porticus Liviae and the Forum Augustum in Rome.[13]

These were only the most conspicuous of the ways in which Pompeii acknowledged the new regime. Further-reaching were the social changes. We now find Pompeii with an extensive paramilitary organization and a new recognition and estimation of the class of freedmen and tradesmen. The office of *tribunus militum a populo* comes into existence under Augustus and is held by five of the most distinguished men of the period, including M. Holconius Rufus, before Augustus's death, when the office seems to have been allowed to lapse.[14] We do not know what the office entailed, but the title was awarded late in life, and probably there were no actual military duties. The Iuventus, on the other hand, an organization from which Augustus hoped to recruit officers for the Roman army, did train regularly and compete in contests.[15] Augustus made his grandsons Gaius and Lucius *principes iuuentutis,* and the officers of the local collegia must have found this one of the stepping stones in a successful

---

[13]*CIL* 10.810–12; L. Richardson, Jr., "Concordia and Concordia Augusta: Rome and Pompeii," *PP* 33 (1978) 260–72.

[14]C. Nicolet, "Tribuni militum a populo," *MélRome* 79 (1967) 29–76; Castrén 98–99.

[15]Consult esp. M. Della Corte, *Iuventus* (Arpino 1924).

cursus. For the mercantile class we find the *Augustales* and the *ministri Augusti* in charge of the imperial cult and the *magistri uici* and *pagi* in charge of the cult of the Lares Compitales, but they probably had other administrative duties as well.[16] All of these offices seem to have been open to freedmen, though the freeborn might hold the higher ones. Some of the lowest were open to slaves. All were considered honors and tend to appear after signatures and on tombstones. With the passage of time they created a middle-class elite.

This new pervasive insistence on enthusiastic loyalty to the princeps is apt to seem a bit sinister in a town as old as Pompeii but must have been no more so than in Rome itself. The opportunists presumably made a good thing of it, and others learned to. Once the adjustment was made, stability returned, for the economy of Pompeii was not highly complex.

Castrén conjectures that the new social order was maintained undisturbed in Pompeii for sixty to seventy years, down to the reign of Gaius Caligula, when in the year A.D. 40 Pompeii suddenly elected the princeps quinquennial duovir together with M. Lucretius Epidius Flaccus (*CIL* 10.904). The *praefectus iure dicundo,* appointed by the princeps to act for him, was M. Holconius Macer, almost certainly the son or nephew of Pompeii's most distinguished citizen, M. Holconius Rufus, duovir in 2/1 B.C. and eventually duovir five times. What prompted this extraordinary appeal to the central government there is no way of knowing, but since the quinquennial duovirs exercised the powers of censors, we may guess that the second generation of the freedman class, some of whom had inherited wealth and a taste for power but were excluded from the magistracies by an alliance of the established families, were agitating for a position of greater importance and the removal of the decayed nobility from the ordo. A curious gap in our knowledge—complete ignorance of the names of the magistrates of Pompeii in the years A.D. 41–50—prevents our examining this incident in greater detail, but social injustice was an evil felt in many places in Italy at this time, and much of Claudius's domestic policy was addressed to rectifying it (Suetonius *Claud.* 14–16; *CAH* 10.685–97). If the problem solved itself at certain times and in certain places, thanks to the liberality of Roman social philosophy and the mobility within Roman society, there must have been others where it did not and where drastic reforms were required.

With the resumption of our knowledge of the names of Pompeian magistrates, thanks to the archive of L. Caecilius Iucundus, we find Q. Coelius Caltilius Iustus, L. Helvius Blaesius Proculus, D. Lucretius Satrius Valens, Cn. Alleius Nigidius Maius, and Hegius (Regu-

[16] On these offices see Castrén 72–78.

lus?) in office. These seem to be a combination of the old and the new. Many of the names are Oscan names not encountered in the annals of Pompeii since the early days of the colony; others are names that seem to have first appeared at the time of the Civil War. One thing is clear: these are not the sons of those at the height of power a generation earlier; but whether they are the descendants of freedmen or simply a new generation of aggressive politicians cannot be determined, thanks to the Roman system of nomenclature, by which all trace of servile origin disappeared within two generations of manumission. A name like D. Lucretius Satrius Valens shows us only a man born into an Oscan family, the Satrii, an old family but one comparatively undistinguished in Pompeii, who has been adopted by a Lucretius, a member of a family that first appears in Pompeii in the Augustan period (Castrén 185). Since both families carry the cognomen Valens, a name fairly common among the decuriones of Pompeii, we might presume them both to belong to the ruling class, but we cannot be entirely certain. The name of Cn. Alleius Nigidius Maius shows that he is the son of an ancient Campanian family adopted by another, possibly his maternal grandfather, a not uncommon occurrence in Rome when there was no son.[17] There is a persistence of Oscan names in Pompeii remarkable when we consider its importance as a port.

The one other bit of history that attaches to Pompeii in the reign of Claudius is the story of the death of the princeps's eldest son, Drusus. If a widely accepted conjecture to improve a corrupt passage in the text of Suetonius (*Diu.Claud.* 27.1) is correct, Drusus choked to death on a pear he was playing with, tossing it into the air and catching it in his mouth, at Pompeii. This might be taken as an indication that there was an imperial property there, a likely enough possibility in any case.[18]

Under Nero, Pompeii seems to have enjoyed a period of new prosperity and optimism. D. Lucretius Satrius Valens became *flamen Neronis Caesaris Augusti fili perpetuus* (CIL 4.1185, 3884, 7992, 7995); Vibia Sabina may have become *sacerdos Iuliae Augustae* (CIL 10.961). A feeling of euphoria seems to have swept over Italy, and Pompeii was caught up in it. Perhaps it was this feeling that the city was entering

---

[17]Castrén (109) asserts that the funerary inscription of Alleius's adoptive parents was found in the tomb of Eumachia in the Porta di Nocera necropolis and identifies them as Cn. (?) Alleius Nobilis and Pomponia Decarchis, she at least being of servile origin. But Nobilis would be a very strange cognomen for a freedman, and it is ordinarily a woman's name, not a man's, while Decarchis seems to be only a slightly affected way of saying "of Puteoli," where we know the Pomponii were established. So the case seems far from proved, and without the stone to examine, this assertion cannot be accepted.

[18]J. H. D'Arms, *Romans on the Bay of Naples* (Cambridge, Mass., 1970) 73–103.

a new flowering that led to its disgrace. In A.D. 59 at a show offered in the amphitheatre of Pompeii by Livineius Regulus a riot broke out between the citizens of Pompeii and those of its neighbor Nuceria that proceeded from insults to brickbats and ultimately to real weapons. The Pompeians prevailed, and the Nucerians had many dead to mourn. They sent a deputation to Rome to show their wounds and protest the outrage, and the matter was passed back and forth, from princeps to the senate to the consuls, and back to the senate for judgment. Finally the Pompeians were forbidden to hold *coetus* of this type for ten years, the collegia that they had organized contrary to the laws were disbanded, and Livineius and those who had fostered the riot were exiled (Tacitus *Ann.* 14.17).

I have argued the historical meaning of this riot elsewhere.[19] A graffito showing a *Campanus uictor* dressed in what is clearly legionary armor (not gladiatorial) and brandishing a palm branch[20] seems to me proof enough that the *Campani* were a *collegium iuuentutis* that was taking part in the amphitheatrical games and whose victory touched off the riot. This will explain their having weapons in hand and why the judgment of the senate should have taken special cognizance of illegal collegia. I have argued that the name Campani was probably loaded with social and political significance and that the three Pompeians we can identify as culpable, Livineius and the duovirs Cn. Pompeius Grosphus and Cn. Pompeius Grosphus Gavianus, were in some way trying to use the collegium for their own advantage by awarding a prize in the competition of the collegia of iuvenes to those whom others were convinced did not deserve it. The whole scheme must have gone awry, for Livineius's hope must have been to get himself reinstated in the Roman senate thanks to the support of a Pompeian constituency. We do not know Livineius's origins; the family had been prominent in Rome since the time of Cicero. He is associated here with a Pompeius Grosphus; that, too, is a striking name. The Greek cognomen indicates a type of light javelin, so it is not to be taken as indicative of a servile origin. Horace mentions a member of the same family in two poems (*Car.* 2.16; *Epist.* 1.12.22); very likely the gens Pompeia was originally Campanian, but members of this family are not known in Pompeii itself until the imperial period. Then they are fairly numerous, though these are the first Pompeii Grosphi there. The son adopted by Pompeius Grosphus, who was his colleague as duovir, came from an old Pompeian family, the Gavii. These men might be presumed to have had connections with the inner circles of municipal power, and the election of father

[19] L. Richardson, Jr., *Pompeii: The Casa dei Dioscuri and Its Painters* (Rome 1955) 88–93.
[20] *Museo Borbonico* 6, "Relazione degli scavi," pl. C; Overbeck and Mau 485, fig. 261.

and adoptive son together to the senior magistracy of the city is striking. Had Livineius seen the way to local preeminence by giving sumptuous games during the magistracy of the Pompeii Grosphi and attempted to curry favor with the innermost circles of the Pompeian aristocracy by awarding little-deserved palms to their sons, that would have made a satisfactory background for what occurred. There is only a little guesswork involved here, and while Roman society was always mobile and we might have thought that by A.D. 59 the Samnite aristocracy of Pompeii would have been completely absorbed into the amalgam that successive waves of new blood had brought, we must remember that the Samnite stock was extraordinarily resilient, as the record shows, and that many of the Pompeian aristocracy tended to be highly conservative, as mansions such as the Casa del Fauno and the Casa del Labirinto demonstrate. That the Pompeii Grosphi had lent themselves to the schemes of Livineius, possibly in the hope of rising together with him, suggests that they were ambitious and willing to take risks.

What the riot cost Pompeii in the long run we do not know. Various scholars, among them Van Buren, have supposed that Nero's second wife, the beautiful Poppaea Sabina, whom he married in A.D. 62, either was herself a Pompeian or had close Pompeian connections and would have seen to the alleviation of the punishment.[21] Certainly there were in Pompeii both Poppaei Sabini and Ollii (her father was T. Ollius; she assumed her maternal grandfather's name after her father's disgrace due to his intimacy with Sejanus). But by the time Nero married Poppaea, Pompeii was struggling in the aftermath of a more terrible catastrophe.

On 5 February A.D. 62 an earthquake of the greatest severity virtually destroyed the city. Seneca (*Quaest.Nat.* 6.1.1–2), our only literary source for this disaster, says that Pompeii was the centre of the destruction, but Herculaneum also suffered, while Nuceria was shaken and Naples escaped without loss of public buildings. He seems more impressed by the earthquake's having occurred in the dead of winter than by the statistics of loss of life, but this was certainly great. There was hardly a building left in habitable condition in Pompeii, while the public buildings around the forum were all but leveled.

But the Pompeians were an indomitable people, and the Sarno Valley was too rich to abandon. The initial reaction, if it was despair, was quickly followed by a determination to rebuild the city in finer form than it had had before. A master plan was drawn up, a scale of

---

[21] A. W. Van Buren, "Pompeii—Nero—Poppaea," *Studies Presented to David M. Robinson* 2 (1953) 970–74.

priorities devised, and work forces organized. For its rebuilding Pompeii drew on the resources of the whole of the Bay of Naples, as is shown by the sudden appearance of the yellow tufa of the northern reaches of the bay in great quantity and by work of some of the same painters who painted in Pompeii also in Herculaneum and Stabiae. At first it probably could draw to some extent on Rome itself, though the great fire of Nero in 64 will surely have meant the end of that supply. Dumps for debris were established around the periphery of the city and even within it.[22] First attention seems to have been given to putting the water supply back into shape and rebuilding the covered food market; probably these works went together. Until there was aqueduct water, deep wells were scattered through the city to draw on, and at first an open market must have been set up, probably in the forum square. Thereafter came public buildings, baths, and temples, but at a pace much slower than one might have supposed. At the time of the eruption of Vesuvius seventeen years later the water system was still being overhauled and new pipe was being laid in the immediate vicinity of the castellum aquae.[23] Around the forum the basilica, the Temple of Jupiter, the Aedificium Eumachiae, and two of the halls on the south side were either under construction or waiting their turn. But at the same time, work was progressing slowly on a magnificent colonnade in two storeys along the west side of the forum; plans were underway for a glorious new Temple of Venus; and the skeleton of a new public bath, the Terme Centrali, was up, more sophisticated in its thermal engineering than one might have supposed to be possible at this date.

At the same time, householders must have had to get workmen when and as they could, bribing and threatening, doing as much as they could with the men of the household and the materials at their disposition, having to wait for long intervals between the completion of one operation and the beginning of the next. A few managed to get a whole house up and decorated before the disaster struck, but these were exceptions. Even in the Casa dei Vettii, where one is struck by the sumptuousness of the appointments, two of what would have been the finest rooms, the exedras in the northwest and southeast corners of the peristyle, were bare of plaster when the eruption came. Almost none of the elaborate terraced houses in the

---

[22] On dumps for debris see Maiuri 1942, 174–75; G. Cerulli Irelli, "Frammento pittorico con il ritorno di Ulisse," *CronPomp* 1 (1975) 151 n. 2; and M. de Vos, "Primo stile figurato e maturo quarto stile negli scarichi provenienti dalle macerie del terremoto del 62 d.C. a Pompei," *Mededelingen van het Nederlands Instituut te Rome* 39, n.s. 4 (1977) 29–47.

[23] On the state of the water system and the castellum aquae at the time of the eruption see Maiuri 1942, 90–94.

southwest sector of the city were habitable, although work was in progress in most of them, and in many houses a suite or block of rooms, enough to make living quarters but only a fraction of the whole house, had been completed, and the rest was held in abeyance. Wherever the work was of more than routine nature, wherever special carving or stuccoing was needed, one had to wait a long time. A good case in point is the room housing the great mosaic representing Alexander's battle with Darius in the Casa del Fauno. The Ionic peristyle of the house had been knocked down in the earthquake, and the Alexander exedra was in a dangerous state, but no one could be found to repair it. So rough masonry buttresses were installed in the fine rooms to either side to shore up the walls,[24] while in front a scaffolding of wooden beams, purchase for them hacked into the footings of fallen columns, supported a temporary roof. And seventeen years later things were still in this condition, though many repairs and remodelings had been carried out in other parts of the house. It was simply that the specially skilled workmen necessary to rebuild this venerable peristyle were not readily available.

The dearth of workmen and materials is a common phenomenon after earthquakes, even today. Long after the debris has been cleared away and life has resumed its normal pace and patterns, the repair of shattered buildings is a slow and painful process. The economy is dislocated; those who have places elsewhere to which they can transfer themselves tend to do so. Even with a well-organized program for recovery things move very slowly.[25]

One of the phenomena produced by the earthquake at Pompeii was the invasion of old domestic architecture by industry, for the most part small industry. Presumably these houses were too poor or too old-fashioned or too badly damaged for their owners to contemplate reconstruction on a grand scale, and presumably the dyers and fullers who took them over found it cheaper and easier to get workmen to patch up an existing building and install there what they needed in the way of furnaces and vats, pipes and tanks, than to build a proper workshop *ex nouo*. One presumes that the fullers of

---

[24] These buttresses of *opus mixtum vittatum* masonry are not shown on early plans and have frequently been ascribed to the repairs and restoration made by the nineteenth-century excavators. But I know of no good parallel for such masonry in nineteenth-century work in Pompeii, while it is typical of work in the last period of Pompeii (Maiuri 1942, 201–2), and early photographs show the walls of this exedra as remarkably well preserved, evidence that the buttresses are ancient (see, e.g., *Pompei 1748– 1980: I tempi della documentazione*, exhibition catalogue [Rome 1980] 50–51; and A. Laidlaw, *The First Style in Pompeii: Painting and Architecture* [Rome 1985] 199). They also fit neatly into the picture of hurried shoring up of the walls and roof to protect the mosaic.

[25] J. Andreau, "Histoire des séismes et histoire économique: Le tremblement de terre à Pompéi (62 ap. J.-C.)," *Annales, économies, sociétés, civilisations* 28 (1973) 369–95.

Pompeii were originally established on the outskirts of town, somewhere along the Sarno River, where there would have been an abundant supply of space and fresh water.[26] But now at least some of them moved into the heart of the city and used the atria and peristyles of once fine houses for their shops. Almost all of those, one notes with particular surprise, lie along the major arteries of town—the weavers' shops at IX xii 1–5 and the Fullonica Stephani at I vi 7 on the Via dell'Abbondanza, the dye shop at VII ii 11 and the Fullonica Vesonii Primi at VI xiv 22 on the Strada Stabiana, the dye shops at V i 4–5 on the Via di Nola, to name only a few. These cannot have raised the tone of the neighborhood or the value of property, for many required offensive materials in their work and must have been noisy and rather dirty. Many Pompeians probably now moved out of town to villas in the surrounding countryside, which by this time was relatively safe from violence, and gave up their houses in town to businesses dependent on retail custom. Workshops, especially small shops, of every sort seem to have sprung up along the Via dell'Abbondanza, and it must have teemed with lively activity most of the time, while hawkers and peddlars mingled their cries with the din of tinkers and carpenters and the babel of the crowd in many tongues and dialects.

The municipal government of Pompeii at this time seems to have been for the most part in the hands of men belonging to well-established families.[27] If one looks down the list of names of candidates known from electoral programmata to have stood for the duovirate in the last years of Pompeii (fair evidence that they had already been successful candidates for the aedilate), one is struck by how many of the names are not only familiar but clearly of Sabellian origin. Names like C. Calventius Sittius Magnus, C. Gavius Rufus, M. Holconius Priscus, P. Paquius Proculus, N. Popidius Rufus, L. Statius Receptus, and A. Suettius Certus leap to the eye. Compared with these, there are comparatively few of presumably servile descent, and these are all the scions of imperial freedmen: Ti. Claudius Claudianus, Ti. Claudius Rufus, C. Iulius Polybius. This phenomenon is even more striking in the list of candidates for the quinquennial duovirate, all of whom seem to have belonged to old Pompeian families long active in local politics: Cn. Audius Bassus, M. Lucretius Fronto, M. Satrius Valens, A. Trebius Valens, P. Vedius Siricus, and L. Veranius Hypsaeus. It looks very much as though in the time of their city's suffering the old families felt their obligation and rose to the

---

[26] Note the large tannery, the only one so far discovered in Pompeii, in block I v near the Porta di Stabia.

[27] See J. L. Franklin, Jr., *Pompeii: The Electoral Programmata, Campaigns and Politics*, A.D. 71–79 (Rome 1980).

occasion, for the chief magistrates in these years certainly would have had to incur extraordinary personal expenses for public works over and above the public revenues, in addition to the onerous duties of overseeing a multitude of undertakings and coping with the complicated legal problems and entanglements such a crisis engenders. It is to the credit of Pompeii's leading families that they responded so well, and another measure of the health and vitality of the city. Not only could Pompeii face rebuilding with the clear goal of making the city a far better place than it had been but its strength was solidly founded on an alliance of all the social orders.

In the morning of 24 August A.D. 79, Vesuvius began to erupt in what was to be one of the worst catastrophes in history. Pliny the Younger, who was staying at the house of his uncle, the encyclopaedist, at Misenum, left us a brilliant eyewitness account of the tragedy (*Ep.* 6.16 and 6.20). Since his uncle was *praefectus classi*, admiral of the Tyrrhenian navy, at the time, and the fleet was marshaled to take a major part in the work of evacuation, he had access to other and more authoritative sources of information than others might. But his account is especially valuable in that it captures the bewilderment of the victims, the alternation of terror and nonchalance, and combines scientific observation with acute penetration of the sense of human helplessness before the larger forces of nature. He tried to give us an understanding of the experience of a cataclysm, and for this he has been attacked as foolish and cowardly. By the time the eruption was observed at Misenum, in the early afternoon, it was apparently well advanced, and before a ship could be readied to explore this extraordinary happening, word was brought from a certain Rectina, whose villa was at the foot of Vesuvius, probably in the neighborhood of Herculaneum, that she was in immediate danger, with all escape except by sea cut off. The fleet was then manned and a full-scale rescue operation got under way.

By the time the fleet got to the disaster zone, it could not be brought in to shore, the volcanic debris in the water proving an effective obstruction. According to Pliny, shoals had formed, thanks to the ruin of the mountain, and the excavations show that rivers of mud that later solidified into stone poured down upon Herculaneum with great speed and violence. But these did not contain pumice in any quantity; they must have struck first in the afternoon of the twenty-fourth and been mainly the work of the intense electric storms that accompanied the eruption, forming mainly around the column of heat rising from the crater. Since Herculaneum was only a small town and very few skeletons have been found there, we may presume that most of its inhabitants, seeing the danger, got away, but recent finds show that many perished on the beach below the town before they could be evacuated.[28] Unable to fulfill his original purpose, the elder Pliny then took the fleet to Stabiae, where the danger was not yet acute. There they found evacuation in progress, hampered by adverse winds. By now it was late afternoon, but during dinner alarming fires, which Pliny assured his companions were from abandoned peasants' huts and farmsteads rather than from the volcano, lit up the scene. There must also have been fearful electrical storms around the crater, but Pliny does not mention these. And during all this time there were earthquakes. Such conditions lasted through the night, and the next morning, though at Stabiae the darkness was still as black as midnight, they set about preparations for sailing. The sea continued to run strong. But now there came a sudden smell of sulphur that drove the others to take flight. Pliny, who had been lying down, was got to his feet but collapsed immediately; he had a history of respiratory trouble. He died on the beach and had to be left there. Three days later he was found, seeming more like one who was asleep than one dead. Evidently his companions escaped and returned to recover his body, so the accumulation of volcanic detritus after this time cannot have been very great.

Vulcanologists believe that the eruption of Vesuvius followed a classic pattern.[29] At first the solidified matter stopping the throat of the volcano disintegrated under heat and pressure and was thrown violently upward in a stream that then lost momentum and billowed out into a great cloud, taking the shape of one of the umbrella pines of the Mediterranean, as Pliny describes it. This rained down on the surrounding countryside in pellets of pumice ranging in size from bits as small as rice grains to lumps as large as the end of one's thumb. There were also occasional larger fragments. The rain of pumice was annoying, and the threat to roofs from the accumulating weight a cause for concern, but there was no great danger. At Stabiae Pliny and his friends tied pillows on their heads to protect themselves when they decided to venture out. They seem to have been worried more about the difficulty of movement in the gathering drifts and the turbulence of the sea than anything else. This phase of an eruption is now called the Plinian phase, and in 79 it seems to have lasted about eighteen hours. Pliny does not mention the electric storms caused by the hot column of pumice, but he does say that the ash and pumice falling on the fleet as it approached the volcano grew

[28] See J. Judge, "A Roman Town Gives Up Its Dead," *National Geographic Magazine* 162 (1982) 686–93; and R. Gore, "The Dead Do Tell Tales at Vesuvius," ibid. 165 (1984) 556–613.

[29] See, e.g., F. Ippolito, "Sul meccanismo del seppellimento di Pompei e di Ercolano," and A. Rittmann, "L'eruzione vesuviana del 79. Studio magmalogico e vulcanologico," *Pompeiana* (Naples 1950) 387–95 and 456–74.

hotter and denser. As long as the pine-tree shape was maintained, however, the pumice ought to have been thrown to such a height that it would have cooled sufficiently before falling to the earth to pose no threat of fire.

From the excavations of Pompeii we get some notion of what was happening there. As at nearby Stabiae, at first the danger did not seem desperate, though everyone must soon have realized what was happening. Some of the lighter roofs probably collapsed, for a great many people took refuge in cellars, baths, and other places where the vaulting seemed likely to be strong enough to withstand the weight. At the same time, there was an orderly, if hasty, organization of relief and evacuation procedures. It is hard to piece together how elaborate and far-flung the efforts to reach people in outlying villas and villages may have been, or how the various municipal authorities may have been involved, but it is quite clear from the finds at the Porta di Stabia and the Porta di Nocera that emergency evacuation points were set up at these gates, and as transport became available, the Pompeians, with whatever portable valuables they could scrape together, were taken off. The scene at the Porta di Stabia is especially vivid. There the Ludus Gladiatorius was pressed into service as an evacuation centre, and the people must have been evacuated by boat from the port on the Sarno River. When the eruption entered its second phase, a great many of those awaiting evacuation were trapped. Men, women, and children, the adults for the most part each with a small hoard of coins or jewelry, perished miserably, giving rise to fanciful stories today about romantic attachments between high-born Pompeian ladies and roughneck gladiators (*PAH* 1.211–18 [29 August 1767–16 April 1768]).

In the morning of 25 August the eruption entered a new phase, the Pelean phase. The plug in the throat of the volcano had now completely disintegrated, and from the bowels of the earth heavy liquid magma shot up in explosions that rained down as ash on Pompeii and Stabiae. From time to time portions of the throat of the volcano collapsed and blocked it, only to be blown out again as pressure increased. These have produced the thin strata of lapilli that divide the accumulated mass of ash where the beds of volcanic matter from the eruption are undisturbed. There seems to be some question as to whether the ash was charged with gas. Pliny speaks of a strong smell of sulphur as prompting Pomponianus's party to flee, but many geologists believe that there would have been no lethal gas and that the Pompeians must have been killed by the heat of the ash flow, which would have been sufficient to destroy life but not to start fires. In the eruption of Mont Pelée in Martinique in 1906, St. Pierre, a town of twenty-three thousand inhabitants eight kilometers distant from the volcano, was wiped out in a matter of minutes. In Pompeii the earlier accumulation of pumice in lapilli reaches an average depth of about 2.60 m, while the depth of the ash is only about 1.10 m.

Whether those who had taken refuge in a cryptoporticus or other strongly built part of their house were more than momentarily aware of the change in the nature of the matter now raining from Vesuvius has been disputed. Clearly Pliny's friends escaped; he seems to have been the only victim of that party. Whatever the force of the ash flow, it cannot have been as swift or as lethal as that at St. Pierre. In the Casa del Menandro a group of three seem to have tried to dig their way through a wall to reach other victims, but with what purpose is not clear (Maiuri 1933, 11–16). Most seem to have accepted death with dignified resignation. It is hard to estimate how many may have perished, either in terms of numbers or in terms of the percentage of the population. Were the numerous skeletons in the cryptoporticus of the Villa di Diomede the farm hands and resident staff of a large estate? or were they a household? A single woman among them seems to have had more than simple jewelry, and hers was not rich.[30] Since many must have lost their lives on the roads or at the port, waiting for means or essaying to escape with inadequate means, the picture must remain hopelessly incomplete. But however many perished, it is clear that many survived.

The eruption lasted two days, and when it was over, Pompeii was buried under nearly four meters of pumice and fine ash. Most of the roofs must have collapsed, though some of the vaults of the Terme del Foro and the Thermae Stabianae survived. The standpipes of the water system, the superstructures of the fortifications, and the upper parts of walls must have stuck up crazily in the midst of desolation. To the Pompeians who returned, it must have seemed a nightmare landscape. The princeps, Titus, appointed a commission of exconsuls to oversee the work of salvage and applied the property of those known to have perished without heirs to the relief of the survivors (Suetonius *Titus* 8.3–4). This historical notice of salvage operations has now been given substance by archaeological exploration. In the forum of Pompeii, despite the numerous bases of honorary statues—sixteen standing figures in the chalcidicum of the Aedificium Eumachiae, fifteen in front of the macellum, at least fifteen equestrian statues around the south and west sides of the forum square, and several larger groups—not only was not a single statue discovered but the marble revetment for only a single base survives. The rest the salvagers recovered. Since the forum was in the midst of rebuilding, many of these may have been stored together in a single

---

[30] *PAH* 1.252–56 (9 March–25 May 1771), 268–78 (12 December 1772–30 July 1774).

place, or a few places, but the salvagers got them all. They took the cult statues of all the temples, except a colossal head of Jupiter and the terracotta images in the Temple of Zeus Meilichios. They got the marble veneer of the curia, the chalcidicum of Eumachia, and the library (Sacellum Larum Publicorum), except for a few flags of the pavement and bits of the baseboard and dado. They so completely denuded the three triumphal arches near the north end of the forum that it is impossible to tell whom they honored or what the program of decoration may have been. They stripped the scaenae of the two theatres of every vestige of statuary and ornament. Their work was very thorough and must have been highly efficient, for excavating in the fresh volcanic detritus was dangerous business; possibly there were even pockets of residual gas that could prove lethal.

At the same time that there was an official ransacking of the public buildings of the city for whatever was valuable and reusable, private citizens were hard at work trying to recover their own property— and that of their neighbors who had perished. Getting at a strongbox or storeroom was a relatively simple matter; the survivors could locate the area very precisely from the landmarks and walls that still jutted up above the deposits and dig straight down in a well just big enough to work in. In some cases, such as at the Casa dei Dioscuri, where the object was a strongbox to which they evidently did not have the key, they dug down behind the wall against which the strongbox stood and tunneled into it from the back. This would seem to be an efficient system, but since the salvagers missed some forty-five gold coins and five silver ones in the process, we may wonder whether these were members of the household. In the Villa dei Misteri they dug a well into the corridor between two storerooms and tunneled into each from that, a very economical system. At other places in the city the salvagers clearly were not members of the household. In the Casa degli Amanti they tunneled from room to room around the peristyle in a frantic search for things of value, while only next-door, in a cellar under the baths of the Casa del Menandro, a large table service of silver, no less than one hundred and eighteen pieces, together with a number of pieces of gold jewelry and a small hoard of coins, lay undisturbed (*NSc* 1934, 336 [O. Elia]; Maiuri 1933, 245–53).

Quite often this treasure hunt proved fatal. Over and over again, especially in the northwest quarter of the city, where there were so many fine houses close to one another, the excavators found skeletons of people carrying hoards of jewelry and coins at levels high above the pavement. At first it was supposed that these were late fugitives trying to make their way to safety over the accumulated lapilli; then it became clear that they were salvagers and looters.

Whether Pompeii came to an end with the ancient plunder of the ruins is not entirely clear. Once the survivors returned and saw the extent of the destruction, they must have decided that systematic excavation and rebuilding on the site was out of the question. But the Sarno Valley was too rich simply to be abandoned. Towns like Nuceria and Nola, which must have suffered extensive damage, continued to exist without any hiatus, so far as we know, and would have required an outlet to the sea of the sort Pompeii had provided. There are some signs, though nothing very much, that for a time people lived in the ruins of Pompeii, fixing them up as best they might. The course of the Sarno River had probably changed a good bit with the deposits of volcanic material, but it was still a considerable stream, and very soon the initially destructive volcanic ash would enrich the soil of the valley. It is impossible to imagine that life here could have come to an end and equally impossible to see clearly the pattern in which it continued. We may suspect that individual villas were quickly rebuilt and restored to productivity; possibly there were even villages, and probably there was at least a fishing community soon built at the new mouth of the Sarno. But these were all dependent on Nuceria; Pompeii had returned to what it had been at the end of the fourth century.

2 · THE SITE AND ITS
GEOGRAPHICAL CHARACTER

Pompeii covers the swelling end of a solidified stream of volcanic material. This was thrown out in successive eruptions by Vesuvius to the southeast of the main mass of the volcano. It must have arrived in a liquid state, or nearly liquid, and has hardened in rounded bluffs. As it descended the lowest slope of the mountain some impediment must have interfered with its advance, for the site is divided by a gradually deepening cleft running northwest/southeast from the crossing of the Via di Nola and the Strada Stabiana to the Porta di Stabia, the lowest point in the city. A second impediment lower down the slope seems to have shaped the bowl of the Theatrum Maius. From the Porta di Ercolano counterclockwise around the site, at least as far as the Porta di Nola and very likely as far as the Porta del Vesuvio, the city defenses follow the line of the brow of this mass; possibly the drop below was sometimes scarped to eliminate irregularities, but for the most part it appears unimproved. Along the southern front of the site of Pompeii is what is commonly called *lava tenera*, or pappamonte stone, a dense black earth heavily peppered with small grains of lime that can be dug out with a spade. Toward the centre of the site it is underlaid by deep strata of lava (trachite), but all over the city wells have been driven through this down to the water table of the Sarno Valley.

The isolated mass of Vesuvius divides the generally flat coastal plain along the northeast side of the Bay of Naples into two broad valleys leading back inland. The strip between the bay and the volcano is narrow—and was narrower in antiquity—and cut by torrent gullies. Therefore many of the cities on the bay originally communicated by water more readily than by land. The northwestern valley was dominated by Naples, the southeastern by Pompeii. West of

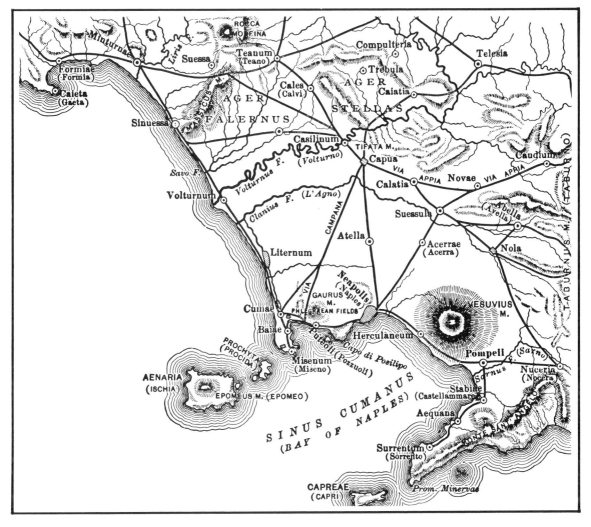

FIGURE 1.
Map of the Bay of
Naples, Showing the
Ancient Sites and
Roads, as Known

Naples begins the great conglomeration of volcanic craters and hills
known collectively as the Campi Phlegraei, stretching from the gates
of Naples to Cape Misenum and continuing beyond in the islands of
Procida (Prochyta) and Ischia (Pithecusa). The south shore of this peninsula, which forms one boundary of the Bay of Naples, is deeply
indented with smaller bays and lagoons, of which the most beautiful
were occupied by the port of Puteoli and the resort of Baiae. Toward
Misenum the great Augustan naval base of the Tyrrhenian fleet was
built in part from existing lagoons and crater lakes, in part by man-
made dikes and moles. Volcanic activity can be observed throughout
this district, and eruptions occur occasionally, though the larger vol-
canoes have not been active in historical time. There is a wealth of
volcanic stones and sands, of which the most famous are the light

yellow tufa of Naples and the grey pozzolana (pit sand) of Puteoli. The former cuts very easily and makes excellent building stone but cannot be carved; the latter makes admirable mortar for concrete.

The southeastern valley is drained by the Sarno River and bounded by the Sorrentine Peninsula, a rugged and dramatic spur of the Apennines that runs out to sea in a direction somewhat south of west and is continued and terminated by the island of Capri. This is all limestone, the principal ridge called Monti Lattari (Lactarius Mons and Surrentini Montes), but in the folds and gullies are deep deposits of volcanic material, including tufa, and mineral springs are frequent in the neighborhood of Stabiae. The south side of the peninsula is gloriously beautiful but inhospitable; along the north side protected bays afford landings for a few towns. Stabiae (Castellammare di Stabia), on the slopes of Monte Faito at the beginning of the peninsula, and Surrentum (Sorrento) are the most familiar. Wine from the neighborhoods of both is esteemed today, as it was in antiquity (Pliny *HN* 14.64; Strabo 5.4.3 [C243]). The higher limestone slopes are also densely planted with olives.

Behind Vesuvius, between the volcano and the ridges of the Apennines that run northwest/southeast, is a valley dominated by the city of Nola that links the upper valleys of Naples and Pompeii. Nola seems to have had little to do with Naples in Roman times and seems instead to have relied on Pompeii for the bulk of its imported goods. A highway that had been important at least since the early Iron Age (witness the Ponte Cagnano necropolis and the princely tombs of Praeneste) ran from the Tiber down the Hernican Valley, through the low pass at Casinum (Monte Cassino) into Campania, to Capua. From Capua it passed behind Vesuvius to Nola and through the pass at Nuceria Alphaterna (Nocera Superiore) to the Gulf of Salerno and on to Paestum (Poseidonia). From here goods could go overland to Sybaris, the mother city of Poseidonia, or be transported by sea.

The importance of this highway is hard to measure and must have fluctuated with a variety of conditions, but it was certainly always very great and continues to be so today. The Autostrada del Sole follows its course. The pass at Nuceria is a particularly vital part, for here the Sarno Valley rises very gradually and connects with a valley draining into the Gulf of Salerno, so that though rugged mountains rise forbiddingly on both sides, through this pass, and only through this pass, one can make one's way easily, even unaware of how far one has climbed, until one emerges high above Salerno on the other side. Nuceria and Salernum must have come into existence to service and protect this road, and Pompeii must have begun either as a watch post on the sea to guard against surprise attacks on the road or as a link with the sea for some of the inland cities along the road. Probably it was something of both, for Strabo (5.4.8 [C247]) tells us that Pompeii's port was in close connection and commerce with Puteoli in the last years of its existence.[1] In the Social War it usurped the lead of Nuceria, and as one of the more important cities in Campania we find it associated with Nola and Capua. Since we cannot trace its existence as a city before the Second Punic War, we cannot say who its founders may have been, but it is scarcely thinkable that before its emergence as a city in its own right its history can have been separate from that of the road. Whoever controlled the road in this sector must have controlled Pompeii.

But it was its suitability as a port that was responsible for Pompeii's emergence as a city. The Sarno River, we are told by Strabo (5.4.8), was navigable in both directions in the vicinity of Pompeii, and its port was in large part a river port, which means that the river must have changed considerably since then, for today it is an inconsequential stream, only partly because so much water is drawn off to water the fields. It can never have been much longer than it is in its main stream, but the character of its system may well have been affected by Vesuvius. If any landmark was needed to mark the river mouth for navigators, this was provided by a small island, Petra Herculis (Isola di Rovigliano) (Pliny *HN* 32.17). Attempts have been made to locate the line of the coast in front of Pompeii in antiquity. The most important of these took the form of a series of fourteen small test pits dug by Ruggiero in 1879. He reasoned that where strata of volcanic debris in a test pit corresponded to those observed in the deposits covering Pompeii, these would have been laid down on dry land, while the same material falling in water, being lighter than water, would have been carried away or confused by currents. On the basis of this investigation, he located the ancient coastline about a kilometer west of the Porta Marina of Pompeii, or half the present distance from that gate to the sea. His findings were later modified by Iacono, whose study of the problem is the most detailed to date and produced the most plausible solution. Iacono put the coastline about seven hundred meters west of the Porta Marina.[2] Finds of fishermen's gear, including a boat and anchor, and storehouses in the neighborhood of the old Sarno bridge on the highway from Torre Annunziata

---

[1] Not only are the frequent mentions of Puteoli and Puteolani in Pompeian graffiti testimony to this but the cache of wax tablets found in excavations near the ancient mouth of the Sarno River, generally known as the archive of the Agro Murecine, is composed almost entirely of documents having to do with the legal and business world of Puteoli (see, e.g., C. Giordano in *RendNap* 45 [1970] 211–31; 46 [1971] 173–82, 183–97; 47 [1972] 167–86; 48 [1973] 307–10, 311–18; 51 [1976] 145–68; and 53 [1978] 249–69).

[2] M. Ruggiero, *Pompei e la regione sotterrata dal Vesuvio nell'anno LXXIX* (Naples 1879) 5–14; Sogliano 17–26.

to Castellammare suggest that here a fishing community must have settled near the mouth of the river and tend to confirm Iacono's interpretation of the evidence.[3]

The port of Pompeii has never been positively located, though a complex of buildings discovered in 1880 and 1881 in which there were a number of skeletons of victims of the eruption carrying gold jewelry not far from the Porta di Stabia (on the near side of the Canale di Bottaro) has been taken to belong to it. Presumably it lay more or less opposite the Porta di Stabia and west of this toward the river's mouth, and since no warehouses or depots cluster inside this gate, the port must have been extensive and efficiently organized. Some slight clue to its complexity is given by the canal recently discovered in the area outside and north of the Porta Marina. This is still unstudied and unpublished, but if canal barges were brought up this far, it seems likely that an arc of commercial establishments ran outside the southwest quadrant of the city.

The Sarno Valley is wide and fertile; it is farmed intensively as far inland as Sarno (Sarnum). Today it is almost entirely taken up with small market gardens that grow a great variety of produce, often as many as five crops a year. These are not, by and large, the crops that were grown in antiquity, but we can presume that there was the same intensive agriculture. At least the villae rusticae that have come to light in the district seem to be more commonly independent farmhouses of moderate size than housing for gangs of field hands.[4] Grain, fruit, vegetables, and flowers will have been grown in the valley, with vineyards and grazing both in the valley and on the lower slopes of the surrounding hills, olives and pasture for smaller animals a little higher up.[5] Because of the tendency of the lime brought down in solution in the Sarno to precipitate out as soon as it reaches the valley floor with its warmer temperatures and numerous warm volcanic springs, drainage ditches and canals have to be dug and the soft travertine that forms removed periodically; otherwise the ground becomes swampy and unusable. The quarrying operation is one more of the annual chores of farm life.

The slopes of Vesuvius above Pompeii are rather different, and to judge from Strabo's description, they must have been very different in antiquity (Strabo 5.4.8 [C247]). The lower slopes were covered with

---

[3]NSc 1880, 494–98; 1881, 25–29, 64–66, 121; 1901, 423–40 (A. Sogliano).

[4]On the villae rusticae around Pompeii see R. C. Carrington, "Studies on the Campanian *villae rusticae*," *JRS* 21 (1931) 110–30; J. Day, "Agriculture in the Life of Pompeii," *YCS* 3 (1932) 165–208; Rostovtzeff *SEHRE*[2] passim; S. De Caro, "Boscoreale," *Pompeii, Herculaneum, Stabiae* 1 (1983) 328–31; and J. H. D'Arms, "Ville rustiche e ville di 'otium,'" in F. Zevi ed., *Pompei 79* (Naples 1984) 65–86.

[5]K. D. White, *Roman Farming* (London 1970) 47–65, 72–73, 82, 272–329.

vineyards and produced a strong, sweet wine. Higher up there must have been some olive cultivation, for an olive pulper and an oil press were found in the Pisanella villa at Boscoreale.[6] Here the land seems to have been divided into larger parcels than in the valley, suitable for one-crop farming, and here the finest villas seem to have been built, where they would catch the breeze in summer and look over the valley and the bay but be close enough to be accessible from the city and to use the city's port for the export of their wine and oil.

Strabo says that Vesuvius was covered with vineyards to its summit, which was in large part flat, bare of vegetation, and cindery, evidence that it had once been volcanic. In the famous lararium painting from the Casa del Centenario a conical mountain is shown that is often taken to be Vesuvius. Its lower slopes are covered with vineyard that gives way to trees, probably either olives or forest, while the very summit is apparently treeless. On Monte Somma today, which must more nearly resemble Vesuvius in antiquity than the ash cone that is so prominent today, above a certain point all agriculture ceases because of the steepness of the slope and the sharp-edged boulders that strew it and is succeeded by chestnut woods, where the only activity most of the year is charcoal burning. Except for the famous umbrella pines, which are ubiquitous and sometimes occur in groves, other timber is comparatively rare. In the paintings of Pompeii we see what are probably oaks, sycamores, poplars, alders, and cypress. Fir and beech were common in the Apennines in antiquity; the latter seem responsible for the name of Monte Faito behind Stabiae. But probably much of the better timber of the slopes of the Sarno Valley was cut in the intensive shipbuilding of the Punic Wars.

Somewhere on Vesuvius we must put the quarries of *lapis pompeianus*. These will not have been far from the city, but far enough that there is no evidence of cutting or working of this stone within the city. The mountain slope rises gently as far as Boscoreale and then becomes steep. The quarries should be on the lower slopes.

As we see the mountain from Pompeii today, it seems to come to an almost perfect peak, a smooth cone of ash of purplish grey with a lesser, more irregular height behind it to the east. This lesser height is Monte Somma, only very little lower than Vesuvius itself, from which it is separated by a depression in part called the Atrio del Cavallo, in part the Valle dell'Inferno. This is the remains of the ancient crater that erupted in A.D. 79.[7] The ash cone is a comparatively recent formation of light and volatile stone around an orifice that has opened inside the great crater.

---

[6] *MonAnt* 7 (1897) 397–554 (A. Pasqui), esp. 496–504.
[7] *Enciclopedia Italiana*, s.v. Vesuvio, p. 248 (G. B. Alfano).

The Bay of Naples looks southwest and is well protected from most other directions by high mountain ridges. Almost the only snow in winter is a cap covering Vesuvius from time to time, and the summer is bearable, hot and bright but tempered by the proximity of the sea, and known for its pleasant evenings. Oranges and lemons, artichokes, broccoli, and fennel in the winter months are succeeded by a great variety of fruits and market vegetables in the spring and summer. Palms thrive. In the landscapes and still-life pictures of Pompeii we see grapes, apples, pears, pomegranates, figs, cherries, and peaches, the last two relatively exotic and recent importations, the cherry having been introduced to Italy by Lucullus on his return from the Mithridatic War in 66 B.C. Mushrooms and asparagus are also shown as delicacies, while a wide range of legumes and nuts have been found in a carbonized state here and there in the excavations. Suckling pig, kid, and hare, as well as a range of poultry, chickens, geese, peacocks, guinea fowl, squab, and several game birds, are shown in the xenium compositions. Duck seems to have been a rarity and was probably not domesticated in Italy. The bay teems with fish and shellfish. It is certainly one of the most productive areas in the world, and its beauty and the intensity of its life impress themselves on every visitor. For the Romans of antiquity a visit to the Crater, as they called the Bay of Naples, was travel abroad, *peregrinatio,* and the Romans today feel much the same way.[8] History may have accentuated the differences, but Naples today and the Neapolitan character must have been shaped largely by the physical environment. With all that life and all that natural beauty surrounding them, the ancient Pompeians must have been as strongly oriented toward exuberance, youth, and love as their modern counterparts.

Pompeii emerges, then, as geographically well blessed, oriented both to the sea and commerce and to the land and agriculture. Its climate was exceptional, decidedly milder than that of Rome yet temperate, not subtropical. Its land was good. Roads connected it to Naples and Sorrento along the coast and to Nola and Salerno up the Sarno Valley. Presumably the coast road was at least as old as the Sullan colony, and Pompeii was linked to the other municipalities of the bay by a convenient land route as well as by water. The graffiti show that the cities and islands of the northern part of the bay figured large in the thinking of the citizenry, who thought of Puteoli as more a rival than a superior.[9] Probably many Pompeians were accustomed to journey to the northern cities for important feasts and games, and contingents from there came to Pompeii in return. The

[8] See J. H. D'Arms, *Romans on the Bay of Naples* (Cambridge, Mass., 1970) passim.
[9] See, e.g., *CIL* 4.2152, 2183, 4262.

record of the cycle of market days in the cities of the area scratched on a Pompeian wall (*CIL* 4.8863) shows that communication was easy and constant. If Pompeii was not so glamorous as Naples and Baiae, nor so historically important as Cumae and Pithecusa (Ischia), nor so cosmopolitan as Puteoli, it had its share of each of these qualities and felt a close affinity with these neighbors.

3 · THE CITY PLAN

The Via di Nola and the Via dell'Abbondanza, the major east/west arteries of Pompeii, are commonly called decumani, and the Strada Stabiana, its single north/south artery, a cardo, but it is widely recognized that this terminology cannot be defended, that the city plan of Pompeii bears only superficial resemblance at best to the castrum plan, and that to use the terms of that plan in describing it is to avoid facing fundamental difficulties. In fact we do not know how Pompeii came into being, how it grew, and how and when the grids and patterns of streets that can be discerned in various sectors were laid down.[1]

Early in this century, with the opening of the Nuovi Scavi, it was observed that the blocks east of blocks I vi and IX v seemed to be laid out aligned to the east/west arteries, at right angles to these and with regular, or nearly regular, dimensions.[2] With the excavation of regiones I and II in the 1950s the correctness of this observation was confirmed; not only do the southern extremities of these blocks run true to plan but two streets laid out parallel to the Via dell'Abbondanza came to light with blocks that conform to the pattern along them. The lines of the blocks are not of constant depth, those in the second line being a little shorter than those along the Via dell'Abbondanza and those in the third line shorter again by about

---

[1] The basic sources on the question up to the present are: F. Haverfield, *Ancient Town-Planning* (Oxford 1913) 63–68; R. C. Carrington, "The Etruscans and Pompeii," *Antiquity* 6 (1932) 5–23; G. Spano, "Porte e regioni pompeiane e vie campane," *RendNap* 17 (1937) 269–361; A. von Gerkan, *Der Stadtplan von Pompeji* (Berlin 1940); F. Castagnoli, *Ippodamo di Mileto* (Rome 1956) 26–32; Eschebach 1970, 17–61; and L. Richardson, Jr., "The City-Plan of Pompeii," in *La regione sotterrata dal Vesuvio: studi e prospettive* (Acts of the International Congress, 11–15 November 1979, Naples 1982) 341–51.

[2] Haverfield (supra n.1) 63–68; cf. Sogliano 38–47.

the same amount, but it is clear that they must all have been laid out together, and irregularities and discrepancies are casual.

F. Castagnoli thought that the dominant line in this quarter was provided by the road leading in from the Porta di Nocera, which would form a cardinal axis, but it is quite clear that the siting of all three gates in this sector—the Porta di Sarno, the Porta di Nola, and the Porta di Nocera—cannot be separated from the street grid.[3] Any attempt to see the gates as determining factors will run into insurmountable difficulties in explaining why the east/west arteries divide the eastern reaches of the city into three bands that at their western end are precisely thirds of the length of the Strada Stabiana. This fact is of the highest importance, for it must mean that the line of the Strada Stabiana antedates and governs the layout without conforming to it.

That this is indeed so is shown by the blocks east of the Strada Stabiana. In regiones I and IX the first two rows of blocks east of this street are rhomboidal, normal both to the east/west arteries and to the Strada Stabiana. Beyond this point block I vii is trapezoidal, clearly with the object of making adjustment between the rhomboid and the rectangular grid. And it looks as though blocks I xix and IX vii will prove, when cleared, to be adjustive blocks of the same sort.

The reason the eastern reaches of the city are not laid out normal to the Strada Stabiana has become clear only recently, though it might have been guessed from consideration of the general configuration of the city. Pompeii covers a peninsula of volcanic effluvium, and it is this that gives the city its shape. From the Porta di Ercolano counterclockwise to the Porta di Nola, as the recent excavations outside the walls between the amphitheatre and the Porta di Nola show, and very probably for some distance west beyond the Porta di Nola, there was an important natural drop just outside the walls. For at least three-quarters of their circuit the fortifications of Pompeii follow a natural line of defense, and if the concentration of towers is valid evidence, only from the Porta del Vesuvio to the Porta di Ercolano was there no natural fosse of protection.

Once it had been decided that the city should occupy the whole of this peninsula, the approximate rectangle of the southeast quarter and the axis of the Via dell'Abbondanza were easy for the planners to see. Had the grid been laid out normal to the Strada Stabiana, the southeast quarter would have been disproportionately large and hard

[3]Castagnoli (supra n. 1) 28–30. He further held that the enlargement of the city to its present size was the work of Greek planners in the fifth century and that there was no intermediate phase between von Gerkan's "old city" and the final plan. In this I believe he was mistaken.

to subdivide into the long thin blocks they preferred, and another artery might have seemed necessary. It having been decided that the Strada Stabiana and two cross streets were to be the basis of the plan, what we see represents simply the most sensible and logical arrangement of these. So the whole city east of the Strada Stabiana must have been laid out in a single operation.

But some features of the northwest quarter of the city must also have been laid out at the same time, for its east/west streets are an extension of the Via di Nola and a street parallel to this, the Vicolo di Mercurio. In this quarter, however, the cross streets, though parallel to one another, are not squared to these arteries; rather, they are canted at a perceptible angle that makes the shops along the front of the Casa del Fauno, for example, seem awkwardly planned. The reason for this is clearly that there was an important preexistent grid that could not be abolished. The axial Via di Mercurio, the Strada delle Scuole, and the precinct of the Aedes Apollinis all have the same orientation, at variance with that of the forum. So do the Villa di Cicerone, the Villa di Diomede, and the Villa dei Misteri in the suburbium. Here we seem to have the remnants of a city plan older than the forum and the fortifications that survived as a few main streets along which old property divisions had to be respected in later days. It is interesting to note that if the towers of the fortifications of the first century B.C. replaced towers of the original construction, then those in this sector were keyed to the street grid and did not follow any rule for optimum spacing.

The planners of the new city were able to bring the northwest quarter into their plan by extending the lines of their new arteries through it, so it is hardly likely that the zone was heavily built up at that time or that more than a few streets that had to be respected existed here. They were certainly free to lay out long thin blocks of the same sort as those in the eastern quarters, but these are exceptionally deep in the row along the wall, so deep that one might have expected another east/west street here.

The whole layout of the city north of the Via di Nola and east of the Strada Stabiana can thus be shown to be the product of a single operation of sweeping scope, obedient to a few normative avenues and concepts and admitting occasional irregularity where an older road, such as the Strada Consolare, cut across the neat rectangles of the new plan or where one section had to be adjusted to fit another.

The same does not seem to be true of the southwest quarter of the city. Here streets wind and jog with seemingly inexplicable capriciousness, widening at some points to make little public squares, narrowing at others until wheeled traffic could hardly get through. The Via Marina, along the Aedes Veneris, is one example of this, the Vicolo dei Soprastanti another. Blocks and streets here are so irregular and illogical that von Gerkan very reasonably decided that this must be the ancient heart of the city, reflecting in its confusions the rebuildings of many centuries.[4] Here were the forum and the most ancient sanctuaries; here should be the nucleus from which the new city expanded. An irregular, apparently continuous street composed of the Vicolo dei Soprastanti, the Via degli Augustali, the Vicolo del Lupanare, and the Via dei Teatri seems to bound this ancient heart and may be taken as representing the line of an ancient wall street that has disappeared on the south and west sides under later building. While von Gerkan recognized that there were difficulties with his theory, it seemed to fit the evidence better and at more points than any other that could be devised.

But the theory depends entirely on looking for a recognizable settlement boundary and a defensible core, a tight compound fortified against the attacks of hostile neighbors and pirate raids. There is no indication that this approach is justified; certainly any reading of the continuous boundary line that von Gerkan saw as a wall street or a survival of a wall street is demonstrably mistaken. It follows no natural contour and offers no advantage for defense. Even its continuity is specious, since it forks at a point where one would not expect a gate to have occurred (the juncture of the Via degli Augustali and the Vicolo del Lupanare), and the continuous stretch runs around only half of the presumed settlement. Moreover, the grid of the streets within this boundary cannot be completed, as he proposed, by connection of the streets on one side of the forum with those on the other; yet the forum is far too big to have served for any settlement of the size we are discussing or for any much smaller than the city at its fullest extent. At point after point von Gerkan's theory proves inadequate. The Vicolo dei Soprastanti runs to the city wall simply to permit the sewer under it to discharge its wastes into the canal below the city at this point and makes an awkward and deceptive elbow in doing so; it and the fortifications here must be contemporary, but it is not a wall street. Recent excavations have shown that the natural edge of the site southwest of this lay along the line of the Porta Marina, well beyond the line of von Gerkan's wall street. And the pattern of streets within the circuit conforms to the distortions of the circuit, not to an axial street or streets. We should do well, therefore, to abandon von Gerkan's theory and seek some explanation for these anomalies.

There can be no question that the oldest settlement on the site of

---

[4] Von Gerkan (supra n. 1) 15–26. The theory seems to have been enunciated first by Haverfield, but von Gerkan is responsible for its elaboration and refinement into a comprehensive scheme.

Pompeii is most likely to have been in the southwest quarter. The archaic material found in the Forum Triangulare and the Aedes Apollinis strengthens this probability, as does the location of the Aedes Veneris and the forum here. So far as we can see, the heart of the city's life was here throughout its history.

The main approaches to an early settlement in this quarter must have been by the Strada Consolare and the Strada Stabiana. The Via Marina we can discount as of small importance; the pull up into the city is extremely steep, difficult on foot and almost impossible for a vehicle. The excavations outside the walls at this point have produced nothing that suggests a lively flow of traffic and trade here, despite the canal that has come to light under the Insula Occidentalis, and inside the gate there is not the concentration of food and wine shops we see at other gates. On the other hand, traffic from the northeast probably would have come down the ridge that was later crowned by the Porta del Vesuvio and made its way over the tableland of regio VI by a route that has disappeared; it is possible, but hardly likely, that the Vicolo Storto was once part of this. There were probably also farms on the slopes of Vesuvius that used this route, but there were no towns out there, and it is not likely to have been heavily traveled.

Along the Strada Consolare, however, came the traffic from Oplontis, Herculaneum, and ultimately Naples. This was an important road and certainly heavily traveled. And by the valley of the Strada Stabiana all traffic from the river port and the farms and villages of the Sarno Valley, in addition to traffic from Stabiae and Nuceria, must have made its way. There was a natural cleft here, the Porta di Stabia lying at the lowest point of the city, and up this a road must have led from the very beginning. We can see that the Strada Consolare must antedate the grid of streets in the northwest quarter, and one can project its line to connect with the forum without much difficulty. But the Strada Stabiana runs in a straight line from the lowest point of the site to the highest without approaching the forum by the slightest deviation in its course. Yet along this road must have passed most of the supplies and commerce of the city. It is easy to say, as many who have dealt with the problem before me have said, that having reached the line of the Via dell'Abbondanza, this traffic simply turned, at what amounts to a right angle, and flowed toward the forum. But in the last period, when that stretch of the Via dell'Abbondanza was closed to wheeled traffic, it would have had to turn into the Via del Tempio di Iside, where the grade is distinctly gentler, and before block VIII iv was built up a road diagonally across that area would have offered distinct advantages.[5] We must therefore try to explain

[5] There is abundant evidence that in the last period of Pompeii the forum was closed

why no such road existed. To resolve the difficulty, von Gerkan postulated preexisting *Landstrassen,* country lanes, along the lines of the Via dell'Abbondanza and Via di Nola, but he does not seem to have appreciated the importance of the natural slope up from the Strada Stabiana and certainly did not take into account the configuration of the hill of Pompeii as a peninsula. We now know that his *Landstrassen* are imaginary.

We would do better to see the irregular streets of Pompeii, not as boundaries of any sort, but as the survival of roads leading to and from centres of activity. Just as the Strada Consolare seems originally to have brought traffic in from the northwest to the Aedes Apollinis and a market in the neighborhood of the forum, so the Via dei Teatri and the Vicolo del Lupanare seem to be vestiges of a road bringing traffic to and from the Forum Triangulare. In part the Vicolo dei Soprastanti follows a natural contour along which an important drain was laid; parts of the Via degli Augustali seem to be branches from the Strada del Foro, feeding into it and governed by it, rather than parts of a continuous circuit. When one walks the lines of von Gerkan's circuit, one gets no feeling of coherence or continuity. It is far more likely that we are dealing with a few well-marked roads along which villagers early established houses and fields in a community focused not so much on defense as on agriculture. In the event of a need to defend themselves, if they could not take refuge in Nuceria, the mother city, then they could withdraw to the natural arx of the Forum Triangulare, where their limited numbers could readily be accommodated and where the only defense work necessary would have been a relatively short wall on the northwest.

When this way of looking at the plan of this quarter of the city is tested, its essential correctness becomes apparent. The somewhat irregular grid of streets within von Gerkan's circuit is seen to be the product of a series of compromises between the irregular lines of the old tracks and a rectangular grid, and the blocks just outside it are shaped by a combination of the old tracks and arbitrary adjustments to fit on the grid of the northern and eastern reaches of the city. In other words, the grid of the southwest quarter must be contemporary with the grid elsewhere.

Thus the Vicolo del Balcone Pensile and the Vicolo degli Scheletri are not normal to the precinct of the Aedes Apollinis and the Via di Mercurio but, rather, basically normal to the eastern stretch of the Via

---

to all wheeled traffic, and the question is, How close to the forum could it be brought and by what routes? At the time of the construction of the Tetrapylon of the Holconii a block was thrown across the Via dell'Abbondanza just west of its crossing with the Strada Stabiana, and vehicles had then to continue to the Via degli Augustali.

degli Augustali. The Vicolo di Eumachia is not at right angles to these or precisely parallel to the axis of the forum because of an adjustment it makes to meet the Vicolo Storto. The Vicolo del Gallo is clearly simply related to the Vicolo dei Soprastanti and the Aedes Apollinis, without concern for squaring with a comprehensive scheme.

Moreover, all the streets in this part of the city show an interesting relationship to the forum: their lines converge on the forum but do not continue across it. It has long been recognized that the failure of the Via Marina and the Via dell'Abbondanza to align is a major obstacle to reading their line as one of the original axes of the city, while precisely the same is true of the Via di Mercurio and the Strada delle Scuole, read as the cross axis in the opposite direction, though the gap between these is greater. Yet so strong is the wish to find in Pompeii a coherent master plan for the archaic community that this is usually put aside with no more than some remark to the effect that in the nucleus of ancient Pompeii axiality was not so rigorously applied as elsewhere.[6] But these streets cannot be made axial by simply introducing hypothetical jogs or bends.

It seems rather that the layout of the forum of Pompeii and the grid of the streets around it must belong to the same scheme as the rest of the city plan, worked out in the same detail and with the same architectonic consideration of organic need. It is a big forum, a forum to serve a city the size of Pompeii in its full extent, and any attempt to reduce it by seeing this or that area as having been a later addition falls foul of the street grid, which cannot be extended across the open area at any point. The forum had assumed its present shape and size before the grid of streets was laid down, and Maiuri's excavations in the late 1930s and 1940s under the present floors of the forum confirmed the antiquity of the general lines of the present square.[7] It always had the long narrow shape Vitruvius prescribes for a forum, never the squarish shape of a Greek agora. Its siting probably goes back to a very early period, a time before any planning of the city, and probably was due primarily to the proximity of the Aedes Apollinis, if the two did not come into being simultaneously as the core of village life.

If the city plan in all its parts and ramifications shows strong signs of being the product of a single, all-embracing conception, we must ask when and why it came into being, when Pompeii would have felt the necessity to set its house in order and anticipated the rapid growth implicit in so grand a scheme. The answer is clear and inescapable: when the fortifications were constructed. For the main ar-

[6]Castagnoli (supra n. 1) 27.
[7]*NSc* 1941, 371–404; 1942, 253–320, 404–15; 1951, 225–60. Maiuri 1973, 53–133, 191–223.

teries and the city gates go closely together, and if the present towers reflect the siting of original towers, these were keyed to the grid of streets. When the fortifications were laid out, a firm city plan became a necessity, and there is every indication that the walls were built in the middle of the third century B.C., between the first and second Punic wars. At that time Pompeii was probably wealthy enough to undertake such a grandiose building program as a result of the First Punic War, and the necessary impulse was given by the influx of immigrants from the uplands and backwaters eager to share in the new prosperity the war had generated for the coastal cities engaged in shipbuilding and seafaring.

Can we say anything positive about the plan of Pompeii before this? Only that the precinct of Apollo, the Via di Mercurio, the Strada delle Scuole, and the villas of the suburbium northwest of the city seem to have conformed to an orthogonal layout of the territory, while a handful of streets in the neighborhood of the forum did not. Presumably the latter represent a very early phase of habitation here, when builders were free to site as they chose, while the former are vestiges of something later. That something seems to have involved centuriation of a considerable area, possibly even all the arable land in the Sarno Valley. Since Pompeii seems to have been a mere village, a dependency of Nuceria, down to the close of the Second Samnite War, it is tempting to see such centuriation as an outgrowth of the Samnite Wars, which brought all of central Italy firmly under the control of Rome, *ciues sine suffragio*, but firm proof is lacking.[8]

[8] The observation of F. Zevi ("Urbanistica di Pompei," in *La regione sotterrata dal Vesuvio*, 353–65) that the orientation of the Aedes Apollinis and the Via di Mercurio is the same as that of three large suburban villas to the northwest must mean that a survey and division into lots of a substantial territory were carried out at the time of the laying out of the temple and the streets obedient to this grid. P. Mingazzini ("Un criterio di datazione della villa di Diomede a Pompei," *ArchCl* 1 [1949] 202–3) would date this to a time before the deduction of the Roman colony, because the Via dei Sepolcri runs at a sharp angle to this grid. He thought the road was cut across ancient rectangular lots and could only have been laid out during the reorganization attendant on the arrival of the colonists. But the road is in all probability a very ancient track, and there is nothing in the architecture of the villas that insists on a date before the middle of the first century B.C. The earliest architectural members, the columns of the peristyle of the Villa dei Misteri, are in a very late Tufa Period style, while Tufa Period architecture may, on the evidence of the tomb of Eumachia outside the Porta di Nocera, extend down to late Augustan times. If what has been argued in this chapter is correct, this survey and division into lots must antedate the fortifications and organization of Pompeii as a city.

4 · THE FORTIFICATIONS

The walls of Pompeii are a famous enigma. Built of heterogeneous materials, with stretches that appear widely different in date, in their totality they still show a unified concept of engineering for defense that is without any important parallel elsewhere, and despite several recent studies of other fortifications, they continue to defy attempts to date their successive stages precisely.[1] Maiuri's patient investigation of them at a series of significant points, while it clarified many details, failed to produce stratified deposits of archaeological material that would permit secure dating; indeed, he was forced to confess that he believed earth for the fills and agger must have been brought from some distant point in the countryside, so sterile was it and so insignificant in stratification.[2] But it must be admitted that he was looking for evidence of a particular sort and may well have overlooked evidence that others would have found more significant.

The walls enclose an irregular oval, the long axis lying northeast/southwest and the short axis, northwest/southeast. The long axis is ca. 1200 m long, the short 720 m. They are a fairly sophisticated, but unusual, system, well preserved around much of the circuit. From the Porta di Ercolano counterclockwise probably as far as the Porta del Vesuvio, they run on the brow of the peninsula of volcanic effluvium that forms the city site and in much of their course are basically a terrace wall. But along the north front from the Porta del Vesuvio to the Porta di Ercolano they are of a complicated hybrid character,

---

[1]The most important studies of the fortifications are A. Maiuri, "Studi e ricerche sulla fortificazione di Pompei," *MonAnt* 33 (1930) 113–290; and F. Krischen, *Die Stadtmauern von Pompeji und griechische Festungsbaukunst in Unteritalien und Sizilien* (Die hellenistische Kunst in Pompeji 7, Berlin 1941) 6–18. Consult also *NSc* 1943, 275–94 (A. Maiuri); C. Chiaramonte Treré, *Nuovi contributi sulle fortificazioni pompeiane* (Milan 1986) 13–50.

[2]Maiuri (supra n.1) 136.

combining a double wall of essentially Greek type with an Italic ag-ger. Along this front there probably also ran a broad ditch, though this may have been filled in in the last period of the city. Where they were terrace wall, they seem to have consisted of a series of rectan-gular compartments built of large blocks of Sarno limestone and No-cera tufa filled with earth. These were probably originally, as later, punctuated with occasional rectangular towers, more guardhouses than defense works, for it does not appear that the Pompeians ex-pected attack along these fronts. The slope of the hill was steep, per-haps scarped in places, and the weakest points, at gates and along the north front, would have been the places to expect any hostile assault.

Along the north front the wall is built in two stout faces of stone blocks with an earth fill between and an earth fill, or agger, behind, sloping down on the city side to a low margin wall. In places, espe-cially just east of the Porta di Ercolano, the inner wall is lacking, and the agger was covered with a steep stair, up which defenders could swarm. Elsewhere the inner wall rises some six courses—more than two meters—higher than the outer and was intended more as a screen for the town against missiles than as a bulwark. Outer and inner walls are of the same character, built of large rectangular blocks with short, stout buttresses projecting inward at close intervals. Maiuri thought the inner should represent a later modification of the system, but the two are so perfectly in harmony that that seems most unlikely, and the inner is based in the earth fill, its foot at the height of the eighth course of the outer wall. The wall walk between the two walls, eight meters high and five wide, was provided with battle-ments, which have now largely disappeared, and was open to the sky; there are rainspouts along it at regular intervals. There is no indication as to how the top of the inner wall was finished. In the last period the agger behind it reached only to the height of the city-side doors of the towers, a half-storey above the ground level, where it leveled off, finished as an auxiliary inner wall walk, the buttressed face of the wall rising naked above it; very likely it was always so, though Maiuri postulated removal of part of the agger when the pres-ent towers were built.[3] It is hard to see what the reason for this would have been.

Of the original towers, only one to the west of the Porta del Vesu-vio has been located.[4] This was roughly square, in bond with the curtains and flush with the face of the wall on the exterior, but pro-jecting inward a little on the city side, more a bastion than a tower.

[3] Maiuri (supra n. 1) 167.
[4] Maiuri (supra n. 1) 187–91 and pl. 6.

FIGURE 2.
The Fortification Walls
and the Porta di Nola,
Exterior

The lower part was filled with earth, probably to the height of the wall walk. None of the superstructure survives. Since this was obviously intended to strengthen the gate, we may wonder whether there were not similar towers at all the gates, but no counterpart to this seems to have stood on the opposite side of this gate.

The present gates all show signs of rebuilding at a late period, but in the vault of the Porta di Nola on the city side are a voussoir of tufa and a keystone decorated with a female head in high relief (Minerva?) that must go back at least to the second century B.C.[5] These are associated with an Oscan inscription describing them as the work of the meddix Vibius Popidius (Conway 45; Vetter 14). The head is much battered but seems to have been of good quality. Why the gates should have required rebuilding is not entirely clear; at least four—the Porta di Stabia, the Porta di Nocera, the Porta di Sarno, and the Porta di Nola—were of the same relatively unsophisticated type, a long and narrow throat with the gate proper at the inner end covered

[5]Several of the gates are well illustrated in Eschebach 1978 figs. 102–10, the Porta di Nola in figs. 105–6.

by a barrel vault. At the outer opening are bastions, and between these and the gate, a sort of court where attackers would be exposed to fire from above from both sides. There are no towers, and the bastions seem insufficient for the mounting of much defensive artillery, yet there is no sign of a vault over the outer end or a portcullis. Stairs to the wall walk appear to either side of the gate, but these are in all cases rather narrow. The gate itself was a heavy, two-leaved door closing against a lintel and a sill block and secured by a transverse beam fitting into sockets to either side. Since all the closures seem to have been extremely simple affairs, we may ask whether they were ever intended to endure a siege. But their siting made the gates naturally strong, and in the event of war it would have been possible to reinforce them in a variety of ways. There is no indication that the town fell to the besieging army of Lucius Sulla.

All these gates show a confusing combination of building techniques in which large blocks of Sarno limestone, large blocks of Nocera tufa, a mixture of the two, and concrete faced with incertum of broken lava with coigning in Sarno stone and Nocera tufa appear side by side. Comparison of one with another indicates that they were all rebuilt at the same time to a more or less uniform pattern. In the vaults over the gates proper the masonry is of broken lava in heavy beds of mortar coigned with blocks of Sarno limestone and tufa. The final form of these gates is usually assigned to the time of preparation for the Social War, and the patchwork effect to haste.

The three gates that do not conform to this plan are the Porta del Vesuvio, the Porta Marina, and the Porta di Ercolano. The first two are of the same general lines and carried a vault over the opening to the exterior, but the gates proper close well inside this, in the entrance throat. The Porta del Vesuvio, however, was ruined by the earthquake of A.D. 62 and never rebuilt, so it is not clear in all details. The Porta Marina is a steep passage covered by a tunnel-like vault from the opening on the exterior back nearly to the top of the rise to the plateau of the city site. Along one side of this a corridor for pedestrians was walled off, while off the other opened a guard chamber. There was ample room for mounting machines on top of the vault, and the whole concept of this gate differs from that of the others. Its construction is very like that of the Theatrum Tectum, and it must belong to the early years of the Roman colony; probably it was rebuilt in connection with work on the adjacent Temple of Venus. At a later period it was extended a short distance and given a new façade with a double vault on the exterior; probably this was at the time of the construction of the Villa Imperiale.[6]

[6]A. W. Van Buren ("Further Studies in Pompeian Archaeology," *MAAR* 5 [1925]

The Porta di Ercolano, on the other hand, is not only different in concept from all the others, it is different in almost every way. It is a triple gate, with symmetrical pedestrian passages to either side of the paved road, an inner-court gate in plan, with a portcullis to close the opening to the exterior and a two-leaved door at the city end. But the inner court was not a trap for an attacking enemy so much as a place where important visitors might be received or duty on freight collected. This was a monumental entrance to the city built in the last period, as the construction faced with opus mixtum vittatum shows, despite traces of what at first seems to be First Style decoration. One wonders whether it was also crowned with statuary.

The towers of the present system show two concentrations, one of four around the bastion of the amphitheatre and one of three between the Porta del Vesuvio and the Porta di Ercolano; elsewhere they occur only at wide intervals. In all, thirteen have been counted, but two of these are rather doubtful. Those that can be examined all conform to a single pattern, and the best-preserved is the first to the west of the Porta del Vesuvio, turris X, which has been carefully studied and partially restored. The towers straddle the walls, projecting beyond them on the exterior by 2.15–2.45 m; to construct them, sections of the wall had to be torn out, and the patch in the curtain to either side is clearly of a build with each tower, the masonry of broken lava in heavy beds of mortar coigned with larger pieces of lava and finished with stucco in the First Style. There are three storeys in each, all barrel-vaulted, connected by interior stairs. The middle storey comes at the level of the wall walk and connects with this by an arched door to either side so troops could be moved along the wall with maximum ease. Along the field face are narrow vertical openings for archers, four on the exposed face and one in each flank. From this storey one could go up or down to another storey. If one went down, one came at mid storey to a door in the city side of the tower from which one could make one's way down the slope of the agger or walk along the top of it behind the inner wall. Since there is no sign of a stair down the agger today, we must presume that there was a wooden stair, which seems a bit odd. Descending below this door on the interior, one came at full storey to a guardroom illuminated by very narrow slits on the field face, not so much openings for archers as peepholes for light and reconnoitering, and from this a ramp led down to a postern in the flank of the tower, from which sorties could

---

105–6) held that the outer frame of a gate similar to the Porta di Stabia could be detected here, but he did not observe that this was provided with installations for a double door, which would make it fundamentally different from the Porta di Stabia in concept, as well as in architecture.

be effected. This storey must have served especially for assembling and marshaling men for sorties. The top storey of each tower was provided with large windows with rounded heads, evidently four in each of the three walls commanding the field, and here, one must imagine, artillery would have been mounted. The summit of the tower was decorated with a Doric frieze in stucco and covered with a roof, which Maiuri restored as a gable, Krischen as a roof of four slopes. It also seems possible that there was a flat roof on which more artillery could be mounted. The finish of the frieze, which is finely worked, the attention to proportion and detail in the finish of doors and windows, the care with which foundations and masonry are laid, all suggest that this was no hasty work put through when danger threatened. It seems rather to have been a major civic project, probably many years in process, and a date after the arrival of the Roman colony will best fit the evidence. Had these towers been in use during the siege of Sulla, we should expect to find the outer walls scarred by the missiles of the bombardment and the plaster of the chambers covered with soldiers' graffiti.

The date of the original construction of the walls is not easy to fix. Maiuri, in his investigations of the structure at many points, originally in 1926–27 but thereafter throughout his career, determined that there were traces of an older wall of Sarno limestone blocks with finished faces inside and out at several points in the western part of the circuit. The most extensive remains of this he found east of the Porta del Vesuvio. This he judged pre-Samnite and dated ca. 550–420 B.C. The original construction of the succeeding wall, which is the one with which we are concerned, he put at ca. 420–300 B.C., with a major modification, the introduction of the inner wall and widening of the agger, ca. 300–200 B.C. The evidence for distinguishing two periods is very slight, and one must be very skeptical about it. Certainly most of the wall is of a single build. Because of the agger, Maiuri thought this had an especially Italic character, but the use of a higher inner curtain behind the wall walk is an unusual feature that is peculiarly Greek. This fortification belongs in a class with the Lycurgan walls of Athens of the fourth century, the double-trace system of Philo of Byzantium, recommended for use on sloping ground, a very costly and elaborate defense system and a very sophisticated one.[7] It seems unlikely that such walls would have appeared in Italy before 300 B.C.; in fact, defense works using these principles seem to have appeared first in Greek Sicily only in the first half of the third century B.C.

Since we now know that the walls of Paestum are not Greek, but

---

[7] See F. E. Winter, *Greek Fortifications* (Toronto 1971), esp. 120–21 and 190–91.

either Lucanian or Roman,[8] we need not suppose that a wall with finished faces inside and out would not have been quite acceptable to the Samnites in the fourth and third centuries. Too little of Maiuri's "pre-Samnite" wall has come to light for us to be able to date it—we have neither gate nor tower—but it need not be of high antiquity.

The original construction of the double-trace defense system is probably to be dated to the third quarter of the third century, when Rome was girding for a showdown with Carthage and every coastal town in Italy was readying itself for the struggle. Here we should expect to find the most advanced system that could be devised and no sparing of effort or expense, which will square with what we see. Such a system will have served admirably for the next hundred and fifty years, and only minor modifications and repairs will have been necessary in that time. But in the siege of Sulla the fortifications of Pompeii must have taken a severe pounding. Military science had made considerable advances, with inventions and techniques developed especially for siege warfare. It is not surprising to find that the walls needed considerable repair thereafter. Nor was it yet safe for a city to dispense with its walls, for the sea was infested with pirates, and Rome was to endure another half-century of turmoil before peace was finally achieved. The new towers, new stretches of curtain, and refurbishing of the Porta Marina must have been among the Roman colony's first works.

[8]H. Schläger, "Zu den Bauperioden der Stadtmauer von Paestum," *RömMitt* 69 (1963) 21–26; idem, "Zur Frage der Torverschlüsse von Paestum," ibid. 71 (1964) 104–11.

5 · THE WATER AND SEWER SYSTEMS

Before the Augustan aqueduct brought a supply of fresh Apennine water to Pompeii,[1] the city was dependent for its water on wells driven through the spur of Vesuvius on which it stands to the water table of the Sarno Valley and on rain impounded in cisterns. Conceivably, some use was made of the Sarno River for laundry and industrial purposes, and one would certainly expect the farms of this valley, which is so rich agriculturally, to have drawn water from it by irrigation ditches, but of these we know nothing. No spring within the circuit of the fortifications has ever come to light, and today water must be piped in for restoration and repair work, as well as for drinking.

The difficulty of digging wells probably varied considerably; the stone of the hill of Pompeii is soft along its edges (pappamonte tufa) but dense in the interior of the city, where softer material overlies strata of lava (trachite), and the wells had to be deep, that at the north end of block VI xvi, near the Porta del Vesuvio, the highest point in the city, descending no less than 38.25 m.[2] Consequently, although they are surprisingly numerous, as numerous as the public fountains supplied by the aqueduct, they tended to be public, or shared in common by more than one household. The most conspicuous well is that at the southern end of block VI i, a small rectangular building (no. 19) covered by a barrel vault of rubble masonry with a large, window-like opening, 1.45 m wide by 1.10 m high, in the side toward the Strada Consolare. Unfortunately, it was abandoned and deliberately filled in long before the eruption of A.D. 79, at which time the pulleys and buckets and other apparatus for raising water were removed,

[1]On the water system of Pompeii see H. Mygind, "Pompejis Vandforsyning," in his *Pompeiistudier* (Copenhagen 1977) 77–157, also published in *Janus* 1917, 294–351.
[2]On this well see *NSc* 1931, 546–57 (A. Maiuri).

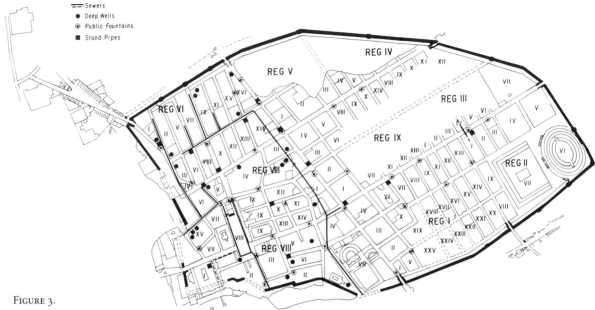

Sewers
● Deep Wells
◉ Public Fountains
■ Stand Pipes

REG IV
REG V
REG VI
REG III
REG IX
REG VIII
REG II
REG I
REG VIII
REG VII

FIGURE 3.
The Deep Wells,
Fountains, Standpipes,
and Sewers in
Pompeii, as Known

and while the contents of the fill are highly informative, assuring us that it was in consequence of the arrival of the Augustan aqueduct that the well was abandoned, today the structure is a mere shell (*NSc* 1910, 563–67 [G. Spano]).

Almost equally familiar is the well covered by a graceful tholos south of the ruins of the Doric temple in the Forum Triangulare. Here the wellhead is a tufa puteal, 0.77 m high, 1.08 m in diameter at its mouth, unfluted and trimmed with simple moldings, while the tholos over it is of the finest Tufa Period architecture, eight Doric columns supporting a plain epistyle and simple cornice, presumably covered with a conical roof of timber and tile. Here again the apparatus for raising water is missing (Pernice 1932, 36).

Other wells are known from their connection with the baths of Pompeii, those of VII i 49 (Thermae Stabianae), VII v 7 (Terme del Foro), and VIII v 36 (Terme Repubblicane). Of these the first was carefully studied in great detail by Maiuri in his investigation of these baths.[3] He was able to determine that the well dates back to the second century B.C. and was originally worked by simple manpower, those appointed to the task hauling water with the aid of only a single pulley. Later an endless chain of buckets was installed that ran round a great wheel and could be worked efficiently by draft animals. Even

[3] *NSc* 1931, 566–69 (A. Maiuri); R. Pemp, *Drei Wasserhebewerke Pompejis* (Würzburg-Aumühle 1940); Eschebach 1979, 27–34.

after the introduction of the aqueduct this seems to have been kept in working condition to supplement the water supply, although the water it provided was probably no softer than aqueduct water.[4] The wells of the other baths were similar, but Maiuri believed that the Terme Repubblicane never actually got a wheel. The least conspicuous and least known of the wells in public areas is that in the southeast corner of the basilica, an area shown on most plans as solid masonry but actually a well and an adjacent tank lined with hydraulic cement.[5] The well was not accessible at floor level, and one might ask what purpose it may have served—perhaps none but to provide water for washing the floors of the basilica and the forum colonnade.

The wells in private houses, on the other hand, in order to be readily accessible to a maximum number of users, tend to be located off the fauces, so that nearby householders could fetch water without disturbing anyone but the ostiarius. They are commonest in the area immediately around the forum and along main streets, but clusters of them (three along the north side of block VII xv and three along the Vicolo del Panettiere) show that they were not a public system designed to distribute water with maximum convenience. There seems to be no record of any payment for the right to use a well, and it is interesting that none has been discovered connected with the Aedes Apollinis, which must mean that the water for this temple had to be fetched from the basilica well.[6]

The water impounded in cisterns seems to have been chiefly rain water collected from roofs. In the public squares and buildings the rain falling on the roofs of surrounding colonnades was regularly collected in gutters along the stylobate, cleared of coarser impurities by settling basins at intervals along these gutters, and drawn off into channels leading back to cisterns under the floors of the porticoes laid out normal to them and provided with drawshafts, usually on the line of the colonnade to cause minimal obstruction. The drawshafts vary in size, the smallest of them barely negotiable by cleaners as thin as chimney sweeps, and are provided with puteals set over them or disc lids fitting into chamfered or rabbeted heads. The cisterns vary in plan but are usually long rectangles, somewhat deeper than wide, of any convenient length. They are lined with hydraulic cement and regularly have rounded corners and are provided with a quarter-

---

[4] For a chemical analysis of well water from Pompeii see *NSc* 1931, 556 (A. Maiuri).

[5] Maiuri 1973, 192–204; K. Ohr, *Die Basilika in Pompeji* (Karlsruhe 1973) 28–33.

[6] Presumably the series of cisterns discovered under the southern part of the temenos (Sogliano 91) is not of great antiquity. Early cisterns, since they had to be flat-roofed, are placed alongside or behind temples (e.g., the cistern of the Portonaccio Temple at Veii). In early times the temple may have had access to one of the wells of block VII xv.

round molding covering the joint of floor and wall as insurance against leaking. They are roofed with vaults of rubblework in which field stones of appropriate size and shape are used as voussoirs, set against wooden centering in heavy beds of mortar and small stone. The water impounded in such a cistern can never have been very pure and must have been used principally for washing pavements and watering plantings.

In private houses the rain falling on the roofs around a compluviate atrium ran toward the compluvium, where usually through spouted terracotta gutters it was thrown into the impluvium basin in the centre of the atrium below. From here it could be conveyed to the street gutter by a drain beneath the floor, usually on the axis of the fauces, or diverted to a cistern through a second channel, usually in the side opposite the fauces, the cistern being immediately adjacent. Occasionally rain collected in the impluvium was diverted to a cistern in another apartment, but this was uncommon. In the peristyles the pattern was usually the same as in public colonnades, though occasionally the water seems to have been collected along the eaves and conveyed to the cistern in a downspout. And along the front of the house shops might collect rain water either from the front slope of the roof or from individual peaked gables; in either case the water was taken in terracotta sleeved pipes imbedded in the fabric of the walls into cisterns under the shops. Not infrequently one finds two shops sharing a single cistern, sometimes with a single drawshaft on the line of the party wall, accessible to both.

This water served a multitude of purposes. It served for washing the pavements and watering the garden. Enough of the cisterns are so located in respect to kitchens as to indicate that it was used at least for washing up and perhaps for other things. Enough tanks have been found near cistern heads to suggest that it was used for what laundry was done in the house. And its uses in Pompeian industry can hardly be estimated. Even after the aqueduct was introduced, rain water served wherever water of the quality of drinking water was not required. Aqueduct water seems to have been restricted for the most part to drinking; fountains, where pressure was necessary; bathing; and fish ponds, which were usually fed by fountains. And it seems always to have been carefully regulated by valves and taps.

Pompeii's aqueduct entered the city just west of the Porta del Vesuvio, the highest point in the city. Here the specus terminated in a castellum aquae that diverted the flow into three channels, the main arteries of the city. The specus itself is high enough for a man to crawl along but not high enough for him to walk upright, but the channel for the water, articulated by a sharp setback, is only about 0.26 m wide at the crown, rounded at the base, and 0.32 m deep at the centre. Clearly, in such a channel the gravity flow on which ancient aqueducts relied would not have delivered sufficient water to supply the whole city, and the main purpose of the castellum was to direct water to different quarters at different times. The castellum itself is a domed circle encased in a masonry square, brick-faced on the main façade, a rectangle trimmed with pilasters and architrave framing three essentially blind arches, but in the interior the ghost of reticulate behind the signinum facing shows through faintly, and the west front is faced with reticulate, while the east is in part a wall of large blocks of Nocera tufa, the remains of one side of the Porta del Vesuvio, with reticulate above. It is a curious structure, evidently post-earthquake and temporary, and before it, in a trapezoidal area of the street marked off by big lava paving blocks set on end at intervals, the pavement has been lifted to permit laying pipe, work we know was in progress at several points in the city at the time of the eruption.[7]

In the interior of the castellum the channel of the specus fans out and down and is then divided by masonry wedges into three channels. At the upper end of these are traces of settings for the metal barriers that must have closed one to open another, while a bit above these, before the channel divides, are traces of another fixture, probably a metal filter. To left and right are platforms protected by low barriers for the attendants, who could easily reach any part of the system by catwalks. The egress of the main channels is ruined, probably a result of plundering, but on the exterior the remains of the three mouths show that that at the centre was considerably larger than those at the sides, so presumably when it was open they were closed, and vice versa.[8]

From here the system of distribution is in part a matter of conjecture. Presumably citizens bought the privilege of tapping the artery nearest them for a specified amount and took the water off in their own pipe, stamped at intervals with their name, but how this was governed, and how far the public arteries extended, we do not know. The artery to the west ran beyond the forum and, after supplying the Terme del Foro and the forum fountains, extended as far as the Aedes Veneris, for there is a standpipe in the little alley along the east side

[7] NSc 1903, 25–33 (R. Paribeni); 1931, 557–64 (A. Maiuri).

[8] The notion advanced by Maiuri (1942, 90–94) that there were only two main arteries, one running down the Vicolo dei Vettii and one down the Strada Stabiana, while the third mouth was for a public fountain in front of the castellum, must be rejected, since all three mouths are of considerable size. Undoubtedly there was to have been a fountain here eventually, but it could have been supplied by a pipe of small bore. Vitruvius (8.6.1–2) is explicit in saying that a city's castellum aquae should supply three arteries, one for the fountains and reservoirs, one for the baths, and one for private houses.

of the temple. But there is no sign of any fountain to mark this artery's end. The central artery must have been intended to supply the two big bath establishments along the Strada Stabiana, though the opening of the Terme Centrali was far in the future and might have required an augmented supply. Presumably it will also have supplied the industrial heart of the city and the complex of public buildings adjacent to the Forum Triangulare. The artery to the east had to supply a district that was largely made up of residences and gardens but included the Palestra Grande, with its huge swimming tank.

To maintain pressure in this simple system, standpipes dot the city in an irregular pattern. Most of these are of concrete faced with small ashlar of Nocera tufa and Sarno limestone and must date from the Augustan period, the time of the original building of the aqueduct. A few show extensive repair or rebuilding with facing of yellow tufa, and two are faced with brick; these must date from the years after the earthquake. But it is interesting that these are so consistent in their masonry and bear clear witness that the maintenance of the system was a municipal affair, though the size and design of the individual towers seems to have depended on the number of pipes each was to serve. Only one standpipe reservoir survived, a rectangular tank of lead in the alley along the west side of the Casa di Loreio Tiburtino (II ii 1), possibly preserved because it was small and stood relatively low. Most probably stood well above the roofs of the houses and were masonry tanks lined with hydraulic cement. No sign of any pump has been found, so one presumes that they were filled by hand; in most cases they are so close to a public fountain that a team of two with a ladder and a bucket on a rope would have been all that was needed.

From these tanks lead pipes of varying diameter descended in rectangular channels in the sides of the supporting tower and at a convenient point near the ground curved away to join the pipes in which they were to maintain pressure. These were mostly laid under the sidewalks close to the surface, and in many places in Pompeii they have been exposed with the passage of time and the breaking up of pavement. The most informative group is probably that on the north side of the standpipe on the east side of the northeast corner of block VI xiii, where pipe was being laid at the time of the eruption and a considerable trench along the north side of the block had been excavated. Here there are stretches of at least six lines of different dimensions, in some of which the enlargements, resembling automobile mufflers, that were to keep the flow even and free of hiccoughs can be seen. This standpipe is a fair specimen of the usual size, square in plan, about 1.15 m on a side, with a generous channel for pipes on its north face and a smaller one on its south face. It is built against the wall of a house for added support and stands across the sidewalk. Its pipe channels show heavy deposits of lime from leakage that spread out over the face of the tower. The four standpipes along the Strada Stabiana all stand free, but they are the only ones that do; they also include an exceptionally large one, the largest in the city if we exclude that in the attic of the Arco di Caligola, at the southeast corner of block VI xiv, 1.48–1.50 m on a side. The smallest is that on the west side of the northwest corner of II ii, 0.86 m by 1.07 m, but only its shallow depth sets it apart. It was rebuilt in the last years of Pompeii and shows very slight lime incrustation in its channels, and in this quarter of the city it cannot have served many buildings, as the half-foot channels in the three exposed faces attest.

The pattern of distribution of standpipes through the city is probably no indication of the system of aqueduct arteries. One line of four stands near the Vicolo di Mercurio: at the south corner of block VI i, the northeast corner of VI vi, the northeast corner of VI xiii, and the southeast corner of VI xvi. One standpipe served the Terme del Foro, at the northwest corner of block VII v; one the quarter east of the forum, at the northwest corner of VII x; two the southwest quarter of the city, at the northwest corner of VIII i basilica and the southwest corner of VIII v (v–vi); and three have been found just off the Via dell'Abbondanza: at the northwest corner of I iv, the northeast corner of I vi, and the northwest corner of II ii. Fifteen are known in the parts so far excavated, and it is certainly conceivable that others in the upper parts of buildings have vanished without a trace.

The most unusual standpipe was that in the attic of the Arco di Caligola, where vertical channels in the masonry betray their purpose by remains of lime incrustation. There are box channels in both faces just at the spring of the arch and continuing down the face, replaced after a meter or so by terracotta pipes enclosed in the masonry, reappearing just above the lava-faced base of the arch's piers as box channels, 0.20–0.25 m wide, 0.29–0.33 m deep, and 0.71–0.78 m high. On the south face toward the Via del Foro a pair of fountain basins seem once to have been set against the piers; shallow vertical beds for the insertion of slabs, one of which contains remains of leading, appear on the lava blocks of the base, but the fountains must have been removed in the last period. There is no way of estimating the size of the tank in the attic, but it appears not to have filled the attic.

Water was taken from the main arteries in property owners' private pipes, but the majority of the citizenry must still have depended on the public fountains for drinking water. Some thirty-two street fountains are known so far. Others in the forum had been temporarily removed for refurbishing or replacement, but clear traces of four, two against the north face of the piers of the Arco di Tiberio and two on the step around the forum square to either side just in front of the Aedes Iovis, still survive. Typically a street fountain consists of four massive slabs of lava fastened together with iron clamps set in lead to form a box a little more than a meter in one dimension by a little less in the other, about 0.70 m deep, floored with tile covered with a thick coat of hydraulic cement and caulked with mortar. The water was delivered through a standard set up at the middle of the rim away from the street, where the sidewalk permitted ready filling of vessels directly from the feed pipe. The standard was ordinarily provided with a backer to protect the feed pipe, and unshaped blocks of lava protected the fountain corners from passing traffic where necessary and provided steps for children wishing to drink and places to rest pots. The standard was carved with an ornamental device, and the fountain rim was cut by a spill channel on the street side under which was a hole to drain it at the level of the basin floor.

There are exceptions to each of these features. Two of the fountains are of marble: those of the southwest corner of block VII xv and the southeast corner of VII ix. In both cases one might advance the proximity of the forum in explanation, and the latter, with its standard of Concordia Augusta, probably was part of the gift of Eumachia, next to whose building it stands. But that in the Vicolo del Gallo was not very conspicuous and is of finer marble and workmanship than the other. Here we may see the hand of a private benefactor. Two are of fine limestone: those of the southeast corner of block VI xiv and the southeast corner of VII iv, the latter with a bowed basin, rather than rectangular, and unique in this. One basin, that at the juncture of the Strada delle Scuole and the Vicolo della Regina in block VIII ii, is entirely of masonry faced with hydraulic cement, while the standard is of tufa and without a device. That in front of the entrance to the Forum Triangulare is caulked with lead. The place of the spill channel and drain mouth vary; the standard may be set off-centre or in the middle of a street side. One fountain, that of VIII ii at the end of the Vicolo dei Dodici Dei, is set very low in relation to an abnormally high sidewalk and was provided with a guardrail set in lead around two sides to prevent accidents. And some fountains are floored with stone.

The devices carved on the standards are of three types: a head from the mouth of which the feed pipe issues, a conventional circular motif from the centre of which the feed pipe issues, and a representation suggestive of spilling liquid. In the first category we have a number of heads of animals; masks, including a gorgoneion (at the southeast corner of the forum on the Strada delle Scuole) and a clipeate head of a young river god, perhaps Sarnus (before the propylaeum of the Forum Triangulare); and even a few heads of divinities. In the second we have shields and rosettes. In the third the most interesting are perhaps a cock with spread wings atop an overturned vase (at the southwest corner of VII xv) and a flying hawk carrying a hare it has caught by the nape of the neck (the feed pipe issues from the hare's mouth) at the south corner of VI iii. An odd one on the east side of VI xvi shows an upright long-necked bottle from the belly of which the feed pipe issues irrationally; probably we should think of it as a leather bottle that has been punctured. With few exceptions the carving is rude but bold and expressive. The figured devices do not seem to repeat, with the exceptions of three heifer heads (in the Vicolo della Regina opposite the Vicolo dei Dodici Dei, the Vicolo di Tesmo opposite the Vicolo di Balbo, and the Via dell'Abbondanza midway along the north side of II i) and a bull's head (at the southeast corner of VI xiii) and two tragic masks (at the northwest corner of I iv and the northwest corner of VII xi). But the device of a shield is known in at least seven examples, several of them in close proximity to one another (at the northeast corner of I v, the northwest corner of I ix, the northeast corner of I x, the northwest corner of I xvi, the northeast corner of IX x, the southwest corner of IX xi, and a limestone standard not associated with a fountain now lying in the Strada di Nola against the sidewalk on the south side of V i). A few fountains did not have ornamented standards. Possibly some fountain devices served to identify neighborhoods, as did such other landmarks as temples and gates.

The fountains are so distributed that no one in Pompeii had to go more than two blocks for water. They are most frequent along the main traffic lanes (six along the Strada Consolare and the Via di Nola, six along the Strada Stabiana, and seven along the Via dell'Abbondanza), but there are at least two in unpaved back streets (at the northeast corner of I v and the northwest corner of I xvi). They were usually located at street corners, but this was not to make them more conspicuous, since they were always set to one side, out of the path of traffic.

The water piped into these fountains was allowed to overflow, spilling into the street by an apposite channel in the basin rim. Since the basins probably served chiefly as watering troughs for the animals, and into them itinerant hawkers of fruit, vegetables, and flowers must have discarded the spoiled and superfluous parts of their wares after refreshing them from time to time under the streams, this will have helped to keep the basin clean, but it also served another purpose as well. The streets of Pompeii appear to have been dirtier than those of most ancient cities, receiving in addition to the wastes of busy city life the dirty water resulting from the washing of pavements of houses and shops. This water was swept into drains that emptied into the gutters through the sidewalks, the mouths of which can still be seen in front of nearly every doorway and along every minor façade. If the sidewalks of Pompeii stand high and stepping stones were necessary to cross them in the heart of the city, this was because the streets were perennially extremely dirty. It is interesting that such stepping stones do not appear in Ostia or in many other Roman cities that have been extensively excavated. It is also interesting that toward the edges of the city they tend to disappear; the northern stretch of the Strada Consolare and the eastern stretches of the Via di Nola and the Via dell'Abbondanza are almost without them, as is the piazza in front of the Porta del Vesuvio. Their distribution corresponds, in fact, to a surface drainage pattern, rather like miniature river systems, and even their height at a number of key points can be shown to reflect the volume of waste that had to pass through this or that gutter. In this drainage system the street fountains played a vital role, their overflow serving to flush the network constantly. Thus overflow from the Fontana di Mercurio at the northeast corner of block VI viii, for example, ran south down the Via di Mercurio to the Arco di Caligola and, passing through this, turned east to run along the Via della Fortuna. Having reached the Strada Stabiana, it turned south again on this and ran as far as the Tetrapylon of the Holconii at the southeast corner of VII i, where it passed into a great underground drain and flowed west to join the great sewer that passed north and south under the middle of the Thermae Stabianae and continued south to empty beyond the city walls, presumably into the river.[9]

One can follow similar meandering courses of the surface drainage everywhere in the heart of the city, but in the western part all converge ultimately on two great arteries, one along the Strada Stabiana that is interrupted at the Tetrapylon of the Holconii but picks up again immediately, its lower stretch emptying ultimately through a great box drain in the west flank of the Porta di Stabia, and one along the Vicolo del Farmacista and the Vicolo dei Soprastanti that emptied out of the elbow bend of the Vicolo dei Soprastanti to the west, presumably into a canal that ran close to the city in this sector. It is interesting that in the eastern stretches of the two great east/west arteries of the city, the surface drainage from which emptied through box drains similar to that of the Porta di Stabia at the Porta di Nola and the Porta di Sarno, refinements were introduced. The Via di Nola received drainage from the side streets leading into it from the north

---

[9]For a map of the great drain of the Via dell'Abbondanza see Mygind (supra n. 1) 190, fig. 7; and A. von Gerkan, *Der Stadtplan von Pompeji* (Berlin 1940) pl. 3.

but east of IX viii did not allow this to flow south with the natural slope of the city, keeping it instead within its own margins and directing it to the Porta di Nola. And in the Via dell'Abbondanza the same was true east of the Via di Nocera, while to the west of this the surface drainage was directed south along those streets that were paved, the Via di Nocera and the street between blocks I viii and I ix.

The network of underground sewers seems to bear little relation to the pattern of surface drainage, though it received the surface drainage at significant points. But while surface drainage ran along the main streets, the underground sewers ran chiefly in the minor streets and alleys and avoided the main streets wherever possible, perhaps because they lay very close under the pavements and heavy traffic was liable to crush their roofs. Thus a main sewer lies along the Vicolo di Mercurio from its crest at the Vicolo di Modesto to a point midway along the north side of block VI xiv, where it turns south and can be followed by relieving arches in the walls over it, especially conspicuous in blocks VII ii and VII i, and joins the sewer of the Thermae Stabianae emerging in the Via dell'Abbondanza in front of VII i 5. This appears again between the Forum Triangulare and the Ludus Gladiatorius at the level of the latter and can be examined there. Presumably it continued beyond the city and emptied into the Sarno River. This main sewer had a number of minor branches, for the most part apparently run under back streets, the northern reaches of the Vicolo della Fullonica, for example, and the Vicolo del Fauno. Another major sewer served the Terme del Foro and can be followed along the Vicolo delle Terme and the Vicolo dei Soprastanti, where it is provided with regular covered manholes. Presumably it was into this system that the sewer under the Vicolo di Narcisso, as well as all the drainage of the west slope of the city, fed. Other sewers emptying south appear under the Strada delle Scuole and the Vicolo dei Dodici Dei. In the eastern part of the city things are rather less clear, but one underground sewer crosses the Via dell'Abbondanza just east of the Via di Nocera.

It must not be thought that Pompeii's sewer system was sophisticated or truly comprehensive. While the overflow of the water supply was fed into it to flush it, and while in a few houses there is evidence that a pipe supplied from the aqueduct was introduced into the latrine to flush it, or water used for washing up in the kitchen was piped into the latrine, most Pompeian latrines depended for this on water brought by hand and pipes that brought rain water down from the roofs. And very many latrines were not connected with the sewer system, but drained into cesspools.

The most sophisticated hydraulic engineering of Pompeii seems to have been the draining of the forum (Maiuri 1973, 63–70). Here the rain was drawn off through inconspicuous mouths cut in the base of the lowest step around the open square into a capacious channel that ran the whole length of the long east and west sides and across the south end and into which the drains from most forum buildings seem to have led. The steps were slightly canted to throw water toward the drain, and presumably the forum pavement was carefully crowned, but there is no cut gutter. From the forum drain water was diverted into large cisterns under the south end to either side and into sewers leading under the Strada delle Scuole and the Via Marina, the sewer under the Via Marina then passing south between the basilica and the Aedes Veneris, where it can be seen at present. The forum cisterns must have served chiefly as a supply for sluicing down the public square, since most of the buildings around it are provided with their own cisterns.

The individual property owners seem to have contracted with the aediles for specific amounts of water, presumably gauged by the size of the lead pipe in which it was drawn off from the artery. Inside the houses one is inevitably struck by the quantities of lead piping that lie exposed in the gutters of peristyles and climb walls and columns, fixed to these by heavy iron staples. One gathers that it was not considered unaesthetic, though pipes were regularly buried under floors so as not to be a hazard. Perhaps pipes were considered a necessary evil, like television antennae. And wherever one is found, it is fitted with valves and taps so the individual streams could be turned on and off and regulated. Perhaps the most striking examples are in the Casa dei Vettii, where a great variety of figures and basins in the large peristyle and an interesting kitchen fountain had to be supplied (*MonAnt* 8 [1898] 267–68, 281–90 [A. Sogliano]), and the Casa delle Nozze d'Argento, where in addition to an elaborate fountain in the atrium, there is a pipe with a nozzle tap brought into the latrine (*RömMitt* 8 [1893] 32–33, 52–55 [A. Mau]). Almost every house of any pretension is provided with fountains, usually in both atrium and peristyle, but these seem seldom to have required very much water; a trickle down a flight of miniature marble stairs, a needle-thin jet from the mouth of a bronze goose or a marble wineskin, was sufficient. Occasionally there were more ambitious displays, like the euripus of the Casa di Loreio Tiburtino (Spinazzola 1953, 1.404–11) and the pool and nymphaeum of the Insula Iuliae Felicis (*RömMitt* 71 [1964] 182–94 [F. Rakob]), but even these, once filled, required little in the way of supply. The euripus was fed by a single, relatively small fountain; the statuary along it was all occasional, not fountain figures. And the upper level supplied the lower with most of its water; only the water pyramid of four flights of miniature stairs will have needed an additional pipe. It is much the same everywhere, leading inevitably to the conclusion that the amount of water delivered to the private houses was small and therefore presumably strictly controlled and possibly expensive as well. Certainly it reflects the limited capacity of Pompeii's aqueduct. What is surprising is that so much of the limited water supply should have been expended on fountains, but here again one notes a curious economy: there are, by and large, only fountains in Pompeii; taps, especially kitchen taps, are extremely rare. To get water even in a great house one would have had to go to the fountains or the cisterns. And the water of the fountains was usually not allowed to run off; instead it was collected in cisterns or capacious reservoirs that were frequently also vivaria for fish.

PART II

The Tufa Period, 200–80 B.C.

6 · THE FORUM TRIANGULARE AND ITS NEIGHBORS

The Forum Triangulare

The Forum Triangulare is really not a forum at all but the roughly triangular precinct of the archaic Doric temple given architectural definition as a public square, partly colonnaded on the two long sides that face toward the city, open on the southwest front overlooking the dramatic panorama of the Sarno Valley and the mountains beyond. At the time the colonnades were erected the Doric temple had already been destroyed, and probably little more survived of it in the area than the four capitals we see there today. The foundations of the long, narrow "cella" in the centre of the frame of steps that was built around it in the Augustan period are typical of Tufa Period architecture, great blocks of Sarno limestone and Nocera tufa in courses that are leveled but laid dry. Seven courses have been brought to light. The five lowest courses are of rough-hewn blocks of Sarno limestone, not intended to be seen; the sixth course is of Nocera tufa, also intended for concealment but better dressed. The seventh course, of Nocera tufa, is set back and properly finished, the base of the wall. Along the exterior of the right wall and abutting on it below ground level is a second base, a short wall of tufa blocks 2.10 m long on a footing of tufa 0.60 m deep. This must have been for some sculpture or offering preserved in view after the destruction of the temple. The temple foundation seems to be the substructure of a building of considerable height and weight, a single-cella Italic temple with a deep pronaos approaching the cella in size, similar in design to the Temple of Jupiter on the forum. The approach would have been frontal, from the southeast, by a stair extending across the whole front. A single Corinthian capital in Nocera tufa is to be seen in the area today; possibly this belonged to this temple. The style is good, fairly close to that of the Corinthian columns of the Aedes Apollinis, less like that of the columns of the tetrastyle atrium of the Casa del Fauno. A date

FIGURE 4.
The Forum
Triangulare, Ionic
Propylaeum

toward the middle of the second century B.C. is suggested. But presumably this temple, like the archaic Doric temple that preceded it,
was in total ruin by the Augustan period; otherwise there is no explanation for its having been exploited at that time to make an ornamental ruin, a platform roughly resembling that of a Greek Doric temple
on which old architectural members could be displayed decoratively.

The colonnades are Doric with an Ionic propylaeum of six columns
opening on the Via del Tempio di Iside. Though the propylaeum was
rebuilt at some time, presumably in the Augustan period, it was
probably always Ionic, and here there may have been an early example of the combination of the three major architectural orders,
with progressively more elongated columns within a single complex.[1]

[1] The three orders are used with great elegance in the terraces of the upper sanctuary of the Temple of Fortuna Primigenia at Praeneste. The colonnades along the ramps
at the base are Doric, the order of the terrace of the hemicycles is Ionic, and the great
colonnaded square just below the temple itself is Corinthian. So the sequence of orders
must have been important in architectural thinking and design in this period. See
F. Fasolo and G. Gullini, *Il santuario della Fortuna Primigenia a Palestrina* (Rome 1953)
passim.

The propylaeum was designed to be seen from the Via dell'Abbondanza, a block away, and to catch the attention of the crowds that thronged the artery. The fact that the east side of the Via dei Teatri leading from the Via dell'Abbondanza to the Forum Triangulare is an uninterrupted line of shops shows that it was in heavy use. As rebuilt, the propylaeum has exaggeratedly high columns with a deep entablature, an architrave of three fasciae and a plain frieze under a strongly projecting cornice, deeply undercut, the salient feature of which is a line of closely spaced dentils. The bases of the columns are Attic, and the lower shafts are reeded, but the reeding belongs to the rebuilding, as the bases of the engaged columns that finished the colonnade at either end show. One of these, now lying just inside the Forum Triangulare, had its fluted shaft cut away to be replaced by a reeded one. The other, with its fluted shaft still intact, lies against the west wall of the propylaeum. The entablature of this porch seems curiously mannered, too high, top-heavy, and quite unlike the best Tufa Period architecture, and we must ask whether originally it was not closer to the colonnade of the Aedes Apollinis in its proportions, especially since the porch and the porticus on the interior are of about the same depth, the porticus being only slightly deeper. The tufa stylobate and step below this are indications that it cannot be very late. Presumably the rectangular public fountain that stands in front of the westernmost column and gives focus to the end of the street of approach is also Augustan. It is remarkable for having been caulked with lead, the only one in Pompeii so treated, and for the grotesque mask that decorates the standard, a young satyrlike face with cheeks puffed out overlying a disc crossed diagonally by a rod. If it is not a satyr, it may be a young water god. On the interior wall of the propylaeum, which is broken by a pair of doors giving access to the temenos, is a series of six marble brackets, presumably intended to carry honorific busts. These must belong to the Augustan rebuilding.

The colonnades on the interior are oddly interrupted and ruinous, though of fine architectural detail. That on the north, six columns at the entrance, is complete, and a stretch to either side shows the lines the long colonnades should follow, but each breaks off after less than a dozen columns. That on the west is picked up by a pair of columns once carrying a section of entablature at its south end; the entablature has now collapsed. The southern column here, though almost complete, was originally engaged against a wall. This was a theatrical touch introduced by Maiuri; these columns do not appear on any of the old plans and presumably were simply transported for this purpose from the remains at the north end of the area. Stylobate and gutter run unbroken to a point opposite the end of the narrow alley between the Forum Triangulare and the Casa di Giuseppe II; beyond this there is no trace of either, which probably means that a wall finished the colonnade at this point. At the south end of the east colonnade three more or less fragmentary columns stand on a continuous stylobate with a gutter like that at the north end of this wing. These are presumably remains of the fourteen shown on the plan in *CIL* 4, supplement 2; unfortunately this end of the precinct has been deeply eroded by landslips, and one must take earlier observers' word for the arrangements. Mau shows this section of colonnade as fronting a long leschelike hall, with six doors giving to the colonnade followed by a large rectangular tower, possibly originally part of the city's fortifications, containing a stair by which one could descend to the floor of the Sarno Valley. This "lesche" appears to have been a comfortable place where those frequenting this area could sit in shelter, quiet and secluded, possibly even a place where a school might have been held at certain hours. That would be in accord with the other arrangements we see here. But the colonnade in front of this may never have been roofed; no part of any entablature is to be found here, and the general effect is of architecture built as a ruin. Between this and the point where the colonnade around the north end breaks off there is no gutter, and the line of the stylobate is marked by a broken series of smaller blocks of tufa and Sarno limestone, poorly laid, more than 60.00 m long. Possibly the colonnade simply ran around the north end of the precinct, much as we see it today, and then broke off, becoming an open promenade.

The architecture of this colonnade is exceptionally elegant and more classical than most Tufa Period architecture. It is Doric, the shafts fluted down to the stylobate, the straight-sided echinus finished with three annulets, into the lowest of which the apophyge merges directly. The architrave is divided into two equal fasciae on both faces. The frieze has three triglyphs between each pair of columns and plain metopes. The cornice is rather severe, with mutules and guttae, otherwise almost undecorated, deeply projecting, with small cymas at base and crown to produce a line of shadow. The roof did not project beyond the cornice. The effect of this architecture is sober and rhythmical; nothing about it suggests that it might originally have been built as a ruin. It looks, rather, as though limited funds were available at the time it was laid out and those responsible built what they could, intending to continue it whenever more money was in hand. But that never happened, and in the course of time the people who frequented this area grew used to using it in its unfinished state and gradually stopped thinking of it in any other terms.

In harmony with the architecture of this colonnade is a pretty little tholos of eight Doric columns that shelters a well in front of, but not

Figure 5.
The Forum Triangulare, Doric Colonnade

centred on, the temple building. This well is one of the deep wells of Pompeii, guarded by a rather plain tufa puteal. The columns are fluted to full height; the entablature is deep and completely plain, without even distinction between architrave and frieze, with a very simple cornice. The roof must have been conical. The epistyle carried an inscription in Oscan characters recording that it was built by the meddix Numerius Trebius (Conway 47; Vetter 15), so the notion that the epistyle might be a late repair must be rejected. This building is very charming, with a sculptural quality that is enhanced by its openness.

Parallel to the eastern portico, a strip wider than the portico is set off by a low terrace wall, ruinous in places, without clear terminations. It has been presumed that this was a racecourse for footraces in connection with the Palestra Sannitica off the north end of the precinct. But there is no starting line nor any other feature one might associate with a racecourse, and the identification of the Palestra Sannitica as such is open to serious question. It seems more likely that this was simply a walk, possibly a place where a market, perhaps a luxury market like that installed in the Saepta Iulia at Rome, could be set up.

The use of this area as a pleasure park is indicated by the tufa schola and sundial installed near the south end of the west colonnade overlooking the Sarno Valley and the port of Pompeii. This was the work of the same magistrates who erected a sundial on a marble column in the precinct of Apollo (*CIL* 10.831). Since this schola runs through the west corner of the lowest step of the temple platform, which is built of secondhand material, including many fragments of Tufa Period architecture, it must antedate this. And since the temple platform seems intimately connected with the rectangular enclosure in front of it, where we find masonry in the small blocks typical of early Julio-Claudian architecture, it has been presumed that this was Augustan work, part of a general refurbishing connected with the erection of a statue of Augustus's nephew Marcellus inscribed PATRONO near the north end of the temenos (*CIL* 10.832). This statue faced a handsome basin of large crystalled Greek island marble into which a pipe threw a stream of water, a feature that cannot antedate the construction of the city's aqueduct in the early Augustan period. It looks very much as though the schola were late republican, and the new temple platform and general rebuilding of the whole area work of 30–20 B.C. Whether the remodeling of the propylaeum with reeded columns can be put so late might be doubted, but a reeded Ionic column not unlike these is used in the tomb of Aesquillia Polla outside the Porta di Nola, which is certainly of imperial date.

The history of the area is then clear. It began as a temple precinct, around an archaic Doric temple of the sixth century. This was taken over by the Samnites and maintained as a place of worship at least down to the fourth century.[2] It then fell into ruin and was plundered for building material until only a few capitals and some deposits of temple terracottas and votive material remained. In the reorganization of the city of Pompeii in the third century the area was set apart as a public square, and in due course a small temple and an entrance porch with the beginnings of colonnades framing the interior were constructed, but this work did not go forward according to plan. The temple, the dedication of which remains uncertain, seems to have been neglected, and the area used more as a public park than as a place of worship. Since there was no other park in this quarter, one can understand how this might have happened. So in the Augustan period, presumably in consequence of M. Claudius Marcellus's acceptance of the role of patronus of the city, it was rebuilt as a park, the temple converted into an ornamental ruin and the cult probably limited to occasional simple ceremonies at the enclosure and altars in front of this. Marcellus's statue was erected just inside the propylaeum, which was now remodeled, and a splendid fountain with a basin of Greek island marble was set facing it. As a park it filled a public need and may also have made a place where a special market could be held.

The So-called Palestra Sannitica

Adjacent to the north end of the Forum Triangulare and accessible from it is a building commonly called the Palestra or the Samnite Palaestra (VIII vii 29), which is very close in architectural style to the colonnades of the Forum Triangulare and must be close to them in date, mid-second-century. At present the main feature is a peristyle of nineteen Doric columns lacking its east portico. Originally it continued east for two more bays and had an east portico, having twenty-six columns in all, ten by five; the east end was sacrificed to permit enlargement of the Temple of Isis. Originally the door to the Via del Tempio di Iside and the statue base opposite it, in front of the south portico, were axial. Today thirteen capitals survive, and differences between this order and that of the Forum Triangulare are sufficient for us to be sure that these were designed by different hands, but the columns are fluted to full height, and at the crown the apophyge is filled, rather than hollowed, in the transition to the annulets, giving the effect of an extra annulet. There are four true annulets; the echinus is straight, the abacus plain. Nothing of the

---

[2]Cf. the terracottas shown in Eschebach 1978 figs. 12–14.

FIGURE 6.
The So-called Palestra
Sannitica, Interior with
Altar

entablature remains. The order is light and graceful; there can have
been little overhang to the roof, for a broad gutter with settling basins
runs just in front of the stylobate.

Off the west portico opens a line of rooms. At the north end is a
blind corridor that is probably a stairwell, followed by a deep exedra,
a large rectangular room, a small square room, and last a lobby giving
access to the Forum Triangulare and the open space behind the Theatrum Maius. In none of these rooms is there any sign of a wash basin
or plumbing of any sort; the material found in them suggests that
they were used for habitation. Since it is impossible to imagine a palaestra without a washroom in a city as sophisticated as Pompeii in
the Tufa Period, we must seek another interpretation for this building
and the Oscan inscription found immured in its east wall.[3]

[3]It should be noted that the building was not without water after the construction
of the aqueduct, but it was not used for bathing. The column of the north portico just
west of the main door was channeled and pierced to take a feed pipe for a fountain,
the basin and pedestal of which were found in the excavation (*PAH* 2.68 [31 August
1797]). The inscription, on a tablet of limestone, beautifully cut in the Oscan alphabet,

Opposite the principal entrance is a high base approached from behind by a small, steep stair. In front of it is an altar. Pernice (1932, 58–60) identified the base as an altar of the best Tufa Period architecture, part of the original design of the building, converted to use as a statue base. The altar in front of this and the stair behind are of a comparatively late date, the altar capped with a seat block taken from the Theatrum Tectum. At various points in the building were found parts of the famous marble copy of the Doryphorus of Polycleitus, slightly over life-size, now in the Museo Nazionale in Naples. It has been presumed that the statue stood on the base and was a cult statue of some sort for the Iuventus of Pompeii to which the victors in contests offered their crowns by climbing the stair and placing them on the statue's head. It is hard to conjecture what the cult would have been, since the divinity is Iuventas, not Iuventus, and the statue's association with the base is arbitrary. The large fragments of the statue were found in the southwestern part of the peristyle, some distance from the base. It seems more logical to suppose that the statue was a votive offering that stood in front of the colonnade and that the cult statue had yet to be installed or was salvaged by the survivors. Pernice's findings show that originally there was no cult statue, only an altar, and that without inscription. Granted the popularity of Hercules in Pompeii, and the association with the *vereiia* of Pompeii, of which, if in fact it was an association of the youth, Hercules would have been the natural patron, it does not seem unlikely that this building is really the Temple of Hercules.[4]

The Theatrum Maius

Because the orchestra of the Theatrum Maius[5] is horseshoe-shaped, and a full circle of the diameter of the arc of its first row of seats could be inscribed in it and not come tangent to, let alone run over, the front of the stage, it has been thought that this theatre must be of high antiquity, essentially a Greek theatre. Nothing, however, in the

was found immured in the east wall of the courtyard (Conway 42; Vetter 11). It states that one Vibius Aadirans (Atranus) left money in his will to the *vereiia* of Pompeii. This money was devoted to this building on decree of the assembly, and the quaestor V. Vinicius oversaw its construction. It has been widely presumed that *vereiia* was approximately equivalent to *iuuentus*, but there is no adequate proof of this. The root seems to be connected with the Latin *uir* and might designate any sort of corporation, possibly the populace as a whole.

[4] Temples of Hercules are apt to take unusual architectural forms. Cf., e.g., the sanctuary of Hercules at Alba Fucens (*MonAnt* 46 [1963] 333–96 [De Visscher-Mertens-Balty]) and that near Sulmo (*AntCl* 42 [1973] 36–48 [vanWonterghem]).

[5] The most important study of the Theatrum Maius is that of Mau (*RömMitt* 21 [1906] 1–56); see also Sogliano 196–209.

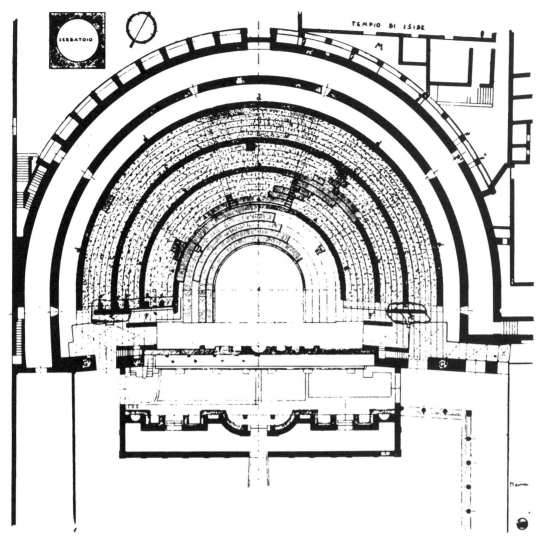

FIGURE 7.
The Theatrum Maius,
Plan of the Final Phase
with Augustan
Modifications

stones or building techniques employed suggests great age. In fact, the oldest materials to be found here are a number of large, well-cut blocks of Nocera tufa reused in masonry of the western parts of the stage building and a keystone with a female head in high relief, a protective or apotropaic divinity, in the outer face of the arch over the exit from the orchestra on this side (Eschebach 1978, fig. 64). These seem to be survivals from the original construction and indicate a date not far from that of the fortifications and houses with tufa façades, in the late third century or the first half of the second century. The odd shape of the orchestra may well have been the result of an attempt to enlarge the seating capacity of the cavea by adding seating in straight sections to an originally semicircular design; in support of this notion it should be noted that the parodoi slope down to the floor of the orchestra, proof that the natural configuration of the slope has been improved by excavation of the orchestra, as well as by grading and shaping of the cavea. Such excavation is not typical of Greek theatres but appears in both the amphitheatre and the Theatrum Tectum of Pompeii, both dated by inscriptions to the early years of the Roman colony. If this theatre was part of the original city plan, as seems very probable, it was at first the only place of assembly designed as such in the city and must have served as the Samnite equivalent of the Roman comitium, a place of assembly for legislative and political purposes and for voting. Moreover, down to the time of the construction of the amphitheatre it would have been the best place in which to give gladiatorial shows and spectacles, as well as plays. Vitruvius (5.1.2) gives prescriptions for the design of fora to accommodate such spectacles, but the galleries from which spectators were to watch the shows did not appear in the forum of Pompeii until a much later period, probably not before the earthquake of A.D. 62. In view of the lack of such accommodations, we must suppose that the Pompeians did not use their forum for these shows, and there is no reason why they should have, with a theatre at their disposal. Rome did not have a stone theatre down to the time Pompey built his in the middle of the first century B.C., and the proliferation of theatres of the Augustan period throughout central and northern Italy is evidence that permanent theatres had earlier been a rarity. This was probably not the case in southern Italy and Sicily, where the Greek cities had had theatrical shows from a very early period, but even the theatre of Syracuse is now believed to be no older than third-century. (*Palladio* 17 [1967] 97–154 [L. Bernabo-Brea]).

The Theatrum Maius as we see it today seems to be largely of the Augustan period. The four lowest steps of seating of the cavea are exceptionally wide. Where the construction is original, it is of blocks of white marble; on these, special chairs for the dignitaries would have been set. The fifth row is a diazoma; the sixth, of narrower marble blocks, preserves on axis traces of the setting of a marble bisellium (?) flanked by an inscription (*CIL* 10.838) recording that this was in honor of M. Holconius Rufus, the preeminent Pompeian of his day, flamen Augusti, tribunus militum a populo, and patronus coloniae, offices indicative of his importance. It seems likely that the general rebuilding of the central core of the theatre was his work and his gift to the city, and he was honored by his fellow citizens in this fashion in gratitude. In the top step of the ima cavea is another setting for an installation of uncertain character that was evidently removed in antiquity. Above this bank of seating in marble only a single patch of parts of five rows of seating in marble blocks appears in the northeast quadrant. One block in the eleventh row carries the numbers xi to xv carved on its vertical face, with the seat widths marked by short vertical grooves. The places of six radial stairs dividing the cavea into cunei are clear, and these, in blocks of tufa and marble, seem to have been complete, though they may have been repaired in modern times. The rest of the seating must have been of wood. The ima cavea is accessible from the orchestra; the diazoma below the media is reached by vaulted ramps off the parodoi. The parodoi have been vaulted and carry tribunals for the magistrates and donors of games. These tribunals are reached by narrow stairs off the parodoi, so those occupying them could appear dramatically at the last minute before the games began. They are edged with marble moldings carved with leaves and modillions that presumably carried a parapet of metal or wood. The parodoi are of good size, but the approaches to them were awkward. That on the east was reached most directly by a long, vaulted corridor from the Strada Stabiana along the north side of which runs a broad, raised gutter of masonry faced with signinum; the wall coats of this corridor are covered with an extraordinary welter of graffiti. Secondary access to this parodos was provided by doors to a porticus running along the west side of the Theatrum Tectum. Approach to the west parodos was still more awkward; it could be reached by a stair down from the Forum Triangulare or by one of the approaches in from the Strada Stabiana. The builders seem to have been unaware of the shortcomings of their design and unable to cope with them better.

The media cavea had seventeen rows of seats. At the top runs a diazoma in front of an annular corridor that carried the summa cavea on its vault, a gallery outside this being supported by vaults on a ring of piers and short spur walls in the western half, by more or less freestanding piers in the eastern half. This annular corridor, though itself fairly spacious, with a bench faced with signinum running its whole length, could be reached only by awkward and sometimes very narrow throats, two from the Forum Triangulare, one from the Strada Stabiana, and one from the Via del Tempio di Iside. The summa cavea could be reached only from behind, by cramped stairs arranged without symmetry, wherever existing building permitted their insertion. Two are in the triangular open area between the theatre and the palaestra/Temple of Hercules, one off the throat in from the Via del Tempio di Iside. Clearly, the annular corridor and summa cavea are a late modification, Augustan to judge from the masonry in small blocks and marble molding. Everything here had to be kept as light as possible, so the seating was entirely of wood. The lower edge of the summa cavea was bordered with a simple marble molding, probably the base of a parapet, while the top of the rear wall was finished with a deep cyma reversa molding in tufa. In from the wall behind the summa cavea project pierced blocks to carry the masts on which awnings for the spectators were rigged, with cuttings in the crown molding to accommodate these. There were thirty-one of them, equally spaced except at the ends, where insertion of an extra one caused the last three to be closer together.

The stage building is relatively simple and typically shallow behind the stage. To the east of the stage building has been set up a copy of a small marble plate inscribed M. ARTORIVS M. L. PRIMVS ARCHITECTVS (CIL 10.841); according to the daybooks (PAH 1.49 [28 June 1792]), it seems to have come from the front of the building. The same man was responsible for other work in the basilica. Probably he built the stage, and from its simplicity we can assign it to the Augustan period. The back wall is a series of only three niches, rather than the usual five, those to either side rectangular, the centre one bowed, and the porta regia framed by a pair of freestanding columns on high plinths set well in front of this. At either end is a large, plain opening. The stage was deep, floored with wood. Along its front is the trough into which the curtain was lowered, and the wall in front of this on the orchestra is carved into a lively sequence of seven small niches, the centre one curved, the second and fifth fitted with little flights of steps. In these niches have been found remains of pipes. Either there were fountains that played in the intervals of the shows to cool the audience or saffron water was sprayed on the audience in the refinement made famous by Nero. At one time, though not in the last period, large tanks for water were installed in the orchestra. Just behind the trough for the curtain is a series of strongly built wells and buttresses under the stage. These must have been for the mounting of machines for spectacles. They show a rough symmetry, but responding pairs are sometimes of different sizes. Behind the stage, the backstage is simply an unfinished space to which the only access from behind is a large door opposite the porta regia approached by a ramp on the exterior. Presumably, heavy scenery and equipment had to be brought in on rollers through the porta regia. The stage building is buttressed on the exterior by pilasters at regular intervals, and the back wall of the stage itself is very heavy; we can take this as evidence that the stage stood three storeys high, which was probably standard at the time it was built.

The stage building stands free in a courtyard the use of which is not entirely clear. Probably scenery was constructed in it, and those to take part in large shows could wait their turn here, but it seems mainly simply waste space, relatively inaccessible. Along the west side runs the great drain from the Thermae Stabianae. Along the east is a Doric porticus that brings the Theatrum Maius, the Theatrum Tectum, and the Ludus Gladiatorius into communication with one another. From the south a branch of the great stair down from the Forum Triangulare debouches into it; probably this served as access to the theatre for a certain number of spectators, and it may have been used by the procession (pompa) with which ludi scaenici customarily began. The magistrates and donors of the games would have made a sacrifice at one of the important temples of the forum area and would have marched in procession down the Via dell'Abbondanza and the Vicolo dei Teatri to the Forum Triangulare, from which the obvious route would lie down the great stair and through the orchestra of the theatre to their places. The participants in the show, if they did not attend the sacrifice, might have waited in the courtyard behind the stage building and paraded through the orchestra from west to east and out the other side to be ready to go onstage.

The large theatre, then, appears to have had three important building periods:[6] an original construction in the first half of the second century B.C., of which very little remains; an enlargement in the early years of the Roman colony, to which belong the approaches from the Strada Stabiana and the excavation of the orchestra; and a refurbishing in the Augustan period, to which we can assign the stage building and the new seating of the ima cavea and the building of the summa cavea. In the earthquake of 62 the summa cavea was damaged, and it had not been completely restored by the time of the eruption. The debris had been cleared away, and the building may have been made to function as a comitium; it may even have been possible to put on plays and spectacles there in the last period of the city.

The Temple of Jupiter Meilichios

The identification of the Temple of Jupiter Meilichios (VIII vii 25) depends on an Oscan inscription found at the Porta di Stabia that is usually interpreted as recording the paving of a road from the Temple of Jupiter Meilichios to a bridge (over the Sarno?) that was the boundary between the territories of Pompeii and Stabiae (Conway 39; Vetter 8). It is, to be sure, always possible that the Temple of Jupiter Meilichios lay somewhere outside the city, but it is highly probable at least

---

[6]Mau (supra n. 5) distinguishes six building periods, but it seems likely that his periods 2, 3, and 4 are all parts of one major remodeling, while 6 is simply work preparatory to the laying of a new pavement in the orchestra that was never carried out, probably postearthquake. Mau would assign the brick-faced stage wall to the Augustan remodeling, but as Maiuri observes, by all the criteria available to us, it, too, should be postearthquake (Maiuri 1942, 78–80).

that the temple near the northeast corner of block VIII vii is the one in question.

It might be described as a minimal temple, an altar and a cella in a tiny precinct, but the architecture has been put together with such finesse that one feels that it is economically and adroitly designed. The precinct is proportionately long and narrow, widening somewhat toward the back with a slight optical illusion of greater size than there really is. The axial door in from the Strada Stabiana gives immediately onto a portico across the front of the precinct, its roof supported on a pair of Doric columns with bases of brickwork and capitals of lava. Off this to the north is a room that must have served as a sacristy, a later addition. In front of the portico is a small squarish court containing a very large rectangular altar of exceptional beauty set longitudinally on axis. This altar is of Nocera tufa, except for a burning surface of slabs of lava, carved with a small Doric frieze just below the crown; it is reminiscent of the altar sarcophagus of Scipio Barbatus in Rome and the use of such friezes in the Temple of Fortuna Primigenia at Praeneste.[7] In Pompeii its closest relation is the altar of the Temple of Apollo, which it resembles in size and proportions, but it is clearly older. Just beyond the altar a dramatic flight of nine steps running the full width of the precinct leads up to the cella. The cella is square, set off from the precinct wall by a narrow corridor that runs around it on three sides. In front a deep apron separates it from the stair; this has prompted archaeologists to restore a line of four columns, making a pronaos in front of the cella.[8] Not only is there no real evidence for this but the two architectural elements that survive here, a jamb capital and a pilaster capital in Nocera tufa, the former found carved with a curious full-bearded head above a row of acanthus leaves, are strong evidence against it.[9] Such capitals were meant to be featured prominently, not hidden under a porch. The masonry base for the cult statue stands against the rear wall of the cella; mortared onto it were found roughly life-size terracotta statues of Jupiter and Juno and a bust of Minerva.[10] In the last period of the city's life this temple had been converted to use as the Capitolium of Pompeii, while the one at the north end of the forum awaited rebuilding.

A number of puzzling questions about this temple still await answers: How typical of Campania was the plan of this temple, which has obvious affinities with the Temple of Augustus on the forum but

[7] Nash 2, fig. 1131; Fasolo and Gullini (supra n. 1) passim, esp. 44, fig. 63, and 150, fig. 225. Pernice 1932, 55–58, dates this altar in the early Tufa Period.

[8] Consult, e.g., Mazois 4, pl. 5; and Overbeck and Mau 110–14.

[9] Mazois 4, pl. 6; Kraus and von Matt fig. 10; Eschebach 1978 fig. 21.

[10] Von Rohden pl. 29; Kraus and von Matt fig. 247; Eschebach 1978 figs. 19–20.

is much older and is otherwise a rare type? Temples in Pompeii being comparatively rare, why should the cult of Jupiter Meilichios, which is uncommon, have got so firm a hold at so early a date? On the other hand, why should this temple have been so unpretentious and set in relative isolation?

The last of these we can probably answer: probably the temple was not originally in the apparent isolation we see it in today. Before the building of the Temple of Isis and the houses to the south (VIII vii 24 and 26), before the building of the summa cavea of the Theatrum Maius, it probably stood in clear relation to the theatre and the palaestra/Temple of Hercules, one of a group of fine buildings of the Tufa Period loosely grouped but with free space to set each off in a large tract that was public domain. The Casa del Marmorista (VIII vii 24) is an old atrium house without peristyle that may conceivably have been built as a residence for the priest of Jupiter; the rest grew up piecemeal, but probably only after the arrival of the Roman colony.

On the evidence of the altar, Pernice assigns the original building of the Temple of Jupiter Meilichios to the early Tufa Period (Pernice 1932, 55–58), and the jamb and pilaster capitals are in accord with this. But the façade and cella are of quasi-reticulate coigned with small blocks of tufa and limestone, masonry characteristic of the early Roman colony at Pompeii. Why a rebuilding should have been undertaken at this time is not entirely clear, but the original plan of the temple does not seem to have been altered at that time.

The Theatre Colonnade

In the angle between the scene building of the Theatrum Maius and the west side of the Theatrum Tectum is a Doric colonnade that has been thought to be the remains of a theatre colonnade that was once considerably larger. Though the alley entered at VIII vii 16 might be a survival from an earlier period and might therefore be taken to indicate the original southern limit of such a colonnade, the ancient party wall between VIII vii 8 and VIII vii 9 opposite the street between blocks I i and I ii is probably a better clue to the original pattern of streets in this area. If a street along it was the original southern boundary of this colonnade, then it was very large. But there is very little here, only a few columns, for the most part of brickwork with footing in mortared rubblework, and a tufa gutter, together with some blocks of an entablature in limestone and tufa piled in the southwest corner against the stair leading up to the Forum Triangulare. The tufa column drums are faceted with twenty narrow flat planes, not fluted, to their full height, like some in the palaestra of the Thermae Stabianae, and the capitals are very plain, some of them without a proper annulet, only an angular step produced in the turning of the echinus on a lathe. The oddest thing about these capitals is a ring cut in relief on the top surface of the abacus in place of the more usual disc. The weight of the evidence suggests that this colonnade is late, not early, built after the Ludus Gladiatorius and the Theatrum Minus to permit the Ludus Gladiatorius to serve as a theatre colonnade for both theatres, but especially the latter. Earlier the colonnade of the Forum Triangulare must have served as a theatre colonnade for the Theatrum Maius.

The Ludus Gladiatorius

The Ludus Gladiatorius is a vast quadrangle surrounded on all sides by a Doric colonnade, with seventeen columns on the short north and south sides, twenty-two on the others.[11] Behind these lie rows of cell-like rooms in two storeys, the upper storey accessible by a narrow wooden gallery, for which a wealth of evidence was found during excavation; it has been reconstructed in the southeast corner. Few of the rooms still had remains of plaster or decoration at the time of excavation; what there was is now badly faded. These rooms are more or less uniform, except on the east, where they had to be fitted into an irregular space, but they are interrupted and broken into groups by other features. In the middle of the south side is a large exedra; in the middle of the west the area of four rooms was filled with earth and served as a buttress to the foundations of the Forum Triangulare colonnade above. At the northwest corner a broad stair descends from the Forum Triangulare; at the northeast corner three steps connect the Ludus Gladiatorius with the area behind the scaena of the Theatrum Maius, while beside these to the east is a colonnaded lobby connecting the Ludus Gladiatorius with the Strada Stabiana at VIII vii 16; this must have been the main entrance to the Ludus. And at the middle of the east side opens a very large trapezoidal room separated from the colonnade in front of it by four piers, around which opens a series of large irregular rooms. There was a second storey in this part that was reached by a fine, broad stair, most unusual for Pompeii.

The columns of the Doric colonnade are tufa with high base drums, either lightly faceted or unfluted cylinders, and upper shafts fluted but squared off under a plain finishing band at the top of the shaft. The capitals are given a cavetto annulet of rather angular pro-

---

[11] Mazois 3.12–15 and pls. 2–5. There are errors in the details of this account and in the drawings. Good general views of the complex may be found in Eschebach 1978 figs. 79 and 81.

file, and the echinus is very straight. These were all heavily stuccoed over in the last period and painted, some red and some yellow, while single columns at the centre of the short sides and pairs at the centre of the long ones were painted blue. The stylobate is of tufa and edged with a tufa gutter with catch basins at the corners and at irregular intervals on all four sides. The water was impounded in cisterns, and there are cistern heads near the southeast and southwest corners. On the stylobate are rectangular cuttings for the setting of statue bases in four series: in the east portico, six in the fourth through the ninth intercolumniations from the north and six in the thirteenth through the eighteenth; and in the south portico, six in the second through the seventh intercolumniations from the east and six in the eleventh through the fifteenth. There are none in the other porticoes, and all had evidently been eliminated in the final remodeling of the building.

In the last period the main entrance of the Ludus lay through the alley leading in from the Strada Stabiana at VIII vii 16. This was found paved with lava, but the blocks were prized up and reused for road construction elsewhere. The alley debouches into a little portico of three Ionic columns. This clearly has been butchered by remodeling, since the southernmost intercolumniation is much wider than the others, and the northernmost distinctly narrower. Originally the intercolumniations must all have been equal, but when the Theatrum Tectum was built and the alley behind its scaena was made the principal approach to the Ludus, the southernmost intercolumniation, opposite this alley, was enlarged, while the northernmost was reduced in order to convert some of the portico's area to use as workspace for the theatre. The wall here runs at an angle and shows many signs of having been an afterthought. The original entrance to the Ludus must, then, antedate the Theatrum Tectum and presumably was monumental. The date of the Theatrum Tectum is fixed in the early years of the Roman colony by a building inscription (*CIL* 10.844).

The Ionic order of the entrance portico is a slightly unusual version of Pompeian Ionic (Eschebach 1978, fig. 80). It shows all of the familiar elements, but the half-palmettes trimming the volutes crowd the ovolo of the echinus and appear very linear; also, they are not pierced. The eyes of the volutes are finished with rounded buttons, rather than conical points, and the collar above the fluting is so deep that the volutes hang only about halfway down it. At present the columns are without bases, descending through the steps that lead down from the entrance lobby to the Ludus floor; presumably their bases are concealed underneath.

Throughout the Ludus the masonry is rubblework of the most heterogeneous sort, employing much secondhand material, coigned at all openings and corners with opus mixtum vittatum. Clearly the building was rebuilt after the earthquake of A.D. 62, a deduction also borne out by the remains of painted decorations, all of which seem to have been in the Fourth Style (Maiuri 1942, 81–83). But all the columns, as well as the stylobate and gutter, must be old.

It is the dating of the original construction of the building that gives the greatest difficulty, and all we have to go on in seeking an absolute date is the style of the order, since except for its relation to the theatre portico and the stair down from the Forum Triangulare, the building is independent or uninformative in its relation to others. Capitals like these do not seem to appear in other public buildings but are not uncommon in private houses; good parallels are found in the Casa del Centauro (VI ix 3/5), for example, the Domus Corneliorum (VIII iv 15), and the Casa del Centenario (IX viii 3/6). All these houses have First Style parts and must be dated not later than the early first century B.C.[12]

The excavation of the building is first reported in the daybook entry dated 25 October 1766, and it continued until as late as 22 May 1794 interspersed with other work, but the majority of the complex had been uncovered by 11 February 1769. The digging began on the south side, apparently near the southwest corner, in an attempt to locate the southern edge of the site and the city walls. Very soon, handsomely decorated armor began to come to light, and the building became known as the Quartiere per Soldati. In the report for 20 December 1766 we find note of the discovery of the guardhouse, with iron stocks for prisoners, together with four skeletons "forse de' carcerati," which shows that there was no convincing evidence. Armor continued to turn up, some finer than other. By 7 February 1767 the excavators had reached the midpoint along the south side and discovered the blue column, while in the report for 14 February we read of the decorations of the central exedra of the south side, including very large trophies and graffiti referring to the gladiatorial familia of Pomponius Faustinus. Every room here seems to have had its share of interesting material; under the date of 12 May we find the contents of a storeroom full of household goods. By 26 September the excavators had turned the southeast corner and were advancing in the direction of the theatre. Then came a surprise. Beginning with the report of 5 December and continuing through that of 16 April a great

[12] On First Style houses see chap. 9. The Second Style seems to have arrived in Pompeii with the Roman colony of ca. 80 B.C.

number of skeletons are mentioned, and together with these, a great deal of portable wealth: a large, elaborately mounted cameo, a gold chain set with twelve small emeralds, a great many gemstones and rings, and some handsomely mounted weapons. In this period the parts being excavated were the large rooms around the middle of the east side, and here at least fifty-two human skeletons were recovered, including some of children, and also some of dogs. This is a very large number, especially to have been found in a place without a vaulted roof. But here we are close to the Porta di Stabia and the port of Pompeii; evidently, in the final disaster this was being used as an evacuation centre, a collecting point from which groups of refugees could be taken to safety as means became available.

But even the building's functioning as a Ludus Gladiatorius is more than a little puzzling. The rooms of the south half seem to have been the parts where the men slept and where the gear was kept. The rooms at the north end of the west wing were the kitchens and latrine. Those in the north wing are something of a mystery, since very little was found here, but they also might have been quarters for the men. But what are the big rooms around the middle of the east side? workshops, or clubrooms for enthusiastic followers of the sport? There is nothing to inform us. And where were the baths? For it is hard to imagine that they could have done without baths. Did they have to be content with washing at a pipe or from a basin after their exertions?

Compared with the wealth of gladiatorial illustrations and inscriptions elsewhere in Pompeii, the harvest from the Ludus is very meager (CIL 4.1084–95, 2464–83), but it was excavated before the art of spotting and deciphering graffiti was far advanced. The painted inscriptions collected from the main entrance, however, are of the highest interest, since they indicate that the familiae of several gladiatorial impresarios were quartered, or at least accustomed to train, here. And they show that N. Popidius Rufus, a member of one of Pompeii's first families, kept a familia.

The monumental stair from the Forum Triangulare not only follows the design of the Ludus but goes together with it. At present it descends handsomely in the width of the north bank of cells of the Ludus to a point eight steps above the level of the Ludus and then breaks into two small makeshift flights, one leading down north to the area behind the scaena of the Theatrum Maius, the other down south inside a cell to the Ludus. Both are difficult to negotiate. But the ends of treads that carried the flight down east in a continuation of the main flight are still clearly visible in the north wall. Once this stair descended monumentally and must have debouched into a lobby of suitable dignity that was an important feature of the Ludus. After the earthquake, perhaps because of the prohibition on public assemblies in Pompeii, the lower part of the stair was sacrificed to make more rooms in the north wing of the Ludus.

7 · THE FORUM AND
NEIGHBORING BUILDINGS

The Forum

The forum of Pompeii, running north and south, long and narrow, has an open area of approximately the proportion 1:4.5, much longer and narrower than Vitruvius prescribes to provide a maximum of place for spectators at games and ceremonies customarily presented there.[1] There is no indication that this forum was used for shows. It lies in the southwest quarter of the city, near the Porta Marina. Since the port of Pompeii is reported to have been a river port, the Porta di Stabia must have been the gate closest to the port, so in its location the forum does not conform to Vitruvius's principle that in a port city the forum should be conveniently accessible from the harbor, but it may well antedate Pompeii's importance as a port.

Whatever its early form and size, it must always have lain along the precinct of the Aedes Apollinis, where temple terracottas and votive material dating back to the sixth century B.C. have been found. Sogliano's attempt to discover its original form and history by connecting the Vicolo del Gallo and the Vicolo del Balcone Pensile, the Via Marina and the Via dell'Abbondanza, and seeing the resulting streets as its southern boundary in successive periods is unconvincing, especially in respect to the first, for it is based on no more than wishful thinking (Sogliano 83–87, 188–90, 253–58). On the other hand, it may be that the forum was at some time extended to the south and that prior to that time the Via Marina and the Via dell'Abbondanza took off from its lower corners. But to assume that these were ever parts of a continuous street is absurd. From the beginning the forum will have dominated the development of streets around it, and these will have come into it along the obvious and convenient lines of access. That the Strada delle Scuole enters the

---

[1] Vitruvius 5.1.1–3. Vitruvius prescribes a proportion of 2:3 for fora.

forum west of its southeast corner suggests that it follows an older line and that the forum has been enlarged and its axis changed. That the Vicolo di Championnet runs just out of the southwest corner suggests that it was a creation of the time of the construction of the basilica. The forum as we see it is in area the forum of the end of the second century B.C., and buildings of fine Tufa Period architecture, the basilica and the "comitium," define its southern extremity.

It is doubtful that the Aedes Apollinis was ever intimately connected with the forum. Even in the days when a series of large openings along its eastern flank may have given a vista of the temple to people in the forum, the wall between the temple precinct and the public square will have been a barrier. Before we could produce a significant relationship, we would have to suppose that the temple was once oriented so as to face on the forum and that a monumental approach led to it. So probably it was always more or less as we see it today and as the Greek temples of Paestum are related to its agora and forum, accessible but set apart, visible but architecturally a separate complex, religiously discrete.

The Aedes Apollinis

The precinct of the Temple of Apollo[2] presented a blank façade to the Via Marina, on which it fronted across a broad signinum sidewalk, the surface thickly sprinkled with chips of white limestone. On the forum along its east flank there seems to have been at one time an alternation of broad openings and stout piers, the piers progressively thicker toward the north in adjustment to the slight divergence in axis between temple and forum. The five southernmost openings were subsequently walled up, the northernmost closed down and fitted with a door. That next to it was converted into a shallow alcove for the mensa ponderaria. Three of the remaining four have sills of lava blocks but no sign of any door; they may have been closed with panels of grillwork secured to the jambs. The main door is framed in tufa blocks cut to make pilasters but not drafted; the eastern jamb capital, which was chiseled away in a redecoration, was certainly originally a plain block capital. But at the southeast corner a handsome Doric pilaster remains, its capital at a level below that of the jamb capital, quite unlike the door jambs in its character, related to, but not identical with, the pilasters decorating the exterior of the basilica. It is hard to reconcile these differences, and the variety of materials and masonry one sees where the stucco has fallen away (large

[2] On the Temple of Apollo see Mazois 4.37–44 and pls. 16–23; and Fiorelli 1875, 237–41.

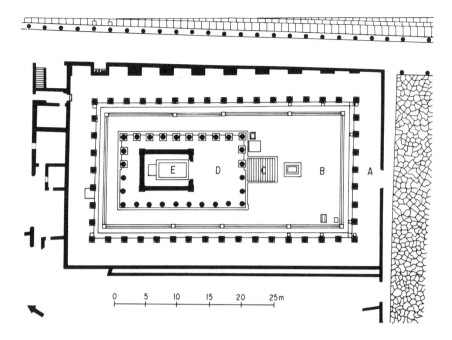

FIGURE 8.
The Aedes Apollinis,
Plan

blocks of limestone and Nocera tufa, small squarish blocks of tufa, and rubblework of every description) looks like a patchwork of many successive rehandlings. The façade was refinished in the last period in a version of the First Style in which above a very high, plain socle courses of ashlar blocks with drafted margins were simply deeply scored into a flat stucco surface. The main doorway, preceded by a single step, has a sill of Caserta stone with cuttings for a great door of four leaves hinged together in pairs.

Inside, a peristyle, nine columns by seventeen, that surrounds the precinct on all sides closes relatively tightly around the temple proper except in front. Originally of finely carved tufa, in the last period it was thoroughly remodeled in stucco. Today most of the column shafts have reeded lower parts, painted yellow, with bases of masonry appliquéd around them, and white upper parts. There are now no remains of the stucco of the capitals of the last period. Originally the colonnade was Pompeian Ionic. The shafts that are bare of plaster show no bases, but each column is set on a plinth carved with an offset disc that might have been stuccoed as a base. The lower shafts have shallow fluting, twenty flutes to a column, without sharply articulated fillets, to a height of 1.24 m; the upper shafts have crisp fillets. The capitals are canonical, with four volutes, not deeply pendent, trimmed with half-palmettes; the echinus is composed of seven small eggs tightly tucked in their cups between each pair of volutes. The echinus was finished with an astragal below, now almost entirely chiseled away, and the upper edge of the abacus was carved in a Lesbian leaf pattern. The entablature, now heavily picked and chiseled for restuccoing, was Doric, a common Pompeian fashion in the Tufa Period. The architrave was in two fasciae, the lower one a wooden beam, as in the south colonnade of the forum. In the frieze there were three triglyphs over each intercolumniation, and the metopes were blank. The cornice has Doric mutules, and in the back of the frieze are cut sockets for the beams of the ceiling. Since these are closely spaced and show no inclination, and there are no beam sockets cut in the cornice, it has been supposed that there must originally have been an upper colonnade, access to which could be found in the stair outside the northeast corner. But that stair is clearly of a late period and almost certainly led rather to the upper storey of the forum colonnade, while the combination we see here of Doric and Ionic elements is not an order that lends itself to multistorey buildings. It therefore seems necessary to restore the peristyle as a single storey and to understand the lift of the temple podium (2.30 m) to more than half the height of the colonnade around it as calculated to make the temple more visible from the forum.

In front of the stylobate of the colonnade is a tufa step, 0.62 m wide, on which a number of votive offerings were mounted, including the well-known bronze figures, slightly under life-size, of Apollo and Diana as archers, mounted on bases of tufa capped with blocks of Caserta stone, a herm of Mercury, and several others. There are at present three bases on the east side, two on the west, and two on the south. In the southeast and southwest corners were deep, rounded basins mounted on fluted marble pedestals. These may have served as fountains, since behind that in the southwest corner is a high, marble-faced base suitable for mounting a fountain figure. But the two basins were not a pair. At least four other dedications stood in the open area in front of the temple, notably a sundial of white marble mounted on an Ionic column with a shaft of blue-grey marble between a white marble capital and base that carried an inscription recording that it was the gift of the duovirs L. Sepunius Sandalialius and M. Herennius Epidianus; a schola and an identical sundial were dedicated by the same men in the Forum Triangulare (*CIL* 10.802).

Below this step is a broad walk of tufa, 0.89 m wide, along the inner edge of which is cut a gutter. If the peristyle roof projected to drip into this gutter, it will have had a total projection of ca. 1.80–1.85 m, an extraordinary depth. At the corners of the gutter and at irregular intervals along the sides are settling basins, showing that the water was impounded in cisterns. Two small drawshafts with modern brick mouths in the open area in front of the third intercolumniation from each end on the south and a larger lava manhole in the third intercolumniation of the north portico from the west seem to mark these (Sogliano 91); one of these has an ancient lava cover.

Between the precinct entrance and the temple building, effectively blocking the approach, stands a large rectangular altar of travertine and white limestone with a marble crown, its long axis coinciding with the axis of the temple. It seems out of scale and out of key, only partly because of its material. It stands very high (1.46 m), trimmed at base and crown with moldings, and the top surface has been fitted with lava slabs in the area where the sacrificial fire would have burned between marble bolsters at the ends. Only a very tall man could have sacrificed here with any ease. An inscription on the west front records that this is the work of the quattuorvirs M. Porcius, L. Sextilius, Cn. Cornelius, and A. Cornelius; the slab on which it is carved is reused and shows traces of an earlier inscription (*CIL* 10.800).

The temple platform is crowded to the back of the space around it, so there is a passage of less than 1.10 m between it and the back gutter, and at the sides there is less than 2.50 m. In front a stair of fourteen steps, the lowest six of blocks of limestone finished as large drafted ashlar along the sides, the rest a reconstruction in brick, rises to the top. Although this does not run the full width of the façade, it is still broad and inviting. The podium is trimmed at the base with a double torus separated by a scotia, like an Attic base, partly carved in tufa, partly constructed in masonry and stuccoed, above a deep step. There is no trace of a crown molding left today.

The temple, though raised on a podium and frontal in the Roman manner, is peripteral, with six columns on the front, the central intercolumniation being noticeably wider than the others, and probably ten columns on the sides. The columns are Corinthian, of manneristic delicacy with an elongated and very beautiful bell. The bases were constructed of masonry; the shafts, like those of the Ionic order of the peristyle, have twenty flutes and well-articulated fillets. The capitals rise in three zones, the ribs of the acanthus leaves in stiff sheaves, the edges breaking into crinkled lace, highly plastic and decorative in its effect. Little is left of the volutes, but they were delicate and given a convex outer face trimmed with raised edges and were presumably corkscrew, like those of the basilica. Nothing of the entablature or pediment survives.

Within the frame of its generous peripteros the cella seems to shrink in upon itself, the line of its front wall coming just in front of the fifth column, so that the pronaos is deep and airy in the Italic manner and the cella tiny, hardly inviting to the visitor. One tends to stay in the generous space within the cage of columns, enjoying the

FIGURE 9.
The Aedes Apollinis,
Corinthian Capital

height and the prospect, strolling around the edge, and bothering to take only the briefest glance inside. The effect cannot have been much different in antiquity, when the cella served merely to house the cult image and such treasures as could not be displayed in the courtyard. The centre is paved with opus sectile in lozenges of black, white, and green set to give an optical illusion of perspective, framed in a plastic meander in colored mosaic surrounded by black and white mosaic. In the slate margin was worked an Oscan inscription recording that this was the work of a quaestor, whose name has been lost, with money belonging to Apollo, so we can be sure that we are indeed dealing with a temple to that god.[3] If we needed further confirmation, a tufa omphalos stands against the west wall of the cella. The cult image was salvaged in antiquity, but its base survives, 1.44 m by 1.15, 1.55 m high. To permit a view of the image to worshipers in the vicinity of the altar, not only was the central intercolumniation

[3]Conway 52; Vetter 18. The pavement is shown by Mazois 4, pl. 23.4. Pernice 1938, 69–70, assigns it to the period of the Second Style, contemporary with similar mosaics in the Casa del Fauno.

of the peripteros widened but the doors of the cella were very wide, 2.20 m.

Inside the cella are remains of First Style plaster, a plain socle and squarish orthostats with drafted margins, 1.46–1.53 m on a side, framed in a raised band 0.15–0.17 m wide. Some of this work is original First Style, some a later repair (Mau 1882, 59–60). On the exterior are remains of fine plain tufa pilasters with Attic bases at the corners, but in the last period these were stuccoed over to make reeded pilasters, and the whole exterior was finished in a stucco relief in which stamped ovolo patterns play an important part, replacing and embellishing the drafting of margins, so that the surface sometimes becomes almost agitated in its complexity. The excellence of the stucco, with its addition of marble dust, intensifies the effect (Mazois 4, pl. 23.1).

Exploration of the subsoil of the precinct has brought to light much interesting material, including parts of earlier building phases (Sogliano 88–92). In the southwest corner of the forecourt a section of worn tufa pavement just below the present floor has been exposed. Along the west flank of the temple, excavation has laid bare a series of sleepers of tufa laid parallel to one another projecting from under the edge of the podium, but it is not clear that these are not simply the foundation of the present structure. Also found was a curious column base, now in the antiquarium, of pale tan tufa; it is composed of a deep base disc surmounted by a swelling quarter round. This appears to be a genuine archaic member, possibly a base for a wooden column.

Besides these things, numerous fragments of black-figure Attic pottery, especially Little Master cups, fibulae, and bucchero, were found. The evidence suggests an early building of the sixth century B.C., largely of wood and other perishable material, rebuilt in its present form no earlier than the last third of the second century, then thoroughly redecorated, but without substantial architectural change, in the last period of the city.

So little of the redecoration survives that it is hard to believe the early descriptions, and the drawings alone carry conviction. The columns of the peristyle were encased in stucco, and the capitals were rendered in a rather heavy, multicolored form of Corinthian. The architrave and frieze were treated with a rich stuccoing showing patterns of palmettes and gryphons, apparently done with matrices (Mazois 4, pl. 21). But if the changes in the architectural decoration were bold, those in the wall painting were still bolder. Here the walls were covered with a Fourth Style decoration in which a set of subject paintings showing scenes from the *Iliad* were the main feature, while others showed Nilotic landscapes peopled with dwarves. Unfortu-

FIGURE 10.
The Basilica, Interior

nately, no good copies of these were made in time, and they had utterly perished by Helbig's day; we must rely for our knowledge of them on old line drawings and descriptions (Mazois 4, pl. 22; Schefold 192).

The Basilica

The basilica of Pompeii, excavated mainly between 15 May 1813 and 17 February 1816, is one of the most splendid buildings of the Hellenistic period.[4] It lies at the southwest corner of the forum, opening to it on a short side, and is framed by the Via Marina on the north and the Vicolo di Championnet on the south, the latter probably contemporary with the basilica. Behind the basilica, between it and the Temple of Venus, is a narrow, paved alley that once connected the flanking streets.

The main façade of the basilica, in large plain blocks of Nocera tufa, opens to the forum by five large doors. These were fitted with shutters, presumably of wood, that ran in vertical slots to either side

[4]The principal studies of the basilica are those of Mazois (3.36–41 and pls. 15–21); Maiuri (1973, 191–223); and K. Ohr (*Die Basilika in Pompeji* [Karlsruhe 1973]).

like a portcullis and were secured at the bottom to lava sill blocks. Traces of the fastening set in lead survive on most of the sills. The cores of statue bases flank the central door, and another stands at the south end of the façade; there is no indication of who was so honored. The lateral and rear façades are in rubble masonry, principally broken lava, at least in the lower parts, stuccoed. There is a large door in the centre of each long wall, but that on the south is a late modification.

From the forum, one entered a broad, plain lobby and from this climbed a flight of four steps to reach the main level of the building. The stair is in blocks of lava, and a line of four large Ionic columns flanked by a door at either end rose from the middle of the stair to carry the roof. These, like the columns of the nave, have cores constructed of pieces of tile as thick as a modern brick made in special matrices of different shapes carefully mortared around central discs of at least two sizes to make a fluted column of considerable size and then deliberately roughened with chiseling for stuccoing. The capitals are of tufa, Pompeian Ionic, flamboyantly carved into corkscrew volutes like ram's horns that are trimmed with palmettes carried on branches that curl back from the volute to bring the palmettes up to the abacus. The echinus is an egg molding of exaggerated plasticity, finished below with an astragal on a deep, plain collar above the top of the fluting. The abacus is a cyma reversa. The general effect is baroque, the designer having been eager to exploit the possibilities of his material.

The main hall of the building consists of a long columnar nave, four columns by twelve, surrounded on all sides by an aisle. The massive columns of the nave, constructed of specially shaped tile, have been reduced to stumps, none higher than a man's head, and stripped of their stucco. No fragment of a capital was found. The bases and fillets show that they were Ionic or Corinthian, more probably the latter. Down the long flanks of the surrounding aisle is an engaged Ionic order similar to that of the entrance. This carried a Corinthian order above in a second storey, of which numerous capitals lie in the building today. The capitals are both clustered in groups of three and freestanding, so the upper wall must have been pierced all around with large loggialike windows that flooded the interior with light.[5] These made a clerestorey over the central nave unnecessary, and since there is no trace of any means of access to a gallery over the side aisles, it is very unlikely that there ever was one. Remains of First Style stucco cover the lower walls (Mau 1882, 11–17).

[5] Ohr (supra n. 4), pls. 18–19, carries these continuously the full length and width of the building, so that only at the tribunal did the roof not seem to hang suspended over the building.

At the far end of the building is a tribunal, on axis, dominating the central nave, flanked by symmetrical exedral rooms from which one could get to the tribunal by a concealed lateral stair and to a vaulted cellar under it, the purpose of which is puzzling. This was certainly not a jail for prisoners awaiting trial, as has sometimes been suggested; such incarceration was not a Roman practice. It was more likely for storage. The tribunal is raised just above head height and has six Corinthian columns across its front, with an engaged order responding to this down the sides and across the back. Above this was a second storey, with an engaged order of uncertain character framing rectangular windows of rather plain design.[6] That the tribunal was not intended primarily for a speaker's platform seems proved by the base for an equestrian statue set on axis between the two centre columns of the nave at this end; this would have interfered with the assembly of a crowd of any size here. Since basilicas were halls for banking and stockbrokerage that might include offices for public magistrates (the tribunes of the plebs had their place in the Basilica Porcia in Rome),[7] we may see the tribunal and exedras as places where the ordinary business of the quattuorvirs and the servi publici of Pompeii was transacted—the drawing up of such leases as those mentioned in the archive of Caecilius Iucundus (*CIL* 4, supp., apochae 138–53), the letting of contracts, and so on. The limited access to the tribunal is also in favor of this interpretation, since it means that these officials would be on public view as they went about the dispatch of public business, but an usher at the approach could keep order and prevent their being presented with more business than they could handle.[8] If this notion is acceptable, we may see the cellar under the tribunal as temporary storage for records, where these could be immediately accessible as long as they were likely to be called for.

A number of oddities about the building need to be noted. First, a series of drains in the floor leads to a channel beneath that runs around three sides of the central nave inside the columns (Maiuri 1973, 204–7). This is carefully leveled and slopes regularly to a point at the southwest end, where there is no sign of an exit. Deposits in it suggest that it may never have had an exit. This was at one time taken

[6] The order of Aeolic character now in place is an invention of the time of Maiuri, as is the north corner of a pediment above it. Neither rests on sound evidence, and the latter gives the tribunal the effect of a building within a building, which is very unlikely to be correct (see Ohr [supra n. 4] 120).

[7] See Platner and Ashby, s.v. Basilica Porcia.

[8] That not all of the business of the magistrates could have been transacted in such surroundings is proved by the tomb of Vestorius Priscus outside the Porta del Vesuvio, where a painting shows the young aedile seated on a small tribunal covered by an awning (see *MemLinc* ser. 7, 3 [1943] 289–92 [G. Spano]).

as evidence that the central nave was unroofed, but it is clearly nothing of the sort. The thick signinum pavement, though broken in many places, is uniform throughout and quite level, strong evidence, if we needed it, that the nave was roofed. The drain must be for water used to wash the floor, and the lack of an outlet, if not a later modification, may be due to an unforeseen impossibility of installing a sewer line to the nearby brow of the city site.

The powerful thrust of the columns of the nave, the evidence for continuous windows in the upper walls of the side aisles, the unified two-storey façade of the tribunal, and the absence of any evidence for stairs in either side aisle combine to make a strong case against there having been a gallery over any part of the side aisles and suggest that the roof was a single longitudinal gable preceded by a single-storey vestibule with a relatively high lean-to roof. The portico on the forum built later in front of this may have carried either a sloping roof at a lower level or an open gallery for spectators at events in the forum. A stair with steps of well-cut blocks of lava that runs along the south side of the basilica on the exterior is support for the hypothesis of a gallery. It was clearly for public use and equally clearly constructed after the basilica.

In the seemingly massive wall at the south end of the vestibule of the basilica is concealed one of the deep wells of Pompeii.[9] Presumably it antedates the basilica and was once the public water supply for this corner of the city. After the building of the basilica, it was completely enclosed and used only to supply a tank adjacent to it that was built well above floor level, from which water could be drawn off for washing floors and similar purposes.

At a late period a door was cut in the middle of the south wall of the basilica to give access to the Vicolo di Championnet. This responds to the door to the Via Marina in the north wall but is of no clear usefulness. Because the floor of the basilica at this point stands high above the pavement of the vicolo, one emerges onto a narrow platform built over the sidewalk from which one can make one's way down a narrow ramp to the west or down a stair to the east. The whole design here is so clumsy that one would like to ascribe it to a date after the earthquake, but to judge from the masonry and materials, it is late republican. Presumably it is in some way connected with the entrance to the Temple of Venus at the end of this alley.

The basilica's architecture is majestic, the very acme of the Tufa Period, and in its proportions it is as fine a building as Pompeii has produced. Some may find the style of its capitals too ornate to compare well with the soberer style of the Forum Triangulare or the atria

---

[9]Maiuri 1973, 192–204; Ohr (supra n. 4) 28–33.

of the Casa del Fauno, but the sweep of its axis in from the forum, with careful consideration and control of the vista at every point from the façade to the tribunal, is an impressive achievement. A series of screens, lines of demarcation, was thrown across the view, but one was constantly aware of the tribunal as the culmination of the axis to which all the rest worked as preparation. The elegant lifting of the nave above the vestibule with a stair punctuated, rather than interrupted, the experience by its line of columns, and the surprise of the spacious interior flooded with light from vast windows set high in the side walls is architecture of a very high order.

We are of course interested in dating this building as exactly as possible. Maiuri made extensive excavations under the floor but was unable to find substantial and readily comprehensible remains of earlier buildings (Maiuri 1973, 212–23). The footing of a long, heavy wall in blocks of tufa that is aligned with the axis of the basilica, perpendicular to that of the forum, can be taken as proof that this area was occupied by a public building before the construction of the basilica, but the character of that building is not clear. The material collected in these excavations was abundant, however, and included a wide range of pottery, roof tiles, and even an antefix of an amorino wearing the girdle of Venus. The sum of the evidence led Maiuri to decide that the basilica could hardly have been built before 150 B.C., but he was reluctant to bring the date lower than 130–120 B.C. In view of the increasing evidence that the last quarter of the second century was a time of extraordinary productivity and inventiveness in architecture in central Italy, one may incline to a date slightly later than 120 but before the end of the century.

8 · OTHER PUBLIC BUILDINGS

The Thermae Stabianae

A. Maiuri's researches into the architecture of Hellenistic Pompeii early on led him to explore the subsoil of the Thermae Stabianae at the crossing of the Strada Stabiana and the Via dell'Abbondanza (*NSc* 1931, 564–75 [A. Maiuri]). The evidence that at the moment of the eruption a gang was still laying pipe to supply aqueduct water (*NSc* 1931, 554–64 [A. Maiuri]; Maiuri 1942, 90–94) and that the bath complex, despite some newly decorated rooms, was far from being in working order (Maiuri 1973, 70–72) and the evidence that a large, deep well off the Vicolo del Lupanare had early supplied water to the baths suggested that excavation might expose a clear series of building periods going back to an early date. Maiuri was able to demonstrate that the baths were probably the earliest building of this type in Pompeii and go back to the second century B.C., but the sequence of building periods is confused. Subsequently H. Sulze and H. Eschebach conducted further investigations (Eschebach 1970, 1979), but their work was vitiated by the conviction that a small cellar is an early chamber tomb and that the fortifications of the town once ran through the middle of the complex, both notions for which there is no substantial evidence.

The original building is represented by five doorways on three sides of the block with fine frames of tufa, those on the Vicolo del Lupanare and the Via dell'Abbondanza surmounted by remains of transom windows also framed in tufa. Three blocks of tufa lintel now lying against the west wall of the entranceway at VII i 8 do not belong to the original building. This entrance was clearly created out of what had once been a shop by closing down the shop door. The main entrances were probably those now walled up near the southeast corner of the block, on the Via dell'Abbondanza between VII i 9 and VII i 10 and on the Strada Stabiana between VII i 13 and VII i 14. Both prob-

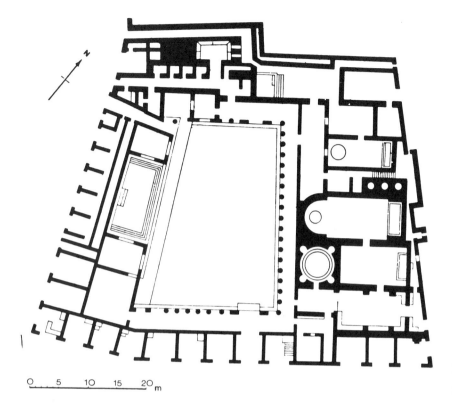

FIGURE 11.
The Thermae
Stabianae, Plan

O   5   10   15   20 m

ably led through lobbies provided with benches for waiting slaves more or less directly to the apodyterium (dressing room) of the principal suite of bath rooms. The apodyterium in turn gave onto the tepidarium (warm room), which gave onto the caldarium (hot room), while the frigidarium (cold room) was off the west entrance lobby, which also gave onto the palaestra.

The furnaces and tanks for hot water to supply the warm rooms will always have lain in a courtyard just beyond the caldarium, and the major rooms will have had vaulted ceilings and been lit by relatively small shafts cut through the west end of each to the area of the palaestra. The apsidal caldarium and conical-roofed frigidarium seem too organic not to have been part of the original design. Access from the bathing complex to the trapezoidal palaestra was probably only from the west entrance lobby, though the palaestra must have been very large from the beginning. Presumably the palaestra did not have any special features; it will have been simply an exercise ground, probably framed on three sides by colonnaded walks.

The women's bath, north of the praefurnium (heating room or heating yard) so that its caldarium could be heated from a central set of furnaces, was smaller than the men's but otherwise similar. The caldarium, though without an apse, had a labrum for cold water at its west end and a bathing tank at the east end. The original entrance was almost certainly at VII i 15, where the door has a handsome tufa frame, and this led to a corridorlike lobby that may have communicated with the palaestra in some way for the convenience of the attendants. But the women's section was otherwise carefully segregated from the men's. The original apodyterium was almost certainly the space south of the entrance lobby later turned into storage for fuel for the furnaces, at which time a new apodyterium with a cold plunge was created west of the original one. Whether the original one included a frigidarium is not clear. From the apodyterium one passed first to the tepidarium and then to the caldarium. Both these rooms were vaulted, the vaults parallel to those of the men's section, the floors raised on suspensurae and the walls hollow.

At the north end of the palaestra was a third bathing complex, a suite of small vaulted cubicles, probably always four in number, for bathing in private, each provided with its own place for a small tub. These lay along a corridor in part vaulted and lit by tiny vents in the vault opposite each door with its own entrance from the Vicolo del Lupanare, and probably originally there was a praefurnium for heating water for these located west of them in conjunction with the deep well, adjacent to the Vicolo del Lupanare, where it would have been easy to bring in fuel, while other offices lay to the south of the corridor. Off the east end of the corridor a stair led up to a second storey, where there is a reservoir adjacent to the deep well. It seems possible that a street or alleyway along the north in continuation of the Vicolo di Balbo once separated the baths from the rest of the block, and the well that supplied the baths and the area in which the men, and later animals, toiled at the water-hoisting device were accessible from the Vicolo del Lupanare by a broad door, so this may once have served as the water supply for the whole neighborhood.

This is a very sophisticated bath for its period, with floors raised on suspensurae and hollow walls in the hot rooms, capable of accommodating a good many people. The cubicles for private bathing have been taken as indication of an early date, a development from the individual larnakes (tubs) of such Greek Hellenistic baths as that at Gela,[1] but they really have nothing in common with these. The arrangement was probably not to satisfy considerations of modesty but to allow for water temperatures different from those in the public rooms.

An inscription found out of proper context in a room on the north side of the palaestra (*CIL* 10.829) attests that in the early years of the

---

[1]See Eschebach 1979, 51–53; and P. Griffo, *Gela* (Rome 1964) fig. 142.

Roman colony the duovirs C. Vulius and P. Aninius rebuilt the porticoes and palaestra and added a laconicum and a destrictarium. The destrictarium, where athletes had the dust and oil scraped from their bodies, we should expect to be in close conjunction with the palaestra, but not a very large room. The laconicum, a dry sweat bath, ought to be a small, closed bath room where high heat could be produced.[2] At what was the northwest corner of the palaestra there is today a pair of rooms built into part of the north portico, one very open, simply a walled-off part of the portico, the other more enclosed but with big rectangular windows to south and west. Here was found a bronze brazier donated to the baths by P. Nigidius Vaccula, a rich citizen who seems to have been alive and active in the years leading up to the eruption (*PAH* 2.649–50 [4 June 1857]). It was out of place, against a wall, simply put there temporarily by workmen to be out of the way, but this room would have made a good destrictarium. A laconicum heated by braziers could have been constructed anywhere in the complex, but one could hardly have been added to the main suite of centrally heated rooms. Perhaps the likeliest place for this is the room created out of a shop between VII i 8 and VII i 9; the small block masonry of the doorway to the interior would suit such a date. The stuccowork in the corridor leading to this room shows that it was one of the public rooms, though the room itself has now been stripped to bare masonry. Eschebach would like to identify the frigidarium as this laconicum and sees the destrictarium as a room north of this in the area later used for the apse of the caldarium. But the circular basin lined with signinum and painted blue that takes up all but a narrow walk around the frigidarium is clear indication that this was especially a cold plunge, while the identifying characteristic of a laconicum was dryness.

Eschebach distinguishes six building periods, the first consisting only of the "Greek" bath with individual cubicles at the northwest corner of the later complex, the fifth the rebuilding by Vulius and Aninius. Between these he sees the development as (1) the addition of a palaestra covering the area of the later palaestra and bath rooms, (2) rebuilding of the rooms north of the palaestra, except for the suite of bathing cubicles and its vicinity, and (3) construction of the first bank of bath rooms along the east side of the palaestra. The lack of architectural logic here, however, is very striking and immediately arouses suspicion, and the perfect harmony of the Tufa Period doorframes strongly suggests that the general organization of the whole complex was carried out in a single operation. If the deep well and the suite of bathing cubicles were older than the rest, they were com-

[2]See Vitruvius 5.10.5.

pletely rebuilt when the later complex was designed, and why they should have been preserved, an outmoded relic, becomes a mystery. It is easier to think that they had a special use from the beginning and kept this down to the destruction of the city. I see the Thermae Stabianae as coming into existence in the later Tufa Period, when bathing first became popular and public baths spread rapidly over Italy, as theatres were to do in the Augustan period. The façade on the Via dell'Abbondanza, though it is of fine tufa blocks, is not decorated with drafting or pilasters and does not continue up either the Strada Stabiana or the Vicolo del Lupanare. The columns of the palaestra are faceted rather than fluted. These are indications of construction in the second half of the second century. Then after the arrival of the Roman colony and a half-century or three-quarters of a century of hard use, the baths required repair and redecoration; this the magistrates Vulius and Aninius undertook to carry out on a large scale with the addition of facilities the old baths had lacked. The baths probably needed repair and repainting again by the time of Augustus, and to this we may ascribe some of the brickwork in the hot rooms and the praefurnium.

At this time aqueduct water became available, and it became possible to make extensive changes and important additions. The area of a house adjacent to the baths on the west was acquired and converted into a swimming pool flanked by large open loggias containing wall fountains with a strip of independent, but interconnected, shops along the Vicolo del Lupanare. Some of these were probably meant to serve the convenience of bathers. A broad walk paved with tufa blocks was added along this side of the palaestra. The whole building was repaired and refurbished. The heating and plumbing systems were overhauled. A new entrance paved with limestone flags and travertine that gives directly onto the palaestra was created out of one of the old shops on the Via dell'Abbondanza. After the earthquake another redecoration was necessary. The colonnades of the palaestra were encased in stucco and finished with reeding and fantastic brightly colored architraves and capitals. Figurative stuccoes of fine workmanship in a fantastic architectural setting typical of the Fourth Style covered the exterior of the loggias flanking the swimming pool and the vaults of the apodyterium and the tepidarium of the men's baths. They are full of interest and include a number of recognizable types and divinities (Silenus, Hercules, Amor), but the program is elusive. All this work is competent but clearly only a refurbishing of an older establishment. There was no general rebuilding nor any attempt to introduce large windows to light the big bath rooms, though they are a feature of the Terme Centrali, and the fine Tufa Period doorways that survived on the façade were either still in use without modification or walled up without disguise. Additions and modifications were made with an eye to practicality and efficiency rather than to aesthetics, and no more was done than was necessary to make the edifice solid and serviceable.

The Temple of Bacchus at Sant'Abbondio

Despite the enormous popularity of Bacchus and the Bacchic mysteries in Pompeii, no temple of that god has come to light within the city or is now likely to appear. Pictures of the abandoning of Ariadne on Naxos and her discovery by the Bacchic thiasos, the education of Bacchus, the triumph of Bacchus, satyrs and maenads, Bacchic trophies, and still-life arrangements of the instrumenta of the mysteries appear in nearly every house, and Bacchus is a very common figure in Pompeian lararia, but his worship was evidently not part of the official religion of the city. So it is all the more gratifying that in 1943 a stray bomb should have brought to light a little rustic temple of Bacchus at Sant'Abbondio, about a kilometer southeast of the Porta di Nocera.[3] This seems not to have been connected with a road of any importance but owes its location rather to a low eminence overlooking the Sarno River. One may suspect that in antiquity it was surrounded by a grove.

The tetrastyle temple is small, frontal in the Italic manner, the single cella preceded by an only slightly smaller pronaos, built of blocks of Sarno limestone. The order is Doric, of Nocera tufa, with an entablature in blocks of the same stone. The pediment, which was recovered in remarkably good condition, is also of blocks of Nocera tufa, carved with figures in high relief.[4] At the centre Bacchus and Ariadne, approximately life-size, recline symmetrically as if at a banquet; he is wreathed and holds a bunch of grapes, while she lifts a corner of her veil coquettishly. He is attended by Silenus, on a smaller scale, and a panther fills the left corner of the composition. She is approached by an amorino bringing her a fan, while a goose, or swan, fills the right corner. The whole group is formulaic and is known in other versions, notably one on a smaller scale from a temple tomb at Vulci in Etruria.[5] The execution is careful but not first-rate and the figures are somewhat wooden.

In the last period of Pompeii the walls and columns of the temple

[3] On this temple, see *Atti del IV Convegno di Studi sulla Magna Grecia* 184–91 (O. Elia); *CronPomp* 1 (1975) 121–23 (O. Elia); and Jashemski 157–58.

[4] A. De Franciscis, *Pompei* (I documentari 15, Novara 1968) fig. 104, published in English as *The Buried Cities: Pompeii and Herculaneum* (New York 1978); Eschebach 1978 fig. 32.

[5] See M. Moretti, *Il Museo Nazionale di Villa Giulia* (Rome 1962) 25, fig. 13.

were encased in heavy coats of stucco painted red in the lower parts, white above, and a high, thick pluteus with a bench in front of it ran between the columns enclosing the pronaos, except at the entrance. This must have made the cella very dark, unless there were windows there, but not enough is preserved to tell. The only feature of the cella preserved today is a large, low statue base. The pronaos is paved with broken chips of limestone in mortar, and in a panel at the entrance is an Oscan inscription worked out in chips of black stone recording its construction by the aediles Oppius Epidius and Trebius Ulezius.

The pronaos is approached by a ramp, at the foot of which was found the altar, of modest size, also of Nocera tufa, inscribed with the name of the aedile Maras Atinius. The ramp of approach was flanked by two triclinia of masonry covered with a veneer of red stucco, which were covered with an arbor over which vines were trained (Jashemski 157–58), and a schola of the same material is constructed against the right flank of the pronaos.

The terminus ante quem for the construction of this temple is fixed by the Oscan inscriptions, but in the excavation were found sherds of both impasto and bucchero pottery, which, although without context, attest to the existence of a shrine here from a very early period. A more precise date is impossible to determine. The romantic treatment of the pediment with its almost feminine Bacchus suggests that the present building is not very early, but any time in the second century B.C. would be an acceptable date for its construction.

9 · THE HOUSES

Introduction

The First Style of Pompeian wall decoration did not go out of common use until sometime in the first century B.C. The arrival of the Roman colony about 80 B.C. is a convenient and likely date for the first appearance of the Second Style in Pompeii; it is not likely to have originated in the vicinity, and no conspicuously early example of it is known here. Thus, through the whole of the second century, the period of the flowering of Pompeian architecture, and down to the beginnings of the first decline of the city as a flourishing urban organism, the First Style was the only decoration known. We might expect to be able to divide it into several phases and several categories, since it lasted at least as long as the other three styles combined and was the only style available during the city's greatest growth and vitality, but though there are about three hundred examples of it scattered through the city from end to end, few houses have more than one or two rooms still preserving First Style plaster, while of the public buildings that must have been built in the time of this style, all except the basilica were subsequently redecorated. The two houses that still have a number of rooms with First Style decoration, the Casa del Fauno and the Casa di Sallustio, were both mansions of the very rich maintained as architectural monuments down to a very late period, in the case of the Casa del Fauno down to the destruction of the city. A number of other fine houses preserve an isolated room in this style that seems to have been a showplace; a cubiculum in the Casa del Centauro is a fair example of these.[1] Few houses in Pompeii, however, preserve both the original architectural lines of a house of this period and substantial remains of First Style decoration. The earth-

---

[1] See *Museo Borbonico* 6, "Relazione degli scavi," 3–4; and Mau 1908, 268–69 and fig. 136.

quake of A.D. 62 cannot be used to explain this, for then more of the damaged decorations would still have been preserved on the walls in 79 than in fact there are, and we are forced to blame their loss on the change in fashion, for a great many houses still show the plan and characteristics of houses of the second century.

The Casa di Sallustio

The best example of a mansion of a single atrium without peristyle is the Casa di Sallustio (VI ii 4),[2] preserved with most of its original decorations and very few alterations in architecture. Additions were made to the original nucleus on three sides in space that must originally have been hortus, but only three rooms of the original atrium complex were destroyed by subdivision, only one of them probably an important room, and despite the later cutting of doors and windows and redecoration of rooms, the architecture of the house in its first period is extremely clear.

The façade is of large blocks of Nocera tufa on a footing of Sarno limestone. The socle is plain and projects slightly; the wall above is of horizontally drafted ashlar, finely finished. This façade runs continuously from the southwest corner of the city block to a point opposite the south corner of block VI i, and the whole southern end of VI ii was clearly a single property from the beginning, though the house occupied only the central portion. On the Strada Consolare were six shops, three to either side of the house door. In the last period that at the northern end was a bakery, probably of relatively late installation; that at the southern end, the corner of the Vicolo di Mercurio, was a cookshop, a good location for this. Only the shops immediately flanking the house door seem likely to have communicated with the atrium from the beginning. The shops are all large, originally squarish in plan; the bakery has absorbed all available adjacent space in the course of time, so as to obscure the original plan of this corner, and the cookshop has annexed the space behind it, presumably for use as dining space. Originally the shops seem to have been uniform, having a big ground-floor room with a wide door that stood open through the day and a loft covering the rear half of this room that was open across its front for light and air. The front of the ground floor served as shop and workshop, the rest as storage and living quarters. The uniformity of the shops must have served to emphasize the axial house door rather than to obscure it.

The house itself stood in the centre of the plot, framed on three

[2] Mazois 2, 75–79 and pls. 35–39. I am much indebted to A. Laidlaw, who has made a special study of the house and its history, for invaluable information otherwise unavailable. Her excavations here have clarified many obscure points.

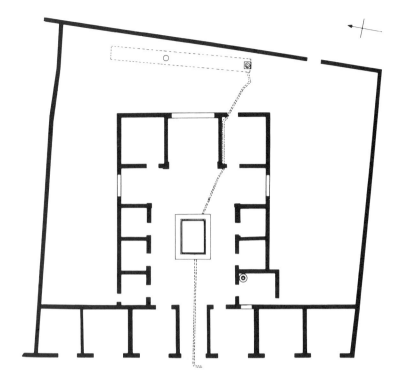

FIGURE 12.
The Casa di Sallustio,
Plan of the Original
Building

CISTERN

PERISTYLE

0   10m

FIGURE 13.
The Casa di Sallustio,
Plan of the Final Phase

sides by open space running to a circuit wall. Though the ground here was sloping, rising steadily toward the northeast, only the area of the house proper seems to have been leveled. The axis of the house is normal to the principal façade, though this made the space around it unequal and irregular. The house door was very large, originally more than a meter wider than it is today, the jambs crowned by figured capitals, one of which was found by the excavators but has subsequently been lost; presumably this was capped with a deep, carved lintel of the type of the house door of the Casa del Fauno. There is no sign of an entrance lobby in front of the door, but the rebuilding of the fauces to open onto the shops to either side of them may have confused the evidence. The fauces were relatively broad with a distinct but gentle slope up to the interior.

The atrium was Tuscanic, very large, with alae to either side off the east end, just in front of the tablinum. There were three cubicula on either side, their two-leaved doors uniform and grand, proportioned to the atrium. The impluvium is of tufa, very large, floored with five great tufa slabs, the margin trimmed with a flattened cyma reversa above a broad, slightly convex fascia. There is every sign that this was part of the original construction, and it is typical of a group of impluvia fairly widespread in Pompeii. There is no cistern in the atrium, and the original drain of the impluvium seems to have led east to a cistern in the garden. The alae, open across their whole front to the atrium, were framed with unfluted pilasters with acanthus-and-volute capitals of pretty workmanship, clearly related to the jamb capitals of the façade, and the walls were decorated in the same scheme as the atrium. The tablinum is large and square, raised a low step above the atrium, the opening framed with broad, fluted pilasters with Attic bases; the filleted fluting suggests a Corinthian order, but neither capital survives. The entrance seems to have been higher than any other on the atrium, the dominant focus. The rear wall has been rebuilt; probably originally it was completely closed. The decoration is related to that of the atrium but not identical to it. The rooms to either side of the tablinum were slightly narrower but squarish in proportion; both have been remodeled, but that to the north shows its original lines quite plainly. Both were originally accessible from the atrium, that at the north closed to the east, that at the south with access to the garden, the only place along this side of the house where the garden could be entered on the level. One thinks of the northern room as a winter dining room, the southern one as a summer dining room. There are remains of First Style plasterwork in two of the cubicula along the flanks of the atrium, one on each side, that to the south very unusual and elegant; these will have been bedrooms. The westernmost room to either side seems to have been a storeroom; that to the south contains an ancient well that was later abandoned and filled in.

The offices of the house, the kitchen, the latrine, and the stables must have been small independent buildings of insubstantial construction in the area of the hortus and must have been destroyed when this was reorganized to enlarge the house. In the last period they were clustered in the southeast corner of the house, and they may well always have been there, since this area has the readiest access to the Vicolo di Mercurio and the sewer under it. If so, the hortus would have been divided into two distinct parcels, but neither of these is apt to have been a pleasure garden. A summer triclinium under an arbor similar to that which now occupies the northeast corner might have been included in one of them, but even in the last period of Pompeii such amenities often appear in kitchen gardens.

This house was typical of a class of mansions of similar scale and similar simplicity of plan. All have very large atria with a large number of cubicula and only a few staterooms, the tablinum and a pair of dining rooms that flank it, with sometimes a third dining room replacing one of the shops that regularly flank the entrance. These houses stand on busy thoroughfares and, despite their lack of comfort and convenience, are noble in proportion and refined in decoration. They are the houses of the rich, and their deficiencies must have been made up for by a large number of servants, but for these there is no more place provided than there is for the animals. If they did not simply bed down on pallets wherever there was a convenient corner, the personal servants in the rooms of those they attended, the rest as best they might, then these, too, must have found their place in sheds in the hortus. *Natus in pergula* was not a vague slur on the dregs of society; it described a common entrance to the world.

The houses of this group that most merit attention are the atrium complexes of the Casa del Chirurgo (VI i 10), the Casa del Marinaio (VII xv 1/2), the Casa del Torello di Bronzo (V i 7), the Casa di Cecilio Giocondo (V i 26), and the Casa del Marmorista (VIII vii 24), possibly also the Casa di Marte e Venere (VII ix 47). Others, especially along the principal arteries of the city, have probably been disguised by remodeling in later periods; among these might be the Casa del Forno di Ferro (VI xiii 6) and the Casa del Gruppo dei Vasi di Vetro (VI xiii 2).

The Casa di Epidio Rufo

The most splendid of all mansions of a single atrium, the Casa di Epidio Rufo (IX i 20) (Overbeck and Mau 297–300; Mau 1908, 325–28), appears to be an anomaly, the only house of its period with a single

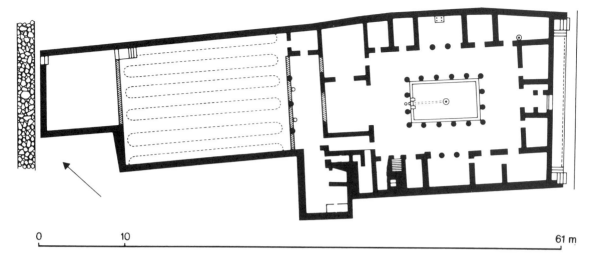

0   10   61 m

FIGURE 14.
The Casa di Epidio
Rufo, Plan of the Final
Phase

atrium that is Corinthian and very unusual in the form of its atrium
and many other features. Since it has been shown to be the house of
the wealthy ancient Pompeian family of the Epidii, it was probably
built as a showplace. It stands on the north side of the busy Via
dell'Abbondanza, a bit east of its crossing with the Strada Stabiana,
but makes no concession to the commerce concentrated here. Instead
an elevated sidewalk along the whole façade, a unique feature, sets
the house off from the world, and the façade behind this seems to
have been essentially blank and forbidding. There was a little lobby
between the façade and the house door from which a small door to
the east allowed entrance when the house door was closed and which
made an alcove for the ostiarius when it was open. The fauces are
short and give immediately onto the enormous atrium, more a peristyle than an atrium, with sixteen Doric columns arranged four by six
around the vast impluvium. Columns, impluvium rim, and basin
floor are all of tufa, the columns of good style, fluted to the floor. The
alae are arranged at the middle of the long sides of the impluvium,
not at the far end; this may have been the rule for early tetrastyle and
Corinthian atria. They are broad in proportion to their depth and
given two Ionic columns in each opening, as well as figured jamb
capitals. The Ionic is typical of the four-sided Ionic of the best period;
the bases are Attic. The figured capitals are not a set of four, but two
pair. Those of the west ala have groups of satyrs and bacchantes, full-
figure reliefs; those of the east have busts above a band of acanthus.
The presumption is that these elements were bought ready-made.
There are remains of First Style stucco in the atrium and both alae
(Mau 1882, 98–100).

The rooms around the atrium, except those at the far end, the tab-

FIGURE 15.
The Casa di Epidio
Rufo, Atrium and
Opening to the East
Ala

linum and the rooms flanking it, were all relatively small. That in the southwest corner appears to have been a winter dining room; that at the southeast was probably once a kitchen, with a well, or cistern, still apparently in use in the last period, although by that time the kitchen had been moved to the northwest corner of the house. There was an uncommon amount of communication among the lateral rooms, and most rooms had a small window to the atrium beside the door, too high for anything but ventilation. These were bedrooms and storerooms.

The tablinum was in the process of remodeling and redecoration at the time of the eruption, and nothing remains of the original architecture except possibly the general shape and the rather coarse mosaic floor (Pernice 1938, 48). The triclinium east of this had a curious ceiling with a low false vault running north and south over the central area, which may have been an original feature; it was probably once windowless. The triclinium that must once have flanked the tablinum on the west has been broken up and rebuilt to create the offices of the house; it is now divided into an andron, two long, narrow closets, a latrine, and part of the kitchen. At the time these alterations were made, a second storey was added over this corner of the house, the closets vaulted in order to support it. As an early example of modification to provide convenience, it is interesting in that it shows how little Pompeian builders relied on timber and what lack of light and air they would endure to avoid its use. Large timbers, we may infer, were very expensive.

Behind the house, running the full depth of the block to the street beyond, is a large kitchen garden, still nearly as large as the house itself but once presumably considerably larger. Portions at the northwest corner clearly were sold off in the course of time, and along the house side a colonnade and a small garden pavilion have been built. Part of the purpose of the colonnade was to allow the opening of large windows in the tablinum and the triclinium, but because the ground rises sharply here, the portico floor had to be excavated out and a retaining wall run between the columns, so as an addition it is less then ideal. It appears to be Augustan in date; presumably the cistern with two lava cistern heads that lies under it and received water from the impluvium is also Augustan. Up to that time the house had run to the north wall of the tablinum and had been a canonical atrium unit, though of unusual form. It is interesting that in size its tablinum is one of the largest in the ancient city, in a class with that of the Tuscanic atrium of the Casa del Fauno.

The Casa della Grata Metallica

I know of only one medium-sized atrium certainly of this period in Pompeii showing clearly the simple atrium-without-peristyle plan.[3] This is the Casa della Grata Metallica (I ii 28), an unusual house with a tetrastyle atrium without alae.[4] This house was much modified in later periods, but the original block seems to have consisted of the atrium and the rooms in front of it and behind it. It had two relatively deep rooms in front flanking axial fauces and a good-sized tablinum

[3]It is probable that a number of other houses preserve an atrium complex of medium size of this period, but remodeling and redecoration have made it impossible to identify them certainly. One of these is the Casa di Ceio (I vi 15), where the plan and façade suggest a second-century date, but inside there are only scant remains of First Style decoration (Laidlaw 61–64; Spinazzola 1953, 1.257–74). Others are the houses in the northern part of block VI ii, beginning with VI ii 11 (see Mau 1882, 66–69).

[4]The house is described by Mau, *BdI* 1874, 249–52.

in back flanked by narrow cubicula, one of which preserves traces of First Style decoration (Mau 1882, 63). There must have been rooms in a second storey both front and back, and there must have been a hortus beyond. One might guess that the latter extended beyond the area north of the tablinum now included in the house, but the evidence is not clear. That this was a known house type seems to be borne out by the Casa Sannitica in Herculaneum, a very similar house with a Tuscanic atrium. One can understand that alae might be superfluous to many households, but the only place in this house where a dinner party might gather was the tablinum, since in this period dining rooms in the upper storey seem always to have been open pavilions for use only in the summer.

The Casa del Cenacolo

A house that is only one remove from the small atrium-without-peristyle is the Casa del Cenacolo (V ii h [or s.n.]), next-door to the Casa delle Nozze d'Argento on the west.[5] Here the atrium is almost square, with rooms flanking the fauces in front and a proportionately large tablinum flanked by narrow rooms behind. One of the latter is a cubiculum that still preserves a First Style decoration, while the other is a passage through to the garden beyond that is half taken up by a steep stair to the upper storey. This upper storey is a true cenaculum, a loggia of four columns and two engaged columns at the ends filling the whole of this end of the atrium. Other rooms in a second storey reached by a stair in the atrium covered the fauces and the rooms flanking it. This would make a perfect atrium-without-peristyle unit of small size, but apparently from the beginning there was a portico along the garden with access to it from the tablinum, as the sill panel in the First Style pavement shows,[6] and a cubiculum at one end of the portico. This, then, is a late First Style house preserving much of the character of an earlier type.

The Casa del Fauno

The house of two atria, one an architectural frame in which the paterfamilias could present himself to the public in his roles of patronus and host, one for the family's use, was an intermediate step between the atrium house and the atrium/peristyle house. It cannot have been a plan that lasted very long in use, since the invention of the pleasure garden was only a short step from the addition of a second atrium and bound to replace it. In fact, one may ask whether

[5] *RömMitt* 8 (1893) 14–27 (A. Mau); *NSc* 1910, 328–30 (A. Sogliano).
[6] See Pernice 1938, 38.

potted shrubs and flowering plants had not been kept in the impluvium earlier and removed only when formality demanded it. Fortunately, the house of two atria, which seems to have come into being about 185–175 B.C., perhaps in consequence of the Romans' increased activities in the eastern Mediterranean in this period, came at a moment when Pompeii was ripe to receive it, and we have been left with three splendid examples—the Casa del Fauno, the Casa della Fontana Grande, and the Casa dell'Argenteria—as well as several less noteworthy or improvised examples—the Casa del Gallo, the Casa del Principe di Montenegro, the Casa delle Danzatrici (VI Insula Occidentalis [hereafter Ins. Occ.] 15–18), the Casa del Marinaio, and possibly the Casa del Labirinto. The first three are architecture of the highest quality for the Tufa Period, and though they have all been modified by the addition of peristyles, their quality seems to have preserved them from the danger of extensive rebuilding down at least to the time of the earthquake.

In these houses the grander atrium is always Tuscanic, and its scale is very impressive. The Casa del Fauno (VI xii 2/5) faces on the Via di Nola (Via della Fortuna), a thoroughfare, and was originally preceded by a row of five shops, the entrance lying between the two westernmost of these, both of which also communicate with the atrium. It is one of the grandest entrances in Pompeii; the doors were so big that each had to be hinged, making four leaves in all. The façade is of blocks of Nocera tufa with a Doric pilaster at either end and between each pair of shops and Corinthian pilasters and a elaborate lintel framing the door. The doorframe was given a thin finish of hard stucco and possibly painted, the rest left plain. An inner door was set behind a small lobby; its door opened outward so as not to hide the decoration of the fauces. The fauces slope rather abruptly up to the north. The atrium is canonically Tuscanic with alae just in front of the tablinum. There are three large doors on either side in rigid symmetry, those to the west to cubicula, those to the east to rooms of about the same size as the cubicula but evidently not bedrooms. At the far end the tablinum, on the axis of the atrium, was set a step above the atrium and trimmed with massive fluted pilasters with Attic bases in stucco. It is flanked by large rectangular dining rooms, that on the east the winter dining room and somewhat larger than the other. All the pavements and sills belong to an early remodeling, probably of the early first century B.C. (Pernice 1938, 90–95).

The secondary atrium is tetrastyle and originally had no entrance of its own from the street, being completely subordinate to, and dependent on, the Tuscanic atrium. The columns are Corinthian, fluted to full height, with Attic bases. The impluvium is of broad blocks of Nocera tufa, floored with five great slabs of the same. The water col-

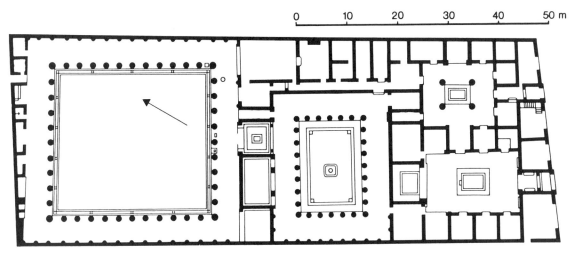

FIGURE 16.
The Casa del Fauno,
Plan of the Final Phase

lected here was not impounded but was discharged through a drain
to the east into the gutter of the Vicolo del Labirinto. The alae were
arranged on the cross axis, and in the western ala opened the door
from the Tuscanic atrium that must have been the principal entrance.
This was not set precisely on the axis, however, but in conformance
with the symmetry of the Tuscanic atrium. There is no tablinum, the
eastern ala apparently serving such a function, if it was necessary.
This ala is trimmed with ornamental jambs with modified Corinthian
capitals in tufa finished with stucco. Though much of this part of the
house is rebuilt, there seem to have been small rooms around this
atrium on all sides from the beginning, but their uses are not clear. It
is doubtful that there was a second storey over any part here until
the last period of the city, and no room here shows any sign of ever
having been a kitchen. A corridor leading back to the hortus on the
north was probably an original feature.

Thus the house consisted of three distinct parts: a grand Tuscanic
atrium, with the three staterooms of the house and a group of bedrooms; the intimate tetrastyle atrium, with the living rooms, storerooms, and possibly smaller dining rooms, as well as extra bedrooms;
and the hortus, occupying the rest of the block, more than twice as
large as the house itself.

The Casa della Fontana Grande and the Casa dell'Argenteria

The other double-atrium houses agree with the Casa del Fauno in
having the principal atrium Tuscanic and the staterooms all arranged
on it but differ in having the secondary atrium directly accessible
from the street by an axial extrance. There were no rooms between

the primary and secondary atria of the Casa della Fontana Grande (VI viii 21/22) (*PAH* 2.164–82; *Museo Borbonico* 4, p. 48 and text pages 15–18), the three doors necessary for the symmetry of the Tuscanic atrium all communicating directly with the diminutive Corinthian atrium, unless one or more of them was a false door. The order of the six columns of the Corinthian atrium is Doric, an unusual order for an atrium, with a plain epistyle and dentil cornice. It originally had a row of small rooms on the south that have been destroyed in rebuilding and probably always had a second storey over the rooms along the street. The back parts have been so thoroughly remodeled that it is impossible to reconstruct their original form. The hortus seems to have been a shallow area to the west, but big enough to plant with a kitchen garden if the offices were crowded into one corner. The garden of the pseudoperistyle of the Casa dei Dioscuri was so planted.

The Casa dell'Argenteria (VI vii 20–22), up the street from the Casa della Fontana Grande, was very like it but on a slightly more modest scale (*PAH* 2.299–306, 333–34, 342–5). Its Tuscanic atrium had only two doors on either side and smaller alae, but the tablinum was very large in proportion to the rest, as were also the dining rooms that flanked it on either side. Since the Via di Mercurio was a quiet residential street, here and in the Casa della Fontana Grande the front rooms were not made into shops, and one of these could be made a dining room for smaller parties. The secondary atrium is a particularly handsome apartment with four Ionic columns at the corners of the impluvium and two Corinthian columns marking the division between an entrance lobby and the atrium. The lobby seems to have functioned as a sitting room in its own right and to have been the principal focus of this atrium. It seems likely that the street door here was not original. At the opposite side there is no tablinum, only a small room, a corridor leading back to the hortus, and a stair to an upper storey. Second storeys front and back seem to have been part of the original structure. The area of hortus behind was only a little deeper than that of the Casa della Fontana Grande. The architecture is worked out with authority, efficient and neat, not experimental, though the house is the only example of its type surviving in Pompeii. It seems not unlikely that the architect learned a good bit from the Casa della Fontana Grande.

In the case of a number of double-atrium houses, presumably either they were enlarged with the addition of a peristyle after peristyles came into fashion, as the Casa del Fauno was, or the owners sold off one of the atria to replace it with a peristyle, if the family was not large. An example of the former is the Casa di Obellio Firmo (Spinazzola 1953, 1.337–65), if I read its complicated architectural history correctly; an example of the latter is the Casa del Torello di

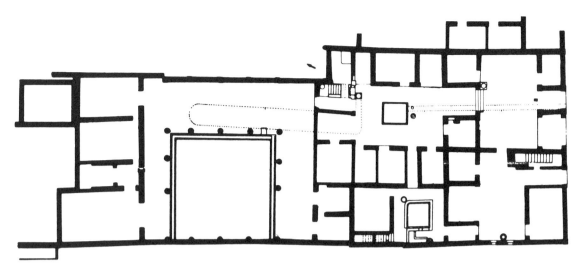

FIGURE 17.
The Casa di Giulio
Polibio, Plan of the
Final Phase

Bronzo (*PAH* 2.329–54), where the minor atrium has been rebuilt to serve commercial purposes. Once the peristyle had been created, a secondary atrium would have few uses that a peristyle could not accommodate more agreeably.

The Casa di Giulio Polibio

An extremely odd house is the Casa di Giulio Polibio (IX xiii 1–3) (Spinazzola 1953, 1.317–34), but the handsome façade with pilasters trimming the corners and the planning of the front parts indicate that it was conceived as a unit and built in the Tufa Period. In front it is a double-atrium house, both atria testudinate, with a single roof of two slopes covering both. Both atria are rectangular, lying across the main axes of the house. The more important atrium is the eastern one, where symmetry is also more strictly observed. One entered through short fauces flanked by symmetrical rooms giving onto the atrium; later that on the west was made into a shop opening on the street. Opposite the entrance the small tablinum, raised three steps above the atrium, has been converted into a broad passage leading back to an impluviate atrium complex beyond by knocking out its north wall. Originally, as the First Style decoration shows, symmetrical doors, one a false door of stucco and paint, flanked the tablinum handsomely. The atrium soars two full storeys, with windows between pilasters around its upper storey, while there were rooms over the dependencies front and back. The minor atrium had an entrance off axis to permit development of a large dining room in the southwest corner and a stair leading to an upper storey to the east. A tablinumlike exedra opposite is only slightly off axis, flanked by a small square cubiculum and a passage back to the hortus. Here we seem to have a perfect double-atrium house of very primitive type.

The first enlargement of the house seems to have been the addition of a Tuscanic atrium complex behind the eastern testudinate atrium and a tiny court for the offices behind the western one. The Tuscanic atrium is not in itself interesting architecturally, being too long for its width and rather small and cramped, evidence that it was not part of the original scheme and had to be adjusted to the space available. The rooms around it are an undistinguished collection of small spaces. The courtyard of the offices is square, with the kitchen built into a small shed against the western wall and the latrine beside it in the usual fashion. A single good-sized room opens north of it. Presumably at the time these additions were made the pseudoperistyle to the north was also added; it has the square proportions and deep porticoes of early peristyles, and a number of the rooms behind the Tuscanic atrium and kitchen court open out onto it, but the bank of rooms on the north portico is probably an addition of the time of the Second Style, a row of rooms for entertaining of the type of the Casa del Labirinto.

Here, then, we have a clear development of the sort we see in the Casa del Fauno in a house of far more modest, but still dignified, size and architecture. It began as a double-atrium house with both atria testudinate, built probably about the same time as the first block of the Casa del Fauno, in the early second century, enlarged late in that century by the addition of a cramped Tuscanic atrium and a little courtyard fitted into the space available and by a generous peristyle and then enlarged again toward the middle of the next century by a row of rooms for entertaining. Though in the course of time there was a good bit of redecoration, it kept its old-fashioned character and venerable façade down to the time of the destruction of the city.

The Casa di Pansa and the Casa dei Capitelli Colorati

The earliest pattern of Pompeian houses built with both atrium and peristyle can be seen in the Casa di Pansa (VI vi 1) and the Casa dei Capitelli Colorati (VII iv 31/51).[7] They are so similar that they seem to be the work of the same architect, and they show a number of identifiably early features, notably the restriction of the garden area in the peristyle and the absence of original vaulted cisterns. Clearly they must be dated just about the middle of the second century. These

[7]On the Casa di Pansa see Mazois 2.82–87 and pls. 42–45; and *Museo Borbonico* 15, pl. 50. On the Casa dei Capitelli Colorati see *PAH* 2.264–88; and *Museo Borbonico* 10, "Relazione degli scavi."

houses are very spacious and handsome, and all the architecture is of generous proportions and fine detail. The Casa di Pansa occupies the whole of a nearly rectangular block facing south on the Via di Nola (Via delle Terme); the plot of the Casa dei Capitelli Colorati probably originally comprised the whole eastern end of block VII iv beyond the Casa dei Capitelli Figurati, an irregular lot with an S curve along the eastern side. When the architect had done, he had carved away parcels for the Casa della Caccia Antica and the Casa del Granduca, as well as converted the oddments of space along the Vicolo Storto into a variety of shops, some of them miniscule cells. It is interesting that he made the house face south on the Via degli Augustali rather than north on the more important Via di Nola (Via della Fortuna) yet made the entrance from the Via di Nola as impressive as a house door, the jambs crowned with a pair of figured capitals.[8]

In both houses the atrium entrance is set between shops, a relatively long throat. In the Casa di Pansa the whole façade is of fine tufa ashlar, with the house door framed with pilasters with fine Corinthian capitals of the class of those of the Casa del Fauno. The rest is divided into shops of nearly uniform dimensions, three to either side of the doorway. In the Capitelli Colorati there are only two shops, both communicating with the atrium, and the façade is unimpressive. On the narrow Via degli Augustali no vista of the door is possible, and the neighborhood is taken up almost entirely with small factories and shops. The atrium is Tuscanic with canonical alae; the impluvium is not especially large. There are three cubicula to either side, and the emphasis is still on the symmetry of the atrium, the cubicula themselves being small and, in the Casa dei Capitelli Colorati, irregular. In the Casa di Pansa the tablinum is generous, and along one side of it at a late period a corridor (andron) was created connecting atrium and peristyle. Though in both houses the wall between tablinum and peristyle has been torn out, so that now one can pass from one to the other by mounting a step, this is evidently a very late modification. The continuance of the axis of the atrium through the peristyle may be taken to indicate that there was always a central opening to the peristyle so that this could be seen from the atrium, but the arrangements to ensure privacy for the tablinum when it might be desirable and the absence in Pompeii of any tablinum open across its whole width to the peristyle that can be dated earlier than the imperial period suggests that this was at first always a window reaching to about waist height that could be closed with folding wooden shutters of the type of which a cast has been obtained in a triclinium of the Casa di Obellio Firmo (Spinazzola 1953,

[8]E. von Mercklin, *Antike Figuralkapitelle* (Berlin 1962) no. 190, figs. 361–64.

1.342 and figs. 391–92). In the Casa dei Capitelli Colorati there is a corridor to either side of the tablinum; the reason for this duplication is hard to see. Originally there was a large triclinium to each side, like that still remaining on the west of the tablinum in the Casa di Pansa, while off the andron was arranged a small winter dining room. The reduction in available space on this side entailed by the creation of the andron was met by this ingenious use; the summer triclinium would now, of course, be on the peristyle.

The peristyles are both rectangular, the long axis continuing that of the atrium, relatively small, with proportionately wide porticoes on all four sides. The order is Pompeian Ionic with Attic bases, six columns by four; the general effect is similar in many ways to that of the atrium of the Casa di Epidio Rufo. In both cases the garden area is confined to a narrow band surrounding a deep rectangular tank that takes up at least a quarter of the open space. In the last period this was piped for a fountain, but if it is an original feature, it may have served as a reservoir for the rain collected from adjacent roofs for use in watering the garden; the cisterns under the porticoes, if we may judge from their drawshafts and puteals, are not original. In the Casa di Pansa garden an interesting feature is the blocks of tufa laid diagonally across the corners, evidently footing for large potted shrubs or trees; this is a feature found in a number of early gardens—the second peristyle of the Casa del Fauno, where they are an architectural feature, offers a good parallel—but so far as I know, none has ever been found that was in use in the last days of the city, perhaps because the eruption occurred in August.

Off the southern end of the peristyle, the portico along the tablinum, open a pair of squarish exedras of about the width of the portico, giving much the effect of the *pastas* of Greek houses.[9] This is an unusual feature, and its exact purpose remains obscure. In the Casa del Capitelli Colorati these have been rebuilt as rooms. Off the eastern one in the Casa di Pansa an inconspicuous corridor leads to the street. Around the peristyle are grouped a few big rooms for entertaining interspersed with small rooms that served as bedrooms, studies, and workrooms. Though the reception rooms have been rebuilt and redecorated with changing fashions in both houses, one notes four reception rooms of different sizes and architecture in the Casa di Pansa and six in the Casa dei Capitelli Colorati; presumably there will always have been about the same number.

The offices in the Casa di Pansa are clustered off the northwest corner of the peristyle, a good-sized kitchen courtyard, through which one reached another service court containing the latrine closet

[9]Cf., e.g., the Maison de la Colline on Delos (Robertson[2] 300–301 and pl. 22).

and the stables. In behind the kitchen a cart must have been kept, to judge from the width of the street door here. The kitchen itself had no direct communication with the street. The offices in the Casa dei Capitelli Colorati were presumably once similarly clustered off the northeast corner of the peristyle, but here rebuilding has obscured the picture. Whether there was a stable, and whether there was egress to the Vicolo Storto, is doubtful but likely enough.

Beyond the peristyle in the Casa di Pansa the rest of the block was given over to hortus, as it still is today. A portico runs along its southern end, but the garden does not seem to have been much used, except to supply the household with edibles. Only one room looks out on it, and only one small one opens off its portico. The corresponding area in the Casa dei Capitelli Colorati, on the other hand, was developed as a second peristyle with a Doric order, much bigger than the first peristyle, five columns by nine, off which on the east opened a vast exedra raised a step above the portico with two columns in its broad opening. This must have been the scene of sumptuous entertainments in the summer. Other than this exedra, the rooms on this second peristyle were little more than closets and cupboards fitted into waste space.

Two other features of the Casa di Pansa must be mentioned. One is the arrangement of three small, independent complexes along the east side of the house. Each consists of a small testudinate central atrium off which open five or six small rooms. The largest of these once communicated with the peristyle of the house and may have been a hospitium, or guest suite, but in the last period none was decorated, and as the block in its entirety was up to let shortly before the destruction of Pompeii (*CIL* 4.138), these may have been left for their new occupants to decorate to suit their taste. They would have made good apartments for dependents of nearly any sort, even perhaps a married son.

The other feature is a cenaculum, a colonnaded loggia in a second storey. Several Ionic elements and one small-scale block capital, in addition to the letting inscription, attest to the existence of an upper storey. The only stair in the principal apartments is in the corridor leading to the posticum (VI vi 8), east of the tablinum, a couple of steps in masonry of a stair that then continued in wood, narrow and inconvenient but adequate to serve what seems to have been a single room or two over the tablinum and the rooms that flank it, raised above the roofs of the atrium and peristyle and open to the north and south to catch the breeze. The letting advertisement speaks of *cenacula equestria;* the reading has been questioned, but it may mean simply that the cenacula had a double exposure, straddling, as it were, the central block of the house. The columns were barely the height of a man and may have been lifted on a parapet, though in the houses where it has been possible to recover the outlines of the architecture—the Casa del Cenacolo and the Fullonica Stephani—this was not the case. Wooden shutters in the intercolumniations would have provided protection against too stiff a breeze.

The Casa del Fauno

At about the same time as the remodeling of the Casa di Pansa as a classic atrium/peristyle house, the house type that was to prevail in Pompeii down to the time of Nero and the earthquake of A.D. 62, the first peristyle was added to the Casa del Fauno (VI xii 2/5). In laying this out, a strip along the east side of the block was reserved for the offices, which were simply arranged in a row served by a single corridor: a stall, in which was found the skeleton of a cow (perhaps because there was a nursing baby in the house); the latrine; the bath; and the kitchen. All are of large proportions for a private house, and the floors of the bathrooms are raised on suspensurae, the fire being stoked through a mouth in the kitchen next-door and the smoke carried off through vents opening high in the wall into the kitchen. The kitchen had a loft over its western half that was reached by a stair in the corridor outside. Whether this was an original feature is uncertain, as is its purpose, but it is clear that the kitchen was from the beginning essentially a courtyard where food could be prepared and cooked and tableware and pots could be washed up, though there seems to have been no arrangement for storing these. It is curious that in a house of this great size there is no oven; one might have expected at least a small one.

The peristyle is a broad rectangle, seven columns by nine, the long axis at right angles to the axis of the Tuscanic atrium, to which it bears no important relation. The order is Pompeian Ionic with Attic bases, with a plain architrave and Doric frieze, a popular combination in late Tufa Period architecture. The peristyle was evidently badly damaged in the earthquake of 62, and work on its reconstruction had barely begun (*PAH* 2.250). The column elements were still piled carelessly about, and a temporary wooden roof to protect the Alexander mosaic had been rigged by cutting mortises for the timber uprights into the column footings in front of the great exedra, while great masonry buttresses were run up in the rooms to either side to shore up the tottering walls.[10] A new edging of fine white limestone was in the

[10] A. Laidlaw informs me that the German archaeologists studying the house consider these buttresses modern, the work of the excavators. But it seems hardly likely that nineteenth-century masons would have imitated ancient work so closely (see Laidlaw 199).

course of installation along the old tufa stylobate, but work on this had not progressed very far. The peristyle and the rooms giving onto it clearly were not usable at the time of the eruption, and their disorder makes reading the history of this part of the house more difficult.

The tablinum and the rooms to either side of it were now provided with large windows on the peristyle, but they were not reoriented to take full advantage of the garden. An insignificant room east of the andron to the tetrastyle atrium was turned to the peristyle. These were modifications of small importance, involving no rethinking of the architecture; the proportions of the rooms and their relations to one another and the atria remained essentially the same. But a row of splendid new reception rooms was now created. The most important of these is the large rectangular exedra of the Alexander mosaic, clearly a creation of this time, as the similarity in the unusual lathing of the drums of the two columns in its opening and the peristyle order shows. The columns are raised on square plinths, with deep simple moldings at base and crown. The capitals are a rather flamboyant Corinthian with corkscrew volutes, close to the capitals of the basilica in aesthetic. Plain pilasters with Corinthian jamb capitals finish the opening to either side. The rooms flanking this were oriented to the hortus, probably having been remodeled at the time of the creation of the second peristyle in the early first century B.C., while the suite of two rooms at the east end is a creation of a still later date, when the Second Style had come into fashion.

If the first peristyle of the Casa del Fauno shows many signs of being a relatively late creation and should probably be dated about 125 B.C., the second peristyle hardly seems to be Tufa Period architecture at all and must have been built at the very end of the prevalence of the First Style. It is squarish, like a good many Second Style peristyles, eleven columns by thirteen. The columns are built of thick terracotta quadrants, stuccoed over, only the capitals carved in tufa. The order is Doric, fluted to the floor. Since the only new rooms opening on this are a collection that simply fill out the slant of the northern end of the block, this was not built to increase the accommodations of the house, and we may presume that the open area continued to be a kitchen garden. Though there are no cisterns serving the first peristyle,[11] there is a cistern under each wing of the new peristyle. These were fed from a gutter with settling tanks that runs around the whole, and part of the purpose of this peristyle may have been to collect water for irrigating this garden. A light wooden fence

[11] I.e., the only cistern fed from the gutter around the first peristyle extends to the east and has its drawshaft in the kitchen courtyard. There is no puteal in the first peristyle.

once ran between the columns most of the way around, presumably to keep people from running carelessly into the garden (*PAH* 2.252), and triangular tufa bases for large pots are sunk into the corners of the garden.

Around the eastern and northern sides of the second peristyle are piled a number of elements of an Ionic second-storey order in tufa; at least fifteen engaged columns are represented. These must be older than the second peristyle and belong rather to the time of the first peristyle than to that of the atria. We have our choice of trying to put the cenaculum they came from over the tablinum wing or over the wing of the Alexander exedra. Stairs of access seem to have been available at the east end of each of these wings, but an inclination to the latter may derive from their style and their location today. In either location the loggia would have been knocked down by the earthquake and so damaged that it was then dismantled in preparation for rebuilding. The front part of the house was got back into condition for use by the time of the eruption, while the Alexander exedra was still only shored up temporarily. Wherever it was, this loggia will have been the largest such apartment in Pompeii; it is seldom that one finds parts of more than three or four second-storey columns.

The Casa del Centenario

One more house should be included in the first group, the very important Casa del Centenario (IX viii 3/6).[12] This is the vast house of A. Rustius Verus, a city magistrate in the last period of Pompeii (Della Corte[3] no. 216; Castrén no. 342), though the family was not numerous in the city. The house is an amalgamation of architecture from a number of periods, the main Tuscanic atrium going back to the late second century, while most of the rooms, indeed all the staterooms, not only were redecorated in the last period but were extensively remodeled or rebuilt. The complex of reception rooms on the south side of the peristyle, the largest one with its own fountain court beyond, was still unfinished at the time of the disaster. Some of the architectural work here was rather less than professional in quality, but the atrium was once a fine apartment with high doors and high, slit windows, and the peristyle, which must have been part of the original house, was also fine. This was almost square, slightly broader than deep, six columns by seven, the order Doric. The north portico carried an Ionic gallery above of remarkable height and singularly grace-

---

[12] *BdI* 1881, 113–28, 169–75, 221–38; 1882, 23–32, 47–53, 87–91, 104–16, 137–48. Overbeck and Mau 353–59. On the age and architecture of the house see Pernice 1938, 43–44.

ful proportions, part of which has been restored. This ran only on this side, as is shown by the gutter, and was accessible only by a stair off the secondary atrium. Examination of the house indicates that though it was from the beginning a double-atrium house, the original communication between the two atria was blocked up in the early imperial period, when there was a general remodeling of these parts. The secondary atrium, with its direct communication with the baths and service quarters so arranged that these parts of the house could be shut off completely from the staterooms, seems to show one more solution to the problem of how to divorce private life from public life, not, however, a very successful one.

The Doric order of the peristyle is deeply fluted with sharp arrisses, while the Pompeian Ionic of the gallery has fillets and Attic bases. The gutter on this side stands nearly a meter out from the stylobate to catch the drip from a deeply projecting cornice, of which some ten blocks have been recovered; elsewhere the gutter fits tight against the stylobate. There are lava cistern heads in the north portico, so set that a low fence could be run between the columns without interfering with these. Two of these out on the garden side were evidently for watering the garden; a third is on the portico side. The Ionic upper storey also had a fence between the columns and must have served as communication to a series of rooms over the tablinum wing. Unfortunately nothing of these survives, but the access to this gallery from the secondary atrium suggests that they were not staterooms, but utilitarian, or family quarters. This would agree with other evidence in Pompeii. The elegance of the Ionic upper storey came more out of consideration for the peristyle as a whole than from the apartments it served.

PART III

The Early Roman Colony, 80–30 B.C.

10 · THE PUBLIC BUILDINGS

The Theatrum Tectum

The two buildings most immediately associated with the deduction of the Roman colony sometime close to 80 B.C. are the Theatrum Tectum and the amphitheatre. Both carried inscriptions on limestone slabs in which the magistrates C. Quinctius Valgus and M. Porcius took credit for having built them. In the case of the Theatrum Tectum there can be little room for doubt: they let the contracts and approved the work (*CIL* 10.844).

The Theatrum Tectum is a broad rectangle, 28.60 m by 30.00 m, with a great gable roof that ran north and south, the lateral walls being three and a half Roman feet thick, a half-foot thicker than any other wall, in order to carry it.[1] The roof must have been trussed, though not necessarily elaborately. The stage was a shallow rectangular platform, originally with five doors of graduated size opening symmetrically in the straight back wall. This was covered with marble revetment at some time, as the appearance of clamp wedges proves. A trough for the curtain and the masts that carried it runs along the front of the stage, accessible by a narrow stair at the east end. The backstage area is an unfinished rectangular hall of the same size as the stage with four doors in its back wall, staggered so they would not be seen through the stage doors. These open to a broad alley behind. There is another door at either end. This seems a very primitive form of stage for this period; the theatre of Scaurus in Rome, built in 58 B.C., when he was aedile, was famous for the splendor of its stage. The floor of the orchestra is sunk three steps below the

---

[1] Consult M. Murolo, "Il cosidetto 'Odeo' di Pompei ed il problema della sua copertura," *RendNap* 34 (1959) 89–101. Murolo concludes from the evidence of strengthening that there was a shallow hip roof at either end, but the roof was essentially a great gable supported on simple trusses. The roof over the stage building he believes to have been a simple shed roof independent of the rest.

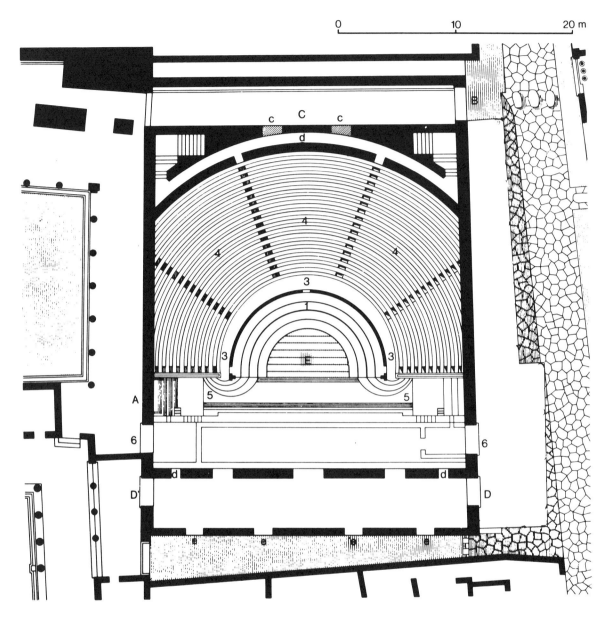

FIGURE 18.
The Theatrum Tectum, Plan

surrounding ground level. The cavea is of normal circular curvature, simply cropped on either side to fit the rectangle. Access to the seats is provided from the orchestra, where semicircular stairs projecting at either side lead up to a balteus set off by a pluteus above the lowest four steps, which are broader than the rest, evidently the place of the decuriones. From the balteus four radial stairs divide the upper cavea into equal wedges. There are also two flights of stairs leading up just inside the back wall from a passageway behind the theatre to the rear corners of the building, and from there to a narrow corridor running behind the top of the cavea, but this is so narrow and inconvenient that it is unlikely that it was much used, and spectator traffic must have snarled here. There are tribunals to either side supported on vaults over the parodoi of the orchestra, accessible only by stairs leading into the wings of the stage. These must have been provided with parapets, perhaps in wood and bronze. The face toward the orchestra was at some time covered with marble veneer, as the presence of clamp wedges shows. The only architectural ornaments of the theatre, apart from the simple molding that trims the seats, are a pair of winged lion's paws, the typical finishing elements of scholae, and a pair of kneeling telamons, all carved in Nocera tufa, which finish the tufa parapet bounding the cavea at either side. The latter are interesting figures related to others in the Terme del Foro and a number of examples from Sicily and central Italy of the Hellenistic period.[2]

The walls of this theatre are of concrete faced with opus incertum of broken lava coigned at corners and openings with brick tailed into the wall in irregular wedges. The lateral exterior walls on which the roof rested are 1.04 m thick, while the back wall of the stage and the back wall of the corridor along the north side of the cavea are only 0.89 m thick. These are the main walls of the building, the others not reaching above 0.59 m in thickness. All openings are covered with semicircular relieving arches. All carved members except the building inscription are of Nocera tufa. The building inscription is of the highest interest:

C QVINCTIVS C F VALG

M PORCIVS M F

DVOVIR DEC DECR

THEATRVM TECTVM

FAC LOCAR EIDEMQ PROB

These men, chief magistrates of the colony, with Roman names, who inscribe their building in Latin, were subsequently to become

---

[2] E.g., the interesting caryatid and telamon figures from the theatre of Syracuse (G. E. Rizzo, *Il teatro greco di Siracusa* [Milan and Rome 1923] 97–104).

quinquennial duovirs and give Pompeii its amphitheatre. They must have been enormously wealthy and important to have been in office at a time when Pompeii was undergoing extensive rebuilding and refurbishing. Since the masonry here is of a family with that we see in the basilica and the towers of the fortifications, but carried out with measurements in Roman feet and with a Latin inscription, we can with considerable confidence ascribe the Theatrum Tectum to the very early years of the Roman colony.

The orchestra pavement of colored marble—fragments of pavo-nazzetto, cipollino, africano, and giallo antico fitted ingeniously together to make flaglike rectangles in a pattern—was installed by the duovir M. Oculatius Verus (*CIL* 10.845) and is no older than the Augustan period.

The Amphitheatre

C QVINCTIVS C F VALGVS

M PORCIVS M F DVOVIR

QVINQ COLONIAI HONORIS

CAVSSA SPECTACVLA DE SVA

PEQ FAC COER ET COLONEIS

LOCVM IN PERPETVOM DEDER

(*CIL* 10.852)

There was evidently no word in common use for an amphitheatre when the amphitheatre of Pompeii was built, and the donors had to fall back on the word for shows, *spectacula*.[3] The masonry we see today in the retaining walls and stairs of approach to the exterior balteus of the amphitheatre is strikingly similar to that of the Theatrum Tectum and should belong to the second quarter of the first century B.C., but the inscriptions on the pluteus around the arena proper (*CIL* 10.853–57) show that little, if any, of the seating belongs to that construction. Probably the duovirs' gift was only the essential core.

The amphitheatre is a great oval bowl, the arena having axes of 140 m and 105 m, in the southeast corner of the city. Earth excavated from the interior was heaped toward the outside as the base for the cavea and was held in place by the city wall on the south and east and by a stout retaining wall around the remaining two-thirds of its circumference. This retaining wall shows a pronounced batter and is

[3] The amphitheatre is described by Mazois 4.77–86 and pls. 43–48; his drawings of details are especially valuable. There are good photographs in Kraus and von Matt figs. 51–52; and Eschebach 1978 figs. 68–71. An exhaustive modern study of it was made by M. Girosi, "L'anfiteatro di Pompei," *Memorie dell'Accademia di Archeologia, Lettere e Belle Arti di Napoli* 5 (1936) 27–57; this is open to question on certain points.

reinforced at regular intervals by radial buttresses joined by barrel vaults, upon which a broad walk circles the whole at a high level, joining the wall walk of the fortifications in the southeast sector. This walk was the main approach for the spectators to their seats in the cavea. The retaining wall is faced with opus quasi-reticulatum of broken lava; the buttresses are faced with small blocks of tufa and limestone and coigned with larger blocks; and the voussoirs of the vaults are of tufa and limestone. During the games the spaces between buttresses apparently were assigned to individual vendors and hawkers by the aediles (CIL 4.1096).

To reach the annular balteus on the exterior, one climbed one of six stairs, four of them arranged in double flights from opposite directions, two tucked into the corners where the amphitheatre abuts on the city wall. These are clearly of a single build with the retaining wall and in harmony with it in masonry, supported on walls and vaulting in line with that of the main buttressing. The treads are of blocks of lava. To reach the arena, capacious tunnels paved with the usual polygons of lava slope sharply down to entrances on the long axis, the northern one straight, the southern obliged to turn at a right angle just inside the arena end. They are roofed with continuous concrete vaulting laid on centering that has left clear prints, reinforced toward the exterior with brickwork arches. They are provided with gutters along the walls, and the north entrance has rectangular mortises cut at intervals along its east side, probably for a wooden stair, since the blocks in which they are cut seem to have been prized up and reset more or less level. Such a stair would have made the descent much easier. The sophistication of the vaulting suggests that they were originally roofed in some other way. They debouch some distance from the arena edge, a little more than halfway back under the media cavea, into open trenches, and there are trimmed with jambs and a segmental facing arch cut in blocks of Nocera tufa.

These were processional ways for the pompa with which the shows opened and for participants in the various individual events, and from these to either side runs a low annular passage just behind the parapet separating the ima cavea from the media. This runs almost all the way around but is broken for a short distance on each side where it would cross the short axis, presumably to prevent congestion of spectator traffic. Thus there are actually four segments, one in each quarter. Those in the western half also communicate directly with the exterior, each by an additional tunnel driven straight through the mass of earth.

From the annular corridor, stairs lead in regular alternation either directly out radially to the ima cavea or in a pair of flights branching to either side to the lowest part of the media cavea, the latter a rather clumsy system, since it wastes valuable seating space and involves in effect a dangerous open trench. Moreover, the corridor behind is dark, lit only by light filtering in from the exits and a series of small windows into this open trench. The vault of the annular corridor is everywhere segmental with a clear sharp shoulder, reinforced at intervals with modern brick arches and coigned with brick at the exits to the media cavea (Maiuri 1942, 83–87). The subsidiary tunnels to the exterior are reinforced with brick buttressing, and brick is employed in coigning the lateral openings along the entrance passages on the long axis of the arena.

The cavea is divided into four sectors by annular baltei and into cunei by radial stairs. In the ima cavea are four plain steps of lava to accommodate the portable seats of the privileged to either side of the short axis, where they would have the best view, and five steps of tufa given the profile of ordinary seating in the end sectors. The ima cavea is separated from the media by a continuous parapet and divided by others into cunei accessible by individual stairs coming up from the annular passage described above. The media cavea is separated from the summa by a balteus edged with a low parapet that makes a back and arms to the seats of the last row of the media. The media consists of twelve rows, the summa of seventeen. The media was accessible from below by sixteen branching stairs from the annular passage and from above by twenty stairs leading down from the top of the earthwork. The summa cavea was designed to be accessible by forty radial stairs from the top of the earthwork, but one could also make one's way up to these from the annular passage below. All the seats surviving in the media cavea and summa are of the same design, a ledge 0.365 m wide and the same high, with a molded edge, behind which is a shallow depression of the same width for the feet of the spectators in the row above.

Above this a superstructure was added in masonry faced with opus incertum of broken lava and limestone coigned with opus mixtum vittatum, presumably work of the last period of Pompeii, as is also shown by the free use of segmental arches and vaults here. It consists of a series of boxlike compartments roofed with radial vaults, those opposite the radial stairs of the summa cavea pierced by doors, that then support an annular walk reached by branching stairs from the perimetral avenue, giving onto substructures for wooden seating. In the floor of the annular walk, tailed under the masonry walls that held the wooden seating, are blocks of lava, 1.04 m long, in which are cut square sockets, 0.21 m on a side, the footings for masts on which the awnings were carried.

The stepping of the cavea is completed very irregularly, and inscriptions on the limestone coping of the parapet around the arena record that this was the work of various magistrates and authorities in lieu of games and illuminations (*CIL* 10.853–57). At the time of the destruction of Pompeii apparently less than half the cavea had stone seats, unless these were removed by salvagers, which seems unlikely. The summa cavea, of concrete with coigning in opus mixtum vittatum, must be considerably later than the rest, but the famous picture of the riot in the amphitheatre of A.D. 59 from I iii 23 and the repeated references to vela in the programmata advertising spectacles in the amphitheatre show that this must have replaced an earlier summa cavea.[4] The lowest bit of the cavea was also torn out at a very late period and rebuilt, presumably using most of the same material, since the inscriptions on the parapet can hardly all belong to the last years of the city.

The arena is a proportionately long and narrow ellipse in comparison with that of the Colosseum, designed especially for gladiatorial combats, since with its restricted entrances it offers limited opportunity for the deploying of riding and marching formations, and the absence of underground chambers and emplacements for cages and derricks makes it unlikely that its builders had any notion of the sort of elaborate effects venationes were to come to include by Nero's time. In its general outline it is not unlike Vitruvius's prescription for a forum, long and narrow, so that spectators could follow a maximum number of the gladiatorial matches. The parapet around the arena floor is more than two meters high; the existing wall, however, has been rebuilt, and the presence of coigning in opus mixtum vittatum all through the ima cavea shows that this was rebuilt at the time of the addition of the superstructure of the cavea, at which time the evidence of the access stairs suggests that the ima was enlarged by the addition of an extra row of seats, so the original parapet will have stood higher. In the middle of the west side, on the short axis of the arena, was the death gate, now walled up, to a narrow passage leading first to a small chamber off to the north for the functionaries who took care of the wounded and the killed and then (with occasional steps along its length) out to the exterior. There is also a little flight of steps connecting this passage with the centre of the ima cavea, possibly for the dramatic entrance of those in charge of the games.

Since there is so little in the way of architectural decoration here— only the single profile of the seats and the molding of the intrados

---

[4]The picture of the riot (Museo Nazionale [hereafter M.N.] Inv. No. 112222) is reproduced in Kraus and von Matt fig. 50; and Eschebach 1978 fig. 75.

and impost of the vault over the arena entrance—it is hard to discuss the aesthetic of the architecture. These members are, however, all in tufa and all very simple in character; their spareness accords well with that of the Theatrum Tectum. This is our earliest amphitheatre; no permanent amphitheatre was built in Rome until Statilius Taurus built one in honor of Augustus in the Campus Martius that was destroyed by the fire of Nero. The nearest in design to that of Pompeii that survives seems to be the amphitheatre of Lucera, also of Augustan date.

The Temple of Jupiter on the Forum

The Temple of Jupiter at the north end of the forum of Pompeii was explored in excavations reported with admirable care and detail by Maiuri (1973, 101–24). He found that it stands on virgin ground, replacing no earlier building, and decided that it should be associated with the reorientation of the forum at the beginning of the Tufa Period but realized that the design of the building was incompatible with a date earlier than the middle of the second century B.C. He was therefore inclined to date its construction 150–120 B.C. After the arrival of the Roman colony, the temple was remodeled extensively according to the taste of the Sullan period and became the temple of the Capitoline Triad.

One can do better than this. The original architecture showed strong classicizing tendencies before any remodeling took place. These do not belong in the second century; they are a Sullan characteristic and are apt to have been learned from Rome, so the temple probably belongs to the early years of the Roman colony. And the masonry faced with opus incertum of broken lava most closely resembles that of the Theatrum Tectum. The appropriateness of a temple of Jupiter as an early building of a Roman colony hardly needs arguing.

The Temple of Jupiter takes the forum as its precinct and dominates it on axis. Since all the buildings in its immediate vicinity are not only of subsequent construction but at least a century later, it is impossible to come to a satisfactory understanding of the total architectural effect of the building when it was new, but even in its ruin it fills the end of the forum impressively for anyone entering at the south end and towers over those who enter from the north, reserving its impact until one can turn to look at the façade. Like so many Roman temples, it is set at the very end of its precinct and can be properly appreciated only from the front. Seen first from the southern end of the forum, it closes the sweep of the open square, rising high on its podium above its immediate surroundings to draw a metaphysical

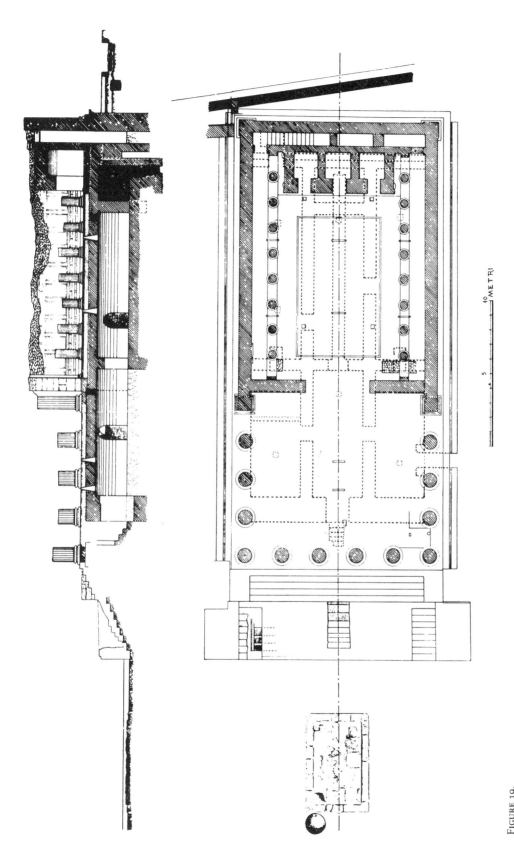

strength from the mass of Vesuvius behind it. It must always have been magnificent.[5]

Today it is approached by a pair of narrow stairs of Nocera tufa, 1.63 m wide, eight steps to each stair, flanking a great transverse platform, 1.89 m high, faced on the front with brick, that must have held the altar, or altars. These stairs are too narrow to have been used by a crowd of people, so we must presume that the public congregation at any sacrifice gathered in the forum, the altar platform and temple pronaos reserved for the priests and dignitaries and for visitors who came at other times.

Beside the little stairs and architecturally almost divorced from the temple jut out rectangular bases, also faced with brick and rising to the same height as the altar platform. These, we know from a relief in the lararium of the Casa di Cecilio Giocondo, carried equestrian statues.[6] All this approach, however, is a reworking and rebuilding of an approach that was originally fundamentally different. At first the stair covered the whole façade and rose eight steps; at this point it divided into three flights, those at the sides continuing to rise seven more steps to the pronaos, that in the centre descending again to a crypt in the basement storey. This crypt, divided into three long, thick-walled, heavily vaulted chambers, runs parallel to the axis of the temple. The chambers are subdivided, but the rooms communicate with one another and are lit by narrow transverse slots through the crowns of the vaults in the floor of the pronaos and the cella. This must have been the aerarium of the city, put under the protection of the god, like the aerarium of Rome in the Temple of Saturn and the private loculi in the Temple of Castor,[7] and this relationship was emphasized in the architectural design. With the remodeling to emphasize the altar platform, the front entrance to the crypt was blocked up and the stair above the platform made continuous across the façade, while a new entrance to the crypt was cut through the east flank of the temple, well back from the façade, where it would be unobtrusive. The altar originally stood out in the forum on the axis of the temple and was a large construction, probably similar in its general lines to the altar of the Temple of Apollo. The foundations for this were discovered by Maiuri (1973, 115–19 and figs. 66–67).

Above the altar platform the temple stair now rises eight steps to the level of the pronaos; along this upper stretch it is flanked by bases

[5] Photographs that suggest the tension for visitors to Pompeii between the temple and Vesuvius can be found in A. De Franciscis, *Pompei* (I documentari 15, Novara 1968) fig. 15; Kraus and von Matt fig. 16; and Eschebach 1978 fig. 5.

[6] See De Franciscis (supra n. 5) fig. 64; Kraus and von Matt fig. 9; and Eschebach 1978 fig. 3.

[7] See Platner and Ashby s.vv. Saturn; and Castor.

that appear to be part of the original construction and may have carried statuary before the bases for equestrian statues were added. The crown molding of the temple podium, a deep cavetto a step below the floor of the pronaos, was originally carried around these bases to finish them. It responds to the base molding, a similar cavetto stepped up by two high steps above the pavement of the forum. The necessity for these steps is evident from the battered condition they are in today, especially the lower one, which in places has all but disappeared. Maiuri was able to recover the original profile of the podium moldings before remodeling; the crown molding was a cyma recta above a bead, the base molding a cyma recta finished with beads both above and below.

The pronaos is exceptionally deep, almost as deep as the cella, roughly in the proportion 7:9, hexastyle on the façade, with four columns and a square anta carried forward from the cella on each side. The order is Corinthian; all the surviving drums and the single capital element are of Nocera tufa, but all the Attic bases are constructed of masonry in which a good bit of tile is incorporated. Presumably they are creations of the time when the floor of the pronaos was raised a step by the introduction of a new stylobate and pavement of travertine and Caserta stone, at least some of the blocks of which came secondhand. On the columns a good bit of hard white stucco survives in protected places; in the undercoat many marble crystals appear, evidently a deliberate admixture. The character of the capitals was similar to that of the Corinthian capitals of the basilica but more classical, if one can trust the drawing of Mazois (3, pl. 35.1). Each was apparently cut in two blocks, of which only one of the lower elements is in place today at the southeast corner, but Mazois shows a Corinthian capital lacking only volutes from the upper block. The acanthus leaves cling close to the bell, their ribs rising in a tight sheaf and their edges breaking into a crinkled, rather linear, frill.

No element of the entablature or pediment remains, and it is probable that these were constructed of wood and rubblework and stuccoed. Certainly the main beams and rafters of the roof had to span distances too great for these to have been beams of stone, and a roof of wood and rubblework masonry could, when stuccoed over, have been made consonant with the rest of the architecture. The relief in the Casa di Cecilio Giocondo shows a crown filling the pediment.

The doorway is wide, and footings with mortises for a wooden frame appear on the interior. In the pronaos against the wall of the cella are travertine blocks with cuttings for the shoes for doorposts about a meter back from the door opening to either side. So there must have been gates here as well as doors.

The cella has files of eight columns running down the sides on a line 1.44 m in from the walls, making a broad nave and narrow side aisles. These lines are set on the crests of the vaults of the side chambers of the crypt, a practice that appears elsewhere in Roman engineering of this period, notably in the basilica of Cosa. The order is Ionic, decidedly classicizing, like the Corinthian of the pronaos (Mazois 3, pls. 35.2 and 35.5). It is an order related to Pompeian Ionic in that there are winglike half-palmettes inserted between volute and echinus, an astragal at the base of the echinus, and a molded abacus, but the volutes lie in a flat plane normal to the axis of the cella and are bigger, more delicate, and more pendent than Pompeian Ionic volutes.

There is no indication of what this order supported—whether there was an epistyle carrying a gallery, possibly with a smaller order above, or a false vault springing high from the epistyle, like that of the tetrastyle oecus of the Casa delle Nozze d'Argento—but the stubby height of the Ionic order and a narrow stair against the back wall suggest the former. The stair led to the top of the statue base, and from there it would have been easy to get to galleries over the side aisles that could have been used for cleaning and decorating. Any upper order would have had to be Corinthian, but no element of one survives, and in all probability there was none.

At the far end of the cella stands a row of three small chambers, uniform in their dimensions, 1.66–69 m by 1.83–85 m, with heavily vaulted ceilings. Each has a door in front that one must stoop to enter, and the roof runs in a continuous flat platform. This is a rebuilding of an older structure, parts of which appear on the face of the walls, while others have been brought to light by soundings in the walls. The basic structure was once columnar, evidently with four columns, ca. 2.38 m high, in front and one at each back corner at least, the whole slightly wider and shallower than the structure that engulfed it. This was then rebuilt twice, once with the addition of rectangular pillars in front of the columns, probably simply to shore them up. In the construction of these pillars one notes the use of several bits of marble, so presumably the date is imperial and the pillar capitals came secondhand. The tufa capitals of three have been immured and survive, Aeolic in character with a rosette between volutes springing from a low band of acanthus like that of most Pompeian figured capitals; the faces of the others have been chiseled away in the building of the present vaulted construction, but the blocks can be identified. But even the first columnar structure, light and graceful as it must have been, probably was not part of the original building, since there is no visible bond with anything around it and the columns are built of masonry, not carved in tufa.

The heaviness of the construction of the vaults suggests that the present structure was intended to carry great weight and that this was, in fact, the statue base. And the fact that there are three chambers has led to the hypothesis that after the foundation of the Roman colony this served as the Capitolium of Pompeii. A dedication to Jupiter Optimus Maximus confirms this (*CIL* 10.796). But one cannot imagine that the salvage workers after the eruption would have left the heroic marble head of Jupiter that was found here—now in the Museo Nazionale in Naples—could they have rescued it, and apparently nothing comparable of any other divinity came to light (*PAH* 1.187–91 [11–25 January 1817]; Mau 1908, 65, fig. 25).

Behind the statue base, accessible by a door in the west aisle, is the stair already mentioned. Its narrow width, 0.90 m, and the care with which it is hidden from view are indications that it was not for public use. Two further slotlike shafts in sequence with the stairwell run down to the foundations of the temple. The central one is windowless and doorless, and it is hard to see what purpose it served. That to the east was originally provided with a door in the east side aisle balancing that to the stair on the west. This has been walled up, but perhaps only recently, since the jambs are finished in large part with brick.

The decoration of the interior of the cella was once Second Style;[8] it is now in ruins, but one can still make out in the side aisles the dado, lined out in imitation of four courses of ashlar, crowned by a yellow stripe and a porphyry stringcourse, with orthostats above. These, originally red, separated by narrow marbleized panels, are now pale pink or a characterless yellow, but their upper limit, well above the height of one's head, is clearly visible and shows that they were ca. 1.50 m high. Of the parts above them only the faintest ghosts remain, and the modillion cornice that crowned the decoration, the only part employing strong illusion of perspective, has entirely disappeared. The nave may have differed from the side aisles in its scheme; the entrance wall shows good remains of rich yellow on both sides from the floor to a height of 2.35 m but no trace of a decorative scheme.

The exterior was decorated in First Style (Mau 1882, 61–62). In the pronaos one sees great relief panels, at present 2.69 m high, that disappear into the floor, probably as a result of the raising of the pavement here. They are separated by channels 0.10 m wide, above which I am unable to make anything out. Mazois shows successive large-scale courses of drafted ashlar in alternate courses of all headers

---

[8]Mazois 3, pl. 36; Mau 1882, 248. Mau holds that the socle is a repair, while a small part of the original socle was preserved in the northwest corner, the repair being of the time of the Third Style. If so, some pains were taken to make the repair harmonize with the older decoration above.

and headers alternating with stretchers. Traces of a similar scheme can be found on all exterior walls. These show that the temple once stood free of all other buildings, as do the fine pilasters with which the back corners are finished.

The building history is fairly easily straightened out once Maiuri's early date for the original construction is eliminated. The temple was built by the Roman colony to give focus to the forum as a civic centre and to emphasize their Roman allegiance. It stood free and took the whole forum as its precinct, an emphatically classicizing building in the high style of its period, both exterior and interior orders being revolutionary for Pompeii. There is nothing to show that it was not from the start intended for the worship of the Capitoline Triad; the fact that it is not a triple-cella temple is counterbalanced by the breadth of the statue base. The severe Second Style decoration of the interior ought to be the style of the time of Sulla. The construction, once completed, stood for three-quarters of a century without substantial change.

Then in the imperial period there was a general refurbishing of the front parts, probably in connection with the triumphal arches that were built to flank the façade of the temple. The stair was rebuilt, and the altar moved back from the open area in front of the temple to a place midway on its stair. The pronaos was repaved with travertine and Caserta stone and raised a step. The statue base was remodeled. And a new entrance was cut for the aerarium. The work was extensive, but it was really aimed only at creating a new backdrop across this end of the forum in which the arches and temple worked together to produce a unified and sumptuous, if theatrical, effect. If we could find a suitable occasion in the Augustan or Tiberian period for a dedication of two arches in Pompeii, we might have a plausible date for this undertaking, but the eastern arch was subsequently destroyed and its place paved over, and the western one was stripped down to its brick-faced masonry core, presumably by the survivors of the eruption. Not a single fragment of any inscription or decorative panel was found. Tiberius and Drusus seem an apt enough pair to have been so honored after Tiberius's triumph in 7 B.C., but there is no supporting evidence.

Thereafter the only modification we note in the temple is the rebuilding of the statue base as a heavy walled and vaulted structure to carry great weight. That must have occurred when the new cult statue of Jupiter of which we have various fragments was presented, and a date for this any time prior to the earthquake of A.D. 62 is acceptable.

In the earthquake of 62 the superstructure of the temple was severely damaged. In the relief in the Casa di Cecilio Giocondo showing the forum in the earthquake we see the temple façade sliding to one side and the equestrian statues flanking the stairs tottering on their bases. After the earthquake the temple was unusable, and the cult of the Capitoline Triad was transferred to the Temple of Jupiter Meilichios. But the statue of Jupiter was still preserved here, as were various inscriptions that show it was the intention of the citizens to restore the temple when they had the opportunity. In the meantime the useless debris was cleared away, and whatever could not be moved elsewhere was put under what protection was available. Thus it is as a shell that the temple has come down to us.

The Porticus of Vibius and the "Comitium"

Around the south end of the forum, from the southwest corner to the Via dell'Abbondanza, ran a colonnade of Nocera tufa, double on the east in front of the "comitium." There was remodeling and modification of this in antiquity, but enough of the original survives for us to be sure of its character. The order is Doric, and the lower shafts are faceted. At the top the fluting is squared off under a plain collar. There is a single, raised annulet, and the echinus is straight. The entablature is in blocks of tufa, and the frieze has three triglyphs over each intercolumniation (Mazois 3, pl. 14 bis, fig. 2). An inscription on a slab of limestone was found in front of the basilica: V·POPIDIVS / EP·F·Q· / PORTICVS / FACIENDAS / COERAVIT (*CIL* 10.794). The lettering and the form *coerauit* indicate a republican date, and it has been supposed that the office of quaestor, unattested in Pompeian electoral programmata, must be a survival from the precolonial government.[9] Therefore this colonnade should be dated in the eighties of the first century B.C. But the fact that the inscription is in Latin means that it itself should not antedate the arrival of the colony. The faceting of the lower shafts of these columns suggests a date no earlier than the late second century B.C., but the reappearance of an old Campanian name for a magistrate would be surprising in the early years of the colony.

The doubling of the colonnade along the east side of the southeast corner of the forum clearly was done in connection with a large building commonly called the comitium. This identification can hardly be right, since there is no provision here for marshaling large crowds of people into readily identifiable groups and none for accommodating an orderly assembly to listen to debate and pass on legislation. Nor does this building have anything in common with the design of Roman comitia that have come to light at Cosa, Paestum, and Alba Fu-

[9] On this question see Castrén 88.

cens, all reflections of the pattern of the comitium of Rome.[10] The large theatre, or even the amphitheatre, could be made to serve far better as a comitium, and it is to be presumed that the former was so used.

The building on the forum of Pompeii is today a naked shell, but once it was completely revetted with marble, as the clamp wedges found inside and out show, and before that it had a fine tufa façade in large, carefully finished blocks along the forum side, while that along the Via dell'Abbondanza was in piers of brick and curtains of rubblework intended to be stuccoed. It is the building technique that gives a clue to the building's purpose. Along the north side, beginning from the forum end, there are three brick piers at regular intervals with light curtain walls between, then a pair of stouter jambs framing a doorway, and then the wall continues to the northeast corner with the thickness of the jambs. Along the forum front are six piers of tufa blocks with light curtain walls or doorways between. Such walls cannot have been expected to carry much weight, certainly nothing so heavy as a roof covering the ample rectangle of this building would have to be; so this must have been an unroofed enclosure. On the street side it is windowless, while on the forum side certain of the tufa blocks suggest that there may have been windows in the curtains that were later walled up.

In the interior the east wall is interrupted by a series of four rectangular niches that have every appearance of having been designed to hold statuary, and the south wall formerly had a similar series of three niches (Mau 1908, 115–16), so one must think of this as a building of public importance. The south wall is interrupted at the middle by a recess filled with a rectangular tribunal raised waist-high above the floor and approached from the main area by a flight of masonry steps, now in poor repair. Opening off to the west from this is a sequence of small closets that one might suppose to have been for storage of furniture, or possibly retiring rooms. The masonry in all these parts is heterogeneous rubblework with reticulate used to face the front of the tribunal.

The evidence indicates that this was an important building. It occupies a conspicuous place on the forum. It was early repaired after the earthquake of 62 and lavishly refurbished with marble veneer inside and out. It could accommodate a large number of people but did not provide them with particular seats or places. The strong suggestion is that this was for the courts of Pompeii, the tribunal being for the magistrate in charge of the court, his attendants, and the court

[10]See F. E. Brown, *Cosa: The Making of a Roman Town* (Ann Arbor, Mich., 1980) 23–24.

functionaries, while the jurors would have sat on benches in an arc in front of the tribunal, and the case would have been pled in the theatre they formed. The corona of spectators could then have gathered freely around this focus, at liberty to come and go but protected from the noise of the forum by a screening wall. It is interesting to note in this connection how the doors are placed so as to give maximum access while at the same time giving maximum protection against distraction to those engaged in the trial. As an unroofed building this would not violate religious dictates that trials had to be held in the open air, and it could have been a permanently inaugurated templum. The storage space at the southwest corner would then be for the furniture of the court, and the niches in the east and south walls would surely be for statues of particularly distinguished magistrates. Moreover, there is no reason why this tribunal could not have functioned as rostra for contiones when court was not in session or why the statues could not have been much like those erected as a special honor on the rostra of the Forum Romanum.

One thing remains to be noted. Along the north front of the building opposite each brick pier is a tufa block sunk in the sidewalk with a square cutting to take the tenon of a stout wooden upright. These are probably survivals from a light portico that once covered the sidewalk, but there is no indication as to when it was built or how long it served.

The construction date of the building can be deduced from the use of a carefully finished façade of tufa blocks on the forum in conjunction with brickwork intended to be stuccoed along the secondary façade of the Via dell'Abbondanza. It should be no earlier than 100 B.C., most probably an early building of the Roman colony, not a survival from Samnite times, and this reinforces our date for the porticus of Vibius.

The Terme del Foro

The only purely utilitarian building associated with the early years of the Roman colony is the Terme del Foro (VII v 2/8/24), a complex in a block adjacent to the forum that includes suites of baths for both men and women.[11] The fact that at this time the Pompeians were able to

[11] The block including the Terme del Foro, the first public bath complex discovered in Pompeii, was excavated, according to Fiorelli, between 26 July 1822 and 5 November 1824. The identification of the centre of the block as a bath, however, seems not to have been definite until the report of 25 July 1824, after which date the discoveries follow in close succession (see *PAH* 2.57–118). Good drawings and descriptions were made by Mazois (3.67–77 and pls. 47–50). A detailed description by G. Bechi, with admirable plan and drawings by P. Valente, is one of the chief ornaments of *Museo Borbonico* 2 (pls. 49–54 with relevant explanation).

rebuild an entire city block just north of the forum is surprising, but one notes that the baths are concentrated in the centre of the block, and around them on three sides are lines of shops that rank among the largest in Pompeii, those on the south having several rooms.

The men's bath shows great efficiency in design. One entered either by a narrow corridor from the north or by a vaulted passage from the east, evidently more regularly by the latter, for it opens to the more important street and has a cubicle for the bathman off it. It gives directly onto the palaestra adjacent to a short passage leading north to the apodyterium. The north entrance leads directly to the apodyterium. The apodyterium is a rectangular, barrel-vaulted chamber with a plaster-faced bench around three sides on which one could sit while dressing and where servants could wait for their masters. A similar bench lies along the exterior of the building east of the north entrance. The appearance of these benches as a regular feature of baths seems to indicate that one seldom went to the baths unattended. Above the bench is a row of rectangular sockets for wooden brackets to support a shelf. The only light in the apodyterium came from a window in the crown of the lunette at the south end. This was glazed with a single pane of glass. As in all the rooms of the men's bath, the lower walls are plain, trimmed with a figured frieze in stucco relief just under the spring of the vault; the lunette, however, is elaborately decorated with an Oceanus head and tritons.

From the apodyterium one had access to either the frigidarium or the tepidarium, as well as to the palaestra, and a very narrow corridor for service led out of the northwest corner behind the hot rooms to the praefurnium. The frigidarium is a circular room with four small, half-domed niches to fill out the corners of an inscribing square. It is almost entirely taken up with a circular pool just deep enough for one to be able to throw oneself in without fear of injury. The niches presumably were for those who preferred to be doused with cold water by an attendant. The room is roofed with a masonry cone that springs just above the crown of the niches, a little above head height. This and the lighting by a window facing south near the apex of the cone give the room a curious subaqueous feeling that is heightened by the cerulean blue with which the basin is painted. The walls and niches were painted with shrubs and trees against a yellow ground; of this almost nothing survives today.

The tepidarium is of about the same dimensions as the apodyterium, similarly vaulted. It is not raised on suspensurae but was heated by braziers. A large, low brazier of bronze with an iron fire pan and two bronze benches were donated by P. Nigidius Vaccula, as inscriptions and allusion to his name in the calves' legs and calf mounts of these bear witness (*CIL* 10.818; Mazois 3, pl. 49; *Museo*

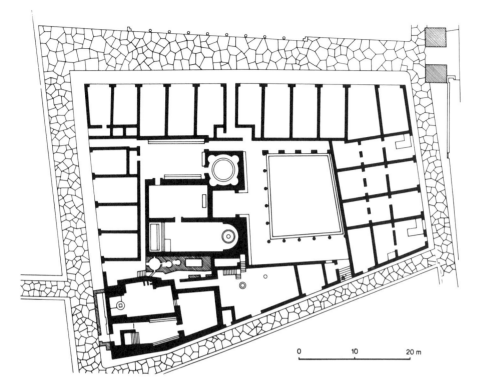

FIGURE 20.
The Terme del Foro,
Plan

0   10   20 m

Borbonico 2, pl. 54). On three sides this room is surrounded by a line
of small rectangular niches separated from one another by terracotta
telamons of three types—some nude, others with breechclouts—but
closely related. It hardly seems likely that these were for clothing;
more probably they were for the sets of strigils and the oil jars one
regularly took to the baths and the towels one would need.[12] The
tepidarium was illuminated by a single window in the southern lunette provided with a bronze frame in which were found four panes
of glass. The ceiling is richly decorated in stucco relief.

The caldarium is the largest of these rooms, about the same
in width as the others but much longer, rather tunnel-like. It too is
barrel-vaulted, and it has an apsidal end at the south, half-domed.
Light is provided by three windows with splayed reveals in the
southern end of the barrel vault and a circular window in the half-
dome. The last may have been equipped with a shield for regulation
of the heat. It must always have been a dark room, and clouds of
steam would have made it almost impossible to recognize one's
friends here. The floor is raised on suspensurae and paved with

[12] The instrumentum of bathers is shown in Eschebach 1978 fig. 47.

white mosaic with a simple black border; the walls are hollow, being covered with tegulae mammatae. The vault is stuccoed in a ribbed pattern, rather severe, the half-dome with figured reliefs. At the end opposite the apse is a large bath basin capable of accommodating at least a dozen bathers. It is lined with marble and provided with steps to facilitate getting in and out and on which one could sit while bathing if one did not wish to recline on the floor of the basin. Water to supply this basin was heated in the praefurnium just west of this room and piped in; a fair-sized drain in the basin suggests that it was changed frequently. In the apse is a marble labrum. An inscription in bronze letters around the lip records that it is the work of the duovirs Cn. Melissaeus Aper and M. Staius Rufus (*CIL* 10.817); other inscriptions show that they were duovirs in A.D. 3/4 (*CIL* 10.824, 893).

The palaestra is small, accessible only from the apodyterium or the exterior. It is bordered on three sides by porticoes, not on the south. The east portico is now arcaded, probably a remodeling of the last years of the city. Around the north end of the palaestra a waist-high masonry pluteus broken only by a couple of passageways runs between the columns; this must have been to keep those exercising, perhaps especially those playing ball, from interfering with those sitting and strolling. A masonry bench runs along the back wall of the portico, and off it opens a deep barrel-vaulted exedra, too deep to catch the sun except when it was very low, toward the winter solstice. This must have been especially for conversation. To what extent the palaestra was actually used for exercise may be questioned; it is inadequate for more than the most limited activity. At the centre of the west side is a small fountain basin, and at the southwest corner is a short corridor leading to a back entrance on the Vicolo delle Terme, off which lies a small latrine.

The praefurnium is an irregular courtyard lying between the men's and women's baths but communicating only with the men's and the exterior. The space in which the tanks for heating water were installed is raised about a meter above its surroundings, and just beyond these is a deep well that was equipped with a wheel device for hoisting water. The great triple-chambered reservoir that lies across the street from the baths in block VII vi must be subsequent to the digging of this well, as otherwise the two would have been located in closer proximity; but the masonry and engineering of the reservoir look to be contemporary with the baths, so presumably the well was here before the bath was built and was one of the factors determining its location. A large trapezoidal courtyard south of the praefurnium and accessible from it, as well as from the Vicolo delle Terme, must have served especially for the storage of fuel, but in the last period a pair of stout columns in opus mixtum vittatum were erected here.

Fiorelli believed that these were to support a channel that conveyed water between the deep well of the baths and the reservoir in block VII vi. This explanation will serve for the northern column, since an arch that carried such an aqueduct across the Vicolo delle Terme is known to have existed and to have collapsed shortly after discovery. But the other column seems more likely to have supported a roof over part of this courtyard. A stairway in the northeast corner leading up to the roof of the men's caldarium was probably installed especially to permit opening of the windows in the bathrooms whenever the weather permitted. Numerous fragments of window glass were collected by the excavators, and the windows in the domes were probably all protected by bronze shields that could be raised and lowered to regulate the amount of light and air admitted (Vitruvius 5.10.5). A stair just inside VII v 7 was probably to provide the same service for the women's section, but it also seems to have given access to a hanging balcony supported on vaulting that ran along the north front of the women's section at the height of the roof, the purpose of which is not clear.

The women's section duplicates the facilities of the men's but is without a palaestra. It is a very solidly built building, independent of the rest of the block, entered only from the Via di Nola by a small door, VII v 8. From an entrance lobby provided with benches, which was evidently an addition of the last period, one passed down a short corridor to the apodyterium, off which the frigidarium was simply a small square basin in an alcove with a vaulted ceiling, hardly a separate room at all. The tepidarium is trapezoidal, the caldarium approximately rectangular, with rectangular niches at the north end and along the east side. Both tepidarium and caldarium are raised on suspensurae and have hollow walls. The northern niche of the caldarium contains a small labrum, and the eastern one is clearly intended for a bath basin, as the flues to the praefurnium show. The absence of any such feature is puzzling; it must have been of bronze and salvaged by the survivors. But in that case it cannot have been very large, perhaps not much larger than the bath basins from the Pisanella villa at Boscoreale and to be used by only one person at a time.[13]

To anyone studying the plan, it is striking that the men's section is arranged in a carefully organized rectangle of maximum efficiency set in the middle of the block so as to interfere as little as possible with the commercial exploitation of the street frontage around it. The bath does not advertise its presence; one has almost to hunt for the entrance. The women's section, on the other hand, is a completely dif-

[13]For the bath basins from the Pisanella villa see *MonAnt* 7 (1897) 421–22, figs. 16–17.

ferent and independent building and takes valuable street frontage, even encroaching on the sidewalks around it. It is also of an irregular plan that suggests expediency rather than design. It can only have been an annex added after the rest had existed for some time, and its masonry and the standpipe built into its west wall suggest that it is no earlier than the early Augustan period. What we must wonder at is that it should have been built at all.

If one now tries to reconstruct the plan of the block at the time of the original construction of the baths, logic demands that the row of shops along the Via di Nola continue unbroken and that the praefurnium be accessible from the west. The great reservoir must have found its place across the Vicolo delle Terme because the space on the east side of the street was needed for something else, but it is by no means clear what that might have been. It is perhaps worth noting that one of the largest cookshops (VI vii 7/8) and one of the largest wineshops (VI viii 9/10) of Pompeii lie just across the Via di Nola from the entrance to the men's bath. This can hardly have been accidental; one finds similar establishments across the Strada Stabiana from the Thermae Stabianae at IX i 3, 6, 8, and 15. Presumably Pompeians, like Romans, were accustomed to spend considerable time at the baths, going nearly as much for business and conversation as for exercise and bathing, and not infrequently wanted something to eat or drink while there.

The capacity of the reservoir of the Terme del Foro appears impressive, but its walls are not thick enough to have withstood the pressure were it ever anything like full. It is sunk nearly a full storey below ground level but rises to the height of two storeys above ground. It is divided into three equal chambers by crosswalls, but the chambers are interconnected, and it is not clear whether they could be closed off from one another in any way. The lower parts are lined with a thick veneer of signinum, the upper not. A masonry stair rose at the south end of the building, and presumably from this one had access to catwalks suspended along the upper part of the walls.

A sewer under the Vicolo delle Terme can be traced by cavities between the paving blocks where its roof has collapsed from a point midway along the block down to the Via dei Soprastanti, where it turns west and runs down this street to the corner between VII Ins. Occ. 15 and 16. Here a surface drain empties into the same channel, and it was carried down the precipitous slope of the city site, presumably to empty into the canal that can be seen running underneath the city north of the Porta Marina. North of the baths it cannot be traced, and presumably it came into existence with them as the main drain for an establishment that required and discharged great quantities of water. This sewer explains the location of the latrine of the baths, and probably all the neighboring parts of the city discharged their waste into it. Since it was a short sewer conveying primarily the waste from the baths, it probably made this part of the city unusually salubrious.

11 · THE HOUSES

Introduction

With the Casa del Centenario (chap. 9, pp. 126–27) we come close to the Second Style. The simplicity of the façade, the proportions and development of its peristyle, the frequency of its cisterns, the use of small secondary courtyards as sources of light and centres of activity, all bring us down close to the time of the Second Style and a new concept in architecture as well as in decoration. In houses of the second century B.C. the emphasis is on monumentality; even the unpretentious house is a formal setting for the salutatio and the cena, and though the secondary atrium and peristyle might have more graceful architecture and more intimate spaces than the Tuscanic atrium, the building and decoration were intended, if not for all time, at least for great permanence. Beautiful as that architecture is, with great refinement of detail and proportion, it lacks warmth. Its spaces demand dignity and ritual; its lines and colors are not to delight the eye and to set off the occupants but to emphasize the solidity of the fabric and the correctness of the volumes.

The Second Style seems to have come to Pompeii with the Sullan colony; presumably it had already developed at Rome. One might expect a wave of building with the arrival of the colonists, but actually there was surprisingly little. While many houses have a room or two in the Second Style, this is usually simply a redecoration of an already existing room without architectural change, and even where there is evidence of architectural change, it tends to be minimal. Consequently, in any discussion of Second Style architecture one is reduced to extrapolation from widely scattered evidence and heavy reliance on a few good examples.

The Casa delle Nozze d'Argento

The Casa delle Nozze d'Argento (V ii i [or s.n.]) is the best-preserved of the Second Style houses.[1] Probably it was built for a colonist. In the last period of Pompeii it belonged to L. Albucius Celsus, a candidate for the aedilate (Della Corte[3] no. 150; Castrén no. 19). The family is not Campanian in origin and had few representatives in the city. The façade is very plain, but the house door is large, and the atrium, the largest in Pompeii, is on a similar scale. It is tetrastyle with Corinthian columns with corkscrew volutes in tufa and a tufa impluvium, the latter deeper than those of the second century and with a rather crisply carved molding. Despite its being tetrastyle, it has alae in the position of those of a Tuscanic atrium, small in proportion to the huge tablinum. The cubicula along both sides of the atrium have been rebuilt in two storeys. In the remodeling the doors were reduced in size and made asymmetrical, and windows were let into the atrium from the rooms above at irregular intervals. The work was a curiously inept job and had given the atrium an incongruous appearance. Thereafter the atrium was repainted with a hybrid Second / Third Style decoration run across the walls without respect for the architectural features. The ala and tablinum openings are trimmed with unfluted pilasters that probably belong to this redecoration; a small patch of Second Style painting appears on the south wall of the east ala. We may presume that originally the doors of the cubicula were three on either side, proportioned to the size of the atrium, and that the cubicula soared.

The tablinum is very splendid, with a pavement of fine white mosaic with a plain black border, judged by Pernice to be Third Style; the painting is of the last period. The large square dining room east of this, though stripped of plaster at the time of the eruption, preserved a splendid mosaic pavement with a sill panel of three-dimensional maeander design and an illusionistic lozenge pattern over the main floor; this is Second Style work of the finest sort and shows that this classic reception room was no longer oriented to the atrium, but communicated with the tablinum by a small door and otherwise was open entirely to the peristyle, a change of considerable importance. Its counterpart on the opposite side of the tablinum has been divided into an andron and a small winter triclinium, neither of which need be original.

The peristyle is the focus of the dining rooms of the house. Besides

---

[1] *RömMitt* 8 (1893) 28–61; 10 (1895) 146–48. *NSc* 1910, 315–30. Mau 1908, 315–24. Mau was of the opinion that the house went back to the time of the First Style, but as Pernice (1938, 50–51) observed, if it did, almost nothing of the original house survived a radical rebuilding. It seems better to regard it as a Second Style construction.

the room beside the tablinum, the tablinum itself may have had a new orientation, for here it is open almost its full width to the peristyle as well as to the atrium, though it cannot be proved that the peristyle opening is original. And off the peristyle are two more grand reception rooms for large parties, one of which is connected *en suite* with a smaller room in a pattern that now becomes common. Also opening off this peristyle are a bath suite, handsomely decorated, a kitchen court, and a kitchen garden. The house has become again a planned and coherent architectural sequence, as it was in the days of the Casa di Sallustio, but enlarged and obedient to a new set of aesthetic rules and demands for comfort.

The peristyle itself is of the class known as Rhodian, having the roof of one portico lifted considerably higher than the others. Here it is the north portico and permits a change in scale. The north portico has only five columns, compared with six in the others, the columns fluted with the classic twenty flutes of the Doric order, while those in the other porticoes are polygons of eight broad facets. The peristyle is surprisingly small after the atrium, but not actually small for a Pompeian garden. Squarish proportions seem now to be in fashion but not obligatory. Unfortunately, the walls were redecorated in the last period.

The grander of the two reception rooms is off the southeast corner, a colonnaded, or Corinthian, oecus. It is a long rectangle with four columns supporting a barrel-vaulted ceiling over a central space behind an entrance lobby. The aisle behind the columns has a flat ceiling at the level of the spring of the vault, while the ceiling of the entrance lobby rises above its crown. The columns are raised on square plinths and given simple schematic bases and capitals, while the shafts are faceted. The room is clearly a dining room, and the rich, rather severe, Second Style decoration and pavement, as well as the architecture, clearly define the place for the service and entertainment in the lobby, in front of the area for the couches of the banqueters. The other reception room, off the southwest corner of the peristyle, is an even longer rectangle, now painted with a Fourth Style black-ground decoration, but the fine mosaic pavement and the Second Style decorations in the rooms adjoining it on either side indicate that its shape is original. The pavement is marked for the couches of the diners, so its purpose is certain. It must always have been a dark room. Communicating with this across the corner of the peristyle by a short, oblique passage is a small room similar to a cubiculum, with a rich decoration and fine mosaic pavement. The pavement has a patterned sill panel, and a place for a couch is marked off from the rest against the back wall. The couch area has a vaulted ceiling, the outer room a flat ceiling at the height of the crown of the vault. In

FIGURE 21.
The Casa delle Nozze
d'Argento,
Colonnaded Oecus

the Second Style decoration the division of the room is further emphasized, the couch alcove being surrounded by strongly illusionistic
Corinthian columns, which are omitted from the decoration of the
outer room. Too richly decorated and too open to be the bedchamber
it first appears to be, the room must have been a dining room for
ladies.

In fact, there are two ladies' dining rooms. At the opposite end of
the south portico is a second, clearly identifiable, which must have
functioned with the colonnaded oecus but is not clearly connected to
it architecturally. Again we see a vaulted niche for the couch, its area
marked off in the mosaic pavement, and in the rich Second Style
painting there are Corinthian columns shown around the couch
niche, none in the outer room. The broad door was provided with a

wooden doorframe, so presumably there were doors here that could be closed when the weather made this necessary.

The remaining room off the south portico is a small exedra painted with a monochrome decoration of yellow base color in the Second Style, a very delicate and elegant scheme. Probably this was a sitting room, perhaps especially for use in the summer. The Rhodian portico would have caught the sun when it was low in the sky in winter and would have been a warm place then to walk and talk. This monochrome exedra with its northern exposure, well protected behind its portico, would have been cool in the summer.

The bath suite along the west portico belongs to the period of the Fourth Style. A small Second Style room next to the southwest triclinium has been incorporated in this, the wall between it and a room to the west having been torn out to make a single long room that must have served as a dressing room. Though baths are a feature of several Second Style houses, and this might have been a rebuilding of an original Second Style bath, we must doubt it. Certainly the tank in the adjacent courtyard that served as a cold plunge would not have been possible before the introduction of the aqueduct into Pompeii. The kitchen is even less informative than the bath; it might be original, as the cistern head against the east wall suggests, but it is a simple, undecorated courtyard with such plain, utilitarian architecture that it could have been built at almost any time. One should note that in the room off the east side of the fauces—a long, low, unattractive room—were found a bronze cooking pot and an iron brazier; so when the weather made cooking in the open difficult, cooking may have been done here.

East of the main body of the house is a large garden, at least half as big as the house itself, reached by a door at the northeast corner of the peristyle. This is regularly shown with a colonnade on all sides, but in fact there is none there today, and there was none there in the last period of the city, although its place was marked by a signinum gutter (*NSc* 1910, 324–28 [A. Sogliano]). Along the west wall is a series of four buttresses making shallow bays that are framed with pilasters, centering on the door to the peristyle, and in the southwest corner was once a door to a corridor south of the garden leading to a posticum on the east that has been blocked with masonry that includes fragments of octagonal faceted columns of the Second Style type characteristic of this house. These might have come from the garden colonnade, but they might equally well have come from an arbor or similar small structure. Today, at the middle of the west side is a masonry triclinium for summer dining built over the gutter and the line of the colonnade. The table had a fountain pipe at its centre, and a tank with a second fountain at its centre is in line with this out in the garden. This garden seems clearly to have functioned mainly as a kitchen garden; its separation from the rest of the house seems a clear enough indication of this.

The Casa del Menandro

According to Pernice, there is no pavement in the Casa del Menandro (I x 4) that need be later than Second Style, while the only pavements that are clearly First Style are those discovered in the excavations under the floor of the great triclinium. The pavements in the atrium complex fit less precisely into the scheme of datable pavements than do the mosaics in the rooms for entertaining, but this is because they are more utilitarian in character. The pavements in the peristyle complex fall into two groups, those in the rooms on the north and east sides, which are all early Second Style in character, and those in the exedras on the south side of the peristyle and in the bath complex, which seem to be later. But we can regard the whole house, despite such alterations as the late floor of the impluvium in the atrium of the baths and a general redecoration of most of the rooms in the Fourth Style, as a creation of the period of the Second Style and an expression of that taste.

The entrance is rather low, the doorway framed by plain pilasters crowned with rather squat Corinthian jamb capitals. Presumably there was originally an ornamental lintel. The fauces are short, flanked by small rooms, and over the front of the house were small rooms in a second storey. The Tuscanic atrium is spacious and lofty with a large impluvium given a marble veneer late in the life of the city. The doors around the atrium vary in height, those along the west side being now lower than those on the east and at the ends, while the opening to the tablinum is dramatically larger, raised a low step above the atrium and framed with Corinthian columns that are engaged but worked almost in the round. This is clearly a development from the First Style tradition of framing the tablinum with massive pilasters that we see, for example, in the Casa del Fauno, but it is almost unique in Pompeii, the only other example known being in VII Ins. Occ. 13. Presumably the secondary doors were originally all uniform. The cubicula are unremarkable, but the single ala on the east is set on the short axis of the atrium. The tablinum is flanked by symmetrical doors, that on the east leading to an andron, that on the west either simply a false door or else leading to a closet, for the body of this corridor was occupied by a vast wooden cabinet that opened onto the tablinum and took up most of its west wall. This was obviously a substitute for the cabinets often found in an ala, and one must ask whether this was part of the original design of the house or an ingenious modification. In defense of the former hypothesis, one must observe that two androns would hardly be needed, but there seem to have been two simply for the sake of symmetry in the Casa dei Capitelli Colorati. At the peristyle end the tablinum had a large opening, nearly the full width of the wall, that was filled with wooden doors.

The Doric peristyle, originally seven columns by eight, the columns spaced at regular intervals, has the squarïsh proportions typical for the period. In the last period the north and east colonnades were rebuilt with irregular spacing to emphasize the tablinum and the big triclinium. The rooms flanking the tablinum are a small exedral room with a rich pavement and pretty early Fourth Style decoration and a triclinium of the deep oblong shape characteristic of the new architecture, open nearly its whole width to the peristyle and with a small door to the andron. The rooms along the east side of the peristyle are a series that include a huge room for banquets with a small room adjacent and in communication with it, clearly another example of the new type of suite for parties, and some smaller rooms of no particular character. Along the south portico opens a series of shallow exedras, hardly more than alcoves, and a single room with a Second Style pavement in which places for large pieces of furniture are marked off along the east and south walls. The pieces of furniture were later replaced with shelving. Maiuri (1933, 88–89) concluded that this was most likely to have been a library, a very attractive hypothesis given the location, architecture, and decoration of the nearby exedras. Originally there were probably large wooden cabinets along the east and south walls to hold the book rolls; later they were replaced by shelves. And the exedras were for the convenience of readers, except the westernmost, which was occupied by a family sacrarium.

Off the west portico of the peristyle is an elaborate bath, once one of the prettiest suites in Pompeii, decorated in late Second Style.[2] It was entered through a diminutive Corinthian atrium with nine columns around a tiny impluvium floored, like the rest of the room, in mosaic. This must have acted as a bath basin; here bathers must have stood, or crouched, to be sluiced down after sweating in the hot rooms. From this, one went south through a vestibule into a tepidarium vaulted east and west; and from this, in turn, into a caldarium,

---

[2]Maiuri 1933, 121–58; Pernice 1938, 60. Pernice was of the opinion that the whole of the Casa del Menandro was essentially a Second Style building, as is shown by the numerous Second Style pavements in both atrium and peristyle complexes. Only the painting he believed to be Fourth Style. Except for a few obvious modifications, such as the pluteus in the peristyle, the house certainly fits well into the canon of Second Style architecture.

also vaulted and given a small apse that one would have supposed was for a labrum, although there is no sign of one. These rooms are also paved with mosaic, the caldarium floor worked with marine motifs and bathing equipment. The wall decorations are fragmentary, except in the caldarium, but are all clearly late Second Style.[3] West of this suite is an open courtyard. Here a semicircular exedra, probably for sunbathing, stands on a raised platform facing south, but it does not seem to have been part of the original arrangements.[4] The lower part of the court served for fuel storage, and from here the fire under the bath floors was tended. The elegance of this bath and the perfection of its proportions is very striking, evidence of the refinements Second Style architecture brought in its course.

The Casa dei Capitelli Figurati

Another town house essentially of the Second Style is the Casa dei Capitelli Figurati (VII iv 57).[5] Here the tufa capitals of the jambs of the house door give the house its name; they probably go back to the middle of the second century, and we should expect a plot so close to the forum of Pompeii as this to have been built up from a very early date, but the arrangements and character of the impluvium and the proportions and decoration of the peristyle are all strongly Second Style, so whatever may survive from an earlier period must have been thoroughly rehandled. And there are traces of Second Style decoration in all parts of the atrium/peristyle complex.

The atrium is Tuscanic, entered down short fauces from the Via di Nola (Via della Fortuna). The rooms to either side of the fauces are

[3] Maiuri 1933, 143–44. Maiuri thought the main body of the caldarium had been redecorated in the Fourth Style because of the green ground. He was mistaken about this, but he has been followed in his error by a great many writers.

[4] Roger Ling ("The Bath of the Casa del Menandro at Pompeii," *Pompeii, Herculaneum, Stabiae* 1 [1983] 49–60) would see this as the beginnings of a laconicum, to be completed as a circular room out of which open four half-domed niches, like the frigidaria of the Thermae Stabianae and the Terme del Foro. But there is no provision for heating, and it is too far from the praefurnium at the west end of the caldarium to have been a laconicum. It might be reconstructed as a frigidarium, but there is no plunge nor any possibility of creating one, and as a frigidarium it would be too large for a private bath and out of scale with the other rooms. Construction was in progress here, but it is hardly likely that a bath on the scale of a public bath was projected. It is more likely that Maiuri was right in suggesting that this was to be a solarium.

[5] The house is largely ignored by Mau in the *Geschichte der dekorativen Wandmalerei in Pompeji* (Mau 1882), though it is not clear why. Pernice (1938, 85) decided that the wall paintings and pavements belonged to the late Second Style or the Third Style, but apparently his notes on the paintings were inaccurate, for he said that there were no considerable remains of First Style or Second Style decoration. We can date the house in the form we see it to the time of the late Second Style. Except for a few interesting pieces, such as the arca from the atrium, the excavation is only perfunctorily reported in *PAH* 2.255–72 (Laidlaw 250–53, with bibliography).

FIGURE 22.
The Casa dei Capitelli
Figurati, Figured Jamb
Capital

included in the house, not let out as shops. The impluvium is of tufa, rather deep, floored with tufa slabs, and drains into a cistern under the atrium with a limestone puteal over the drawshaft cut in the southern rim of the impluvium. The alae preserve traces of identical Second Style decorations with columns, and there are traces of another in the winter triclinium in the northwest corner of the house, a long rectangular room. The other rooms on the atrium seem to have been cubicula and storerooms, at least one of which on the west side preserves traces of Second Style painting. The arrangement of the tablinum wing seems to be original, and there are traces of Second Style painting in the two big rooms flanking the tablinum. The tablinum is open its full width to both atrium and peristyle, and small doors at the peristyle end communicate with the big rooms to either side, a Second Style feature. An andron runs just west of the tablinum, and the big dining rooms now virtually turn their backs on the atrium in order to face the peristyle and open nearly full-width to it.

The peristyle is a pretty Ionic apartment, squarish, six columns by six, but the width of the property has forced suppression of the west

FIGURE 23.
The Casa dei Capitelli Figurati, Ionic Order of the Peristyle

portico. In its place is an engaged order, and between the columns of this appears an illusionistic Doric order on a smaller scale, worked out in stucco relief. At first glance this appears to be First Style, but the character of the moldings, simple cymas without dentillation, proves that it is Second Style. In the open area was a pergola, an arbor supported on six columns of masonry with faceted shafts, like those of the Casa delle Nozze d'Argento. Only stumps of these remain, but one can suppose that the arbor was intended especially to shelter a triclinium in the summer, a triclinium with couch frames of wood that would be dismounted and stored when not in use. The offices of the house must always have occupied the area around the southeast corner of the peristyle, where later a small building facing on the Via degli Augustali was annexed. This part of the house is confused, but it is of only minor interest.

The identifiable elements in the development of house architecture in the Second Style are, then, not many. The relationship between the atrium and the peristyle was not fully thought out, and it was not to be for at least a hundred years yet. Down to the destruction of Pompeii most houses still showed a sharp separation of the two and a change in architectural approach as well as in decoration as one moved from one to the other, the emphasis in the atrium being on a handsome dignity and axial rigidity, while the architecture in the peristyle was relaxed, sometimes almost playful in its freedom from symmetry. There was little change in the design of atria and their dependencies from the time of the First Style. An andron to the peristyle now seems to have been a regular feature, as does a cistern in the atrium. But the peristyle had now come into its own and was the focus of all but the most enclosed winter triclinia. Dining rooms had now in large part grown away from the squarish rooms of the First Style toward the long rectangle that was to remain standard through the rest of the city's history, but the exact formula had not yet been reached. A ladies' dining room had now become a common adjunct to a state dining room, but the precise relationship of these was still experimental. Baths were now commoner and more spacious. Nothing positive can be said about improvements in kitchens and the other domestic offices. Pleasure gardens now seem to have been commoner, but a space was probably still regularly set apart for a kitchen garden if one did not have a garden plot or a farm out in the river valley.

The Casa del Labirinto

Two peristyles of houses of the Second Style show the development of the emphasis on this part of the house. The earlier is that of the

Casa del Labirinto (VI xi 9/10),[6] a great house just behind the Casa del Fauno. The house is an agglomeration of various periods, with a tetrastyle main atrium of the middle of the second century B.C. and a minor atrium that was once part of another house. These seem to have been put together and the peristyle added in the time of the Second Style, perhaps the middle of the first century B.C., and thereafter other rooms were added and modifications and redecorations carried out. But the peristyle and the suite of rooms along the north side of this area are a particularly informative example of a Second Style complex. The peristyle is squarish, eight columns by nine, Doric, with a cistern head in the middle of each side, evidently all original. The order is constructed of masonry, not cut stone, and an engaged order in the decoration responds to the colonnade along each long side. There are bases for potted shrubs or trees in the corners. The peristyle was damaged in the earthquake of 62 and had not yet been repaired by 79; the west colonnade was still without stucco.

Five rooms open onto the north portico, all with fine decoration. Beginning from the west, the first is a long, narrow triclinium with places for the couches marked in the pavement. The decoration is rather severe, but illusionistic Corinthian columns in the main zone set off the couches. The second is larger and finer, squarish, with a mosaic pavement with a deep maeander frame and a deep illusionistic decoration employing Corinthian columns and responding porphyry pillars. These two rooms communicate with one another at the forward end and with a cubiculum with a simple Second Style decoration behind; these relationships are puzzling, and for them there is no obvious explanation. The third room is squarish, a ladies' dining room, as is shown by the mosaic pavement, where an area paved with black-and-white diaper pattern is set off for the couch. In front of this the rest is in a labyrinth pattern with an emblema in tiny colored stones at the centre showing Theseus wrestling with the Minotaur. The painted decoration here was very fine, with vistas of architecture including telamon figures of sea gods mounted on ships' prows and Ionic columns with shafts wound with gilded ivy. This room communicated with the fourth, the finest room of all, a Corinthian oecus with columns on the three sides away from the peristyle door. Here the pavement is of mosaic with a maeander border between the columns and a centre panel of square plates of colored marble. The painting shows vistas of architecture, a temenos containing a tholos flanked by symmetrical panels of cityscape. Off the back corners of the room open two small rooms, both richly decorated, whose use is obscure; Overbeck and Mau (336) suggest that one

[6]On the date of the peristyle and its dependencies see Pernice 1938, 35–38.

FIGURE 24.
The Casa del
Labirinto, Corinthian
Oecus

might have been for the final preparation of food, the other a dressing room for the entertainers, but it does not seem very likely. The
last room in this suite is a second ladies' dining room, with the couch
area given a vaulted ceiling and set off by a panel of scale pattern in
the mosaic floor. The painted decoration here includes some curious
monochrome grotesques, as well as architectural elements and sug-
gestions of vistas.

These rooms, many of them communicating with one another and
all focused on the peristyle with its garden, so clearly formed a suite
for entertaining that we must wonder at the duplications among
them and the lack of variety in orientation. The Corinthian oecus was
clearly the most splendid room, and the labyrinth room approaches
it in sumptuousness. Why, then, is the decoration not harmonious?
One gathers that it is because variety was still admired and the idea
of harmony had not yet taken real shape. The decorations in the Casa

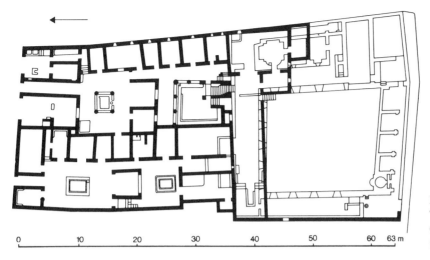

0, 10, 20, 30, 40, 50, 60, 63 m

FIGURE 25.
The Casa del
Criptoportico, Plan of
the Final Phase

delle Nozze d'Argento seem also to bear this out. But why should there have been two ladies' dining rooms flanking the great oecus? Was it perhaps because a large company including many ladies would be expected on the occasions when that hall was used but architects had not yet devised a ladies' dining room with more than one settee? That is what the evidence suggests. Fine as all these rooms are, they seem not yet assured in their architecture, and we may here be dealing rather with two suites than with five rooms.

The Casa del Criptoportico

The second peristyle of interest, that of the Casa del Criptoportico (I vi 2/4)[7] in the new excavations, belongs to the later Second Style, perhaps the time of the second triumvirate. The house of which it was part has been almost completely destroyed, and one can barely make out that it was probably once a double-atrium house occupying the whole eastern half of block I vi. The terrain here is sloping, the land falling off sharply to the south, so the squarish peristyle was arranged in two storeys, with a cryptoporticus in the lower storey that lifted the main storey level with the atria. Of the main storey all that survives is a pair of finely decorated dining rooms, a large rectangular triclinium painted with a curious megalography, including a panel showing a pair of elephants symmetrically flanking a candelabrum, connected with a ladies' dining room with a pretty monochrome decoration in red and green. These opened south onto the peristyle but have now been walled off.

[7] A full description of the pertinent parts of this house is given in Spinazzola 1953, 1.451–525, 549–69; see also *NSc* 1933, 252–76 (A. Maiuri). On the dating of the Second Style rooms and pavements see Pernice 1938, 51–52, 62.

THE HOUSES • 167

The lower storey is better preserved, though it is quite clear that it was out of use in the last period, except as a cellar. It once consisted of a corridor lit by small windows set high in its vaulted ceiling around three sides of a square and a row of rustic rooms making the fourth side of the square. The walls of the cryptoporticus proper were painted with a fine Second Style decoration including herms and a set of illustrations of the *Iliad*, and the vault was richly stuccoed, left white to contrast with the painting. Off this in the middle of the north wing opened an exedra, while the east wing ran to a magnificently decorated triclinium at its south end. This was decorated in a scheme similar to that of the corridor, painted herms with lively gestures seeming to support the elaborately stuccoed barrel vault, and between them, small rectangular still lifes and figure compositions in bright colors in pinakes. This was clearly once a fine reception room. North of it is a suite of four small rooms that Maiuri identified as a bath, though the evidence is really only the shape and sequence of the rooms (*NSc* 1933, 266–69). The decorations seem to me too fine to have been thrown away on so humble a function; the stuccoes are rich, and the architectural frames are worked out in elaborate perspective and peopled with a great variety of rather enigmatic figures, the most sophisticated of the decorations surviving from this house, looking forward to the Third and Fourth styles at no great remove. Moreover, there is no plumbing here, nor are there any clearly identifiable heating arrangements, so it did not continue in use as a bath. Nor is there clear architectural sequence. If these were not a suite of little sitting rooms, they seem likely to have been heated rooms with bathlike architectural form to conserve the heat. The true bathroom of the house is the little mosaic-paved caldarium at the southwest corner, of which only the pavement, with its typical subject of fish and swimmers, and the heating chamber underneath survive; fortunately, this is so close to the mosaics of the baths of the Casa del Menandro across the street as to leave no doubt about its purpose and its date (*NSc* 1933, 269–71).

The Casa del Fauno

While a few examples of Second Style decoration show that there were real changes in architecture in the development of the Second Style, most of our remains of the style come from the redecoration of a room or two in an older house or survive as a room in a house later extensively rebuilt after the earthquake. Thus, in the Casa del Fauno (VI xii 2/5) the rooms at the southeast corner of the second peristyle were now rebuilt as a suite of banquet hall and ladies' dining room in the new style. The big triclinium was stripped for redecoration in

FIGURE 26.
The Casa del Criptoportico, Southeast Triclinium, Detail of the Painted Decoration and the Stuccoed Vault

the last period, but its proportions as a long rectangle, its opening its full width to the peristyle, and its communication with the ladies' dining room next to it are still clear. The ladies' dining room still preserves ghosts of its Second Style painting, the plaster laid over a base of pan tiles to protect it from the damp. Except for repairs in the fauces and the Tuscanic atrium and in a cubiculum off the Tuscanic atrium, this is the only Second Style decoration in this house (Mau 1882, 263–64).

12 · THE VILLAS

Introduction

No villas of the First Style have been found in the vicinity of Pompeii, which is hardly surprising when one remembers that the seas were infested with pirates as late as the time of Cicero, and what villas there were along the coast had to be prepared to defend themselves against armed attack. The earliest villas we have in the neighborhood of Pompeii are the Villa dei Misteri and the Villa of Fannius Synistor at Boscoreale, to which we can now add the Villa di Oplontis at Torre dell'Annunziata. None of these is older than the Second Style.

The Villa dei Misteri

The original structure of the Villa dei Misteri was believed by Maiuri, who excavated it, to go back to the Samnite period of Pompeii,[1] but his reasons for this are not valid, and the plan he produced of the original building is quite preposterous, based in great part on the big symmetrical doors that line the atrium, which even a cursory examination will show to have been purely ornamental and part of the Second Style decoration. The openness of the architecture, the use of a cryptoporticus to support the sea front of the house, the orders of the peristyle and the second-storey loggia, the character of the dining rooms, all show that this villa is not older than the middle of the first century B.C. and must be contemporary with the brilliant sequence of Second Style decorations that adorn its staterooms.

It was entered from the east through a triangular courtyard prob-

[1] Maiuri 1931, 37–40, 99–101. Pernice (1938, 55–58) very correctly observed that the building is remarkably homogeneous and, except for minor alterations and additions that are easy to identify, is a post-Sullan construction with walls faced with opus incertum approaching reticulatum, relieving arches over lintels, and Second Style pavements that go with the Second Style decorations. The essential character of the villa was preserved with remarkably little change down to the earthquake of 62.

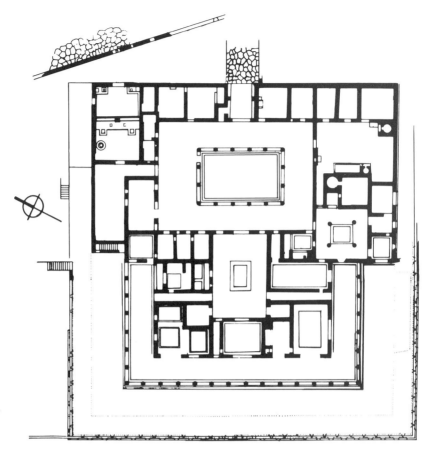

FIGURE 27.
The Villa dei Misteri,
Plan of the Original
Building

ably originally developed as a farmyard surrounded by utilitarian sheds and outhouses, since the main block of the building had no provision for carts or animals. The main entrance to the villa proper is a broad, vaulted tunnel provided with masonry benches along the sides, outside and in, a rather uninviting approach that may have been made more attractive by a Doric loggia or loggias in the second storey (Maiuri 1931, 41–42, 71–72, 89–101). Numerous elements of such a loggia very close to the order of the peristyle in its style lie in the peristyle and areas to the south and east of this. Presumably this was dismantled at the time the new farm buildings were constructed around the entrance court after the earthquake, the pieces reserved for a use elsewhere, to which they were never put. Since, given the conspicuous absence of stairs, such a loggia can hardly have been built over any of the western parts of the house, we must find a place for it around the peristyle, and a location over the eastern wing seems most likely (Spinazzola 1953, 1.83–92, 120–21, 372–73, and pls. 50, 51, 60, and 79).

Through the entrance tunnel one passed a cell for the ostiarius and came out in the peristyle, its colonnade a broad rectangle, six columns by four, set at right angles to the axis of the entrance and the atrium, which is continuous. The peristyle order is a form of Doric, but it has been given a broad, flattened torus base and fillets between flutes, and the capital is schematic, with a deep, scalloped necking ring. The whole effect is fussy and odd and is increased by the entablature in wood and masonry, ornamentally stuccoed in panels with molded borders. A high pluteus has been run between the columns around the whole peristyle, so that the view of the atrium from the entrance, once free and important, is now interrupted. This was done early enough to be given a Second Style decoration, presumably a modification introduced to increase the division between the working and the living quarters (Maiuri 1931, 66–71). The eastern half of the peristyle was given over to the workrooms, the wine press at the northeast corner probably having been rebuilt in its original location. The portico of the peristyle is perceptibly broader on this side and was certainly always so, and the economy of the villa was almost certainly always based on wine. While one might wish to include a press, with its complicated machinery and channels and pits in need of constant cleaning and attention, under the main roof, one had also to have immediate access to a courtyard full of dolia for the process of fermentation. This was evidently just to the north in an area only the edge of which has been excavated (Maiuri 1931, 92–99).

On the opposite side of the peristyle from the wine press was the kitchen, a large courtyard paved with herringbone brick with both a bread oven and a smaller pastry oven, as well as a large hearth platform. Clearly food for a large household was prepared here, although there were numerous small kitchens for smaller units (tenant families?) in the rooms off the peristyle. Off the large kitchen are storerooms, and a corridor in the southeast corner leads back to a large latrine at the east corner of the house, also accessible from the farmyard at the entrance (Maiuri 1931, 77–82, plan p. 356). Between the kitchen and the living rooms is a small bath suite (42–44) so arranged that the fire could be stoked from the kitchen (Maiuri 1931, 61–66). The proportions of the bath seem very small; the rooms could not have been used by more than a small number of bathers at a time. The hot room is a tiny circular laconicum with a bell-shaped ceiling with space for only one or two occupants. This bath opens off a pretty little square peristyle of four columns that may have doubled as a frigidarium. Off it also open some nicely paved rooms with windows looking south that might have been bedrooms (45–47). Three more bedrooms decorated in simple Second Style decoration are lined up along the north end of the west portico of the large peristyle (19–21). Except for one beautiful bedroom on the atrium (3), these are the only bedrooms in the nobler part of the house.

The atrium opens directly onto the peristyle in the sequence prescribed by Vitruvius for country houses (Vitruvius 6.5.3; Maiuri 1931, 42–46). There are three doors, a great central one flanked by a pair of smaller side doors. The atrium is very large, Tuscanic, but without either tablinum or alae, though perhaps there was once a tablinum (Pernice 1938, 56; Maiuri 1931, 52–53). This, if it followed the lines of the room that replaced it, as it must have, was very broad in proportion to its depth. In the time of the Third Style the door to the atrium was walled up, and the room thus created was repaved and redecorated with a dramatic black-ground painting with very delicate and elegant details. Its use in this period becomes enigmatic, and it may be significant that after the earthquake the owners seem to have intended yet another remodeling.

Down either side of the atrium stood a line of four great double doors, after the fashion of First Style atria, and there were at least doors responding to the side doors to the peristyle at the opposite end, but most of these doors were not functional, being there simply for symmetry. Some of them functioned in part, a small door being cut in the larger, but only three seem ever to have been what they appeared. Thus the atrium was not the lobby it appeared to be and was in other houses. Instead it had become a room in its own right, and communication among rooms was largely by means of a portico that ran around three sides of the house at this end and afforded a magnificent view of the sea (Maiuri 1931, 46–52). Since the ground is falling away in this direction, the house had to be terraced, and to support the terracing there is a cryptoporticus faced on the outside with essentially blind arches; this was accessible but was not used or decorated (Maiuri 1931, 86–89). Since the outer face of this cryptoporticus lies nearly five meters out from the house proper, we must presume that it was designed from the beginning to carry a parterre garden, an effect a later version of which we see in the sea-front houses of Herculaneum. One could thus walk among the beds and along the parapet to enjoy the view or savor it from the shelter of the portico. The portico had simple Doric columns, Sarno limestone cores rendered in stucco, but the pavement is very handsome Second Style (Pernice 1938, 55).

Off the atrium open corridors to each wing of the portico, an undecorated storeroom (18), and two decorated rooms; off the southwest corner of the atrium a cubiculum (3) handsomely decorated in monochrome, yellow and green (Maiuri 1931, 54–55); off the northwest corner a small square room (15) with simple architectural decoration in polychrome with dark red orthostats (Maiuri 1931, 60). This seems most likely to have been a winter dining room, the only such room in the house, and may be evidence that the house was not intended to be much used in winter. The other rooms in this part of the house are all dining rooms, arranged in three pairs, a men's dining room next to a ladies' dining room. The men's dining rooms vary in shape, perhaps in consideration of the exposure; the ladies' dining rooms are all similar to one another. The simplest men's dining room (6) is a long rectangle, the shape that becomes increasingly popular in this period, with an architectural decoration with black, dark yellow, and porphyry orthostats. To go with it was a ladies' dining room off the peristyle of the bath (Maiuri 1931, 58, 73). This had two niches for settees at right angles to one another, a square cupboard for tableware filling the angle between them. Once again the decoration is architectural, rather heavy and severe. The connection between the two has been obscured somewhat by remodeling, but the blocked door in the east wall of the men's triclinium is clear. The second pair is made up of the famous room of the Dionysiac frieze (5) and its companion (Maiuri 1931, 54–58). This room, occupying the southwest corner of the house, enjoyed a view in two directions, and the south and west walls were opened up to take maximum advantage of this. The megalographic decorations of life-size figures against a ground of cinnabar orthostats has sometimes been thought to represent a Dionysiac liturgy, but without sufficient grounds; the appropriateness of Dionysiac figures and scenes to a banquet hall is self-evident. The ladies' dining room that adjoins this is similarly decorated at a reduced scale. Again there are places for two couches at right angles and a cupboard for tableware. The most sumptuous of these suites was that at the northwest corner, an L-shaped banquet hall cut up into four small rooms in a remodeling in the Third Style (Maiuri 1931, 59–60). Originally two full triclinia must have been set up there in the ells, with a square space between them for service and entertainment, but the obvious awkwardness of this arrangement must have been responsible for its remodeling. The original decorations, of which only a few fragments survive, were extraordinarily fine. The companion room (16) (Maiuri 1931, 60–61) still preserves its decoration, perhaps the most famous of all architectural decorations in the Second Style, highly plastic in its perspectives in the niches for the couches, with arcuated colonnades, syzygia thrust forward behind open façades, and a wealth of interesting architectural moldings, brackets, and figured capitals. This faced onto the north portico behind a shallow vestibule that seems likely to have served as a stage for performers, though probably we should not think of anything more than musicians during the meal.

In its heyday this was a house where the owner spent comparatively little time; probably he came mainly for the vintage. It is a house in which to entertain, but it is not one designed for house parties. In the course of time modifications were introduced, diaetae (9, 10) built into the corners of the seaward portico and a new long colonnade built along the south side (Maiuri 1931, 48.59, 82–85). The experimental banquet hall was broken up to make more usable rooms (11–14), probably bedrooms, and the tablinum was rebuilt, enclosed, and redecorated, apparently as a sitting room. New doors were cut in various places, and others blocked, and it seems that in the last period of the city the owners had in mind a complete overhaul of the house, construction of an elaborate belvedere in the middle of the sea front and general remodeling (Maiuri 1931, 53–54). They had got as far as refurbishing the utilitarian parts when the eruption occurred. But it is a mistake to say, as Maiuri did (1931, 100), that the villa had fallen on evil days and was converted to purely agricultural uses; the existence at the time of the eruption of two rooms on the atrium that had been filled with furniture, and their doors walled up, in the owners' absence shows that even in the last period the house belonged to people of wealth and taste. The furniture was worth their digging a well down after the disaster in order to salvage it.

One last question that one should raise in a discussion of the Villa dei Misteri is that of water supply. Although there was abundant roof surface from the beginning, there seems never to have been any effort to conserve rain water. The impluvium was stripped of its revetment in antiquity, but there is no sign of a cistern anywhere here. Water from the exterior portico on the north was channeled from its gutter through to the peristyle, as breaks in the pavement show, and that from the peristyle was piped through the kitchen. Nowhere here do we find a cistern. Nor is there any evidence of a connection with the municipal aqueduct; there is no pipe or fountain in this house. We must conclude that there was an abundant spring nearby and that the household was in no way dependent on rain or the public water.

The Villa of Fannius Synistor at Boscoreale

In 1900 on the outskirts of Boscoreale, northwest of Pompeii, a large villa with elegant architecture and a bank of staterooms all painted in fine Second Style was discovered. It is now generally known as the Villa of Fannius Synistor, although the identity of the owner has been disputed. The walls had masonry faced at least in places with opus reticulatum, and the paintings are consistent in style and quality, so it seems likely that we are dealing with a villa of a single build in the period of the second triumvirate in which there was little subsequent

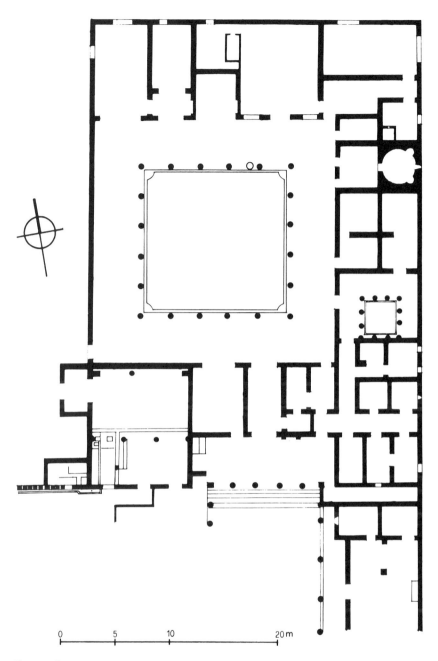

0   5   10   20 m

FIGURE 28.
The Villa of Fannius Synistor at Boscoreale, Plan

alteration. Moreover, the architecture is extremely orderly and shows planning of a highly professional sort. Since the paintings were removed and the villa itself was reinterred, it cannot be examined firsthand, and for an account of it we must rely on the report of F. Barnabei made to the minister of public education on behalf of the commission of investigation with regard to permission for exportation of some, or all, of the paintings salvaged.[2] Fortunately, Barnabei was a skilled archaeologist and an astute observer.

The villa was not completely excavated, but it appears that the unexcavated parts were principally farmyards and outbuildings, while the residential area was completely explored. It consists of a square peristyle with banks of rooms along three sides, an entrance wing to the south made up of living rooms, workrooms, and storerooms, a suite of noble rooms to the north, and a bath complex and storerooms to the east.

One entered through a deep porch of four columns between square pillars at the top of a flight of five steps in lava blocks. Other colonnades led south from this, apparently communicating with outbuildings. To the east are kitchens with a bakery, while to the west is the torcularium with places for two wine presses and a channel leading west to carry the juice to the fermentation yard. Evidently the villa's economy was based on wine. The porch was painted with a Second Style decoration, and a lararium filled the northwest corner. From the porch one passed by an andron on axis with it, also painted in Second Style, to the square peristyle with six columns on each side, surrounded by deep porticoes. The peristyle was not on axis with the andron; one came into it near the southeast corner and had the principal living rooms then opposite. The peristyle itself was richly decorated and provided with fountains, clearly a pleasure garden. The ceilings of the porticoes were coffered, and the richly carved architrave was gilded. Once one had arrived in the peristyle, there was no direct connection with the working parts of the villa. All the rooms were for the use of the owner's family.

Just west of the entrance andron was a decorated room with a wide door to the peristyle the purpose of which is uncertain. Off the east portico lies a small peristyle with porticoes of four columns on a side (except for the south, where the order is engaged) between a bath suite and a group of storerooms and offices, including the latrine. The peristyle gives access to both. The bath is extraordinarily complete, including a circular frigidarium as well as two hot rooms raised on

---

[2]F. Barnabei, *La villa pompeiana di P. Fannio Sinistore* (Rome 1901); see also P. W. Lehmann, *Roman Wall Paintings from Boscoreale in the Metropolitan Museum of Art* (Cambridge, Mass., 1953) 1–22 and passim.

suspensurae, but there is no mention of any decoration in this part of the villa.

The bank of decorated rooms along the north side of the peristyle is reminiscent of the similar bank in the Casa del Labirinto. Beginning from the west, it is made up of a triclinium of long rectangular shape and a ladies' dining room—now reconstructed as a bedroom in the Metropolitan Museum of Art—which connected with the triclinium through a little lobby. The triclinium was decorated with vistas of columnar architecture, while the ladies' dining room had tholoi and landscapes in the couch alcove and cityscapes in the rest of the room. Next came an exedra on the axis of the peristyle that once connected with the rooms on either side by doors that were later walled up, and then a large square banquet hall with a door flanked by symmetrical windows to the peristyle but no window to the exterior. This was decorated with life-size figures against panels of cinnabar, a megalography reminiscent of the great triclinium of the Villa dei Misteri. What figures remain have been divided between the Museo Nazionale in Naples and the Metropolitan Museum of Art. The original appearance of the room was reconstructed carefully by Andreae.[3]

Out of the northwest corner of this great room a short passage led past a closet to a handsomely decorated little room with a window. P. W. Lehmann would see this as "a kind of sacristy or green room" for what she calls "the hall of Aphrodite" next-door.[4] One can agree that the closet was probably for furniture and implements, but what the small room really reminds one of is the little decorated rooms off the Corinthian oecus in the Casa del Labirinto. It served some important function in connection with the entertainments given there, but it is difficult to say what that function was.

The remaining rooms in this series are a triclinium with a scaenae frons decoration including important doorways and masks, one wall of which is preserved in the Museo Nazionale in Naples, and a small but elegant cubiculum.

The pavement of the peristyle was of signinum with a band of white mosaic edged with black along the walls and panels of white mosaic decorated with a maeander pattern in the intercolumniations. The pavements of the finer rooms were of white mosaic with black stripes and panels with black-and-white geometrical patterns touched with color. These all appear to have been Second Style in character.

The Villa of Fannius Synistor thus appears to be a rare and precious document of Second Style architecture and decoration. The

[3] See Andreae and Kyrieleis 71–92.
[4] Lehmann (supra n. 2) 77.

square peristyle with deep porticoes, the small but elaborate bath complex with its own peristyle, the tightly organized bank of rooms for entertainment, which includes a variety of shapes and sizes as well as a broad range of types of decoration, all seem to be characteristic of this period. And it is especially interesting that so many of these rooms have large windows to the exterior and accommodated the painted decoration to the inclusion of these. Clearly the view was always a consideration, and people felt quite safe in country houses remote from the city at the time it was built and decorated. In contrast to the Villa dei Misteri, where the staterooms turn to a view of the bay, the focus of the staterooms here is the peristyle and its garden, where a planned vista could be arranged. But at the same time the rooms are also given windows to make the architecture as light and airy as possible, to provide glimpses of the slopes of Vesuvius and a sense of the Campanian countryside.

The Villa di Oplontis at Torre dell'Annunziata

The remarkable building recently discovered near the hospital of Torre dell'Annunziata and now widely known as the Villa di Oplontis[5] deserves some mention, even if whatever is said must be tentative. Circumstances have not permitted the excavation of the south (sea) and west fronts of this extraordinary complex. While there are indications that very little of the south front still remains unknown, the west front may be very distant indeed. The building is very extensive, even as known, with additions, sometimes also extensive, at various points in time. At the time of the eruption it was undergoing massive rebuilding and redecoration, including the addition of an enormous summer banquet hall on the axis of the Second Style atrium, a room for which the only good parallel in scale is the garden banquet hall in the Casa dei Cervi at Herculaneum. And its purpose remains in question, for it was certainly not a villa in the ordinary sense of the term, being focused neither on agriculture nor on the exposure to the sea. It included a vast pool surrounded by gardens and porticoes on which front elegant little pavilions that are virtually independent units but connected to one another and the rest by colonnades and corridors; a very large service quarter forming in effect a separate wing around its own peristyle; seemingly endless walks, some in the gardens under trees or framed by hedges, others in colonnades looking toward the sea or toward Vesuvius, and one entirely enclosed, a viewless crytoporticus at ground level. One feels that dozens of people must have strolled constantly here, perhaps on

[5]See Andreae and Kyrieleis, 9–38 (A. De Franciscis); and Jashemski 291–314.

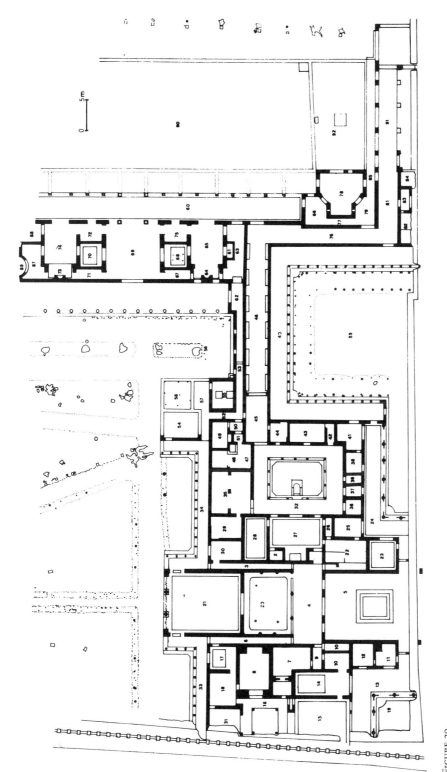

FIGURE 29.
The Villa di Oplontis, Plan of the Final Phase, as Known

orders from their doctor, for there is something of the air of a spa or sanatorium about the place. But if so, where did they sleep and take their meals? There seems to be no provision here for their living. Can we think of this as the central block of a sanatorium/hotel in which separate buildings scattered off among the gardens afforded privacy and independence, while entertainment and treatment were brought together under a common roof?

Be that as it may, all that concerns us at this point is a group of rooms centering around a large Tuscanic atrium decorated with a fine late Second Style decoration. These are all decorated in a consistent style and show every sign of being the remains of a fine villa. The atrium had three doors at its landward (north) end, like those of the atrium of the Villa dei Misteri, but then none along the sides to a point beyond the impluvium where symmetrical doors to either side gave out through short corridors onto symmetrical colonnaded porticoes of which only limited portions have been uncovered. It may be that these porticoes ran around the seaward end of the atrium and joined one another; all the columns are painted uniformly with a Second Style scale pattern. Or there may have been rooms south of the atrium that opened both to the atrium and to the sea. The scaenae frons decoration in the atrium takes the place of the more realistic architectural setting we see in the atrium of the Villa dei Misteri; there is a certain gaiety and playfulness about it. The impluvium is framed with a maeander border in colored mosaic with a strong effect of plasticity, excellent Second Style work. East of the atrium the only Second Style room still preserved is a small square one next to the atrium opening to the colonnade (23), but the colonnade itself is Second Style, and the room at its east end (41) has all the earmarks of a ladies' dining room of the type with places for two couches at right angles that we see in the Villa dei Misteri. Presumably once there were several Second Style rooms along here.

West of the atrium the Second Style rooms are more numerous. Balancing the square room on the east (23) is a ladies' dining room with places for two couches at right angles (11). The decoration is restrained in its development of vista but lively in color. The couch alcoves have low segmental vaults framed with rather heavy moldings, including dentillation, left white but with richly colored painted coffering. This opens both south, parallel to the axis of the atrium, and west on the colonnade, as does 23, presumably to provide a view for each of the couches. Off the west arm of the colonnade, which now turns at a right angle, are two more Second Style dining rooms, one (14) a long rectangular triclinium with places for couches and entertainment carefully marked out in its mosaic pavement, the other (15) a banquet hall of impressive dimensions open both to the colonnade in front of it and to a small water garden behind that is on axis with it and the same in width, so we are probably justified in seeing the two as created as a suite. Both the triclinium and the banquet hall are decorated with very complex architectural vistas in which trompe l'oeil effects are introduced. The water garden is square with a portico with a light roof supported on slender columns at the corners around it. The centre is filled by a deep square tank enclosing a large shallow circular trough in two rings with a jet of water at the centre. It is all built of masonry given a very heavy coat of unpainted stucco; presumbly the trough was for potted water plants. The whole arrangement is very unusual, and the tank may be a comparatively late modification, but the garden is probably part of the original architecture.

There is not a great deal to go on here, but it is enough to show that in the time of the late Second Style a new concept was coming into villa architecture, the porticus villa with reception rooms ranged in lines behind colonnades to take advantage of the view. We see such villas in landscape paintings. Here it is possible that there was originally a peristyle north of the atrium and that the original villa did not differ greatly from the Villa dei Misteri in plan and development. Judgment on that will have to wait for the complete publication of the complex and study of the masonry and footings. But as things stand at present, it certainly looks as though we are dealing with a significant innovation. If the water garden should turn out to be part of the original building, we should want to date it quite late, 30–20 B.C. at the earliest and perhaps 20–10 B.C.

13 · THE TOMBS

Altar Tombs

The oldest monumental tomb still surviving in Pompeii seems to be that of M. Porcius, number 3 on the south side of the Via dei Sepolcri (Kockel 53–57).[1] It was a fairly imposing affair, a large altar tomb constructed of blocks of tufa with decorative parts in white limestone. Not much of it survives, the main die of the tomb being reduced to a block of the base molding, but pieces of a small Doric frieze decorated with boucrania, paterae, and rosettes, of the crown molding, and of the pulvini decorated with scale pattern lie in front of it. The inscription on two lava cippi with crowded letters in a republican alphabet (*CIL* 10.977) informs us that the burial plot was granted by decree of the decuriones, which makes it all but certain that this is the tomb of the magistrate responsible for the Theatrum Minus and the amphitheatre and should be dated about the middle of the first century B.C. The small-scale Doric frieze is popular in Sullan and post-Sullan architecture.

Aedicula Tombs

The second oldest tomb on the Via dei Sepolcri seems to be the Tomba delle Ghirlande, number 6 on the north side of the street (Kockel 126–51). This probably fell outside the pomerial zone and was a work of entirely private enterprise, not very large but very handsome. Above a high foundation the square die of the tomb steps back above a base molding. It is trimmed with an unfluted Corinthian pilaster at each corner and in the middle of each side and two in front. Between the capitals on the sides are swung narrow garlands wound with ribbons

---

[1] There are no monumental tombs in Pompeii of the Samnite period or earlier. Eschebach's wish to see in a little cellar under the Thermae Stabianae an Etruscan chamber tomb is certainly mistaken and widely recognized as such.

with fringed ends. In front these were replaced with a large inscription, or possibly three inscriptions, to judge from the shape of the cutting, presumably on marble, sunk into the face. It is now missing.

Above this Kockel posits a Doric frieze and cornice of which nothing survives. Blocks of an epistyle with an architrave in two fasciae and a frieze decorated with stylized vine scrolls, acanthus leaves, rosettes, and bunches of grapes lie along the street in front of it, for the most part of tufa but one, evidently from the main façade, of marble, set up on a pair of Attic bases of marble. There are also blocks with Corinthian pilasters seen from the bolster end and roofing blocks with coffered soffits decorated with rosettes in lozenge-shaped frames. These are edged with a cornice of which the most conspicuous element is a line of dentils. Kockel would therefore restore this as an aedicula, the rear half an enclosed niche, the front open, supported on two columns with unfluted shafts of breccia corallina and two "chimaera" capitals known to have come from the Via dei Sepolcri but now reused in the forum entrance to the macellum. The last are of Pentelic marble and are judged closest in style to certain figured capitals at Eleusis; they are therefore believed to have been imported especially for use here. The date of the tomb is uncertain; Kockel concludes that it should fall between 90 and 60 B.C. and is inclined to date it after the arrival of the Roman colony. Since so much of the stone here is Luna marble, of which the earliest dated use in Rome is 48 B.C. (Pliny *NH* 36.48), we should incline to a later date. Moreover, the taste of the coffering of the ceiling belongs together with that of the Casa del Criptoportico rather than with that of the Temple of Fortuna Primigenia at Praeneste, and so does the megalographic painting of the back wall, so far as the miserable remains permit judgment. Finally, it seems unthinkable that the heirs of the munificent M. Porcius would have been content to erect so modest a monument to him if so splendid a tomb had already been built for a private individual of no special distinction, so far as we know. We may therefore incline to a date a little after the middle of the first century B.C. The early occurrence of tombs of this form is supported by their occurrence in the Porta di Nocera necropolis. Whether the "chimaera" capitals belong is an open question.

In the Porta di Nocera necropolis are at least half a dozen tombs of apparently republican date, of which three are of the type of the Tomba delle Ghirlande.[2] The first two of these flank the tomb of Eumachia, that to the east, west 9 (9 OS [D'Ambrosio and De Caro]), a

<hr/>

[2] The tombs of the Porta di Nocera necropolis are described in detail by A. D'Ambrosio and S. De Caro in *Un impegno per Pompei; Fotopiano e documentazione della necropoli di Porta Nocera* (Milan 1983). This work is without pagination, but the tombs are set in sequence according to their code numbers.

rectangular aedicula on a high die with two columns of brick finished with stucco and Pompeian Ionic capitals of tufa of late type. The aedicula contains two enthroned statues, evidently man and wife, of very provincial style. The man is togate, but his toga is the toga exigua and does not cover his lower legs. A small tomb chamber in the base was accessible from the back of the tomb. The other tomb, west 13 (13 OS), is a large aedicula with four columns and three shallow rectangular niches but otherwise similar, with high podium and brick columns finished with stucco. Below the base molding of the die are four low, arched niches for tombstones. A marble plate informs us that this is the tomb of M. Octavius and Vertia Philumina. In the niches of the aedicula are three standing statues of tufa, a woman in modified pudicitia pose and a togatus in toga exigua flanking a cuirassed soldier. Seven tombstones are associated with this monument, four feminine and three masculine. Further to the west, tomb west 29 (29 OS) is of the same general type, a single-niche aedicula, and similar construction but with extensive brickwork coigning. The inscription on a circular marble table leaf records that it was built for Annedia and her husband, L. Caesius, the duovir, in recognition of which the inscription was flanked by fasces in stucco. This man seems to have been duovir shortly after the deduction of the Roman colony and was probably responsible for the construction of the Terme del Foro (Thermae Minores)(CIL 10.819). Unfortunately, this tomb was found without statues or other embellishment and badly ruined. Tomb west 27 (27 OS), to the east of this, may have been very similar but now lacks its whole superstructure. Tomb west 1 (1 OS), in a prominent position with respect to the city gate, may also have been very similar; it would have been much the largest of the tombs of this type.

Tombs of Other Architectural Forms

The most remarkable of all the republican tombs at Pompeii is tomb west 3 (3 OS), in the Porta di Nocera necropolis, set well up along the rise of the road leading out from the city gate toward the southeast, where it would have been conspicuous. Above a square base faced with opus incertum of lava originally 1.56 m high, in the north face of which open two arched niches for gravestones, rises a die trimmed at the base and crown with simple moldings. The base was finished with plain white stucco, the die with stucco imitating four courses of drafted ashlar masonry under a plain stringcourse. Above this are the ruins of a tholos, a low drum finished with a single course of ashlar blocks trimmed with moldings at base and crown and a ring of four columns in a semicircle, the ring completed by a curving wall connecting the two outer columns to make a solid background for the statues that stood within the tholos. A Corinthian capital on a base in the shape of a truncated cone at present lying near the street crossing may be part of the finial of a conical roof. The tomb inscription on a plate of marble identifies this as the tomb of L. Ceius Sarapio and his wife Helvia; he was a freedman of L. Ceius and a moneylender (*argentarius*). The use of incertum and stucco instead of tufa may have been a measure of economy rather than an indication of date, and in the absence of capitals and carving one must be hesitant, but Ceius's inscription is in a good classical alphabet. De Caro observes that the terrace wall to the north of this tomb covers the lower part of the tomb wall with its niches for gravestones and must therefore be later than tomb west 3 but earlier than, or contemporary with, tomb west 9. This indicates a republican date for tomb west 3, and this is confirmed to some extent by its relation to tomb west 1, which restricts the view of it.

The architectural form of this tomb is closely related to that of several famous mausolea of the Roman world, all of which are later, notably the great mausoleum of Aquileia and the monument of Iulii at Glanum in southern France.[3] In a larger context one might also adduce the Monument des Alpes at La Turbie and the Mausoleum Augusti in Rome. They are all multistorey buildings that change as they rise, solidity giving way to lightness, simplicity to architectural grace. Ultimately they have their architectural roots in the Hellenistic east, especially the mausolea of Asia Minor at Halicarnassus, Belevi, and Mylasa. But in the Pompeian example we may not be wrong in seeing some influence of such classical buildings as the monument of Lysicrates in Athens.

Tomb west 7 (7 OS) in the Porta di Nocera necropolis is a block of rubble masonry pierced by a low arch framed on the façade with lava jambs and voussoirs. Off the central passage lie roughly symmetrical chambers to either side roofed with a single barrel vault above the roof of the archway, the floors sunk below the floor of the passage. Each chamber is surrounded by three arcosolii for the urns. On the exterior the façade is broken by numerous small arched niches in two zones, that above stepped back from that below. The lower zone has a series of three niches to either side of the central arch, the zone above an unbroken series of eight. Some of the lower series contained tombstones, some of the upper, busts. Inscriptions inform us that the tomb was built by freedmen P. Flavius Philoxenus and Flavia Agathea during their lifetime and that they found their final resting place here

---

[3]G. Brusin and V. De Grassi, *Il mausoleo di Aquileia* (Padua 1956); H. Rolland, *Le Mausolée de Glanum* (*Gallia* supp. 21 [1969]).

after death. The tomb type is a forerunner of the columbarium, a republican version in which busts of the defunct ornamented the façade, and seems to have been popular especially in southern Italy, but this one is unique in Pompeii. That it seems to have been designed for a number of burials but to have been little used until at a late date a series of poor burials was permitted in front of it is interesting.

Tomb west 31 (31 OS) in the Porta di Nocera necropolis is a high podium revetted with blocks and plates of tufa with moldings at base and crown. This is surmounted by a pair of small funerary lions in tufa that crouch symmetrically with one paw on a goat's head. In the base of the podium are three arched niches for tombstones. The inscription carved directly on the revetment informs us that the tomb was built by the freedman M. Stronnius Meinius for his patrons C. Stronnius father and son and for himself and Stronnia Acatarchis, presumably his wife. The alphabet is strongly republican in character, and the tomb should be dated before the middle of the first century B.C. Since the Stronnii belonged not to the tribus Menenia, the tribe of Pompeii, but to the Papiria, their early appearance in Pompeii is interesting; they must have been one of the leading families in early colonial times.

In the late republican period, then, there is evidence for five types of monumental tombs, the aedicula tomb, far the most popular, the altar tomb, the tholos tomb, the arch tomb, and the die tomb, the last three probably serving nearly always as bases for a display of statuary, not necessarily an elaborate one. The simple bustum without architectural embellishment was probably also very widespread, but evidence for it is lacking. The most remarkable of all is the tholos tomb, which, since elsewhere it seems to be an Augustan type, we probably should think of as appearing only in the last years of the republic.

PART IV

Julio-Claudian Buildings, 30 B.C.–A.D. 62

14 · THE PUBLIC BUILDINGS

Buildings on and in the Vicinity of the Forum

The Temple of the Genius Augusti (Templum Vespasiani)

In the Julio-Claudian period there was an almost total rebuilding of
the east side of the forum in a series of monumental edifices to serve
the public interest, the first two, at least, built by public-spirited
priestesses. These replaced a line of shops and converted the forum
square from a hub of commerce that radiated out into the blocks
around it into a civic centre where the emphasis was on religion,
municipal administration, and the amenities of life.

The first in this series was the Temple of the Genius Augusti (VII
ix 2),[1] built by the public priestess Mamia, whose schola tomb in a
plot awarded by the decree of the decuriones is just outside the Porta
di Ercolano. It used to be thought that the tomb was so much older
than the temple that it must belong to another Mamia, but since the
discovery of the tomb of Eumachia outside the Porta di Nocera the
Augustan lettering of the tomb inscription and the architecture of
the temple are now seen to fit together in a perfectly consistent picture.

The temple presents a blank façade to the forum, the temenos wall
being so high that the temple within was completely concealed. This
façade was revetted with marble that was salvaged by the survivors,
and even the pattern of the plates is indistinct, but since in front of
the façade a deep apron of approach interrupts the colonnades along
this side of the forum, its revetment was probably especially rich. The
slightly rhomboid temenos respected the public street along its
southern flank, while the front portion and chalcidicum of the Aedificium Eumachiae ran over it at its western end and turned what had
been a minor entrance to the forum into a blind alley. This is an in-

---

[1] On this temple see Overbeck and Mau 117–19; CIL 10.816; and Maiuri 1973, 88–91.
On the tomb of Mamia see Kockel 57–59.

FIGURE 30.
The Temple of the Genius Augusti, Interior

dication that the temple was the older building, though it need not have been much older.

From the forum one entered through an axial door to a porch running the whole width of the temenos raised a step above the open area beyond. This is very like the porch of the Temple of Jupiter Meilichios, except that here there is no indication of columns. Presumably, therefore, there was a light wooden roof supported on posts. The small square altar stands at the centre of the courtyard to allow a maximum number of worshipers to participate, but the relief on the front showing the sacrifice of a bull marks it clearly as the principal face. On the sides are reliefs showing the implements of major Roman priesthoods—patera, lituus, guttus, mantele, and acerra—and on the back is the *corona ciuica* between two small laurel trees. The sides and back of the temenos are divided by pilasters into shallow bays finished with pediments alternately triangular and segmental.

The temple proper is a small building raised on a head-high podium revetted with white marble accessible from the back by stairs along the flanks of the temple so that the pronaos might serve as a speaker's platform from which to address assemblies in the temenos. This is so common a device in Caesarean and Augustan architecture—one might cite the Temples of Venus Genetrix and the Deified Julius in Rome[2]—that it does not help in dating the construction. The side walls of the little cella projected in antae, and there were pilasters down the sides on the exterior, but there is no sign of columns. Since the whole building was despoiled of almost all its marble veneer inside and out and only the shell remains, one cannot be sure whether there were columns; they would have been so small that there might have been no need for footings. Rather oddly, the rectangular Augustan statue base suggests a seated figure. Behind the temenos, entered by a small and inconspicuous door just south of the temple, is a sacristy built in the last period, three unremarkable rooms in sequence running the width of the temenos.

The identification of the temple is provided by an inscription on a broken block of uncertain provenience, probably an architrave block:

M(AM)IA P. F. SACERDOS PVBLIC. GENI(O AVG S)OLO ET PEC

(*CIL* 10.816)

We know that M. Holconius Rufus was Augusti Caesaris sacerdos (*CIL* 10.830) and flamen Augusti (*CIL* 10.943–46) during his lifetime and that M. Holconius Celer was sacerdos divi Augusti (*CIL* 10.945–46), so we can be sure that the cult of the princeps aroused a lively

---

[2]On the Temple of Venus Genetrix see, e.g., G. Lugli, *Roma antica, il centro monumentale* (Rome 1946) 252; and *MAAR* 13 (1936) 215–20 (O. Grossi). On the Temple of the Deified Julius see Nash 1.93, 512–14.

interest in Pompeii. Whether with the passage of time and change of principes and dynasties the temple was ever rededicated we do not know, but it seems to have been repaired after the earthquake of A.D. 62, which suggests that it may have been rededicated to Nero, a popular favorite in Pompeii whose flamen was D. Lucretius Satrius Valens (*CIL* 4.7992, 7995). In that case it was probably rededicated to the genius of Vespasian after the damnatio memoriae of Nero. While the fabric of the temple had been repaired after the earthquake, only the exterior on the forum and the temple building seem to have had their marble veneer. The rest was covered with roughcast.

The Porticus Eumachiae (Aedificium Eumachiae)

The second building in this series, the Aedificium Eumachiae (VII ix 1),[3] was built by the public priestess Eumachia in her name and that of her son M. Numistrius Fronto, as an inscription in large letters on the architrave along the forum and a smaller copy over the rear entrance from the Via dell'Abbondanza announce (*CIL* 10.810, 812–13). These also tell us that the complex was made up of three parts—a chalcidicum, porticus, and crypta—and was dedicated to Concordia Augusta and Pietas.

The three parts are easy to discern. The chalcidicum is the extraordinarily deep porch on the forum with a Doric colonnade of fine white limestone, sixteen columns on the forum front, and a back wall broken into a series of niches, some rectangular, some bowed, varying in size. All but the northernmost of these must have been for sculpture; the inscription for one of the smaller niches just north of the main entrance was recovered in fragments and proved to be for a statue of Romulus, a duplicate of the inscription used for his statue in the Forum Augustum in Rome. Presumably this was for a reproduction of the Roman statue on a smaller scale. Although the survivors had salvaged all the statuary, as well as the marble veneer that once covered this porch, the façade of IX xiii 5 was decorated with paintings showing, on one side of the door, Romulus bearing the spoils of Acron, and on the other, Aeneas leaving Troy (Spinazzola 1953, 1.150–55), so probably we can with confidence restore Aeneas in the balancing niche to the south. The large niches seem too big for anything less than groups, but here we have simply no evidence. The northernmost was made a speaker's platform at shoulder height in the last period. Opposite these, against the columns of the colonnade, is a row of smaller bases for standing figures, and another marks the middle of the south end. The whole must have amounted to an impressive gallery, and since all the bases against the colonnade

[3]See Overbeck and Mau 131–36; Maiuri 1942, 40–43; *RendNap* n.s. 36 (1961) 5–35 (G. Spano); and Maiuri 1973, 91–99.

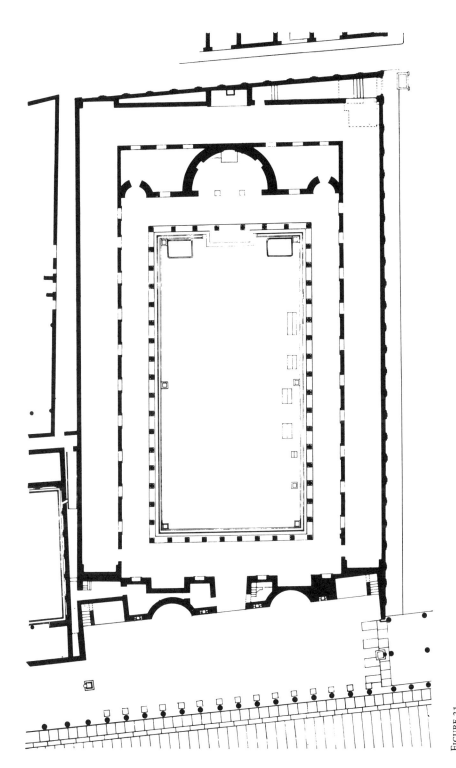

FIGURE 31.
The Aedificium Eumachiae, Plan of the Final Phase

are identical, we must suppose that there was a well-defined program. But whether that entailed balancing distinguished Pompeians
against the legendary heroes of Rome or whether the debt to Augustus's gallery of great men in Rome was even greater we cannot say.
Though the revetment of the façade seems to have been completed
and the statues seem to have been in place there, the columns of the
colonnade had still to be fluted, and the statue bases in front of it
look unfinished. Consequently, we cannot say much about the large
metal gate or fence that closed the colonnade on the south, the cuttings for which are unmistakable. Obviously it would not have kept
people out, nor would it have helped to define the building. Probably
its real function was to prevent people from entering the forum from
the Via dell'Abbondanza, especially men with hand barrows or pack
animals on their way to the macellum, and taking a shortcut through
the chalcidicum rather than going by way of the open area of the
forum. The chalcidicum was a formal, ceremonial space; open as it
might be, it was not to be treated as a thoroughfare.

From the chalcidicum a single large entrance leads to the interior.
This has a marble frame carved with acanthus scrolls peopled with
birds, small animals, and insects, a very pretty relief that owes something to the acanthus scrolls of the Ara Pacis Augustae in Rome. Just
inside this is a cell for a doorkeeper to the south, and a chain of irregular spaces opens to the north, leading eventually to the Vicolo degli
Scheletri. These spaces are carved out of the thickness of the wall, as
it were, which here makes the adjustment between the alignment of
the forum, on which the chalcidicum is laid out, and that of the Via
dell'Abbondanza, to which the rest of the building is squared. They
probably served only for storage.

The main building consisted of a large colonnaded porticus surrounded on three sides by a cryptoporticus. Both were found
stripped of plaster and veneer, simply the shell of the building that
was to be, with vats of lime where the masons were mixing mortar
scattered here and there, some seven of them. The building had been
badly hit in the earthquake and was being rebuilt, in large part from
the very foundations. Maiuri's explorations under the floor showed
that a central rectangular niche at the far end was now replaced by a
semicircular one, and similar minor modifications were introduced
here and there. But the architectural program for the building is clear:
it was to be a single-storey porticus raised on two steps above the
rectangular courtyard that it framed, with special emphasis at the far
end, where a large semicircular niche is flanked by smaller ones, and
secondary emphasis at the entrance, which is flanked by large rectangular niches. The central niche at the end seems to have been for a
major statue on a projecting base framed by shallow niches, flanked

by smaller ones, and fragments of a statuette less than life-size that carried a cornucopia and would fit the Concordia type were found in the excavation (*PAH* 2, pt. 4, 19 [17 March 1820]). If Concordia and Pietas were only supporting figures for the statue that stood on the central base, the central figure may have been Livia, who dedicated her porticus at Rome to Concordia Augusta as part of the celebration of the triumph of her son Tiberius in 7 B.C.[4]

Behind the porticus the cryptae must have been especially for use in bad weather. These open by big rectangular windows to the porticus and are as wide as the porticus. Off the east wing of the cryptoporticus, in line with the main apse of the porticus, is a deep rectangular niche in which stood a statue purporting to be Eumachia herself, erected in her honor by the fullers of Pompeii. It is a Hellenistic female type, not a true portrait. South of this a corridor, in part ramped, in part stepped, leads to an ample rear entrance from the Via dell'Abbondanza, where a marble fountain bears a relief of Concordia on its standard. A large vaulted room beside this rear entrance seems almost too big for a doorkeeper but can hardly have been for anything else. The exterior walls on the sides and back are finished in shallow relief with pilasters and bays crowned with pediments, alternately triangular and segmental, identical with those lining the temenos of the temple of the Genius Augusti immediately to the north.

The building is rather wasteful in its planning. To accommodate niches of curved plan and to regularize angles where the city blocks are not true rectangles, dead space and light wells are included, and for reasons that are far from clear, there was access to the cryptoporticus only at the west end or through the rear entrance, though the windows lighting it made one constantly aware of its presence. The religious import of the dedication to Concordia Augusta and Pietas seems to have been more token than real, since any worship was confined to a niche that gave visual focus to the building without being obtrusive.

The building had a complicated history. It must have been built after 7 B.C., when the porticus of Livia in Rome was dedicated to Concordia Augusta as part of the triumph of Tiberius, and after 2 B.C., when the Forum Augustum, with its gallery of the triumphatores and summi viri, was opened. And it was built by a priestess and dedicated in her name and that of her son, and not that of her husband, who was duovir in A.D. 2/3 (*CIL* 10.892; Castrén 197–99), so presumably it must be dated after that. The porticus suffered heav-

[4]See L. Richardson, Jr., "Concordia and Concordia Augusta: Rome and Pompeii," *PP* 33 (1978) 260–72.

ily in the earthquake, and it was decided to gut the interior and rebuild almost from the ground up, but the exterior wall, with its shallow bays and typically Augustan masonry with coigning in small blocks of tufa and limestone, was kept and repaired. The rest was leveled, and a new building in rubble masonry with coigns of brickwork and finish in marble veneer took its place. For the most part the plan was not altered, except that the central niche containing the statue of Concordia was made semicircular. But the gutting of the building in preparation for rebuilding, the removal or salvage of most columns and all entablature elements, and the deliberate lack of haste in the reconstruction, with completion of the porch on the forum, where it would need to be weighed in relation to other façades in the development of a new monumental square before the interior was more than a skeleton, all suggest that no expense was to be spared and the materials were to be the finest obtainable.

This was the principal porticus of Pompeii and must have served many purposes. The dedication of a statue to Eumachia by the fullers suggests that cloth fairs were held here. Probably fairs of leatherworking, cabinetmaking, metalworking, and a number of other trades in portable goods were held here, for the building lent itself to these. But most of the time it was a place to walk and talk, to meet one's friends and stroll. The popularity of porticus in Rome goes back to the early second century B.C. but received fresh stimulus in the Augustan period, when Agrippa's Saepta Iulia and the porticus of Octavia, of Philip, and of Livia vied with that of Augustus around the Temple of Apollo on the Palatine. These were all remarkably splendid buildings, and the porticus of Eumachia was unquestionably built in imitation of these, a Pompeian priestess's attempt to bring some of the amenities of the new capital to her own town. Several of the porticus of Rome came to house markets of one sort or another, for example, the market in luxuries in the Saepta and the market in hair goods in the porticus of Philip. It may be that the porticus of Eumachia did too, but if so, we do not know what it was and have no way of telling; it would have had to move somewhere else in the last period of the city.

The Macellum

The third building in this sequence was the macellum (VII ix 7/8), formerly called the Pantheon, the central food market of Pompeii.[5] There must have been other markets, small street markets at strategic points, possibly one in the broad avenue north of the Palestra Grande

---

[5]On the macellum see Overbeck and Mau 120–28; Maiuri 1942, 54–61; and Maiuri 1973, 75–88.

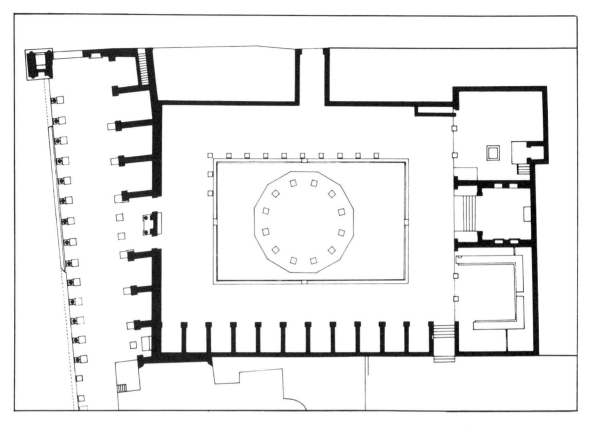

FIGURE 32.
The Macellum, Plan of
the Final Phase

in regio II, possibly another in the little square just inside the Porta del Vesuvio, places where it would be easy to bring in produce and where a neighborhood could be provisioned conveniently. There must have been shops selling particular sorts of foodstuffs—fruit sellers, poulterers, oil merchants, and many others—here and there all over town. And many foodstuffs must have been hawked in the streets by itinerant peddlars, as they still are in southern Italy. But the central market, the place where presumably one could find everything available, was the macellum. Here there were large shops lining both interior and exterior, presumably rented out for fixed periods; a broad rectangular porticus where barrows could be set up; and special provisions for fishmongers and butchers. In all there were about thirty shops for large-scale dealers and place for twice as many small-scale ones.

The date of the building is a mystery. The façade on the forum, with its relieving arches of voussoirs of tufa over fillings of masonry faced with reticulate of yellow tufa, must be postearthquake, as must the Fourth Style decorations in the interior. So also, one would think, must be the Corinthian colonnade in white marble along the forum and the figured capital including an eagle from the aedicula in the main doorway. But there is much to show that the building is a good bit older. A bronze coin, badly worn by use, extracted from the masonry of the wall along the entrance from the Via degli Augustali proved on cleaning to be of late Tiberian date, and a date for the original construction under Gaius or in the first years of Claudius is acceptable.

The macellum is located at the northeast corner of the forum. Originally it had fronts on two streets leading into the forum, as well as the main façade on the forum itself. Later the little street on the south was truncated in the construction of the large building VII ix 3, though an entrance to the macellum from it was maintained, perhaps especially for the convenience of butchers, who could bring their meat in here, rather than for the public. The façade on the forum was monumental, a colonnade of sixteen white marble Corinthian(?) columns with rows of statue bases against them and against the wall opposite, making a gallery. Unfortunately, we do not have any idea who may have been so honored. The column shafts are handsomely carved, very classical, reeded to one-third their height above Attic bases. The capitals are modern, of stucco. A second storey seems to have been an open gallery with an ornamental base over each column; at least this is how it has been restored. The remaining base is decorated with reliefs. The main door to the interior is axial, recessed, divided by an aedicula with figured capitals. This has been wrongly restored at present with capitals belonging to a tomb, the proper capital decorated with the figure of an eagle being in the marble deposit on the opposite side of the forum.[6]

It seems almost unthinkable that a row of shops dealing in fruit and vegetables could have opened on so fine a gallery, so perhaps one should think of these rather as offices, or perhaps the shops of dealers in spices and foodstuffs less untidy than cabbages and game. If the identification of the Via Biberatica in the Mercati di Traiano in Rome as a spice market is correct, Pompeii would have required at least a small area devoted especially to spices.

The interior of the macellum is a spacious rectangular court with a large central tholos. At its far end (east) opened three big subsidiary halls, and along the south side opened a row of eleven shops of uniform plan. There must have been a deep porticus around all four sides supported on wooden posts, presumably a temporary structure that the Pompeians intended to replace with something more permanent at a later date. Only the gutter that caught the drip from the

---

[6]See Mercklin 228, no. 556, and 248, no. 602; and Kockel 126–51, esp. 127.

eaves remains to indicate its line. The west (entrance) and north walls, at least, were covered with a fine painted Fourth Style decoration that made allusion to the purpose of the building by the introduction of huge still lifes of foodstuffs, quite out of scale and character with the rest of the scheme, in the upper zone.

The purpose of the tholos was proved by the discovery of quantities of fish scales in the drains leading from it: this was the fish market. It consisted of a ring of twelve wooden posts, or columns, raised on individual masonry plinths, that carried a light roof, probably conical. This building almost fills the width of the courtyard and is raised a low step above it. Since the drains and the scales in them indicate that the fish were cleaned here, one presumes that they were bought live, and there must have been a source, or multiple sources, of running water, but all trace of such has disappeared today.

Of the three halls that open at the east end of the macellum court only the southernmost was devoted to commercial use; it was the meat market. One entered by a wide doorway divided into bays by two columns. The central area was framed by a counter revetted with broken marble on which the meat was displayed and behind which ran a narrow aisle for the merchants. There are passageways through the counter but no sign of a source of water.

The axial centre hall was some sort of shrine, a raised cella approached by a flight of five steps. In the interior are two large rectangular niches in each side wall and a statue base at the centre of the rear wall. A male and a female statue found here were assigned to the niches on one side and were early identified as Marcellus and Octavia, identifications for which there is no justification. The male is youthful and heroic, half-nude, his garment kilted about his hips. The female is also youthful, fully draped and with her head veiled, her hair done in ringlets framing the face, an Augustan style. One's feeling is that these are members of the Julio-Claudian house, but it is impossible to say which members. There is no altar in evidence anywhere; therefore it may be that this was not a cult centre, but simply a hall decorated with honorific statues where the various guilds of tradesmen whose activities centred around the macellum could meet, the fruit and vegetable dealers, the *pomarii, lupinarii,* and *aliarii* of whom we read in the electoral programmata of Pompeii (*CIL* 4.149, 180, 183, 202, 206, 3423, 3485), and others.

The northernmost of these halls was an unroofed court entered by a broad doorway divided by two columns balancing that to the meat market on the south. This court, a slightly irregular rectangle, contained a small templelike shrine facing the door but somewhat off axis to the south. On the axis of this shrine is a square altar, large in proportion to the shrine. Clearly this was a cult centre closely connected with the activities of the macellum; one thinks of Pomona, Flora, and half a dozen other suitable divinities.

Off the middle of the north portico opens a broad secondary entrance, probably at least as much used as the forum entrance, for it gives onto the Via degli Augustali, a street lined on both sides with shops and workshops, many of them with small houses attached, one of the main shopping streets of Pompeii. A dozen large shops were built together with the macellum itself, and while there is some difference in interior arrangements, these all seem to have been shops with mezzanine lofts where the shopkeeper's family lived or goods were stored.

The planning of the complex shows certain small irregularities that suggest that at the time of its reconstruction after the earthquake it was modified but not replanned. The south entrance (VII ix 42) looks as though it had once been a shop. The courtyard of the shrine seems makeshift, as though it had been created out of space designed for other use. The tholos seems to have been too big for the courtyard in which it stands. These things suggest that the macellum had existed before the earthquake with the same general design and that no need was felt for very much change when its ruin offered the opportunity. But a few innovations seemed desirable. Whether in the long run the change in proportion entailed in the enlargement of the tholos would have been felt intolerable we cannot say, but the use of light roofs supported on wooden posts shows that the Pompeians did not regard the reconstruction as definitive.

The Aedes Fortunae Augustae

The Aedes Fortunae Augustae (VII iv 1), at the southeast corner of the crossing of two very important streets, the Via di Nola (Via della Fortuna) and the Via di Mercurio/Via del Foro, lies a short block from the forum but still very much within the centre of municipal life.[7] Across the street from it are the Terme del Foro. Just beyond it the Via di Mercurio is spanned by a large commemorative arch, the Arco di Caligola. And it is more or less connected to the forum by the Porticus Tulliana.

The temple is especially precious for providing us with a construction date. An inscription with a consular date records that the first Ministri Fortunae Augustae made a dedication in the year A.D. 3/4 (*CIL* 10.824). A second tells us that M. Tullius, who was duovir and duovir quinquennalis, built the temple on his own land and at his

---

[7]On this temple see Overbeck and Mau 114–17; *RömMitt* 11 (1896) 269–84 (A. Mau); and Maiuri 1942, 67–68. On the Porticus Tulliana see Maiuri 1942, 176–77.

FIGURE 33.
The Aedes Fortunae
Augustae

own expense (*CIL* 10.820). Since the latter inscription was on the architrave of the aedicula that housed the cult statue, and since this is proved by a wealth of evidence to have been rebuilt in the last period of the city, R. Schöne, who edited these inscriptions, thought that only the aedicula and the apse in which it stands might be meant, but Tullius was also tribunus militum a populo, an honor that seems to have been awarded only in the Augustan period, so if the inscription belongs to the last period, it must be a copy of an earlier one.[8]

The temple façade projected into the street enough to call attention to itself without seriously interfering with traffic. Stone bollards protected its corners from damage by passing vehicles. There is no sidewalk in front of it, but along its flank on the Via di Nola there is a broad sidewalk with an ornamental pavement made of water-rounded pebbles set in mortar. It was a frontal podium temple in the Roman imperial idiom, prostyle tetrastyle with a deep pronaos. The

[8]*CIL* 10.820–22; Nissen 178–84; Della Corte[3] 122–24; Castrén 231.

podium rose in two storeys, the lower a mass of concrete faced with blocks of fine limestone projecting in front of the rest as a platform on which the altar stood flanked by symmetrical stairs of approach of four steps. In front of the altar the platform is finished with a simple crown molding; otherwise it is plain. This platform was enclosed on the three exposed sides by an iron fence, of which stubs remain. It ran across the top of the stairs with double gates a bit less than half the width of the stairs set at the interior angles. The altar stood on the axis of the temple, a core of tufa blocks once faced with marble, but all but the core was salvaged in antiquity. The upper storey of the temple podium was a mass of concrete faced with marble, of which almost nothing remains. The facing seems to have made a plain block with base and crown moldings but no other articulation. The pronaos was approached by a flight of nine steps running across the full width of the façade. The squarish pronaos is presumed to have had four columns in front, with a somewhat wider intercolumniation between the central pair, and three, including the corner column, down each side. Three Corinthian capitals of two slightly different types, one a replacement for the other, remain there today, along with three pilaster capitals of the later type. The corners of the cella and the jambs were finished with fluted pilasters.

The cella is a broad rectangle with an apse opening on axis at its far end; the apse encloses an aedicula raised on a high base. The cella walls were covered with marble outside and in, and though the plates were salvaged, much of the pattern is clear. Pilasters at regular intervals broke the wall into bays. There were five pilasters along each long exterior wall, including those at the corners. The lower part of each bay was filled with a large, square orthostat above which ran a deep band between projecting cornices. Above this there seems to have been another series of large plates. The core of the cella wall is of concrete faced with opus incertum, coigned at the corners with small blocks but at the doorway with brick. The latter is probably a postearthquake repair. In each side wall were two rectangular niches large enough to hold life-size statues. Statues of a togatus and a woman in the pudicitia pose were found in the excavation, the female statue faceless, the orginal face evidently cut away in antiquity for replacement with another (*PAH* 2, pt. 4, 95 [20 February 1824]; Ruesch 16, no. 48, and 260, no. 1095). The back wall originally ran straight, but in the last period it was broken by a curved and half-domed apse supported below on a vault that makes a little cellar underneath. The quantity of yellow tufa and reticulate employed in this masonry is sufficient indication of its late date. Filling the apse was an aedicula of two Corinthian columns supporting a triangular pediment on a high base. This would have held the statue of Fortuna Augusta holding a cornucopia and a steering oar.

Although the temple was being restored at the time of the eruption, and although after the disaster survivors salvaged as much usable material as they could, including the cult statue, enough elements of the main order and the aedicula were left to permit Mau to make a complete reconstruction of the temple with very few uncertain details. The pavements, on the other hand, and the veneer of the walls are entirely missing, so we do not know what stones may have been used. When we ask what the style of the temple was—Augustan or Flavian—and what it can tell us about Pompeian architecture, we find that the combination of elements is formulaic and not very informative. But the simplicity of the moldings and the balance in the design of the capitals is more reminiscent of Augustan than of Flavian taste. If the restorers had it in mind to modernize the aesthetic of the architecture, they had not yet put hand to the task. It is more likely that enough of the marbles of the original building survived in usable condition to make it sensible to repair, rather than rebuild, the temple, and that except for the introduction of the apse, they intended to keep the lines and style of the original building. We should, I believe, accept this as an example of the Augustan style in temple building in Pompeii, in which no expense was spared.

In the temple were found two inscriptions of the Ministri Fortunae Augustae (*CIL* 10.824, 825) similar in content to three found elsewhere in the city (*CIL* 10.826–28). These include consular dates, the earliest for A.D. 3/4, the latest for A.D. 56. There are sometimes three ministri named, sometimes four. The earliest were all slaves; thereafter there seems to have been a mixture of freedmen and slaves. It is not clear how appointment to the office was made. In one inscription a quaestor, also probably of servile origin, is named: Q. Pompeius Amethystus. Since the cult was closely bound up with the worship of the genius of the princeps and a fragmentary inscription shows that there was a dedication here to Augustus as *pater patriae* (*CIL* 10.823), the ministri were officials of some importance in the state religion, though they acted always on orders of the magistrates of the colony or the decuriones. The fact that according to the inscriptions they were obliged *ex lege ministrorum Fortunae Augustae* to dedicate *signa* from time to time suggests that they were also rich. There are parallels for this college elsewhere in Italy; evidently they were organized as part of Augustus's attempt to involve the whole population in his religious revival. The fact that some of the Pompeian inscriptions were broken up and sold as secondhand marble may indicate that the college had been dissolved by the time of the earthquake, but the temple was not abandoned. The cult of Fortuna was always enormously popular, and Fortuna Augusta, though looking especially to Rome and the principate, would have shared in this popularity.

Adjacent to the temple of Fortuna, but distinct from it, was the Porticus Tulliana, a portico spanning the sidewalk on the east side of the Via del Foro from VII iv 2 to VII iv 12, leaving only a short space the width of three shops between its end and the entrance to the forum. This was supported on two columns and eight piers of brick, all the piers except those at either end with an engaged column to either side. The end piers are L-shaped, one built around a brick column, the other with an engaged column on the north side; the columns stand opposite the doorway to a small irregular house, VII iv 10. All have Doric capitals cut in lava; for the piers a single block carries all the elements for each. A single pier has an Attic base carefully constructed of brickwork and mounted on a lava plinth above its companions. There are ten piers, with a walk the width of an ordinary sidewalk behind them fronting a collection of shops including a cookshop, a small house, a back alley, and a stair to an apartment in a second storey. It seems that the ornamental porticus had little to do with the buildings behind it but was simply added to make a handsome approach to the temple. Maiuri pointed out that while the end piers and columns preserve patches of plaster, the rest do not and must be work of the last period, probably here replacing columns that were thrown down in the earthquake.

The Forum Arches

Around the forum of Pompeii are remains of four monumental arches and traces of a fifth; these must be presumed to have honored members of the imperial house, since none appears to be of republican date. The oldest, that on axis with the Temple of Jupiter, at the south end of the forum, is low and rather squat in its lines, dwarfed by the statue bases that flank it to either side. It has lost most of its attic and remains a single fornix arch, square in plan, of masonry faced with opus incertum and tile. The marble revetment and anything it may have carried were removed in antiquity. A. W. Van Buren identified this as the janus of Pompeii,[9] but there is little to support such identification. It does not lie at a crossing of any sort and has none of the earmarks of a sacred building. There is no sign of doors, no indication of a precinct, and no place for a cult statue or herm. The passage is an uninviting tunnel, designed rather to lighten the effect of the

---

[9] A. W. Van Buren, "Studies in the Archaeology of the Forum of Pompeii," *MAAR* 2 (1918) 22–23.

mass than to suggest entrance. Mau saw it as the base for a colossal standing figure of Augustus,[10] but as Van Buren points out, Augustus would not have been likely to permit erection of such a statue in his lifetime, and it would have been sadly out of scale with the buildings close to it, none of which is very grand. Probably the same could be said about the nearby statues; certainly the equestrian statues that immediately flanked it were no larger than life. It seems likely, then, that like most arches, it carried a group, the princeps and his family or a triumphal car. It could be Augustan or Tiberian in date; Mau compares its masonry to the older parts of the Aedificium Eumachiae. As probably the only statuary group in the forum at the time of its erection, it must have had a singular interest, as well as axial importance, but the figures need not have much exceeded life in scale. The arch served to raise the statuary to the height of the upper storey of the forum colonnade, to lift it above the heads of the crowds in the square.

At the opposite end of the forum square, flanking the stair of approach to the Temple of Jupiter, were originally two single fornix arches, probably twins. But that to the east had been removed and its place paved over before the earthquake, for it does not appear on the lararial relief of L. Caecilius Iucundus showing the forum in the throes of the earthquake.[11] The other is shown with a high attic, the arch framed with pilasters and an archivolt within a triangular pediment that extends the full width of the piers and is supported by other pilasters at the corners. The crown of the attic is trimmed with a molding, but statuary does not appear atop it, perhaps because of the exigencies of space on the narrow plate on which it is carved. Today it is a naked skeleton of masonry faced with brickwork, the arch coigned with an irregular double row of broken tile set on centering, like voussoirs, the attic reduced to a thin slab. A single small fragment of a fluted marble pilaster adorns the north face. There is no indication as to whom it and the balancing arch on the east might have been dedicated; one thinks of numerous pairs among the Julio-Claudian family. But both arches were rather shallow, and an equestrian statue of any size would have had to be set broadside to the forum, which seems aesthetically unattractive. So perhaps again one should think rather of standing groups of the imperial family.

At the northeast corner of the forum, between the Temple of Jupiter and the macellum, the forum entrance is defined by a broad arch, usually called the Arco di Tiberio, through which one descended two

[10] A. Mau, "Die Statuen des Forums von Pompeji," *RömMitt* 11 (1896) 150–56.
[11] See, e.g., Maiuri 1942, pl. 1.a; and M. Brion, *Pompéi et Herculanum* (Paris 1960) fig. 13.

broad steps of Caserta stone to enter the forum proper.[12] The broad, high arch is flanked on the forum side by two deep, square-headed niches for statues and on the street side by a pair of square-headed niches that in a remodeling were piped and fitted with basins lined with signinum. The overflow spilled into a large basin at street level, and this was evidently the main water supply for the public in this neighborhood, the nearest public fountain in the last period being at the corner of the Via degli Augustali and the Vicolo Storto. The broad, well-proportioned centre arch, not quite a barrel vault, flanked by deep niches, gives something of the effect of a triple arch. The base is revetted with blocks of Caserta stone capped with a heavy projecting stringcourse on which stand plinths and two fragments of shafts of an engaged order of Ionic or Corinthian marble columns that framed the niches. Of the lowest parts of the revetment above the base only a few bits remain today, but enough to show that the whole was covered with a sumptuous architectural decoration entirely in marble. The use of brickwork to face the masonry throughout and of flat arches together with relieving arches over the fountain niches, as well as the lavish use of marble, suggests a date well into the first century A.C., and Tiberius, Germanicus, and Nero have been variously suggested as likely to have been the person honored by it. Some importance has been given to a fragmentary inscription found nearby: . . . FLAMINI AVGVSTALI SODALI AVGVSTALI Q (*CIL* 10.798). This has been interpreted as referring to Nero, the son of Germanicus, elder brother of Gaius Caligula, who was born in A.D. 6 and died in A.D. 30. But he seems not to have been prominent enough to be honored with so important a monument, and he seems to have been rather too early for an arch of such highly developed architecture. Besides, there are other bases in the vicinity that could have carried his statue.

Up the Via di Mercurio from the Arco di Tiberio, just north of the crossing of this and the Via di Nola, stands the skeleton of yet another arch of a single fornix, known as the Arco di Caligola (Eschebach 1978, fig. 77). It seems excessively high for its width, which gives the architecture a feeling of delicacy, the fornix soaring above the street. It is built of brick-faced concrete, the arch decidedly segmental. The attic once held a reservoir for water, and the arch acted as a standpipe for the neighborhood. The remains of terracotta pipes appear in deep rectangular slots in the north face that seem to have been left for servicing. Although all the marble revetment of the arch was removed by salvagers, they left the lava blocks with which the foot is

---

[12] For views of this arch see Kraus and von Matt figs. 16, 20, 24; and Eschebach 1978 figs. 7, 77.

revetted, showing not that this was probably less sumptuous than the arches on the forum, where we find Caserta stone, but that the danger of damage from traffic was much greater. In the vicinity were found fragments of an equestrian statue in bronze; this was early identified as showing Gaius Caligula, hence the name given the arch. But the identification is not certain. The restored statue is in the Museo Nazionale in Naples;[13] the horse is nearly complete, but the figure is not and lacks any really identifying traits. Still it is gratifying to know that this arch was indeed a statue base.

But it must be confessed that these arches add little or nothing to our knowledge of Pompeian architecture. Many of the proportions are uncertain, and practically all the decorative finish is completely lost. It is interesting to observe how they were located and to compare them with one another and on the basis of this comparison to try to arrive at dates for them. The arch at the south end of the forum is certainly earliest and most experimental in design. But is the Arco di Caligola, with its soaring passageway looking forward both to the Arch of Titus in Rome and to the Arch of Trajan at Benevento, earlier or later than the Arco di Tiberio, with its deep niches that put one in mind of the Porta Maggiore in Rome and the Arch of the Gavii in Verona? To such questions there is no clear answer. If we knew that the arch that once stood east of the stair to the Temple of Jupiter had been destroyed at the time the Arco di Tiberio was constructed, or that it was demolished so that it would not detract from the new arch, then we could say that its more important location would have been the first to be occupied with an important new dedication. But were the old arch still in place, the location of the Arco di Caligola, flanked by the handsome façade of the Temple of Fortuna Augusta and with the sweep of the Via di Mercurio and turris XI of the city walls as a background, would seem to have offered greater advantages.

Pompeii was uncommonly rich in arches, and possibly some of them were only ornamental gateways, not triumphal arches. One might prefer that explanation at least for those flanking the Temple of Jupiter.

The Forum Pavement of Caserta Stone

The pavement of the forum in large blocks of white limestone must go back in part at least to the Augustan or the Tiberian period, since it was installed after the arches to either side of the Temple of Jupiter were erected but antedates the dismantling of the eastern arch. It is curiously patchy. The areas to either side of the Temple of Jupiter are paved solid, though that on the west ends on an arbitrary line half-

---

[13]M.N. Inv. No. 5635 (Ruesch 199, no. 803); *PAH* 2, pt. 4, 86 (7 November 1823).

way back along the cella of the temple; for this there seems to be no ready explanation. In front of the temple it is completely lacking. Along the west side of the forum there are small patches of half a dozen blocks or so, usually in conjunction with a statue base or bases, and around the south end of the forum, where there are a number of bases of larger monuments, it is fairly solid. Elsewhere there are only single blocks scattered here and there and occasional groups of blocks. Most of these seem to be leveled and to have been intended to provide guide points for workmen laying new sections of pavement. But the whole forum is well metaled with a rudus of broken stone and tile, and this is crowned so that even today heavy rain is carried off by the drains around the edge of the forum and there is minimal erosion of the surface.

Van Buren observed the large letter Q cut in the surface of a block adjacent to the single large base along the west side of the open area and found parts of four more letters on blocks in buildings around the forum (*MAAR* 2 [1918] 70–71; 5 [1925] 104–5 [Van Buren]). These he identified as remains of an inscription commemorating the paving of the forum. Such inscriptions are known from the Forum Romanum, for example, and the forum of Terracina.[14] But if he is right, the paving blocks in the area of the inscription were laid in staggered lines, so that some letters came in the middle of the blocks, while others were divided between two blocks. In all the areas where paving is still in place the blocks are aligned with one another. Possibly the inscription was in more than one line, in which case it seems odd that a line should have been cut across a joint, or these blocks came secondhand and the inscription has nothing to do with the forum of Pompeii. Possibly the pavement was done in sections, the north end at least with blocks aligned, a middle section with the blocks staggered, in which case we should have to assume that it was decided that it should be made uniform and the staggered middle section was lifted to be relaid. The latter explanation seems most plausible, and if it were possible to lift the blocks in place at the southern end of the forum, some of them might be found to have letters on the undersurface. In any case it is evident that the forum of Pompeii was never paved completely with limestone; had it been, blocks of this pavement would be lying about in quantity. Nor was it anticipated that it soon would be so paved; the metaling was too carefully and thoroughly carried out not to have been intended to serve for a number of years anyway.

[14] On the Forum Romanum see *CIL* 6.37068: L.NAEVIVS L.F. SVRDINVS PR. INTER CIVIS ET PEREGRINOS; cf. Nash 1.397, fig. 485. On the forum of Terracina see *CIL* 10.6306: A. AEMILIVS A.F. STRAVI(T).

Other Public Buildings

The Palestra Grande

The so-called Palestra Grande of Pompeii (II vii)[15] was certainly not, properly speaking, a palaestra at all. Not only does it not include any of the arrangements and appurtenances for a range of sports and athletics within its own walls but there are no dressing rooms or baths, and none have been found in the adjacent blocks. There are no running tracks or discus and javelin ranges, and the great swimming tank at the centre is so very shallow at one end as to suggest that it was designed especially to let animals descend by this slope to be loaded with water. One may compare a similar tank on the north side of the forum of Paestum, similarly puzzling, and unlikely to have been used for swimming.[16]

The building consists of a large rectangular open area surrounded on three sides by lofty porticoes with floors raised several steps above the open area. These porticoes are of thirty-six columns on the short north and south sides, forty-eight on the long west side. The columns are built of brick veneered with stucco, with composite capitals built up in stucco over masonry capped by rough Ionic capitals of tufa, probably the earliest composite capitals known (*NSc* 1939, 179–82 and figs. 6–9). The shafts are reeded their full height, and over the reeding are applied rather crude Attic bases. The Ionic upper element of the capital is four-sided but more classical in its general design than most Pompeian Ionic, the egg molding strongly convex, the volutes without trimming palmettes, the middle of the abacus ornamented with a rosette on each face. Below this was a deep zone of acanthus leaves, nowhere well preserved today, rising from a bead molding. No color is preserved on the capitals; the shafts are white. The columns of the southern half of the west portico and the central six of the south portico are stripped cores and were clearly awaiting the stuccoists at the time of the eruption, yet all the others of the south portico are deeply gouged and scarred by wear where people fixed pegs in them and ran rods between them as though they were of no importance and were soon to be restuccoed. The bases of the stuccoed columns all show repair; evidently they had all tipped outward in the earthquake and were straightened and strengthened with wedges of lead run in at the base but had yet to be redecorated at the time of the eruption (*NSc* 1939, 178–79; Maiuri 1942, 87–89).

---

[15] This building was excavated in 1935–39; the excavation is reported in detail by A. Maiuri in *NSc* 1939, 165–231; see also Jashemski 160–62.

[16] See M. Napoli, *Paestum* (I documentari visioni d'Italia 27, Novara 1967) figs. 70–74.

FIGURE 34.
The Palestra Grande,
Order with Composite
Capitals

The columns stand on a stylobate of broken lava and limestone masonry, and the wall behind is of similar construction throughout, coigned at corners and openings with brick keyed neatly into the adjoining walls, except around the doors on the north side, where there is coigning in small blocks of tufa and limestone. There are lava cistern heads with disc lids at irregular intervals along the stylobate of the north and west porticoes and stairs in lava blocks leading down to the open area wherever a door from the exterior pierces the circuit wall. Except for the north wall, the consistency of fabric is remarkable, and one would be reluctant to try to distinguish any difference in building periods from the slight variations.

There are five entrances on the east side toward the amphitheatre, where there is no portico; two on the north; three on the west; none on the south. On the east the building faces an open area lying between it and the amphitheatre that was planted with occasional trees. On the north it faces a broad unpaved avenue between it and blocks II ii, II iii, and II iv that is planted with trees in a regular row down the middle toward the east end. On the west another broad unpaved avenue separates it from blocks II viii and II ix, but this is interrupted by arrangements at the end of the street between these two blocks, where a ceremonial entrance to the building and what looks like a gatekeeper's lodge intervene, and the southern end of the avenue was walled off to make an enclosure, perhaps a place where one could tether animals. On the south the only door leads to a latrine as large as the public latrine of the forum; obviously a great many people were expected to gather here. Another large enclosure fills the rest of the space between this building and the street along the city wall on the south, but it is not clear whether this ever belonged to the complex.

If there was a main entrance, it must have been that at the middle of the west side, the readiest access to the Porta di Nocera. Here there are a large statue base still preserving some of its marble revetment, presumably for a statue of the builder, and an axial approach emphasized by columns in the opening from the antechamber and a pair of columns engaged against piers in the colonnade opposite these. Probably there was also some special treatment of the roof here; perhaps a pediment was introduced. The interesting thing is that this entrance turned in rather than out; its importance could be appreciated only from the interior open area.

The entrances on the opposite side, however, the eastern gates on the side without a portico, face handsomely in both directions. They are imposingly framed in brick but without any trace of stuccoing, consisting of jambs framed by pilasters (in the case of the centre gate, by engaged columns) that support attics surmounted by shallow pediments. On the interior the three central gates project inward and are vaulted. The effect is almost grandiose without being ponderous. Along the crest of the circuit wall on this side stand small merlons capped with blunted pyramids, built of small blocks of tufa and limestone, which add considerably to the effect.

In front of the three wings of the building lined with porticoes the open area was planted with lines of trees, well spaced, many of the roots of which have been recovered by casting. The casts show that these were very large trees. There were eleven (of an original twelve?) in front of each short portico, four symmetrically arranged in front of the west entrance a little less than halfway between it and the swimming tank. Originally there may have been a double line running around all four sides. They must have provided a well-shaded promenade where considerable numbers could stroll.

The focus of the whole complex is the great rectangular tank at its centre built of masonry of broken lava lined with hydraulic cement, rounded against leakage at the corners and capped with a margin of tufa slabs. It is plainly a water container and slopes down gently from almost ground level on the west to a depth of more than two meters on the east. On the east a setback 0.38 m wide half a meter below the upper margin has been interpreted as a diving ledge or starting platform for swimming races, but since the depth of the tank at the shallow end would hardly permit swimmers to turn here, another purpose should probably be sought. The waste from this tank was piped to the latrine to flush it. In size and effect this tank may be compared to the pool in the Pecile at Hadrian's villa near Tivoli.[17]

The walls of the porticoes inside and out are for the most part bare today. The north wall, however, collapsed inward in the eruption and lies today as it fell, a great tilted slab, somewhat crumpled. This, one can see by peering underneath, was covered with plaster and painted, and the excavators salvaged some parts and restored a section at the east end of the north portico. Its decoration is advanced Third Style, approaching Fourth Style in some of its effects, but still quite clearly Third Style (*NSc* 1939, 185, fig. 11).

It remains to ask when this building was built and what purpose it may have served. The original construction seems clearly Julio-Claudian, especially the use of small tufa and limestone blocks in conjunction with facing of incertum of broken lava,[18] but the decoration can scarcely be early Augustan, and the composite order of the columns is surprising. Elsewhere the earliest dated appearance of the composite order seems to be in the Arch of Titus in Rome (Crema 272). But the building must antedate A.D. 59, for it is shown in the famous painting of the riot in the amphitheatre,[19] and the size of the trees is such that one would like a relatively early date. Perhaps a late Augustan or Tiberian date will best satisfy the evidence.

As to its purpose, that must be inferred chiefly from the graffiti that cover its columns. It was a place where people loitered, for many of the inscriptions were casual pastimes. It does not seem ever to have been used as a market, for there is no possibility of bringing in wheeled traffic and no running water other than that in the swimming tank. In the event of bad weather it must have been used as shelter by the spectators in the amphitheatre. Della Corte thought it should properly be designated the campus of Pompeii (*RendLinc* ser. 8, 2 [1947] 555–68; Della Corte[3] 398–408), but one might question the propriety of having a campus within the circuit of the city walls at this date. It is clearly in large part a public park, and its closest con-

[17] Consult S. Aurigemma, *Villa Adriana* (Rome 1961) 51–58.

[18] Maiuri (*NSc* 1939, 202–14) would put the original construction at the beginning of the Augustan period. In this he was especially influenced by the size of the trees, which is clearly an unreliable criterion for precise dating.

[19] M.N. Inv. No. 112222; Kraus and von Matt 51, fig. 50; Eschebach 1978 fig. 75.

geners are the Palestra of Herculaneum and the Pecile of Villa Adriana.[20] Simpler than the former and adapted to a smaller range of uses, it is perhaps more nearly akin to the latter, but the disfiguring of the south portico by scribblers suggests that it was not simply a public park, unless we are to assume that following the earthquake it was thrown open to the temporary use of the homeless and they installed crude curtains and partitions there that have left their scars. And in that case it is rather odd that they did not build better partitions.

The Tetrapylon of the Holconii on the Via dell'Abbondanza between VII i and VIII iv

The Tetrapylon of the Holconii is probably Tiberian in date, rather than Augustan. The Holconii were a well-established family in Pompeii and evidently derived their wealth from the production of wine, for a grape that did especially well in Campania, the Orconia, was named for them.[21] The man responsible for the Augustan restoration of the large theatre, M. Holconius Rufus, held the highest municipal offices and was made Augusti Caesaris sacerdos (CIL 10.830) and later flamen Augusti (CIL 10.943–46). His son—or brother—succeeded him, becoming sacerdos divi Augusti (CIL 10.945–46). Evidently most of the family were staunch supporters of the Augustan regime and public benefactors. It has been presumed that in their honor a curious monument, probably a four-sided arch, was erected on the Via dell'Abbondanza where it meets the Strada Stabiana.[22] The stretch of the street where it was built was closed to wheeled traffic, and effectively all traffic, by a steep drop in the pavement along the line of the Strada Stabiana, and it widens to make a small, well-paved public square in front of the Thermae Stabianae. A house nearby, VIII iv 4, is erroneously identified as the Casa di Olconio in the older literature. The location of the monument was chosen for its public importance; we do not know where the Holconii may have lived.

The monument was light and graceful, four brick-faced piers, one of which preserves patches of plaster facing, in a rough square presumably joined by arches above, in front of which were erected statues with inscriptions recording the careers of those honored. The one surviving statue, of M. Holconius Rufus, shows him in later life,

---

[20] See A. Maiuri, *Ercolano: I nuovi scavi (1927–1958)*, 2 vols. (Rome 1958), 1.113–43; and Aurigemma (supra n.17) 51–58.

[21] On the Holconii see Della Corte[3] 239–42; and Castrén 176, no. 197. On the Orconia grape see Pliny *NH* 14.35; and Columella 3.2.27.

[22] The ruin of the monument with the statue of M. Holconius Rufus in place is shown in Eschebach 1978 fig. 100; the statue itself (M.N. Inv. No. 6233) is shown in Kraus and von Matt 38, fig. 25.

going bald, his face deeply lined. He wears a cuirass and military boots, doubtless in allusion to his office as tribunus militum a populo. He is also described as patronus coloniae. Who the other three honored here may have been we do not know. A fragment of a female statue found nearby has led to the supposition that they were other Holconii, but in that case it is curious that the most distinguished member of the family should have been left in place when the other statues were retrieved. It seems more likely that this was a monument to the tribuni militum a populo or the patroni coloniae.

The Theatrum Maius

In the Augustan period the Theatrum Maius[23] was remodeled. Three inscriptions record that part of this work was paid for by M. Holconius Rufus and M. Holconius Celer and consisted of a crypta, tribunalia, and a theatrum (CIL 10.833–35). Since there is no mention of the scaena, we must conclude that it was not included, but an inscription found in the vicinity with the simple legend M. ARTORIVS M. L. PRIMVS ARCHITECTVS (CIL 10.841) has been interpreted as referring to the scaena, and a copy of this is immured near the east entrance to the orchestra. Moreover, the general character of the scaena strongly suggests that it was also rebuilt in the Augustan period.

The work of the Holconii will have been the construction of the vaulted annular corridor behind the top of the media cavea (crypta) supporting the summa cavea, which was accessible by a gallery supported on arcading over spur walls and columns. This summa cavea is probably the theatrum of the Holconii. Since buildings already framed the theatre, the space the builders could utilize was limited, especially toward the west, where the theatre adjoins the Forum Triangulare. Access was difficult to arrange, and narrow, inconvenient stairs had to be tucked in at three points approximately equally spaced around the exterior, with a fourth at the southwest corner built into the thickness of the wall between the theatre and the Forum Triangulare. In all, the summa cavea had only four rows of seats, with the narrow gallery of access reached by doors at the top of these. Around the inner wall of the gallery was a series of stone blocks with piercings in which were stepped the masts that carried awnings to shade the spectators (velaria). The men who manipulated these worked on a platform over the gallery. The construction of the summa cavea is of concrete faced with broken rubble coigned with masonry of small blocks and brickwork.

The tribunalia are small, high platforms of rubble masonry faced

---

[23] See esp. Overbeck and Mau 156–71; RömMitt 21 (1906) 1–56 (A. Mau); Sogliano 196–209; and Maiuri 1973, 183–89.

with reticulate and brick carried on vaults over the parodoi, accessible by narrow stairs off the parodoi on the scaena side. A fence of metal must have run around the edge of each. Sure traces of another such fence in metal can be seen in the marble coping in front of the lowest row of seats in the summa cavea.

Whether one should ascribe to the Holconii as well the facing of the four steps of the ima cavea with blocks of white marble is questionable. These are low, broad steps to accommodate the bisellia to which members of the ordo were entitled, and just above them in the centre of the first row of the media cavea is an inscription: M. HOL-CONIO M.F. RVFO / IIVIR I. D. QVINQVIENS / ITER QVINQ. TRIB. MIL. A. P. / FLAMINI AVG. PATR. COLO. D. D. (*CIL* 10.838); evidently he was awarded this place of honor in perpetuity.[24] Since Celer is not included in the honor, it must have been bestowed on Rufus for other benefactions, and it may be that it was in gratitude for the honor that he and Celer then undertook the remodeling of the theatre. Just possibly his earlier benefactions included rebuilding of the scene building.

The scene building today is in a sorry state, a mere ruined shell stripped of every vestige of ornament. But the architectural form is still clear and interesting. The stage was deep but very low, raised only four steps above the floor of the orchestra. Its front wall is broken into a series of shallow niches, that at the centre the only one of bowed form, and a flight of steps to either side permitted performers to move back and forth from the stage to the orchestra. Immediately behind this proscenium wall is the trench for the stage curtain. Remains of the back wall of the scaena are limited to the lowest storey, but there must have been at least two. The central door, the valva regia, is set in a broad bowed niche and was preceded by a porch supported on a pair of columns on rectangular plinths. To either side of this is a flanking door, valva hospitalis, also apparently originally framed by a pair of columns. Between central door and side doors is a pair of rectangular niches for statuary, while a bowed niche for statuary finished the wall at either end. Along the face of the wall, except where steps leading to the three doors interrupted it, runs a broad, high plinth that must once have carried a line of columns, perhaps as many as twenty-four. The end walls closing the stage to either side are straight, each with a very wide door to the wings. This is a very typical Augustan stage building in its plan and most of its details, as

[24] Overbeck and Mau (163) hold that the inscription was cut to either side of an honorary statue, there being four holes still visible for securing the base of this. It seems more likely that the holes were for the feet of a bisellium. This was traditionally the place of honor in a Roman theatre, and a statue would have been better placed somewhere in the scaenae frons or around the periphery of the cavea.

far as these can be made out. It is very close to the scheme of the stage building of the theatre of Herculaneum on the one hand and to the Agrippan theatre of Merida in Spain on the other.[25] Possibly these all ultimately derive from the scaena of the theatre of Marcellus in Rome.[26]

The stage proper was of wood, as one should expect, and the area under it excavated to different depths, shallow in the western half, deeper toward the east where two stone bases, probably footings for stage machinery, are found. The fixtures in the trench for the curtain, two lines of stone sockets, one of nine tight against the proscenium wall and one of eight behind these, are puzzling, as is a low, vaulted corridor under this trench in which men might have worked, but only with difficulty.

To this period must also belong the reservoir that stands in the open area northwest of the cavea, between it and the Forum Triangulare, a square of masonry coigned with small blocks of tufa and limestone framing a circular tank, 4.45 m in diameter, 3.65 m deep, faced inside and out with a heavy veneer of signinum. This must have supplied fountains that have since disappeared, probably along the front of the proscenium and perhaps in the circular basin that was found buried under the orchestra, on axis, 7.10 m in diameter, 0.75 m deep. This too was faced with signinum and painted blue. It apparently served especially to collect the water of the fountains, which was then channeled back under the stage to a large central drain into which others from the scaena fed.

The Villa Imperiale outside the Porta Marina

The Villa Imperiale della Porta Marina, a public construction just outside the walls of the city, in fact incorporating a stretch of the walls in its fabric, was discovered during the clearing of debris from the bombing of 1943 and excavated, but only in part (La Rocca, de Vos, and de Vos 90–92; Schefold, 290–93). It had been abandoned by the Pompeians after the earthquake of A.D. 62 and used as a dump for building material from the city once it had been plundered of attractive parts of its architecture and decoration, but it is evidence for an architectural trend of importance.

It consisted of a very long colonnaded promenade, the columns of heavily stuccoed brick, above a broad paved roadway that plunged sharply downhill and could not be followed beyond the twelfth column of the portico. The portico is reached by either of two narrow

---

[25] For the theatre of Herculaneum see de Vos and de Vos 305–6; for that of Merida see M. Bieber, *The History of the Greek and Roman Theater*, 2d ed. (Princeton 1961) 202 and figs. 680–82.

[26] See P. Fidenzoni, *Il teatro di Marcello* (Rome n.d.) 40–43, esp. fig. 21.

stairs just outside the Porta Marina; the walls of both stairs are painted with the characteristic zebra striping of utilitarian rooms. Some forty bays of the colonnade could be uncovered, but it breaks off abruptly within a few meters of a niche tomb below it, and we have lost the terminal feature, whatever it was. It seems to have been a walk, especially for those who wished to contemplate the seashore and the shipping activity at the mouth of the Sarno River. A canal ran around this end of the city, part of which, with stone rings for mooring the vessels immured in the side, can be seen in the excavation to the north of the Porta Marina road, and the lively and varied activity around here must have been a source of endless interest for strollers. The portico itself was rather severely decorated with a black-ground painting in the Third Style. Off the southern stretch of this portico opened a second of at least two wings at right angles to one another, one of which ran back to back with it. Only one corner of this has been excavated, and at least part of it was obliterated in the construction of the foundations of the Temple of Venus, which interrupt it after the seventh column, but the suggestion is that this originally ran for a considerable distance and was comparable to its neighbor, affording a view of the river valley and the port near the river mouth. The two together must have run out to a belvedere with a panoramic view, perhaps a circular pavilion like that of the Villa dei Papiri at Herculaneum or the end of the Pecile of Hadrian's villa near Tivoli.[27]

In the area behind the meeting of the two porticoes were discovered three decorated rooms and part of a fourth, and there might originally have been a good many more. They are framed by corridors that isolate, rather than connect, them, which we may guess were for servants in attendance rather than for any company assembled here. The most impressive of these is a great banquet hall, barrel-vaulted over the area for the dining couches, with a very fine early Third Style decoration with large subject pictures. Even the ceiling is elaborately painted. The predominant color in the main zone is cinnabar. South of this is a ladies' dining room with a cream-ground decoration and delicate architectural motifs and figures in pastel colors. There is an alcove for the settee and windows looking west and south. Down a short corridor to the east is another room with important mythological landscapes in a red-and-black decoration. This is a rather small room with a triple window of unusual form, with rounded heads to the lights, that looks out to the other portico. Next to this on the east are the butchered remains of the largest room of all, reduced to stubs of walls.

[27] D. Comparetti and G. De Petra, *La villa ercolanese dei Pisoni* (Turin 1883) pl. 24; Aurigemma (supra n. 17) 51–58.

From the decorations and proportions of these rooms we must conclude that they were all dining rooms and all for more or less elaborate entertainments. The ladies' dining room might have been used *en suite* with either of the others. The great barrel-vaulted hall is provided with a special area for entertainers with exits to either side. If these rooms were not for the public banquets of the magistrates of Pompeii, those occasions when they were obliged to entertain public heroes and benefactors, we may guess that they could be hired for an evening by a collegium or sodalicium that had no clubhouse of its own. It is certainly not beyond the bounds of possibility that this building belonged to the Temple of Venus, although no direct connection between the two can be seen today. The absence of a suitably impressive entrance from the direction of the Porta Marina helps to reinforce that suggestion.

15 · THE HOUSES

Introduction

The Third Style is presumed to have been in fashion from the middle of the Augustan period to the fire of Nero in A.D. 64.[1] It was slow in evolving, as the number of transitional decorations that bridge the gap from the Second Style to the Third Style shows. Most of these come from Rome, the most notable being perhaps the Casa di Augusto, the Casa di Livia, and the Casa della Farnesina,[2] but at least one good example is known from Pompeii, the Casa di Obellio Firmo,[3] which seems to have undergone extensive remodeling in the transitional period, and one from Herculaneum.[4] One might have expected this to be a time of peace and prosperity for Pompeii, when the future seemed secure and building throve. It is disappointing, therefore, to have to report that houses with extensive remains in the Third Style are a rarity and that those there are are almost all diminutive. Many of the finest pictures in the Third Style come from rooms that were the only examples of this style with figurative paintings in their houses—the tablina of the Casa di Amore Punito, the Casa del Centauro, and the Casa del Granduca di Toscana and the triclinium of the Casa della Grata Metallica (Mau 1882, 409–44). Clearly these can tell us little or nothing about the architecture of the period; they were simply decorations in the latest style introduced where the most important reception room in a house had come to look so shabby or old-fashioned that it warranted redecoration. Only two houses of

[1] A. Ippel, *Der dritte pompejanische Stil* (Berlin 1910).
[2] See, e.g., H. G. Beyen, *Die pompejanische Wanddekoration vom zweiten bis zum vierten Stil*, vol. 2, pt. 1 (The Hague 1960) 20–23 and figs. 217–64; and R. Bianchi Bandinelli, *Roma, l'arte nel centro del potere* (Milan 1969) 119–29.
[3] See Spinazzola 1953, 1.337–65.
[4] Andreae and Kyrieleis 115–18 (A. Allroggen-Bedel); *Pompeji: Leben und Kunst in den Vesuvstädten*, Villa Hügel (Essen 1973) 7 and no. 206; Maiuri 1953, 41.

considerable size seem to be creations of the Third Style—the Casa di Spurio Messore and the Casa di Iasone.[5]

The Casa di Spurio Messore

The Casa di Spurio Messore (VII iii 29) is very irregular, clearly put together from bits and pieces of other buildings.[6] The façade may go back to the period of the First Style, but the Tuscanic atrium, with its small, square impluvium and patches of masonry in small ashlar, is not older than the Augustan period. It preserves traces of a Third Style decoration with a black dado and a red main zone. The tablinum is small and low and has ceased to function as a room in its own right, being rather a lobby of access to rooms around it. Still, its jambs on the atrium are trimmed with painted pilasters, and there are remains of a Third Style decoration with porphyry dado and red main zone. There is a single ala on the east. The rooms around the atrium are for the most part small and had rooms in a second storey over them that gave onto the atrium for light and air but were accessible only by inconvenient stairs tucked into corners. Probably a wooden balcony reached by a stair beside the fauces ran across the entrance end of the atrium, giving access to the second storey rooms here; it did not, however, run down the sides of the atrium, and there is little indication as to how many rooms there were in the second storey. The room over the tablinum was accessible by its own stair, being possibly a single cenaculum. There is no clear order to the rooms around the atrium other than the tablinum and the slightly displaced ala. One can distinguish two cubicula and a winter triclinium preceded by an anteroom, but none of these is remarkable.

[5] The Casa del Gruppo dei Vasi di Vetro (VI xiii 2) was completely redecorated, including pavements (Pernice 1938, 111–12), in the time of the Third Style, but everyone is agreed that the architecture is much older. The Casa (or Scavo) del Principe di Montenegro (VII Ins. Occ. 15) may be a creation of the time of the Third Style, but it is so poorly documented and ruinous, and has been so neglected by Pompeianists, that its evidence must be treated with suspicion. It was excavated at a time when the records were perfunctory at best, 27 September 1850–20 March 1851, and thanks to its having been on the edge of the city site where the accumulation of volcanic debris would not have been so great as elsewhere, it seems to have been thoroughly ransacked in antiquity. It was ignored by Fiorelli (1875) and Pernice (1938), but according to Mau (1882), it was decorated entirely in the Third Style. It seems to have consisted of a large atrium with tablinum, but without alae, flanked by numerous small rooms that then gave by a broad corridor onto rooms beyond arranged on a terrace facing out over the sea. This is a plan one would be happy to find in the time of the Third Style.

[6] See Fiorelli 1873, 43; Fiorelli 1875, 206–8; Pernice 1938, 78; and Della Corte[3] 148–49, no. 261. Della Corte is of the opinion that M. Spurius Messor (or Mensor) was not the owner of the house but a mosaicist who signed his work there. In that case we have no identification of the owner or his place in the life of the city.

Wherever legible traces of the decoration are left, it is Third Style. No room seems to have included pictures; most show traces of the low ceilings with segmental vaults that are typical of the Third Style.

The great rooms of the house are a pair of dining rooms opening on a small rectangular garden off to the east of the main block. These are accessible from a small, square lobby containing a lararial niche off which also opens a small prettily decorated room in black and yellow that may have been a ladies' dining room. The larger banquet hall opens directly to the garden by a large window with a low sill and has a fine black-and-red decoration, the colors reversing between service end and couch area. The smaller banquet hall is preceded by a tiny portico of two columns between it and the garden, so arranged as to frame the view. The decoration was once very fine, with large subject pictures in the centre panels and wonderful vistas of delicate architecture in the upper zone. Only ruins of this now remain, but drawings were made of it when it was freshly excavated (Mau 1882, pls. 11–12).

The Casa di Iasone

If the Casa di Spurio Messore seems to us makeshift and ill-conceived, despite its size and the relative affluence of its owner, the Casa di Iasone (IX v 18–21) must seem to us revolutionary.[7] Here, again, the house was clearly created out of bits and pieces of other properties. The original property lines seem to have run through the block from north to south, and this house would have been created in the hortus area of two lots. It has no atrium at all nor any of the requisites of an atrium complex. Instead, the main apartment is a small rectangular peristyle entered by short fauces and dominated on the long axis by a vast triclinium. The other rooms of the house are all small, but the triclinium takes full advantage of the view of the peristyle; clearly this was considered the most important room in the house. But two other rooms as well had fine Third Style paintings: the cubiculum of Europa, west of the fauces, and the cubiculum of Medea, in the southwest corner of the house. The latter clearly is not a true cubiculum but a ladies' dining room, and one may wonder about the use of the other. There is no clear and unequivocal example of fine pictures in a bedroom in even the most sumptuous house. Here there seems to have been a bordello in the upper storey, but we do not know that this would have made a neighborhood disreputable in Pompeii (Della Corte[3] 162, no. 287).

[7] *BdI* 1880, 19–26, 73–87, 184–86 (A. Mau); Mau 1882, 443; Pernice 1938, 117–18; F. Zevi, *La Casa Reg. IX.5.18–21 a Pompei e le sue pitture* (Rome 1964).

The Casa della Fortuna

Yet a third house that seems to have been essentially a creation of the Third Style is the Casa della Fortuna (IX vii 20).[8] Here too there is no proper atrium, the atrium having become merely a rectangular lobby separated from the peristyle by a pair of columns. It is entered by short fauces, and off it open four small rooms, some of which had pictures too fine for bedrooms. South of the atrium lobby is a second lobby of the same size that appears to have been an unroofed court-yard, off which open the offices of the house. The peristyle is the chief ornament of the house, a long rectangle with a different number of columns on each side, three and four on the short ends, five toward the atrium, and seven on the opposite side, which is arcuated, one of very few arcuated colonnades in Pompeii,[9] though arcuated colon-nades were already shown in Second Style wall decorations, so the idea was not a novel one. Off this peristyle open two dining rooms, one a large room in the Fourth Style for parties, the other for more intimate occasions.

Small Houses in the Third Style

If large houses in the Third Style are disappointingly few, small houses are relatively common and range from such early examples as the Casa di Sulpicio Rufo, through classic houses such as the Casa del Frutteto, to late examples such as the Casa di Marco Lucrezio Frontone and the Casa dei Calavi.

In the Casa di Sulpicio Rufo (IX ix b/c [or s.n.])[10] we again find no atrium but rather a small rectangular peristyle on which open all the rooms, the living rooms in front, the kitchen and offices behind. The ground plan is very irregular, cutting in and out erratically, so the builders must have had to work against difficulties. There are four well-decorated rooms, two triclinia and two cubicula, all excellent ex-amples of the Third Style.

The Casa del Sacerdote Amando (I vii 7)[11] consists of a tiny square atrium approached by long fauces and a small pseudoperistyle at right angles to this. Off the atrium open a row of tiny cubicula and

---

[8] *BdI* 1882, 195–200, 217–22; 1883, 52–56, 71–77 (A. Mau). Pernice 1938, 118. Sche-fold, 270–71.

[9] Other arcuated colonnades in Pompeii can be found in I iii 8, I xvii 4 (the Casa degli Archi), and VII v 2 (Terme del Foro). In every case the arcuation is confined to a single wing.

[10] This is also called the Casa del Porco, from the lararial painting in the kitchen (*RömMitt* 4 [1889] 101–17 [A. Mau]).

[11] *NSc* 1927, 18–32 (A. Maiuri); Pernice 1938, 101. See also A. Maiuri in *Monumenti della pittura antica scoperti in Italia: Sezione III: Pompei* (Rome 1936–) fasc. 2 (1938) 3 ff.

offices and one fair-sized triclinium with mythological landscapes paired with a small ladies' dining room. A tablinumlike room links the atrium with the peristyle; this has a simple black-ground decoration with a single fine landscape. The peristyle is rectangular with porticoes east and north, an engaged order on the west, and none on the south. The order is a schematic Doric worked in stucco. In the garden a lararium is engaged in the west wall, and the excavators were able to cast the shape of a sizable tree root. The room to the west and those off the northwest corner were found stripped for redecoration; one presumes that they were to be a dining suite. A gallery ran over the portico on three sides, and off this may have opened rooms over all those in the lower storey. Though the house is diminutive and obviously makeshift in many ways, it maintains its scale throughout and has a certain gracefulness combined with restraint. There are remains of early Third Style decorations in most of the rooms, including cubicula, and the house can be regarded as the creation of a skillful builder with a well-developed aesthetic. The predominant ground colors are red and black, with some yellow and white. It is interesting that no garden painting is used on the blank wall of the pseudoperistyle.

The Casa del Frutteto (I ix 5/6),[12] on the Via dell'Abbondanza, is basically an old house, perhaps of the years just before the arrival of the Roman colony, redone at the time of the Third Style and awaiting a fresh rebuilding at the time of the eruption. Many of the rooms had been stripped or covered with roughcast, and piles of chunks of broken pavement awaiting use as building material were left in the atrium. The Tuscanic atrium was entered by short fauces, the house entrance being high, with jambs crowned with simple block capitals of tufa and a handsome lintel. Fauces, atrium, tablinum, and the single ala are paved with chips of limestone in mortar decorated with large black tesserae set at intervals. Occasionally frames, sill panels, and emblemata in mosaic appear. West of the fauces seems to have been the kitchen; east of the fauces is a shop connecting to both the atrium and the first cubiculum east of the atrium, which is unpainted and may have served for storage. The second cubiculum was evidently a ladies' dining room. It has a mosaic floor with place for the couch marked off at the east end. The walls are covered with a fine garden painting in the Third Style. Above a black dado with plants a fence of canes separates us from a grove of trees and shrubs against a rich blue ground. Egyptian columns and statues have been introduced, as well as Dionysiac reliefs mounted on colonettes. In the up-

[12] No full description of this house has been published to date. The best account of it is in La Rocca, de Vos, and de Vos 224–26, where it is called the Casa dei Cubicoli Floreali. See also Maiuri 1953, 44, 124, 127; and Kraus and von Matt fig. 297.

per zone large realistic birds, together with vases, theatrical masks, and Egyptian reliefs, stand on the architrave.

The tablinum, though stripped, shows signs of having once been a fine room with a splendid pavement and fluted pilasters to frame the door. It is open its whole width to the atrium and evidently had wooden doors in the opening to the garden. To the east of the tablinum is an andron; to the west a stair led up from the garden end to rooms in the second storey. Between the tablinum and the garden is a porch as deep as the tablinum paved with signinum, with two columns to support the roof. The columns are rendered in stucco with faceted red bases, white reeded shafts, and bell capitals with a single deep band of acanthus leaves. There is no other portico on the squarish garden, and the garden is undecorated. In the garden area is a stack of about thirty-five amphoras of three or four types, and a heap of lime and a stack of five wine amphoras in the northwest corner obstruct the stair to the upper storey. Off the porch to the east opens a suite of dining rooms, a men's and a ladies', connected by a small door. The men's triclinium has a signinum pavement with fine lozenge pattern worked in mosaic tesserae. The decoration is on a black ground throughout with large mythological landscapes and beautiful landscape sketches. The ladies' dining room is vaulted east and west and has a mosaic pavement, with the place for the couch raised a low step above the rest. The decoration is black ground in the main zone, a garden decoration in which a light architecture divides the walls into panels, each of which is filled with a single tree around which perch birds. The effect is highly stylized, a stylization emphasized by a broad band of garden vista below this that has no relationship to it but shows cane fencing, ornamental urns, and large flowering plants. Whether we are in some way to read this as a contrast between a garden and a wild landscape is not clear, but the difference and clash in perspective from one zone to the other is typical of the Third Style.

There are remains of First Style plaster high on the wall in the small room south of the ladies' dining room, but the room was remodeled and repaved at the time the Third Style decorations were installed elsewhere. The lower walls are now covered with coarse plaster. The next room was a storeroom and is full of amphoras. South of the garden was to be a great oecus with a broad view of the garden. It has an ornamental pavement including bits of oriental alabaster, but the walls are now bare of plaster. At the southeast corner a small lobby with steps descending to the east gave access to a latrine and a large stable with a broad posticum, big enough to have accommodated a small cart. A second storey over much of this part of the house was accessible by means of the stair west of the tablinum and perhaps another in wood in the stable lobby. Nothing positive can be said about this or about the second storey attested by a hanging balcony along the principal façade. Since it is clear that the one shop here was closely connected with the activities of the owner of the house, we should presume that this balcony too was part of the house proper, possibly accessible from the kitchen.

To sum up the impression given by examination of this house: it may have been built as much as a century before the arrival of the Third Style, and the house plot was probably always the size it is today. But the house was so thoroughly redecorated at the time of the Third Style, the work extending even to a complete repaving, that we can suppose that the architecture would have been brought into line with the latest taste, as far as that was feasible. And though the house must have suffered in the earthquake so much as to warrant extensive redecoration, if not remodeling, we still see the basic outline of a Third Style house, as well as three fine rooms. The oecus south of the garden will have been a new creation; the rest is a fine small house of our period.

As examples of relatively late Third Style houses we may take the houses of L. Ceius Secundus and M. Lucretius Fronto, both known to have been candidates for the aedilate in the last years of Pompeii and therefore presumably men of wealth and political ambition.

The Domus Ceiorum, also called the Casa della Regina Elena (I vi 15) (Spinazzola 1953, 1.257–81; Pernice 1938, 101–2), has a façade finished in the First Style with block capitals to the jambs and is flanked on the west by a house in a poor state today but showing considerable ancient masonry, on the east by the peristyle of the Casa del Criptoportico. We may therefore presume that there was once a medium-sized house here of the type of the Casa della Grata Metallica or the Casa Sannitica in Herculaneum that was more or less gutted and rebuilt in the time of the Third Style. The garden area appears to have been somewhat enlarged at this time at the expense of houses facing on the Via dell'Abbondanza.

The atrium complex as we see it today is a good example of a small house, the tetrastyle atrium squarish, approached by short, steep fauces with doors at either end. The impluvium is square, rimmed with a band of fragments of terracotta, perhaps sherds of amphoras, set on edge close together in mortar. The columns are set on footings of tufa blocks, rendered in stucco and crowned with only an abacus instead of a capital. In the centre of the impluvium stands a small marble fountain with a central jet. Throughout the atrium complex the floors are of signinum ornamented with borders and patterns in mosaic tesserae. The rooms flanking the fauces are a rustic service room containing a latrine and a stair to the second storey on the west and a squarish, handsomely decorated room on the east. The second storey in this part appears to have run across the whole front of the house; it is not clear whether it was divided into rooms.

At the far side of the atrium there was no tablinum, only two sizable dining rooms with an andron between them, the andron off axis to permit differentiation in the character of the triclinia. The larger had a big window to the atrium, as well as a broad door to the garden; the smaller was evidently essentially for winter use. On this side too there was a second storey, but this was a late modification, perhaps of the last period, made only after the decorations in the Third Style had been carried out. The garden has a deep porch without columns on the atrium side and is separated from this by a masonry pluteus. The porch has Third Style decoration, but the big garden paintings are later. A little pavilion in the southwest corner of the garden is also Fourth Style, but the room at the east end of the porch is Third Style, with a simple black-and-white mosaic pavement. Thus, though the garden was in the process of remodeling, it still preserved most of its Third Style architecture and character.

The Casa di Marco Lucrezio Frontone (V iv a [or 11])[13] is very familiar. The whole atrium complex appears to be of a single construction, though a deep jog in the south side shows that it had to be fitted to its surroundings. Here the second storey overhung the sidewalk along the façade and protected it. The fauces are short and steep, the Tuscanic atrium squarish with a deep impluvium faced with blocks of white marble and framed with a guilloche in black-and-white mosaic.[14] On the east rim stands a marble cartibulum with four fluted legs ending in lion's paws. There are rooms along only one side of the atrium, as well as front and back, and no alae, though the tablinum is canonical. In front, north of the fauces, are a small vaulted cubiculum and the wooden stair to the second storey, while south of the fauces are a storage closet and a large triclinium filling the southwest corner of the house, next to which is a small squarish room with an elegant Third Style decoration, probably a ladies' dining room. On the east side of the atrium is the tablinum, axial, the entrance, like the fauces, framed with unfluted pilasters. The decoration here is extraordinarily rich, but the room is rather low, as there was a second storey over this. The opening to the garden rises a step above the rest and was closed by wooden doors. The tablinum is flanked on the north by an andron, now without finish, and on the south by a small room given a Fourth Style decoration, but a room in the upper storey that covered this and the tablinum, a large loggia, still preserves re-

[13] NSc 1901, 145–70 (A. Sogliano); RömMitt 16 (1901) 333–60 (A. Mau); Della Corte[3] 11–12 and nos. 161–62; Pernice 1938, 96–97.

[14] Pernice (1938, 96–97) believed this impluvium to be a later modification, probably of the time of the addition of the Fourth Style rooms.

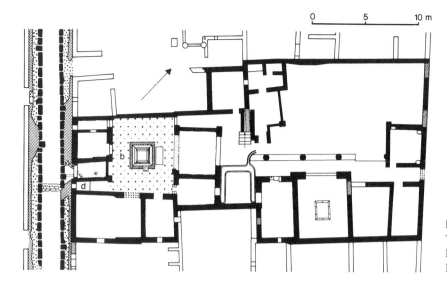

FIGURE 35.
The Casa di Marco
Lucrezio Frontone,
Plan of the Final Phase

mains of a Third Style decoration. This room must have been reached by the masonry stair on the east side of the porch east of the tablinum, the only possible access. The rest of the house is entirely a creation of the Fourth Style and need not occupy us here; there is no indication of what the garden area and garden rooms might have been like in the period of the Third Style or, indeed, of how much of the irregular space that these now occupy then belonged to this house. Throughout the atrium complex the decorations are in a consistent Third Style, all relatively rich, especially in the rooms for entertaining, all clearly part of a single plan, and the pavements throughout are of blackish signinum ornamented with bits of colored marble or patterns of tesserae with occasional use of mosaic.

To this period we can also assign the atrium complex of the Casa dei Calavi (I vi 11) (*NSc* 1929, 404–27 [A. Maiuri]; Pernice 1938, 106) and I vii 19 (*NSc* 1929, 354–79 [A. Maiuri]; Pernice 1938, 107), a small house attached to the Casa dell'Efebo, both apparently rebuildings of older houses.

Multistorey Houses Built on Terraces

Along the edge of the city site from the Porta di Ercolano to the Forum Triangulare a series of remarkable houses interrupted occasionally by public or semipublic buildings crowns the walls of Pompeii and spills over these in descending terraces that have a commanding view of the Bay of Naples and the valley of the Sarno River, with the magnificent mountains of the Sorrentine Peninsula beyond. The fortifications of Pompeii show numerous signs of a complete re-

FIGURE 36.
The Casa di Marco Lucrezio Frontone, Atrium

modeling and modernization after the siege of Sulla, therefore probably after the arrival of the Roman colony, and they are not apt to have seemed expendable before the Augustan period. The earliest building to be constructed in encroachment on them may well have been the Villa Imperiale at the Porta Marina, which is decorated in fully developed Third Style.[15] Therefore the criteria for dating used by Noack and Lehmann must be abandoned. None of the terraces built over the city walls will have been republican, and the great majority will have been created in the first half of the first century of our era and can be considered Third Style architecture. Only a few of the houses in block VIII ii were in usable condition at the time of the eruption, perhaps only nos. 1, 3, parts of 22–24, and 39. Most were a welter of naked masonry, broken floors and plaster, and building equipment and material. But Maiuri to the contrary notwithstanding (1942, 138–44), few of these ever seem to have been houses of the rich or noble. Many of them were multiple-family housing, essentially apartment houses. Such must have been VIII ii 14–16, 29–30, 36–37, and VII Ins. Occ. 12–15. Others seem to have been broken up into apartments later.[16]

One that was probably a single-family dwelling throughout its history is VIII ii 28 (Noack and Lehmann 70–77 with earlier bibliography; Neuerburg 131). One entered the tetrastyle atrium by fauces stepped up from an open outer vestibule, off which to the east opened a small corridorlike room with a bench built into the northeast corner, an anteroom to the kitchen. The kitchen lies east of this room and must have been at least in part an open court, since the windows in the north wall were walled up in the last period. The hearth platform is against the east wall, the latrine a closet with a tiny window built into the northeast corner. A masonry basin with rounded corners in the northeast corner was apparently for washing up. Along the south wall is a stair that must have turned at the southeast corner and continued in a second flight, with perhaps a gallery or a loft along the north side. The upper storey seems to have covered only parts of the service rooms.

The atrium is tetrastyle with a big tufa impluvium that was later veneered with marble. The columns were originally Ionic or Corinthian but baseless and heavily stuccoed in the last period.[17] As is

[15] See K. Schefold, *Pompejanische Malerei* (Basel 1952) 105–9; Schefold 290–93; and Kraus and von Matt figs. 128–30. The relation to the city walls of rooms in VIII ii 0, west of VIII ii 1, with First and Second Style decorations (Laidlaw 262–64) cannot be determined.

[16] The largest of these, VII Ins. Occ. 16–19, the Casa di Fabio Rufo, is not yet available for general study, and those in VI Ins. Occ., which were excavated in the eighteenth century, are now poorly preserved and inadequately published.

[17] Noack and Lehmann (72) made the astonishing statement that there was probably

often the case in tetrastyle atria, the alae are located in the centre of each side to make a cross axis, and here they were framed with pilasters. The rooms on the west side of the atrium are much shallower than those on the east. Here the rooms flanking the ala were storerooms, while those on the opposite side were cubicula. The room west of the fauces had a window to the street and may have been a small dining room. In the northwest corner of the atrium, between this and the storeroom next to it, a lararium was built in the last period. At the south end of the atrium the tablinum was open across both front and back, perhaps with a folding grillwork across the atrium end, where the sill preserves cuttings for some sort of closure. It also has doors to either side at its south end, so it was very open in plan. East of it runs an andron, off which open a cubiculum and a small exedra facing south to the view across the deep apron of the terrace. West of the tablinum is a larger exedra of the size and proportions of a triclinium, also open across its whole south side to the view.

Beyond this bank of rooms stretches a broad, flat terrace that must have been finished with a parapet or fence, no trace of which survives. Along the west wall a stair leads down to a single storey below. This consists of a single important room, a triclinium embellished with a nymphaeum, and dependencies. One came first to a small square vestibule from which a narrow vaulted passage led around the back of the nymphaeum to a couple of small rooms on the far side that must have been used chiefly for storage in the last period. The passage evidently served for control of the water supply and fountains, as did another cellar under the andron; it seems to have been a rather complex system. The fountain room has a barrel vault covered with rustication, and the pavement and walls were largely veneered with marble. The water entered by a water stair in a deep vaulted niche and fell into a narrow basin that extended across the width of the room, its front wall being broken into niches, rather like a theatre stage. The nymphaeum was enriched with rustication varied with painting, mosaic, and veneering. Small windows to either side of the water source may have served for special lighting effects. Opposite the nymphaeum a large rectangular window commands the view.

In plan and appointments this house is graceful but hardly pretentious. The family seems to have been a small one that entertained

no tetrastyle atrium in Pompeii of the Tufa Period, none before the beginning of the Second Style. Not only does the Tufa Period continue through the time of the Second Style but such tetrastyle atria as those of the Casa del Fauno and the Casa dell'Argenteria are certainly very ancient, to be dated in the first half of the second century B.C.

only on a limited scale. The traditional arrangement and proportions of rooms in an atrium plan were kept throughout its history, and when it became possible to build over the walls of the city, a simple terrace was added. The fountain room seems to have been invented late as a whim, almost a private folly, designed as a surprise for visitors. It cannot have been usable as a dining room except in the summer months, and indeed there is much about the openness of this house as a whole that suggests that through much of the year it would have been uncomfortable. It seems to have been generally redecorated after the earthquake of 62, tastefully but not lavishly, as would become a conservative family of moderate wealth.

The Casa di Championnet (VIII ii 1) preserves elements of considerable antiquity (Noack and Lehmann 110–21 with earlier bibliography). In the last period it boasted a tetrastyle atrium with a small square impluvium veneered with marble. The order is not known, as the columns awaited final stuccoing. The atrium is entered through short fauces between small cubicula lit by high slit windows. There are rooms only along the east side of the atrium, a triclinium of canonical shape with segmental vault in the northeast corner lit by another slit window, a large square cubiculum communicating with the rooms to either side, as well as the atrium, and an ala, into which have been built a pair of small closets. Opposite the entrance are an axial tablinum open across both front and back; an andron to the west of this; and a cluster of small rooms to the east carved out of what was probably originally a small dining room entered from the atrium and looking out on the peristyle, and a stair leading down to a lower storey to the east of this that debouched in the ala. In the last period a new entrance corridor to bring people directly from the street to the lower storey had been built along the east side of the house, opening at VIII ii 2, and a piece had been taken from the north side of the dining room to make a new access to the stair from the atrium. Moreover, a second-storey room seems to have been installed above the dining room and the closets built into the ala, accessible by a stair over the stair to the lower storey leading up from the northeast corner of the peristyle.

The peristyle is square, four columns on a side, the columns almost excessively delicate, footed on a masonry pluteus outside which runs a broad gutter. What would normally be garden space is sunken and paved, and a light is arranged in each intercolumniation to light a cryptoporticus under the peristyle. Four circular light wells symmetrically placed light rooms under the open area. South of this everything is in a ruinous state, but the south portico of the peristyle seems to have given access to rooms a half-storey lower overlooking the view, their axes turned at 45° to the rest to obtain the best prospect, so they must be presumed to have been reception rooms. Here also a stair of five steps led up to a terrace at a higher level covering this mezzanine.

The lower storey was once an arcaded court under the peristyle surrounded by a vaulted passageway off which opened a few insignificant closets dug into the bedrock to the north, while a fair-sized room opened off the stair of access a little more than halfway down. Presumably, therefore, the large rooms to the south of which only ruins remain were original parts of this storey. In the last period the sunken court was divided into four square rooms that did not communicate with one another but only with the cryptoporticus, each given a barrel vault. These would have made a cool retreat from the summer heat. Beyond the south wing of the cryptoporticus, facing the Sarno Valley, a large vaulted room a half-storey lower than the cryptoporticus was accessible by a sloping corridor opening out of the southeast corner of the cryptoporticus. This was certainly a triclinium for banquets and had a wide door in its south wall commanding a view over the Sarno Valley. The other arrangements and rooms in this wing are not clear, and the evidence has been confused by modern repairs and rebuilding. A very few remains of Third Style decoration survive in dependencies of the arcaded lower court, while the atrium and almost all the rooms around it, including the tablinum, the little dining room, and the great new triclinium in the lowest storey of the terrace, have remains of Fourth Style painting.

Overall the house gives an impression of some decline and decay from the days when the peristyle stood over a sunken court with arcades and rooms in at least two storeys gave onto the view to the south. The new entrance from the street to the lower storey and the filling in of the sunken court make it very probable that this was now either a hospitium apartment or let out to a tenant, a clumsy and arbitrary agglomeration of spaces hardly worthy of the name architecture, with only a single fine room. The atrium also, despite redecoration, shows a certain decline from better days in the remodeling of the ala and the chopping up of the dining room east of the tablinum. The novelty of the engineering of the rooms filling the open court is only superficially attractive. Through most of the year what had earlier been a court at least as interesting as those in the houses of Bulla Regia in Tunisia now would have been a sequence of dank cellars, and the division of the fine rooms between the two apartments gave neither tenant much choice when it came to entertaining. What before the earthquake had been a spacious and gracious house was now undistinguished middle-class housing for a couple of families.

Although the Casa di Giuseppe II (VIII ii 39) may have been the elegant residence of a rich family as late as the earthquake of 62, by the time of the eruption it was, as Noack and Lehmann observed, well on its way to becoming little more than slum tenements (Noack and Lehmann 18–30 with earlier bibliography; Maiuri 1942, 144). Noack and Lehmann distinguished seven building periods, beginning with a very ancient house, for most of which the evidence is slight or dubious, and the dating of the major building periods requires revision. The expansion of the house by the addition of lower storeys cannot be republican, nor is it likely to have occurred before the middle of the first century, since the apartment created in the first of the lower storeys is a medianum apartment. The medianum form, not really represented elsewhere in Pompeii, became prevalent in the high-rise insulae of Ostia and Rome; here it seems to have been used as an addition to the main house.

In the last period of Pompeii the atrium complex kept little of the splendor it once boasted. The façade was plain, bare of plaster, the fauces short and somewhat closed down at the outer end by a jamb in opus mixtum vittatum to make a lodge for the doorkeeper. The Tuscanic atrium kept its original dimensions, but most of the rooms around it were rebuilt in one way or another. The handsome old impluvium with tufa rim and floor was unaltered, and a series of engaged columns with fine Corinthian capitals raised on high plinths that trimmed the openings to the alae and the corners of the atrium was for the most part preserved. The quarter-column in the northwest corner was sacrificed, as were the half-columns that once embellished the opening to the tablinum.

In the northwest corner of the house a shop was built by opening a door in the façade on the Vicolo della Regina. This is not so wide as most shop doors, and the room itself being small, a narrow door in the south wall gave access to the atrium and a narrow, awkward stair leading up to the west, then back to the east. Tile-lined beam holes in the west wall of the shop at a level well below the top of the second flight show that there must have been two storeys here, a mezzanine and a true second storey. These probably covered only the area of the shop itself, since the kitchen next to it is windowless. In connection with this shop the three cubicula on the west side of the atrium were converted to use as storerooms for stock, given a high signinum dado and fitted with shelves along the walls. The front wall of the first has been torn out to the height of a low pluteus, presumably for the installation of a wooden counter on which to display goods. All of this makes one suppose that the shop was not likely to have been run by the occupants of the rooms on the east side of the atrium. The upper storeys over the shop will have provided all the living quarters necessary for the shopkeeper.

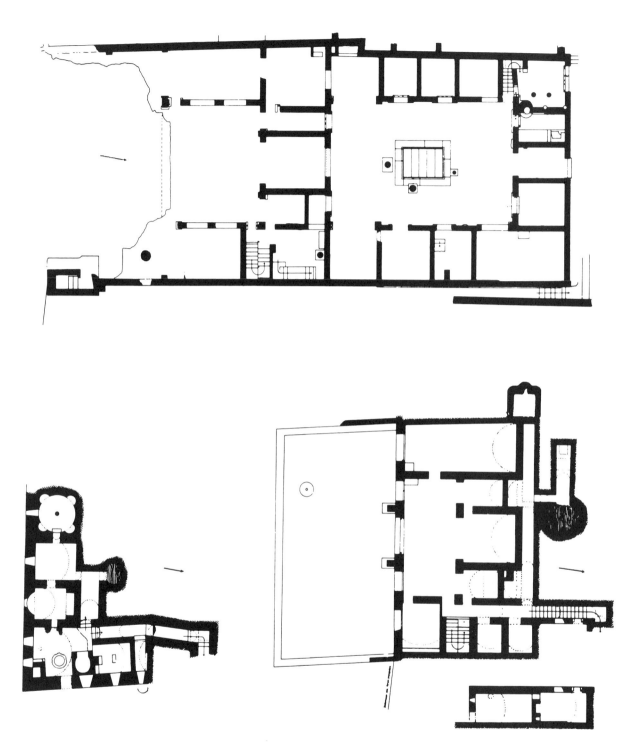

FIGURE 37.
The Casa di Giuseppe II, Plan of the Successive Storeys

On the east side of the atrium we find first a square cubiculum beside the fauces where Mau saw an altar, then a large rectangular triclinium with an unusually broad door, a cubiculum remodeled to serve as a stairwell, and a cubiculum with doors to both the atrium and the east ala. The stair led east, then north, and the second storey will have covered only the northeast corner of the atrium, possibly only the triclinium, and consisted at most of a couple of rooms. Therefore it seems logical to see the kitchen and latrine installed west of the fauces as in common use by the tenants on both sides of the atrium. The east ala served as a sitting room for the apartment on the east side; the west ala, which probably from the beginning had a niche in its southwest corner for a cupboard that at some later time was fitted with shelves, may have served as more storage space for the shop or as a sitting room, possibly both.

The tablinum opening to the atrium was walled up and the tablinum turned to face south, though a large window in this wall still looked into the atrium. The tablinum now became the central room of a separate apartment entered through the old andron. This apartment, the handsomest in the house, was remarkably symmetrical. The tablinum was axial, open across nearly its whole southern front to a courtyard. West of the andron and accessible from it was a square oecus that opened by a window in its north wall to the west ala and by a door in the south wall to the room next-door. This room probably served as a dining room, and the little room east of the tablinum where a place for a piece of furniture along the north wall is marked off in the mosaic floor must be a ladies' dining room. This had once been used in connection with a men's triclinium east of it, an area with which it still communicates by a narrow door but which in the last period became a stairwell with stairs leading both up and down, a public lobby accessible from both the atrium and the tablinum apartment.

East and west of the tablinum courtyard were large rectangular rooms that opened by a door and a pair of ample windows to the court and across the whole south end to the view. These can only have been reception rooms, and the treatment of the south walls seems to force the conclusion that there can have been little, if any, obstruction between them and the edge of the terrace covering the storey below this. The architect must have been reluctant to load the vaults. These have almost entirely collapsed, so it is impossible to tell whether there might have been light pavilions and diaetae of the sort that one finds in the sea-front houses of Herculaneum, but enough survives for us to be certain that the plan of the storey below was not reproduced here. The colonnade that Noack and Lehmann restored along this front and the row of rooms behind it (pl. 21) are entirely imaginary and preposterous. On the other hand, Noack and Leh-mann made the sage observation that the plan of the rooms in the lower storey so closely reproduces the plan of the tablinum apart-ment as to constitute strong evidence that it derives from it, in which case we can trace the evolution of the medianum plan directly from the atrium-peristyle house. It was an adaptation of the bank of rooms between atrium and peristyle turned to face the peristyle and taken together with a small piece of the peristyle.

Since this apartment seems to consist entirely of public rooms and reception rooms, we must presume that its bedrooms were arranged in the upper storey, accessible by the stair along the east wall of the lobby off the southeast corner of the atrium. This led up to the north, turned along the north wall, and then seems to have turned again along the west wall, bringing its head between the ladies' dining room east of the tablinum and the stairwell down to the lower storey. There can have been only a couple of small bedrooms here in the immediate vicinity of this, as the tablinum and the windowed room to the south would have required lofty ceilings if they were not to appear cramped.

The stair to the floors below led out of the same lobby. People could reach this directly from the atrium, so there would have been minimal disturbance to people in the northeast apartment and even less to those in the tablinum apartment. Along the stair down, two small rooms connected in sequence led off to the east midway be-tween the floors, and two others at the same level seem to have been accessible only by ladders from the narrow corridor that runs behind the lower apartment. The former may have served as bedrooms, though they would hardly have been comfortable bedrooms; the lat-ter and the corridor itself, aside from its value as insulation against the damp of the bedrock, can have served only for storage. The cor-ridor runs the full length of the apartment and has vaulted bays under the ends of these mezzanine rooms as well. The stair de-bouches into a corridor of its own width that runs south to a blank wall. Along it two very small square rooms open off to the east and the aforementioned corridor to the west, while at its southern end two doors on the west give access to the apartment on this level and to the east a stair leads down to a second lower storey.

The apartment here consists of a large central lobby, a room at either end, and three rooms behind the lobby that received their nat-ural light only from it. The lobby, or medianum, is lit by a large cen-tral door flanked by symmetrical windows opposite the openings to the rooms behind. The room off the far side of the lobby is the largest of all, a great barrel-vaulted rectangle lit by a very large window at its south end, clearly the main reception room, what in a medianum apartment is called an exedra. In an Ostian apartment the room at the opposite end would be similar but smaller, the second largest room. Here it is very much smaller, not so large as the tablinumlike exedra on the axis of the lobby, and might be thought of as a bedroom were it not for the large window designed to command the view. The "tablinum" seems now to have been converted into a triclinium and communicates with a small exedra that must be a ladies' dining room to the west of it. A similar, slightly smaller exedra to the east also communicates with the corridor of access by a small door whose purpose is unclear. All rooms except perhaps the lobby are vaulted, some with barrel vaults, some with segmental vaults. Whether the lobby was vaulted is unknown, as this part has collapsed completely.

From the lobby a large central door of two leaves led out to a terrace over the storey below. The door is flanked by deeply projecting unfluted pilasters that Noack and Lehmann suggested carried a pediment, a rather unlikely feature for a Pompeian door. It is more likely that they carried a cornice or a shed roof. The terrace is virtually featureless, a rhomboid, almost a rectangle, surrounded by a low masonry pluteus into which protrude the tip of the cone of the roof of the frigidarium of the baths and two pipes from the crowns of the vaults of the praefurnium and the caldarium set close to the pluteus. All three served for ventilation.

The lowest storey was reached by a stair at the end of the corridor of approach to the storey above, a stair that doubled back upon itself and was continued by a long sloping corridor with occasional steps along its length. It is vaulted, and off it opens a narrow closet with a splayed window at the end, evidently for storage. The corridor debouches into the praefurnium, a room with a large oven of typical form built into the northeast corner. A large masonry bin fills the southeast corner, and the mouth of the firebox under the caldarium opens in the middle of the west wall. The room is well lit by four windows in two walls. Behind the oven is the workroom where the bread must have been mixed and kneaded. Out of the northwest corner of the praefurnium a short corridor leads west and at its west end has narrow doorways to either side. That to the south leads to the tepidarium of the bath suite, a square room slightly larger than the others, presumed on this account to have served as an apodyterium as well, but the entrance corridor could also have been so used. The door to the north now leads to nothing, and whatever the builders had in mind, it would have had to be a windowless cellar of little usefulness, except for storage. To either side of the tepidarium are other bath rooms, a caldarium to the east with an apse for a labrum and a rectangular niche for a tub opposite this. Over the labrum is a circular window. To the west of the tepidarium is a circular frigidarium with a conical ceiling and four niches for bathers. According to Mau, there was a fountain in the centre of the room, but it has left no trace. This bath suite is unusually sophisticated. Few private houses have so elaborate a bath complex, perhaps only the Casa del Centenario and the Casa del Menandro. Perhaps this should be taken as indication that in the last period this bath was at least semipublic and run for profit and that bread was baked for more than the household here.

The contrast between this as a private house of many splendid rooms and luxurious appointments and its final remodeling into shop and apartments could hardly be more dismaying. Yet it must be pointed out at once that these apartments were not squalid; in fact they were spacious and must have commanded relatively high rents. From the beginning this was a fine house of generous proportions, and when the lower storeys were added, it became a mansion. The similarity in plan between the tablinum and its neighboring rooms and the medianum apartment below it suggests that the expansion was to accommodate a son's family. The addition of an elaborate bath suite at the same time indicates that these were rich people as well. Like many spacious houses of fine plan and construction, it lent itself to breaking up when the earthquake destroyed so much of the city and the need for housing became acute. Whether it would ever have been restored to anything like its former grandeur is a question that must remain unanswered.

Conclusions

When one tries to summarize and synthesize one's impressions of Third Style domestic architecture, one is immediately in trouble; it is a style full of contradictions. Clearly the old conception of the house as a frame for the Pompeian gentleman as patronus and *hospes* has little continuing validity. In house after house we find the tablinum either eliminated or reduced in importance to function as an alcove or a comfortable sitting room fairly sharply separated from the atrium. The atrium tends to be diminutive even in houses of importance, and the emphasis on monumentality seems to have entirely disappeared. There is a greater interest in gardens, especially ornamental gardens, so increased that it is now possible to have a house of some pretensions without an atrium, a peristyle replacing the atrium. Earlier we might expect to find an atrium without a peristyle, but hardly the reverse. Dining rooms now, if they are not winter dining rooms, almost without exception look to a garden, though the garden is seldom axial with relation to a dining room. Houses tend to be intimate and comfortable, with small rooms, easily heated; they would have required comparatively few servants. But almost every house has one big room for dinner parties, usually with a ladies' dining room adjacent. One feels that money has disappeared from Pompeii, that few people thought of living lavishly, that the most they aspired to was a pretty house full of bright color, sparkling with freshness. The delicacy of the architecture in the decorations, the tiny figures in jewel-like colors, the use of white marble in impluvium frames and marble tables and bits of colored marble to enhance pavements, all combine as parts of a single aesthetic. But on occasion there might be a very sumptuous and spacious room, almost a revival of the majesty of the past.

16 · THE VILLAS

Introduction

Fortunately, two villas of the Third Style have been discovered near Pompeii; unfortunately, neither of them is accessible today. The more noteworthy of these, the Villa di Cicerone on the Via dei Sepolcri, was in one of the earliest excavated parts of Pompeii, and when it had been looted of its contents and decorations, the excavations were filled in again, and they have never been cleared since then. But the finds were impressive and enrich the collections of the Museo Nazionale, and the excavators kept a record of work and prepared a plan of the parts of the villa they explored, so we have some knowledge of it. The other, the Villa di Agrippa Postumo, was discovered on private land at Boscotrecase in 1902. Between 1902 and 1905 a peristyle, a domestic quarter, and part of a series of decorated rooms opening on a long terrace were excavated, and various paintings and panels of decoration were removed. These came ultimately into the collections of the Museo Nazionale in Naples and the Metropolitan Museum of Art in New York. The house was then covered by a flow of lava in the eruption of Vesuvius in April 1906, and no further effort at excavation has been made since. Though all we have left is a sequence of four rooms, these rank among the finest decorations in the Third Style, and their attachment to a historical figure of known dates, a member of the Julio-Claudian house, gives us reason to suppose that they might belong to a villa of the finest architectural quality as well.

The Villa di Agrippa Postumo at Boscotrecase

The parts of the Villa di Agrippa Postumo excavated were clearly divided among three units, none of which was the main body of the house.[1] The land sloped sharply to the south and somewhat less sharply to the east. What was explored seems to have been the eastern wing, while important parts of the nobler apartments continued to the west, and very likely the atrium and its dependencies stood to the north, higher on the slope.

The domestic quarter was entirely utilitarian in its architecture, a courtyard with deep porticoes on two sides and a part of a third, with a kitchen and latrine, places for animals, and a row of uniform cells along one long side. Clearly divided from this and accessible from it only at the southeast corner was a row of rooms of uniform depth and nearly uniform size fronting south on a long raised terrace commanding a panoramic view. The terrace had a low parapet but seems not to have been decorated. The decorated rooms all had black-and-white mosaic pavements and were decorated in the Third Style. The first two from the east end had very wide doorways and communicated with one another. Their decoration was especially handsome. Next to them was a room of the same size and architectural character, also with a mosaic pavement, but converted to use as a passage connecting the terrace with the peristyle behind this row of rooms and with walls faced with plain white plaster. Following this was another undecorated room, then two decorated rooms a little smaller than the first pair flanking a corridor leading north to a group of small rooms of uncertain character.

The peristyle was square, with five columns on a side. What rooms may have used it as their focus and how it was built into the plan of the whole is not clear. According to Della Corte, it had a Second Style decoration of a rather severe sort, with painted columns responding to those of the portico (*NSc* 1922, 476). Given the proportions of the peristyle, this is not improbable, but the description of it makes one suspect that it was actually Third Style: "for each actual column of the portico there corresponded on the wall a similar painted column, in such a way as to have the illusion of a double portico on the background which was treated in great black marble plates, 0.87–0.90 m wide, between the frieze, which has completely disappeared, and the socle treated as a high projecting base constructed of smaller ashlar blocks of polychrome veined and breccia marble." It certainly was not normal Second Style.[2]

We have here a clearly transitional building that unites elements of the villa rustica, the traditional republican villa designed around

[1] *NSc* 1922, 459–78 (M. Della Corte); P. H. von Blanckenhagen and C. Alexander, *The Paintings from Boscotrecase, RömMitt* supp. 6 (1962), esp. 9–17.

[2] Cf. the decoration of the interior of the Temple of Jupiter and Mau's comments on this in Mau 1882, 248.

peristyles and farmyards, and the portico villa, in which rooms are arranged in banks on successive terraces to take advantage of the view. The earliest instance of such a portico villa may be the imperial villas on Capri. Here we see it in very tentative form, and the date of ca. 12 B.C. given the villa by von Blanckenhagen may be supported by this. A little later we see the architectural type fully developed in the Fourth Style Varano villas at Stabiae.

The Villa di Cicerone on the Via dei Sepolcri

The approach to the Villa di Cicerone[3] is not known, except that it opened off the Via dei Sepolcri. It was preceded by a row of seven or eight more or less uniform shops behind a covered walk, an arcade similar to one on the opposite side of the road. The house itself was oriented toward the sea and the view over the bay, its service quarters, storage, and sleeping apartments were probably placed between the road and the living rooms around one or more utilitarian courtyards and peristyles. What we see on the plan is a small peristyle of six columns with a fountain basin revetted with marble in the middle, approached by a long corridor from the direction of the Via dei Sepolcri along which open rooms of irregular plan and no clear pattern. From this peristyle one could pass north through a bank of rooms, some of them large and paved with mosaic, to another court, or atrium, parallel to the little peristyle. This would appear to have been the heart of the house, and from it there was access west to a large T-shaped room where the Dioscurides mosaics were found set into the pavements of the arms of the tee. This gives on the southwest onto a large square room with a big opening in the middle of each wall, exposed to the view on three sides and surrounded on these three sides by a terrace. The large emblema from the centre of its floor was evidently retrieved by the survivors. The terrace was paved with mosaic and colonnaded on all three sides. The symmetry of the planning of the rooms in this part of the house is striking. To the southeast was a suite of two dining rooms with decorations on a black ground, including miniature dancers, satyrs, centaurs, and so on, that are now one of the great prizes of the Museo Nazionale. The room balancing these two on the opposite side of the house does not seem to have been richly decorated, though it had a mosaic pavement. Northwest of this block at a lower level was found a large sunken garden sur-

---

[3]*PAH* 1.1.7, 150–58; 1.2.102–10. Herrmann and Bruckmann 1.119–24. The excavation of this building is very confusing, though La Vega's notes in *PAH* explaining the plan of the complex are extremely helpful and go far toward explaining what happened and where things were found.

rounded by an arcade, nine piers by eleven. Our general impression of the house is that space was available and exploited not only to take advantage of the most commanding views and greatest privacy but as an element in itself. In this it is unlike all other private buildings in the Third Style.

17 · THE TOMBS

Altar Tombs

In the Augustan period the altar tomb seems to have suffered some slight decline in popularity, but if it did, it had certainly recovered before the earthquake of A.D. 62. Along the Via dei Sepolcri, tombs north 1 and 3 may be the ruins of Augustan altar tombs; so Kockel would reconstruct them and date them (Kockel 111–15, 117–18). But 3 is a small affair, reduced to a rectangular footing of concrete faced with blocks of lava surmounted by a base molding of tufa, with only two sides—south and east—still preserved. There is a strong suggestion that the tomb was destroyed in antiquity to make room for others; it is shown as complete by La Vega but not by Mazois (Kockel pl. 69c; Mazois 1, pls. 1–2 [Kockel pl. 1a]). A fragment of a pulvinus decorated with a divided scale pattern for which there is no other readily available place might have come from the superstructure. Tomb 1 consists of a rectangular base faced with tufa blocks and trimmed with limestone moldings. Kockel would restore this as an altar tomb about 4.10 m high, but there is no real evidence. Against it are piled four large unfluted drums of a tufa column that might have been a monumental funerary column from a tomb, a tomb of the same type as that of Septumia outside the Porta del Vesuvio (*NSc* 1910, 406–9). Some of the drums were already there in Mazois's day (Mazois 1, pl. 2 [Kockel pl. 1a]). Accessible by an inconspicuous door in the east wall, 0.60 m high, is a small vaulted tomb chamber built into the concrete core. This contained urns that held ashes, fragments of carved ivory, probably from the funeral couches, and coins, the latest of which was struck between 23 B.C. and 7 B.C.

In the Porta di Nocera necropolis, tomb west 17 (17 OS) is a handsome die of concrete faced with opus incertum of broken lava revetted on the front and sides with seven courses of drafted blocks of Nocera tufa finished with base and crown moldings also of tufa. It stands on a footing of concrete faced with blocks of lava. It was surmounted by a superstructure that stepped back from the top of the die in at least two steps, above which modern restoration has confused the evidence. The height of the die and the stepping back of the superstructure make it seem likely to have been an altar tomb. Just below the crown molding on the front a long plate of marble was let into the revetment. This carried at least six inscriptions—five of which survive—of members of the gens Tillia, one of whom, apparently the man who erected the tomb, was duovir. His brother was tribunus militum in the tenth legion, Julius Caesar's favorite; and his father was twice duovir at Arpinum. The family had apparently moved to Pompeii in the time of the late republic but were still proud of their earlier distinction at Arpinum and Verulae. The tomb chamber is entered at the back of the monument, a comparatively large one with a barrel-vaulted ceiling.

Just west of tomb west 17, west 19 (19 OS) is similar. Above a footing of concrete faced with opus incertum of broken lava that was meant to be concealed runs a socle of roughly finished blocks of Nocera tufa capped with a base molding similar to that of west 17. Above this rises a die of concrete revetted on front and sides with plates of tufa finished to simulate drafted ashlar. Parts of four courses survive. In the front is a small recess for an inscription, now lacking. The tomb chamber was entered from the back of the monument. It looks as though west 19 and west 17 were built in conjunction with one another, 19 being slightly older than 17, which projects in front of it a little and was apparently slightly higher. There is a suggestion that the families of the two tombs were connected.

If none of these tombs need have been an altar tomb, two very handsome ones that belong close in date to the earthquake certainly were. On the Via dei Sepolcri, tomb south 16, the tomb of Umbricius Scaurus, the garum (fishpaste) manufacturer, stands by itself in a very large trapezoidal enclosure not aligned with the road. (Kockel 70–75). It consists of a plain die revetted with plates of tufa with offset socle and simple crown molding, above which the crown steps back in two steps revetted with marble and is surmounted by a small funerary altar elegantly finished with marble on all sides, although much of the material came secondhand. The inscription that, with its frame, filled the front of the altar informs us that Scaurus was duovir and that the decuriones voted him both plot and monument, plus a sum of money for his funeral and an equestrian statue. The tomb chamber is accessible from the back, barrel-vaulted, sunk to half its height below ground level, with five small niches for urns.

The tomb of Naevoleia Tyche, tomb south 22, farther along the road, was built by her for herself and C. Munatius Faustus, Augustalis, and their freedmen and freedwomen (Kockel 100–109). But in fact Munatius Faustus was buried in a much simpler tomb, Via di Nocera necropolis 9 ES. Naevoleia Tyche's tomb stands at the front of a small enclosure, its walls embellished with merlons capped with pyramids at the corners. The base of the tomb proper is faced with blocks of tufa with lower offset footing and crowning courses. At the crown it steps back in two steps revetted with marble and is surmounted by a small altar decorated with reliefs framed with acanthus scrolls on three faces. On the front is a small bust of Naevoleia Tyche, full-face, in a pinax above the inscription, and below it is a long panel showing, as Kockel rightly saw, a distribution of grain. On the left side is shown the bisellium voted to Munatius Faustus by the decuriones, on the right side a merchantman under sail manned by six sailors. The altar is finished with pulvini decorated with acanthus leaves. One entered the enclosure to the left of the tomb by a large, well-framed door, and the tomb chamber from behind by a similar door. The chamber has a segmental vault and is surrounded on three sides by a bench under which there are arched niches for urns; in the walls above there are more niches, arched, except for a large central rectangular one in the end wall. The reliefs decorating the altar must refer to events in the life of Munatius Faustus—a distribution of grain, perhaps on the occasion of his receiving the bisellium, the bisellium itself, and the sea commerce that was probably the source of his wealth. In the tomb were found a glass ash urn and numerous lamps, while in the enclosure were three gravestones. A number of details, including the hair style in the reliefs, date the tomb toward A.D. 60.

Aedicula Tombs

The aedicula tomb continued to be very popular in Augustan and Julio-Claudian times. On the north side of the Via dei Sepolcri, well out from the city, just beyond the point where the road forks, stands a group of closely connected tombs raised on a low, terraced elevation, tombs 38–43 (Kockel 173–84). The most pretentious of these was 38, probably the tomb of M. Popidius, an aedicula tomb of which only the ruined base now remains. This was a high, plain die of concrete faced with opus incertum of broken lava surmounted by a second storey stepped back only slightly from the first, the corners trimmed with pilasters and the lower half of the panels between these divided again by short pilasters, two on the short sides, three on the long, crowned with a straight cornice. Some of the lower panels thus formed were filled with grillwork lattices in stucco relief, others with figures, including an armed soldier with his horse. On the front of the tomb above the cornice were garlands swung in loops framing shoulder busts, of which only the shoulders remained at the time of excavation.[1] To the superstructure might belong a fragment of a marble column or a block of tufa roofing with simple coffering that lie in the vicinity. Nine funerary statues were found in the area: three of marble, of which two were togati and one was a woman in the pudicitia pose; five of tufa, of which three were togati and two were women in the pudicitia pose; the ninth a togatus of uncertain material. The togati all wear the toga exigua without sinus, the right arm pulled close to the chest, and must be late republican or early Augustan. A marble togatus and marble female statue (Kockel nos. 1 and 2) are probably to be associated with this tomb, although Kockel's assertion that they come from the same workshop seems improbable. The tomb chamber was accessible by a small opening high in the west side. It has a small arched niche in the east wall.

Tangent to this at its northwest corner, tomb north 39 is a long rectangle in plan with two storeys, a plain die base and an upper storey set back from this above a beveled joint. There are brickwork coigns in the upper storey. Probably it was crowned with an aedicula of three niches behind a façade of four columns of brick. The tomb chamber is accessible from behind, transverse and barrel-vaulted with seven rectangular niches in the south wall. Generally associated with tomb north 39 is an inscription on marble identifying it as the tomb of L. Ceius Labeo, a quinquennial duovir (*CIL* 10.1037). Also in the vicinity were three gravestones of Ceia, daughter of Lucius, L. Ceius Communis, Servilia, and Lucceia Ianuaria. The tomb is later than north 38, but probably only very little later.

Tomb north 43 strongly resembles north 39 in almost every particular. A long rectangle in plan, it now consists of two storeys, the lower a plain die, the upper set back from this and coigned with brickwork. The upper storey may have been trimmed with stucco pilasters at the corners and must have carried an aedicula; west of the tomb lies a column of brickwork with stucco fluting. One can envisage an aedicula of three niches behind a façade of four columns. The tomb chamber was accessible from the east and lay three meters below the level on the exterior. With the tomb is associated an inscription for P. Sittius Diophantus, Augustalis (*CIL* 10.1034). The tomb appears contemporary with, and a twin to, north 39, although one might wonder a bit at the association of a freedman of the Sittii with the quinquennial duovir Ceius.

North 42, along the road in front of north 43 and blocking the view of it from this side, is a diminutive example of the same type. Mazois

---

[1] See Mazois 1, pl. 16, figs. 1 and 2 (Kockel pl. 64, figs. c and d).

shows it as a single storey with plain pilasters with Corinthian capitals at the corners, the space between finished with stucco showing low socle, high orthostats, and three courses of running ashlar (Mazois 1, pl. 4, figs. 1 and 5 [Kockel pl. 67b]). The orthostats of the façade are embellished with a pair of elongated fasces, and an inscription on marble identified it as the tomb of M. Arrius Diomedes, freedman of Arria, magister pagi Augusti Felicis Suburbani. Mazois restores it with a simple triangular pediment. In view of its small size, it seems unlikely to have had a second storey and should be read instead as a rendering in stucco of a prostyle distyle aedicula, a simplified form of the aedicula tomb later than the others in this group by perhaps half a century.

In the Porta di Nocera necropolis we also find some notable examples of the aedicula tomb belonging to this period. Tomb west 23 (23 OS) is a shallow aedicula tomb raised on a high base faced with opus incertum coigned with brickwork. The aedicula is a simple rectangular niche in antis with a triangular pediment, now largely restored. Moldings and other decoration were carried out in stucco. In the back of the monument opens a niche for burials. Within the aedicula are three headless statues of tufa, two togati with sinus and umbo, one a woman wearing chiton and mantle carrying a torch. The inscription identifies the tomb as that of P. Vesonius Phileros, Augustalis; Vesonia, his patrona; and M. Orfellius Faustus, amicus. A second inscription hints at a bitter tale of friendship betrayed. The base of the tomb and the enclosure in which it stands were largely buried in antiquity, and secondary burials were made at the new level. Despite the small size of the monument, it seems to have been used for at least fifteen burials. A Julio-Claudian date is indicated.

Another tomb of such date is tomb east 13 (13 ES), a square die tomb of concrete faced with opus incertum of lava coigned with brickwork. Above the footing two molded steps trim a very high die finished with stucco. Pilasters with Corinthian capitals frame each face, and in the centre of the front is a panoply of arms in stucco relief. The die was finished at the crown with a molding, now replaced by modern brickwork. It seems likely that the die carried an aedicula for two statues with two columns in front. The inscription is lacking, but the monument was repaired in antiquity; the damage seems likely to have been in consequence of the earthquake of 62.

Tomb east 1 (1 ES) is a low die tomb in a very large enclosure surrounded by a high wall, so that now it almost seems to crouch behind it. The base is of concrete faced with opus incertum of lava and finished with a molding of travertine in front, above which the body of the structure steps back sharply. There is nothing to show how it should be completed, but it seems most likely that this was the base of a large aedicula. It is located to be conspicuous to persons coming out the Porta di Nocera, and the height of the enclosure wall suggests that the tomb must have risen well above it. But no elements of an upper storey lie nearby. In the front of the base are two small arched niches for gravestones, and in back, off-centre, the entrance to the tomb chamber. Parts of five gravestones were found in the vicinity—four still *in situ*, three of lava and one of limestone—all uninscribed. Also in the area of this tomb was found a fine male portrait in limestone of an elderly man with sunken cheeks and temples and receding hair (Excavation Inv. No. 10942), a splendid example of the veristic portraiture supposed to derive from funerary masks. This is exceptionally well designed, reading well from all sides, and of an uncommonly lively expression and vigor. The material and appearance of this head in a cemetery are surprising and make the likelihood that the tomb was a major Augustan monument even stronger.

Arch Tombs

A form that continued to be used in the Julio-Claudian period, although not so popular as one might have supposed, was the arch tomb. Pliny (*NH* 34.27) says that the arch was from the beginning essentially a base for the raising of statuary above men's heads, and we might expect to find it so used very widely in cemeteries. But in fact the arch is never a common form of tomb in Pompeii. A small group is found in Porta di Nocera necropolis, in most of which the arch is the base for an architectural superstructure of different form, for example, a tholos (tomb east 4 [4 EN] and Fondo Pacifico no. 1) or an aedicula (tombs east 6 and 12 [6 EN and 12 EN] and Fondo Pacifico nos. 2 and 4), and with the reduction of the fornix in architectural importance it loses its essential character. But in one case the arch seems to have been true and traditional (Fondo Pacifico no. 5) (*RömMitt* 1888, 132–34 [A. Mau]). It is a small monument, only 3.25 m wide and 1.40 m deep, with a barrel-vaulted fornix and simple cornice, above which are three rectangular niches for statuary opening in the front, that in the middle half again as wide as those flanking it. The inscription on marble informs us that this is the monument of P. Mancius Diogenes, a freedman.

Tholos Tombs

The tholos tomb continues in esteem for very monumental tombs, although clearly only the very rich could afford the expense and exposure it entailed. Close to the Porta di Ercolano we have two splendid examples. The more prominent, tomb north 4, is unidentified, but it is a building of the highest interest from a number of points of view. A large square base, over nine meters on a side, of concrete faced with plates of tufa above a low socle of blocks of lava on the front and all of tufa elsewhere rose for more than three courses. In the interior a circular space was left free but divided by heavy walls into four irregular segments. It is clear that this carried a circular superstructure, a tholos of Ionic columns, many elements of which were found nearby. These had Attic bases, shafts reeded full-height, and Pompeian Ionic capitals. Today the surviving elements have been reerected as the superstructure of the tomb of the Istacidii, south 4A, across the road, where they clearly do not belong. Architrave and frieze seem to have disappeared, though Kockel found mention in old reports of a frieze decorated with vine scrolls (Kockel 122–23). Two blocks of a circular cornice now lie in front of tomb north 5, together with the lower part of the finial of a conical roof in the shape of a pinecone decorated with deep bands of acanthus. The last Kockel would support on the unfluted drums piled against north 1, but against this are the aesthetics of the open monopteros and the laborious hollowing out of the core of the finial, which was certainly intended to lighten it. The tholos must have held statuary at a considerable height above the heads of passers-by. As reconstructed, this tomb is very large, and like the monument of the Iulii at Glanum in southern France, it will have seemed heavy compared with the airy mausoleum of Aquileia, the columns short, the decorative carving crowded, but that is probably because of its comparatively early date and the taste that was responsible for the heavy-headed propylaeum of the Forum Triangulare. Kockel wished to set two small tufa altars that stand on the street in front of tomb north 5 at the front corners of this monument, but they might also belong to north 5.

Across the Via dei Sepolcri, on land behind the tombs of M. Porcius and the priestess Mamia that was certainly pomerial, is the tomb of the Istacidii, south 4A. It stands within an artificially terraced enclosure, almost rectangular, surrounded by a parapet wall pierced with round-headed slots at regular intervals to make a balustrade. Only the lowest storey of the tomb survived at the time of excavation, square in plan, raised on a socle of tufa blocks in front, elsewhere of concrete faced with opus incertum coigned with brickwork. Above this rose the die faced with incertum and brickwork, punctuated by an engaged colonnade on a core of brickwork, four columns to a side; the order may have been either Doric or Tuscan. All early observers agree in making the upper storey round, but Maiuri's mistaken restoration of it in the 1930s has confused the evidence. The presence of Corinthian capitals in the neighborhood in the early reports and drawings suggests that the upper storey was a tholos of Corinthian columns and conical roof. The tomb chamber was entered from the east, a barrel-vaulted corridor around a stout central pier with small niches in three walls and a single large one in the north wall. A great many gravestones were found here; Kockel lists nineteen, for members of the gentes Istacidia, Melissaea, and Veneria, the Istacidii the most numerous. Parts of at least seven statues of marble and limestone were also found. It is presumed that they stood in the intercolumniations of the tholos, and so they are restored by Mau (1908, fig. 254 [Kockel pl. 13c]).

The interior of the tomb is said to have been decorated in the Third Style, but Mazois's drawing does not permit a clear decision (Mazois 1, pl. 8.2 [Kockel pl. 12a]). At least one of the togati wears the full imperial toga with sinus and umbo. Kockel would date the construction of the tomb to the second quarter of the first century of our era. In the state of our knowledge and lack of evidence one would not wish to disagree. A close parallel to the tomb of the Istacidii was discovered in the part of the Porta di Nocera necropolis brought to light in 1886 in the Fondo Pacifico. This is Fondo Pacifico 6, the largest tomb of this group, square in plan, 4.75 m on a side. The footing is travertine, the die of the lower storey faced with white stucco. This is ornamented with an engaged order with Doric fluting, four columns to a side. The door was in the centre of the front, treated decoratively with limestone frame and finely carved leaf, complete with the paneling of a double door. This led, not to the tomb chamber, but to a stair that led in successive flights to the upper storey. From the upper storey were recovered five small-scale Corinthian capitals in tufa, a curved tufa epistyle block, and three limestone statues, two male and one female. So the tomb consisted of a cubical base storey with an engaged order and an open tholos, presumably with a conical roof (*RömMitt* 1888, 134–36 [A. Mau]). Sogliano and Mau assign it a Tiberian date, but it is not clear on what grounds other than its similarity to the tomb of the Istacidii. The lack of a tomb chamber suggests that this was the tomb of a single individual. The stair probably led to a place or tube for libations.

A fourth round tomb of this period is found in the Porta di Nocera necropolis, tomb east 3 (3 ES), the tomb of Veia Barchilla and her husband N. Agrestinus Equitius Pulcher. It consists of a drum of masonry raised on a low square podium faced with opus incertum of broken lava. In the front of the base open three small niches for gravestones. The drum is faced with opus incertum of lava and finished with stucco to show socle, zone of orthostats, and two courses of running ashlar blocks, all parts above the socle with drafted margins. A projecting molding decorated with astragal and ovolo finishes this zone, above which the drum continues, stepped back a little, to make a low parapet around a flat roof. The tomb chamber was entered from the west through a low arched door. The interior was divided into three equal chambers by radial walls. These communicate with one another and are lit by small shafts through the segmental dome of the roof. N. Veius Barcha is known to have been a candidate for the duovirate in the early years of the colony (Castrén 86); it is presumed that Veia Barchilla must be either his daughter or his granddaughter. The type of the tomb is new in Pompeii but familiar from the vicinity of Rome, where the most famous examples are the Mausoleum Augusti and the tomb of Caecilia Metella. A date in the Augustan period seems logical, and the conspicuous location of the tomb will support it.

Schola Tombs

A tomb form that evidently did not make its appearance in Pompeii before the Augustan period but then became popular was the schola, an unroofed curved bench raised a step above the road, a place for travelers to rest, a form that seems to have been rare elsewhere. Just outside the Porta di Ercolano on the Via dei Sepolcri on land that was certainly pomerial are two examples, tombs 2 and 4. Tomb south 4 is the simpler and handsomer, a semicircular bench of blocks of Nocera tufa finished with massive winged lion's paws at either end and with an inscription in beautiful, very large-scale Augustan letters carved in a single line directly onto the back. It tells us that this is the tomb of Mamia, sacerdos publica (presumably of Venus Pompeiana), the place for burial granted by decree of the decuriones. This is probably the Mamia who built the temple of the Genius Augusti on her own land and at her own expense (*CIL* 10.816); her family was prominent in Campania in Samnite times, and Castrén thinks it one of the first of the old families to reach office again under the colony. The relationship of the tomb to that of M. Porcius, with which it is approximately in line, suggests that they once stood here alone.

Tomb south 2 is a similar bench, but of tufa backed by a buttress of rubble masonry. It has similar terminal lion's paws, and at the midpoint a tufa base rises behind the bench. This carried the inscription on a marble plate and must have been surmounted by a column or statue, now missing. The tomb is that of A. Veius, duovir quinquennalis and tribunus militum a populo (*CIL* 10.996). The latter office puts him in the Augustan period, but the tomb, which is canted from the line of tombs 3 and 4, seems somewhat later than these.

Just outside the Porta di Stabia, along the east side of the road leading out from the gate, another pair of tufa schola tombs came to light in 1888–90. One of these carried a large-scale inscription carved

FIGURE 38.
The Schola Tomb of
Mamia, Detail

directly on the back telling that it was the tomb of M. Alleius Minius, duovir, the place of burial granted by decree of the decuriones. It is in every way very like the schola of Mamia. The other, closer to the gate, is identified by a pair of lava cippi, one to either side, as the tomb of M. Tullius, the place again given by decree of the decuriones. M. Tullius appears to have been the man who built the Aedes Fortunae Augustae, three times duovir and tribunus militum a populo, therefore Augustan. Both tombs were no longer respected after A.D. 62 but were buried under dumps of debris from the earthquake. The schola of Tullius has remains of a rectangular base behind the midpoint that probably carried another inscription, and it gives the general impression of being the later of the two, built when the pomerial strip was no longer needed (*NSc* 1889, 280; 1890, 329–31; 1891, 273–74).

Just outside the Porta del Vesuvio another schola came to light in 1908. It is a semicircular bench of tufa terminating in winged lion's paws, then thickened to either side to make a place for a marble inscription. Behind the midpoint is a base on which a column was mounted; this has an Attic base and unfluted shaft and may have carried an urn or other embellishment. The inscription informs us that this was the tomb of Arellia Tertulla, wife of Veius Fronto, the place granted by decree of the decuriones (*NSc* 1910, 404–6). The heavy wear the monument shows suggests an early date, but while presumably Arellia Tertulla died while he was in office, Fronto's career is not well documented.

The reservation of schola tombs for persons publicly honored may be illusory. The land at the disposition of the decuriones for honorific burial plots was the pomerial strip, and benches out of the way of traffic outside the city gates, where people would be apt to have to wait and also to arrange to meet friends, would be only logical and sensible. It is surprising that we do not find them everywhere.

Monuments of Unusual Form

Among tombs of unusual form, first place must go the tomb of Eumachia, tomb west 11 (11 OS) in the Porta di Nocera necropolis, the largest of all Pompeian tombs. It is a monumental exedra raised on a low terrace coming to the edge of the roadway, the terrace wall faced with opus incertum coigned with brick at the corners. This is finished at chest height with a simple molding in blocks of lava. At the centre of the front a low doorway framed in blocks of lava and closed by a monolithic lava door admits to a stair leading to the top of the terrace. Along the sides are low parapet walls. The exedra fills the back of the terrace. A curved wall continued by short straight stretches to either side is set on a rectangular platform. The lower part of the exedra is revetted with slabs of Nocera tufa simulating two deep courses of drafted ashlar above a handsome base molding, but above this only the concrete core survives, the superstructure having been robbed in antiquity. There appear to have been three large niches in the curved wall. The straight back of the monument was divided by six engaged columns with Attic bases into panels that were finished as false windows. Fragments of Corinthian capitals and a dentil cornice suggest how it was finished above. The tomb chamber is entered at the centre of the back and follows the line of the exterior, so that there are in effect two symmetrical tomb chambers, each with nine niches for urns. A large rectangular enclosure frames the exedra at the back and sides. The façade of the superstructure was probably of limestone, as the inscription on the front of the front terrace is on plates of limestone: EVMACHIA/L F//SIBI ET SVIS. Several fragments of sculpture were found here, including fragments of a limestone frieze showing an Amazonomachy and some fragments of marble sculpture in the round. Ten gravestones were found on the front terrace, five of lava, two of white limestone, two of marble, and one of unknown substance. Three more come from the southwest corner of the enclosure. The inscriptions on these show a close relationship between the family of Eumachia and the Alleii. Behind the tomb were two round altars of Nocera tufa decorated with friezes of erotes carrying animals and garlands and surmounted by omphaloi around which serpents coil. A third tufa altar is tipped up against the west side of the terrace.

As reconstructed, this is the most sumptuous of all Pompeian tombs. It has no close relations, being neither a schola nor a nymphaeum in design, although it has been likened to both. For reasons I do not understand D. E. E. Kleiner in her work on the Philopappos monument in Athens, of which it is clearly an important antecedent, dismissed the relationship as superficial.[2] But the date of the Philapappos monument is Trajanic, while that of the tomb of Eumachia cannot be far from that of the Aedificium Eumachiae on the forum of Pompeii. The dedication of the Aedificium to Concordia Augusta and Pietas and its clear echoes of the Forum Augustum in Rome place it in the late Augustan period.

A second tomb of unusual form is that of Septumia outside the Porta del Vesuvio, erected by her daughter Antistia Prima on a plot granted by decree of the decuriones (*NSc* 1910, 406–9 [G. Spano]). It consists of a large plain base with offset base and crown strips faced with stucco surmounted by a slender column of Nocera tufa with Attic base and reeded shaft. The capital and whatever it may have carried are missing. That the base of the tomb was covered with dipinti and graffiti and debris from the earthquake of 62 was heaped casually around it shows that we are dealing with a monument antedating that catastrophe. The inclusion of a single column in the design of some schola tombs of Augustan date, though not the earliest of these, indicates that any date thereafter would be acceptable.

Busta

Of course the simple bustum also continued to be extremely common in this period, but its architecture was seldom graceful and never really monumental. A few examples may serve to define the type. On the Via dei Sepolcri beyond the fork in the road, tomb south 21 is the bustum of N. Istacidius Helenus, a freedman who rose to be *paganus* of the *pagus Augustus*. It is a slightly trapezoidal enclosure surrounded by a thick wall faced with opus incertum, with merlons once capped with pyramids decorating the front corners. There is no entrance; a ladder must have been used to get in. A marble plate let into the façade identifies the chief occupant and specifies the measurements of the plot. Within the enclosure three gravestones with marble plates in front of them marked the individual burials.

[2]D. E. E. Kleiner, *The Monument of Philopappos in Athens* (Rome 1983), esp. 64–65.

In the Porta di Nocera necropolis a pair of twin enclosures, tombs east 11 and 9 (11 ES and 9 ES), have walls of broken lava and square doors framed with lava blocks under low triangular tympana into which are sunk the inscriptions of A. Veius Atticus, Augustalis, and C. Munatius Faustus, Augustalis, and his wife Naevoleia Tyche. The latter was awarded by decree of the decuriones. A. Veius Atticus is known from the archive of L. Caecilius Iucundus for the year A.D. 56/57, as is another occupant of this tomb, A. Veius Nymphius. Tomb 11 ES was repaired in antiquity, and both tombs have stamped moldings around the tympana that belong to the time of the Fourth Style. Therefore, a date just before the earthquake is indicated.

In 1976 outside the Porta di Nola, along the road branching off to the north, was found the bustum of M. Obellius Firmus, duovir, surrounded by a high (1.96 m) wall heavily plastered. There is no door, but a break in the triangular capping of the wall indicates that it was to be approached by ladder from behind. The main front is crowned by a low tympanum framed with a stamped molding into which is sunk the inscription recording the multiple honors accorded Firmus by the decuriones, the pagani, and the ministri. In the interior was only a marble gravestone and a pair of tiles, one having a hole over the mouth of a terracotta pipe for the libations. The large covered cinerary urn underneath was of pale blue glass. So even people of great distinction might be suitably honored with a simple bustum (*CronPomp* 5 [1979] 65–79 [S. De Caro]).

The evidence shows that existing tomb forms continued to be employed in the Augustan and Julio-Claudian period—the altar, the aedicula, the tholos; that to these forms were added the schola and very occasionally a tomb of unusual form, such as the exedra of Eumachia; but that the cemeteries of Pompeii were not the playground for architectural fancy and experiment that those around Rome had become by this time. As in other things, in their taste in tombs the Pompeians were conservative.

PART V

From the Earthquake to the Eruption, A.D. 62–79

18 · THE PUBLIC BUILDINGS

Buildings on and in the Vicinity of the Forum

Introduction

After the earthquake of A.D. 62 left the forum of Pompeii a shambles, the Pompeians seem to have worked out plans for a monumental reconstruction of the whole area in some detail. A few buildings would have to be put into working order as soon as possible. Then, if eventually they proved inadequate or unworthy of the grand scheme the planners had in mind but had not developed completely, these could be rebuilt later. Such were the macellum, the court building (the "comitium"), and the curia, all necessary to the orderly working of daily life. The Temple of Apollo was also refurbished at this time, perhaps because damage to its structure was relatively slight, and with the vogue for brightly painted stuccowork that seems to have been a phenomenon of the period, it could be given a veneer and a new appearance in the current architectural idiom fairly easily. The Temple of the Genius Augusti was also repaired. Here too the damage seems not to have been serious; the masonry is largely Augustan. There is also the strong possibility that earthquake relief and urban reconstruction was overseen by an imperial commission and financed with help from Rome, so there may have been considerations of a suitable show of gratitude involved. The Capitolium, the basilica, and the Temple of Fortuna Augusta were cleared of debris but otherwise left untouched for the time being. Doubtless people wanted to see what the effect of the new colonnades around the forum would be before they tackled the rebuilding of so important an element as the Capitolium.

The Forum Colonnades and Square

On the west side of the forum the planners decided to erect a two-storey colonnade running the whole length of the forum. There had

FIGURE 39.
The Forum, Unfinished West Colonnade

evidently been some colonnaded porches on the east side of the forum at least from the early days of the Roman colony, and gradually that side had become increasingly handsome, until it was lined with fine façades, most of them employing columns and marble. The west side of the forum, thanks to the presence there of the basilica and the Temple of Apollo, fine Tufa Period buildings, had been neglected in the march of progress, and now it was decided to try to bring the two sides into balance by this means.

It is commonly said that colonnades that framed the fora of Italy were introduced in the Hellenistic period and that the forum of Pompeii is an excellent example of this. The notion is that ceremonies and gladiatorial shows being regularly staged in the forum, such colonnades would support galleries from which spectators would have an excellent view of the proceedings.[1] In Rome itself, however, such galleries were always arranged only in connection with individual buildings, such as the Basilica Aemilia, and it is impossible to find any forum that was provided with extensive colonnades, let alone designed as a colonnaded square, before the imperial period. Certainly Pompeii's forum could boast no colonnades at all before the late second century at the earliest, and even in the last period the plans for rebuilding called for a unified colonnade of two storeys only on the west side. Around the south end there was already the colonnade of Vibius, built almost certainly in the early years of the Roman colony, 80–60 B.C., a single-storey colonnade, very probably with an open gallery above, at least over the east wing. But along the east side of the forum what colonnading there was, was in conjunction with the individual buildings and was interrupted and changed its character repeatedly.

A broad, continuous step of fine white limestone, however, ran around the whole forum, interrupted only for a very short distance where the Via dell'Abbondanza came into the forum, and even this gap looks as though it were intended to be filled in later. The blocks of this step are laboriously cut to fit around the footings of the columns of the porticus of Vibius, remains of blocks of a tufa stylobate cut down to make a disc under each column (Maiuri 1973, 71–72 and figs. 34–35). So at least at this end of the forum there was earlier a similar step at the same height. A second broad step below this runs around the south end of the forum from the Via dell'Abbondanza to the "suggestus" midway along the west side and thereafter in patches as far as the Capitolium, where it is abruptly reduced to utilitarian width and as such continues to the north end on this side. On

[1] Vitruvius 5.1.1–2; Robertson[2] 194, 379 (s.v. agora); Boethius and Ward-Perkins 121–27; Ward-Perkins 31.

this lower step toward the middle of the west side are set five small statue bases. Their placing looks tentative, and in relation to the row of seven equestrian statue bases in the open area of the forum in front of them they would have made a poor show. A little south of the point where the width of this step is reduced there was once a large public fountain of the usual rectangular form, 1.18 m by 2.58 m in interior dimensions. The floor of limestone blocks and the bedding for the slabs of the basin are still clear, but in the last period this had been removed, and there is no way of telling whether it was of finer material or workmanship than the ordinary street fountains. For a considerable stretch on the west, between the fourth equestrian statue base from the south and the fourth from the north, this lower step is incomplete. On the east side of the forum the upper step of limestone blocks runs continuously and in line in front of the Aedificium Eumachiae and the Temple of the Genius Augusti. It is then interrupted in front of the bibliotheca, but the line is maintained by a heavy rubblework foundation wall into which are let massive square blocks of lava at regular intervals, clearly column footings. In front of the macellum the limestone blocks reappear as a lower step in front of a stylobate veneered with marble and then run to the north end on this side. Although the place for the lower step is plainly visible all along this side in the unsightly exposure of the rubble foundations of the upper step, it is completely missing, except in front of the macellum, where it is reduced to utilitarian width. At the southern end of this step was once a public fountain balancing that on the opposite side of the forum, mentioned above. This too had been dismantled in the last period.

The west colonnade of the forum was in the process of a monumental rebuilding at the time of the eruption. Blocks of the entablature and cornice of the lower order line the west side of the forum, and there are even some massive unworked blocks near the end of the Via Marina. But column elements, especially of the upper order, are in short supply, possibly because they were retrieved in antiquity. There would have been no less than forty-nine columns in each of the two storeys here, Doric in the lower storey, Ionic in the upper. The footings for all of them are already in place, though their stylobate was not completed at the north end. The footings are of lava, for the most part of the characteristic keyhole shape that was apparently to counteract any tendency of the columns to lean outward, the limestone stylobate blocks being cut to fit around them. Most of the columns of the lower order have at least a drum in place, but there are a number of gaps, especially toward the north end. The lower order is rather heavy in effect, with pronounced entasis. Characteristically, each column is of three drums and a capital cut together with a short section of shaft, but the individual drums show great variation in height. Fluting had not yet been begun, but the capitals show an echinus of cyma recta profile above a simple apophyge. Architrave and frieze were cut in a single block, the architrave of two fasciae inside and out trimmed with a cyma and a fillet, the frieze plain. The blocks are cut diagonally, so that between each pair of columns one hangs as a keystone in a continuous flat arch. The cornice is generally Doric in design, with mutules of eighteen guttae in three rows of six, but with the addition of small cymas at base and crown. It is cut separately in blocks of uneven length. In the back of the entablature between frieze and cornice are cut rectangular sockets for the heavy beams of the floor of the upper storey. These are very closely spaced and carried flooring almost as thick as they are high. The upper order is Pompeian Ionic with Attic bases, extremely light in contrast to the lower. The shafts, all still unfluted, show perceptible entasis. The capitals have pronounced convexity in the echinus, which is carried out beyond the shaft by a deep apophyge. The volutes are disclike but have plump half-palmettes tucked against them, and there is a pronounced curvature to the line of the abacus. No element of the entablature of the upper order is preserved.

The portico was to run the whole length of this side of the forum, crossing the Via Marina, where a wider intercolumniation is necessary, on columns set to either side of its opening. Access to the upper storey was given by a masonry stair with lava treads along the south side of the basilica and possibly by a stair between the Aedes Apollinis and the market building at the northwest corner of the forum. The latter especially seems inconvenient and ill-planned. Probably the principal means of access had not yet been constructed at the time of the eruption.

To go with the new west colonnade there was a remodeling of the porticus of Vibius along the south side of the forum. Evidently this porticus originally had been single on the south, double on the east. It was now proposed to make it pseudo-double on the south. Behind the front line of columns, which remained unchanged except for the installation of a new stylobate in white limestone, a second line was erected, a partial line broken in front of the two easternmore of the three halls opening behind it to make areas where small crowds could assemble. Some of the columns of this line are of a fantastic order of the last period rendered in stucco; those flanking the central hall are engaged against square pillars to take the weight of the massive beams they must have carried. The engineering of the roof must have been a delicate problem in statics. But the reasons why the designers went to all this trouble are obvious: they wanted to make the approaches to these two halls suitably monumental, and because they proposed to burden this end of the forum with an assembly of very large groups of statuary on high bases that would inevitably have crowded and darkened this portico, they decided to double its width in compensation.

At present the inner aisle is narrower than the outer, but evidently the builders originally proposed to make them the same in width, for the easternmost hall (VIII ii 10), the only one finished at the time of the eruption, was once four feet shorter than it is at present. At a late date the front wall was torn out and moved to the north, perhaps because large spaces in both directions in the porticus were found difficult to manage. In its new position the front wall is in line with the fronts of the buildings to the west of it, which must therefore be dated after this modification.

The colonnades on the east side of the forum are best described individually, since they differed markedly from one another. That in front of the Aedificium Eumachiae, sixteen columns long, is of white limestone, Doric, similar to the lower storey of the west colonnade, but each column is raised on a low square plinth and trimmed at the base of the shaft with a single torus. The entasis of the shaft is less marked than that of the west colonnade, and the echinus is straighter and more flaring. The architrave is almost identical with its counterpart on the west; and the frieze is similarly plain, but here it carries the building inscription in large letters that fill the field. The cornice, however, is Ionic, with a row of square-ended dentils the dominant feature. There is no element of a second storey, and the depth of the chalcidicum of which this is the façade is so great that a second line of columns would have been necessary were any considerable weight anticipated. Rather we should think of this as being roofless; there are no cuttings for roof joists in the back of the entablature. Behind each column of the façade is a base for a standing statue, and the back wall is carved into a succession of niches, large and small, curved and rectilinear. All of this seems to have been in working order at the time of the eruption. The imprint of the plates of the marble veneer and the bits of marble that secured the clamps for the plates are everywhere in evidence. But the excavators found the broken inscription of only one of the statues, a less than life-size Romulus that stood just north of the main door of the building. And the columns had not yet been fluted.

North of the Aedificium Eumachiae, in front of the Temple of the Genius Augusti, there was no colonnade, simply a deep apron before the modest door leading into the temple precinct. The façade of the precinct was veneered with marble, probably richly colored and in architectural designs, but the area seems to have been otherwise featureless and must have broken the rhythm of the columns to either side of it rather abruptly.

The bibliotheca, north of this, had a façade with at least one storey of columns and probably two. The square lava blocks that served as footings for the eight columns of its façade are all in place, imbedded in a continuous foundation of rubblework, but no fragment of either columns or entablature was found, which is hardly surprising, since this is one of the buildings that was most completely stripped in antiquity.

Finally, in front of the macellum a line of seventeen Corinthian (?) columns of white marble made a sumptuous porch before the monumental entrance to this complex and the line of tabernae that flanked it to either side. These stand on low individual marble plinths and have Attic bases. The shafts are beautifully fluted, reeded to a third of their height. The architrave is in three fasciae, with astragals to separate these and a Lesbian leaf trimming the crown. The frieze is plain, the cornice deeply projecting and richly carved with ornamental moldings. Since the entablature and cornice are the same inside and out, it is clear that there was no floor at this level. In the restoration of 1930 a fragmentary base with remains of a sculptured panel of sacrificial implements on the front was mounted on the cornice. This is square in plan with a small projection to either side, as though it were the post for a parapet with panels of metal fencing. No other fragment of such a base is known, but almost all of this colonnade was removed in antiquity. But it cannot have stood in this position unless the colonnade was unroofed and simply an ornamental screen like that in front of the Aedificium Eumachiae. Unfortunately, one cannot examine the top of the cornice today to see whether there are traces of the setting of such bases,[2] but it seems unlikely that there would have been a second storey of columns here.

In the interior of this porch there is a statue base for a standing figure against each of the columns except the northernmost, and facing these is a second row of such bases between each pair of tabernae, with two more in the bay before the door to the interior. These are for the most part reduced to their masonry core, but the gallery of portraits that once stood here must have been impressive. Between the two doors to the interior a higher base with a pair of marble columns at its outer corners stands in front of a shallow niche.[3] This has been interpreted as a lararial shrine, but in this context it seems more

[2] See, e.g., *BdA* 25 (June 1931) 563–72 (A. Maiuri); *Le arti* 1 (1938) 72–74 (A. Maiuri); and *PAH* 1, pt. 3, 203–5 (5 May–7 June 1818). Maiuri never published any account of this particular restoration.

[3] These were wrongly restored by Maiuri in 1929–30 with capitals from the Via dei

likely to have been for the portrait of some specially honored person, perhaps the donor of the macellum.

Around the open square of the forum, pushed, except for two, toward its margins so as to leave as much space unencumbered as possible, are a number of bases, but no statue was found in conjunction with any of these, and most have been stripped to the masonry core. Some of these are in series, others in a variety of symmetries. Along the west side of the forum beginning from the north are first four rectangular bases lined up at regular intervals that one would suppose were for equestrian statues, then three of similar dimensions but more widely spaced. Roughly midway along is a large construction that L. Iacono proposed might be the rostra, or suggestus, of Pompeii (*MemLinc* 1925, 267–69, [A. Sogliano]). This is an attractive suggestion, since it is set wide of other constructions, but its low height, ca. 1.23–1.26 m, which is less than that of the other bases here, its limited size, and the absence of a stair leading up to it militate against the identification, and the altar platform in front of the Capitolium would have made a better speakers' platform. It is more likely that this is the base for a large group that was never finished, as the masonry superstructure at its south end, 0.63 m by 1.64 m, suggests. Beyond it, as one approaches the Via Marina, is another pair of equestrian bases, and beyond the end of the Via Marina a single base, balancing the base of Q. Sallustius (*CIL* 10.792) on the opposite side of the forum, the only one with its africano marble revetment and inscription preserved when found, though some of those on the south side preserve parts of their finish.

Across the south end of the forum was an elaborate symmetrical arrangement. In the centre was built an arch, the masonry core in large part faced with brick, but the whole completely sheathed with marble, as bits of the baseboard within the fornix and chunks to secure the clamps of the veneer scattered over the surface attest. The fornix is 1.58 m wide, on the long axis of the forum. To judge from the proportions, we have lost not only the statuary that crowned it but better than a meter of the attic as well.

This arch was flanked by two very large, high bases brought forward slightly with respect to the arch, that on the west somewhat larger than its mate. And each of these was flanked by smaller bases, probably for single equestrian figures, pushed back toward the colonnade. One sees the scheme here quite clearly, but not the rationale that determined it. The statue on the arch, triumphal or not—and it

Sepolcri. The capital that belongs here is von Mercklin's no. 556, fig. 1049, now in the storehouse of marbles on the west side of the forum of Pompeii (VII vii 29) (see Mazois 1, 1812, pl. 6; and Kockel 127).

is too modest a monument to have been covered with important reliefs—dominated this end of the forum without overwhelming it, only slightly, if at all, more important than the groups that flanked it to either side. Out in the open square two bases larger than the other equestrian bases, but hardly big enough to have carried groups, stand on the main axis of the forum, one toward the south end in front of the arch, one toward the north end, but with a good distance between it and the Capitolium.[4]

The large bases, except the arch and that in the middle of the west side of the forum, are of masonry faced with reticulate and coigned with opus mixtum vittatum, masonry characteristic of the last period of Pompeii. Most of the smaller bases are faced with incertum or a combination of incertum and small blocks. One has a base faced with brickwork. Only this and the arch seem likely to antedate the last phase of the city.

The Three Apsidal Halls at the South End of the Forum

The three large halls fronting on the porticus of Vibius from the south are architecturally similar but structurally separate and different. That at the southwest corner of the forum is separated from the house west of it by an isolating passage accessible only from the house and separated from its neighbor on the east by an angiportus with pavement and sidewalk closed by a door at the forum end. This led to the back parts of various houses lying just off the forum. The middle hall is separated from the eastern one by an isolating passage, a cul-de-sac that runs to a buttress bracing the loaded shoulders of the buildings to either side. The easternmost is separated from the street east of it by a narrow stairwell, which gave access to the upper gallery of the forum colonnade, the only obvious access to it in this part of the forum, and from the house south of it by an area made irregular by the arc of its apse that does not seem to have served any particular purpose. We may best think of this as storage space for all the movable furniture and equipment the courts and municipal life in the forum would require, as the cul-de-sac west of this building

[4]Iacono observed that originally there were six rectangular "equestrian" bases of uniform size and spacing at the south end of the forum flanking the central arch. Of these, two were left in place beside the arch, two were moved to the extreme ends of the south side, and two, including that of Sallustius, were moved to symmetrical positions at right angles to the others. This is shown by the fact that the four displaced bases are footed on the limestone pavement, while those in the centre descend below it or overlap it. The bases on the west side of the forum, including the "rostra," all rest on the pavement, as do also the two bases in the middle of the forum (see *MemLinc* 1925, 263–64 [A. Sogliano]; and Maiuri 1942, 29–30). The argument obviously is not conclusive. Mau's suggestion that the large bases were for colossal statues of the Augusti has not found much acceptance (see *RömMitt* 11 [1896] 150–56).

clearly served as its storage space and is in communication with it by a small door in the northwest corner. The forum of Pompeii is not otherwise generously provided with such storage space.

The hall in the centre (VIII ii 8), is the easiest to read first.[5] It is preceded by a platform the width of its broad doorway, ca. 0.85 m high, reached by a ramp or stair up from either side, now too badly ruined to determine which.[6] The platform is clearly a suggestus, as the arrangement of an unobstructed space in the colonnade in front of it confirms. Inside, the hall is rectangular with a rectangular niche opening in the centre of the end wall, into which is built a raised platform, more than 1.90 m high, probably too high to have served as a tribunal, that projects forward into the room and dominates it. Behind this platform, in the back of the niche, runs a second deep platform three-quarters of a meter higher. Along each side wall runs a brick-faced wall 1.58–1.60 m high with rectangular projections, rather like pilasters, at regular intervals. There is no trace of any finish—either marble veneer or stucco—anywhere, and clearly the building was still in construction at the time of the eruption, but a patch of pavement in flags of africano lies west of the central platform.

There are strong indications that this was the tabularium, or record office, of Pompeii: its dominant position, its provision with a small suggestus in front for a magistrate who might need recourse to the city records, its ample size, and the constructions along its lateral walls, which are almost certainly the bases for a continuous series of large wooden cabinets, as a similar arrangement in the Schola Iuventutis (III iii 6), where the cabinets were still in place, shows (Spinazzola 1953, 1.135–47, esp. 142–44). Here there would have been seven to a wall, and here the acta and tax records of the municipal government would have been filed.

The approach to the western hall (VIII ii 6) is undramatic but convenient to both the tabularium and the basilica.[7] On entering the broad door, one mounts from a vestibule paved with grey-and-white striated marble to the main room by two steps of white marble and

<hr />

[5] On this building see Overbeck and Mau 139–42; and Maiuri 1942, 36–37.

[6] It is shown with ramps by Mazois, who made a plan of it ca. 1814 (Mazois 3, pl. 38); with stairs on a plan (by Gandy?) dated 1816 (see *Pompéi, travaux et envois des architectes français au XIXe siècle*, exhibition catalogue [Naples 1980] figs. 28, 34). The truth is probably that it was a combination of steps and a ramp (see *Pompei 1748–1980: I tempi della documentazione*, exhibition catalogue [Rome 1980] 194, fig. 5).

[7] On this building see Maiuri 1942, 37–38. Maiuri would hold that this should be the curia because of the magnificence of its architecture, but he does not assign any specific function to the eastern hall. De Vos and de Vos 37, following Overbeck and Mau 142, see the eastern hall as the office of the duovirs, but such magistrates regularly had their tribunals in the open air.

finds oneself looking across a broad space toward a shallow apse in which has been built a base, ca. 1.39 m high, presumably for a statue. In front of this at floor level lies the molded marble slab that was the footing of another statue base. On either side are three rectangular niches, into which are built projecting masonry bases ca. 1.20 m high. These would suit for either statuary or cabinets, and at first it seems impossible to determine which they held. The architecture is the classic architecture of libraries and Augustea (centers of emperor worship); one sees its congeners in the libraries of Trajan at Rome and the Augustea of Gabii and Velleia.[8] At Pompeii the hall was faced with brick throughout its lower parts, and its grey-and-white marble pavement was already laid, but decoration had not yet begun. Blocks of white marble worked as cornices of two sorts, one with dentils, one with modillions cut to a rake; a length of molding; a column base; a section of column shaft; and an engaged Corinthian capital are scattered about. Presumably these were pattern pieces for the marble revetment of this hall, although there are no blocks or slabs in the course of cutting. But there is no more than a single specimen of any member, and they all seem consistent in scale, style, and material.

In addition to these, there are a fragment of a cipollino base with the fragmentary inscription "Imp.Caesari" and a broken piece of a standing, half-nude male statue, with drapery from waist to knees kilted about the thighs and gathered in a soft roll at the waist. The top surface of this is cut as a socket to receive the base of the nude torso, cut separately, so the statue was heroic in concept. Taken together with the inscription and the architecture, this gives us reasonable assurance that this was the Augusteum of Pompeii.

The easternmost of the three halls (VIII ii 10) was the only one in active use at the time of the eruption.[9] Whereas the others were in the process of being completely rebuilt from the ground up, it may be that only the façade of this one was rebuilt, on a line 2.22–2.28 m north of the line of the original façade. The rest of the side walls are of rubblework coigned with brick, while the new façade was brick-faced throughout. The interior was covered with marble revetment to the height of the lintel that spanned the opening to the apse. We see only the clamp chunks and bits of broken plates imbedded in the stucco undercoat until we get down to the baseboard, for the survivors stripped this revetment very thoroughly. The bit of baseboard still in the northwest corner explains why, for it is of dark blue-grey

---

[8]On libraries see, e.g., Crema 367–70. As far as I know, there is as yet no special study of Augustea, but see F. Yegül, "A Study in Architectural Iconography: *Kaisersaal* and the Imperial Cult," *ArtB* 64 (1982) 7–31. On the Augusteum of Gabii see E. Q. Visconti, *Monumenti gabini della Villa Pinciana* (Milan 1835).

[9]On this hall see Maiuri 1942, 35–36.

marble with lighter veining capped with a molding of white veined with delicate blue; clearly the revetment was precious. On the outside we see good remains of a baseboard and a high dado of mottled grey-blue marble, each finished with a white molding, above which the façade was stuccoed. But the doorway was framed with marble, and the two steps by which one approaches it are still veneered with marble, some of the plates evidently secondhand. The remaining orthostat of the dado is a particularly fine piece, cut so the veining runs diagonally.

The architecture seems simple and straighforward at first glance but becomes more complex with study. We have to do with a large rectangular hall, only slightly deeper than broad, two steps up from the forum colonnade, with a very large apse opening out of the middle of its south wall, defined as a separate entity by projection of the wall to either side in a sort of pilaster. This apse was not vaulted, and as the remains of a stout relieving arch to either side show, the entrance was given a flat lintel at a relatively low height. Inside the apse a series of nine beam holes at regular intervals at the level of the lintel show that the ceiling was flat, and around the apse is built a tribunal, ca. 1.19 m high, at first curving along the line of the apse, then cut straight across in a chord where the magistrate would sit. The front of this tribunal shows no trace of marble revetment, while the wall behind and the jambs of the opening to the apse do, so we must presume that the tribunal was given a wooden floor and that a flight of wooden steps across its front mounted to it; the space is entirely adequate for this. The main hall was paved with white marble lightly streaked with grey, but there is no sign of any other architectural feature. The ceiling stood somewhat higher than anything that is preserved today; only the shoulders of the relieving arch over the opening to the apse are preserved.

A sizable assembly hall with its focus on an elevated tribunal and otherwise featureless, this can only be the curia of Pompeii. The undifferentiated equality of place for those assembled in the main hall and the provision of place for very few on the tribunal support this identification, as do the magnificence of the decoration and the fact that after the earthquake it was restored to working order at a relatively early date. There was no permanent furniture, and the benches for the assembly were probably kept in the narrow throat between this and the next hall, to which a small door in the northwest corner leads. The wide doorway raised two steps above the forum porticus would have permitted a number of spectators to follow the proceedings, as they did at the meetings of the senate in Rome. Surrounded by the life and business of Pompeii, this hall commanded attention without insisting on it. Facing the Capitolium, it drew authority and protection from that prospect. And at the same time, it was set apart from the noise and confusion of the forum, a place for discussion and debate, august, even severe.

In front of the curia on the line of the inner file of the forum colonnade are three blocks in which are cut rectangular sockets, the outer ones wide of the doorway and with larger sockets (0.16 m by 0.18 m) than the middle one (0.09 m by 0.10 m), which is centred on the door. Presumably in these could be set up a barrier that would frame the door, behind which a crowd could assemble and be addressed from the door.

The Bibliotheca

The only building on the east side of the forum that seems to have been a new construction of the last phase of the city is the so-called Sacellum Larum Publicorum (VII ix 3),[10] a great apsidal hall between the macellum and the Temple of the Genius Augusti. Mau claimed to have found remains of a Third Style decoration in one of the secondary rooms at the back and therefore thought this building must antedate the earthquake; he ultimately settled on a date of A.D. 20–50. But it is next to impossible to accept this. The boldness of the architectural concept and the inclusion of a good bit of yellow tufa in the masonry both strongly suggest a date after the earthquake. Moreover, as Maiuri observed, the construction is harmonious throughout and presents no sign of repair or rebuilding. It is impossible to think that a roof as ambitious in its engineering as this space would have required could have survived the violence of the earthquake of 62, and in its collapse it would surely have cracked and damaged the walls. Yet the only lesions to be seen today are at the back and sides of the central apse, which are unrepaired and therefore to be assigned to the time of the eruption. The masonry of the walls is concrete faced with reticulate in beds of yellowish mortar with extensive coigning in brickwork at all corners. There are flat arches in brickwork over all the niches, with relieving arches above them. The only deviations from the original architectural scheme are a walled-up door at the east end of the north wall and the insertion of a brick-faced projecting base under each of the minor niches. The former is unimportant; the latter is to be seen as a minor change in design made during construction, for the bases are all uniform and agree with the brickwork elsewhere. This building antedates the repair of

---

[10] On this building see *RömMitt* 11 (1896) 285–301 (A. Mau); Maiuri 1942, 49–53; and *Archaeology* 30 (1977) 394–402 (L. Richardson, Jr.).

the macellum, however, for the south wall of the macellum incorporates the back wall of the north bay of this building on a slightly different line, while the portico in front of the macellum was extended beyond the façade of that building to connect with the colonnade of this one. But probably the difference in date was no more than a year or two.

In plan the building was essentially a square off which opened large bays, rectangular on either side, curved at the back. But the walls are so enlivened by eight niches, some brought forward into the main room by projecting bases, others receding, that there is a baroque quality to the architecture. The large side bays had pairs of columns in their openings and were probably roofed at a lower level than the rest. Against the centre of the back wall of each is a base for a statue. The curved rear bay, so big it nearly fills this wall, held at its centre a broad rectangular niche, almost certainly once framed by a pair of columns and a pediment, while along the wall to either side of this at the same height runs a continuous plinth that must have carried a line of columns. Within the niche is a high narrow step that does not seem designed for the display of statuary. This bay was probably covered by a roof on radiating beams, like that of the apse of the curia at the south end of the forum, rather than a half-dome, since it is very large and the wall is not thickened or buttressed.

The building was open to the forum across its whole west side but preceded by a colonnade, the eight footing blocks of which are still in place, probably with a second order above. The columns and all the veneer that once sheathed the walls were removed by survivors, but a small part of the marble pavement was recovered. It was in alternating squares and circles within squares, related to the pattern of the pavement of the Pantheon in Rome. The whole must have been roofed with a great wooden gable; the lateral walls were thickened to take the weight of this, and the area to be covered is not so great as that of the Theatrum Tectum. In the centre of the main room is a stepped square base revetted with marble of uncertain purpose, but certainly not an altar and probably not a statue base.

The openness of this building, the multiplicity of small niches, and the unusualness of the architectural form, which seems to anticipate the great trilobate banquet hall of Hadrian's villa,[11] have puzzled archaeologists ever since the building's discovery. It seems to be in masonry of the last period. On the north it runs over the line of a street that must once have been a fairly important entrance to the forum.

[11] S. Aurigemma, *Villa Adriana* (Rome 1961) 75–77; H. Kähler, *Hadrian und seine Villa bei Tivoli* (Berlin 1950) 122–28.

In the space behind it were run up numerous dependencies that do not look like habitation but might be workspace. The best suggestion for its purpose is that it was a public library, the multiple niches being housing for wooden cupboards in which the cylindrical capsae in which book rolls were kept were stored and the bays providing space for more. These would at the same time have protected the papyrus rolls from damp and facilitated the filing and retrieval of books. The closest parallels for this building are the library of Celsus at Ephesus and the library of Timgad.[12] They suggest that there would have been two storeys of niches for book cabinets, the upper reached by a gallery, and a colonnade of two storeys on the forum. Light would then have flooded the building, an obvious advantage for readers who had to contend with books written by hand on papyrus. Vitruvius (6.4.1) warned that private libraries should face east, since in those facing south and west there was a danger of bookworm and damp, but with the books doubly protected this way, that danger would have been diminished.

The Buildings at the Northwest Corner of the Forum

Opposite the bibliotheca on the west side of the forum and running back almost to the Via degli Augustali is a large utilitarian building commonly called the *granaio* (VII vii 29) (Maiuri 1942, 30–32). It measures 34.83 m in length by 8.87 m in breadth and is used today as a storehouse for marbles collected from various places in the city. It is constructed of rubble-faced concrete with brick coigning. There is no sign of finish of any sort and no interior architecture. It opens to the forum by eight broad doors that in effect made up the whole east wall. One thinks of a market shed where trestle tables could be set up and goods could be displayed. Certainly one of the principal aims of the builders was maximum freedom of circulation.

Maiuri suggested that this was the forum holitorium of Pompeii, designed especially for the sale of grains and similar dry stores, but such commodities are heavy and difficult to transport and also require protection from damp and vermin. Probably they were always sold in well-built shops, as they are today. It is more likely that this was for a market in fresh fruit and vegetables, which could be brought in daily and were light enough to transport with pack animals.

Maiuri observed that the building was not yet in use. There is no

---

[12] On the library of Celsus at Ephesus see Boethius and Ward-Perkins 397–98 and pls. 209, 211. On the library of Timgad see *MAAR* 9 (1931) 157–65 and pls. 16–19 (H. F. Pfeiffer); and P. Romanelli, *Topografia e archeologia dell'Africa romana* (Turin 1970) 202–3 and pl. 153.

plaster anywhere, and the putlog holes of the scaffolding have not been plugged. There is no sign of roofing, and the floor is simply beaten earth. Moreover, the forum colonnade in front of this building was a shambles, blocks of the entablature being lined up along the stylobate, but without common elements of any sort. Since such a market would bring a lot of traffic and, unless restricted, overflow into the portico and perhaps the forum square as well, it is unlikely that this building could have been in even limited use. Probably in the years after the earthquake the fruit and vegetable market was set up in the open area of the forum and dismantled entirely each day.

Between this building and the Aedes Apollinis opens a corridor (VII vii 30) leading back to a large irregular courtyard with a roofed shelter along the entrance side, a very large, square shed opposite this, and three smaller rooms along the south side. This has been converted to use as a storehouse for some of the humbler materials from the excavations, and the installation of shelving and roofs makes close examination difficult. It may have been the place where tradesmen were to leave their animals during market hours. These would certainly have created a problem, and there is no other provision of stabling near the forum. It was clearly rather a makeshift building, but in a very valuable location.

The only other buildings north of these fronting on the forum are a public latrine (VII vii 28), and a cellar of two low chambers in the substructures of shops VII vii 24 and VII vii 25 (Maiuri 1942, 32–34). The latrine proper is preceded by a vestibule, the doors from the forum colonnade to the vestibule and from the vestibule to the latrine being staggered so that passers-by would not look into the interior. The latrine itself is surrounded by a sewer trench on three sides and could accommodate at least 20 persons. Like the market next door, of which it was essentially an extension and of similar construction, it was unfinished at the time of the eruption. The walls were bare of plaster, and water to flush out the sewer had not yet been laid on.

The cellar beyond is entered by a door framed in rough blocks of lava, so small that one must stoop to enter. Maiuri decided that this should be an aerarium, a replacement for the aerarium in the substructures of the Capitolium, which he believed had had to be dismantled. But the Romans always put their aeraria, both public and private, under the protection of a divinity, and the ruin of the temple does not seem to have extended to the aerarium. Nor would it have affected its sanctity. It has also been thought to be the carcer of the city, where runaway slaves and petty criminals could be temporarily confined, but there is nothing to prove that it was not simply storage space. The door had to be low and inconvenient because of the floor level of the shops above it.

Other Public Buildings

The Temple of Venus Fisica Pompeiana

For our knowledge of the Temple of Venus Fisica Pompeiana we are largely dependent on the authoritative study of Mau.[13] He was present during the excavation, which continued from 1898 to 1900, and made a careful record and analysis of the evidence as it came to light. Later, in the excavation of the Villa Imperiale di Porta Marina following the disastrous bombing of the ruins in 1943, the substructures of the temple precinct along the main south façade were exposed. Unknown to Mau, these not only give us a correct south boundary for the temenos built upon a series of intercommunicating chambers with barrel-vaulted roofs but show that the south side of the precinct was almost certainly not closed by a portico, as Mau supposed, but developed as a broad, open terrace projecting beyond the rest of the precinct at either end, making a promenade on which visitors could stroll at leisure and exposing the temple's façade to view from the port at the mouth of the Sarno River.

The temple precinct was concealed from the city by the high walls of the enclosing porticoes. It was accessible at its northeast corner by a broad door to the Via Marina and at the middle of the east side by a door to the Vicolo di Championnet, the narrow street along the south side of the basilica. Originally a paved street along the east side of the precinct connected the Via Marina and the Vicolo di Championnet and perhaps continued south beyond this, but in the rebuilding of the last period this was blocked off at the Via Marina end and in large part absorbed into the enlarged temenos, so that it became an angiportus, a mere slot separating the basilica from the temple. Originally, one might imagine, processions formed in the forum, proceeded down the Via Marina to the west end of the basilica, turned south into this alleyway, and entered the precinct of Venus on the line of the temple's façade and at a right angle to it. Later such processions would have had to enter the precinct at the northeast corner

---

[13] For this building see *NSc* 1898, 333; 1899, 17–23; 1900, 27–30 (A. Sogliano). *RömMitt* 15 (1900) 270–308 (A. Mau). Maiuri 1942, 64–67. The epithet Fisica borne by the goddess remains mysterious (cf. *RE* s.v. Venus 838–44 [C. Koch]), the more so because it is also borne by the goddess Mefitis at Grumentum (*CIL* 10.203). If it is to be related to the stem of *fides*, as many have maintained and others have denied, it would probably link the goddess with Dius Fidius Semo Sancus in her functions, a protectress of oaths, while her statue type shows her as a queen (jeweled crown and scepter), mistress of good luck and patroness of sea traffic (steering oar), protectress of vegetation (spray of leaves), goddess of love (Amor), and commander of the arms of Mars (shield). If Fisica is connected with *fides*, its application to Mefitis is probably palliative. Whatever it is, it probably indicates that the cult of Venus was older in Pompeii than the Roman colony (see also M. Della Corte, "Venus Pompeiana," *Ausonia* 10 [1921] 68–87; and idem, *Iuventus* [Arpino 1924] 71–97).

FIGURE 40.
The Temple of Venus,
Corinthian Capital in
Marble

and proceed down one of the lateral porticoes to swing around and approach the temple on axis. In view of the fondness of the Romans for counterclockwise movement, such processions probably would have entered at the northeast corner and marched the full length of the north and west porticoes before emerging and crossing on the south to the temple's axis to approach the altar. The temple seems to demand a main approach from the south, a monumental stair or series of ramps, but of such there is no trace, possibly because the final rebuilding was still in its early stages.[14]

[14]It is interesting to note in this connection that the paving blocks of the Via Marina from the forum to the northeast corner of the precinct of the Temple of Venus are snecked with bits of white limestone, which produces a surprisingly handsome effect and shows that it was a processional way. It does not continue beyond this point.

Mau distinguished three major building periods: First, an original construction of the second quarter of the first century B.C., the early years of the Roman colony. For this construction the area was cleared of buildings, presumably for the most part houses, and a temple in a precinct framed by colonnades was erected. The second was a rebuilding of the early imperial period, perhaps the time of Claudius. In this rebuilding a temple faced with marble was substituted for the original building, and the colonnades were redesigned and rebuilt in marble. These colonnades were not completed by the time of the earthquake of A.D. 62, and both temple and colonnades were evidently severely damaged in the earthquake. The third was a rebuilding of the final period, when the debris of the earthquake was cleared away and the temple was enlarged. Most of the architectural members of the colonnades were removed, and a new design for these may have been in hand. The substructures of the south front and the perimeter wall are faced entirely in yellow tufa reticulate coigned with brick and small block (Maiuri 1942, 64–67 and pls. 13b and 15a). But the temple podium was not yet completed at the time of the eruption, and it can be presumed that work on the colonnades had scarcely begun.

Of the temple of the first period only enough remains to indicate its date. The precinct seems to have been approximately the same size as that of the rebuilding in the early imperial period, but it was not quite rectangular. While the north wall lay parallel to the Via Marina, those of the east and west sides were parallel to the back wall of the basilica and the street along it, hence diverging from the perpendicular somewhat to the west. Nothing remains of the temple building, and only parts of the gutter and foundations of the stylobate of the colonnades remain on three sides, the south side having disappeared. Behind the east colonnade lay a series of rooms, some of them exedral, of the same depth as the colonnade, but there does not seem to have been a balancing series on the west. In front of the east colonnade are remains of bases for statues and dedications, and on the axis of the temple is the core of a large rectangular altar, which was faced with travertine, its short side turned to the temple. The precinct was paved with a mixture of mortar and crushed lava (lava signinum).

The temple of the second period survives in enough detail to be described and reconstructed. It rose on a moderately high podium, frontal in the Roman manner, prostyle and with a deep pronaos, preceded by a stair across the whole façade. Pronaos and cella were of approximately equal depth. There seem to have been six columns across the front of the pronaos, four down each side, running to a deeply projecting anta. Pilasters framed the door, and there seem to have been gates across this, as well as doors in the opening. The cella was square, with an elegant pavement of small square plates of marble set in a frame of simple white mosaic with a black finishing band. The centre of the pavement is missing; there may have been a large emblema here. Against the back wall stood the base for the cult statue, which was not large-scale. If Mau is right in his identification of architectural members found in the vicinity, the order was Corinthian and of white Luna marble.

According to Mau, this temple was framed by colonnades that corrected the lines of the original colonnades to make a rectangular temenos. Along the back was a single colonnade, along the sides double colonnades, all three wings in two storeys but without flooring between, the walls in the ground storey lined with pilasters and those in the upper storey lined with half-columns. All of these were Corinthian and of Luna marble. Plates of marble, some bits of which remain, covered the walls.

In the last period the temple podium was enlarged by the addition of a heavy wall of blocks of lava that ran around the old podium, encasing it, while a crosswall of the same blocks was installed in a cut in front of the line of the old cella wall. The temple now measured 29.15 m by 15.05 m, comparable to the Capitolium, large but not the largest temple in Pompeii. The builders evidently had it in mind to deepen the cella, making it a rectangle, and to make the combination of stair and pronaos equal in depth to the new cella, a more balanced design than before. But even the podium was never completed, so it is impossible to discuss architectural innovation and new aesthetic effects with authority.

The phase that is vital to our understanding of the temple is the second one. If Mau is right, the multiplication of Corinthian orders is rather puzzling. Through the Hellenistic period the Pompeians had observed the canonical sequence of orders very loyally, despite a curious fondness in the second century B.C. for putting a Doric frieze on Ionic columns. In the west colonnade of the forum, begun after A.D. 62, the lower order is Doric with a Doric cornice, the upper Ionic. But Augustus had combined Corinthian orders of two scales in the colonnades of his forum and the Temple of Mars Ultor, and one can find such combinations in late decorations in the Second Style. By the time of the Flavians it seems to have become quite common (see, for example, Porta dei Borsari in Verona [Boethius and Ward-Perkins 308 and fig. 166]), and through the second century we find it repeatedly in such buildings as the Pantheon. Still, such a proliferation of Corinthian orders without variation is very unusual and in the present state of our knowledge must be regarded with suspicion. If it is correct, however, it must be taken as indication of a strong wish on

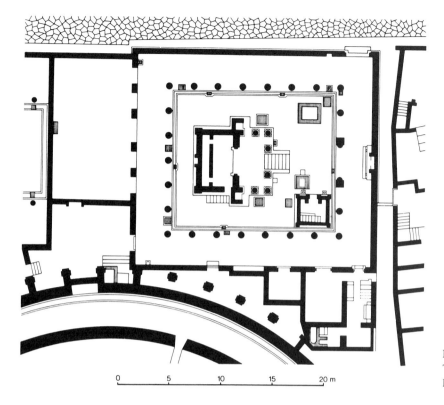

FIGURE 41.
The Temple of Isis,
Plan

the part of the Pompeians to make the temple of their patron goddess very avant-garde.

Set on the brow of a hill, raised on a podium, framed at the back and sides by colonnades, the effect of the temple from a distance must have been very imposing, similar to that of the Temple of Hercules Victor at Tivoli or the Temple of the Deified Claudius in Rome. With a suitably grand approach from the front, it would have accorded well with the great sanctuaries of Latium.[15]

The Templum Isidis

The Temple of Isis in Pompeii (VIII vii 28)[16] is in almost every way an anomaly, diminutive, axial in its main lines but with important additions that obscure the axiality, hybrid in its architectural forms, a cu-

[15] One might compare the approaches to the Temple of Fortuna Primigenia at Palestrina (F. Fasolo and G. Gullini, *Il santuario della Fortuna Primigenia a Palestrina* [Rome 1953] esp. pl. 3), to the Temple of Hercules Victor at Tivoli (C. Giuliani, *Forma Italiae: Tibur*, pt. 2 [Rome 1970] 164–201, esp. 197, fig. 22), and to the Temple of Juno at Gabii (R. Delbrück, *Hellenistische Bauten in Latium*, 2 vols. [Strasbourg 1907–12], 2.5–10).

[16] On this building see Overbeck and Mau 104–10; O. Elia, *Le pitture del tempio d'Iside* (Monumenti della pittura antica scoperti in Italia, ser. 3, fasc. 3–4, Rome 1942); Maiuri 1942, 68–70; and Tran Tam Tinh, *Essai sur le culte d'Isis à Pompéi* (Paris 1964) 30–39.

rious mixture of the Greco-Roman koine and Egyptianizing motifs in its decoration, with extensive stuccowork and some important paintings. It stands just north of the Theatrum Maius in an area between the "Palestra" and the Temple of Jupiter Meilichios and was accessible from the Via del Tempio di Iside by a wide doorway closed by a door of three leaves at the northeast corner of the temenos. Over the doorway was an inscription on a plate of marble recording that it was rebuilt *a fundamento* by N. Popidius Celsinus, son of N. Popidius, at the age of six (*CIL* 10.846). In return for his munificence Celsinus was co-opted into the ordo of the city gratis. His temple replaced an earlier one on the same site destroyed in the earthquake.[17]

The main axis of the new temple lies east/west through the centre of an enclosing peristyle of seven columns by eight, one column being omitted in the middle of the east side and the architrave here lifted higher to give special emphasis to a large painting in the portico. This shows the worship of Harpocrates and was framed by pilasters supported on consoles and a projecting lintel. Opposite this, a little west of the centre of the precinct, rose the temple proper, frontal, raised on a podium trimmed with a base step and crown molding. Pronaos and cella are broad and shallow, of equal depth. There were four columns on the façade, with the central intercolumniation wider than the others. On each side of the pronaos were two columns and an anta, but the anta both was and was not a continuation of the line of columns, having a second lower Corinthian pilaster engaged against it, one of a pair that, with a triangular pediment they supported, framed a small niche with an arched opening projecting to either side as a sort of side chapel. These effectively filled the view for worshipers gathered at the east end of the precinct. The divinities worshiped here are not known. The pronaos was approached by a narrow flight of eight steps the width of the central intercolumniation, and a somewhat broader door led to the cella. In the interior of the cella a broad, high podium runs along the back wall its full width. This contains a vaulted chamber accessible by a low flat-arched door at either end. On the top of the podium are two small bases, but the cult images were missing. At the east end of the south wall of the cella a small door leads to the exterior, where a narrow stair of seven steps leads down from it, concealed behind the south lateral niche. This must have served for priests, who could

---

[17] The reading of the remains of the earlier temple has been much disputed. Overbeck and Mau (105) cite traces on the stylobate of a peristyle of eight columns by ten and the unfluted column elements reused in the pronaos. The latter are very unusual and probably no earlier than the middle of the first century B.C. Extensive excavations under the floors of the temenos in ca. 1949–50 seem to have done little to clarify things, and the results were never published.

Figure 42.
The Temple of Isis,
Temple Building

open the temple doors dramatically from the interior to reveal the divinities within to the worshipers or for other theatrical effects. Behind the temple, in the centre of its back wall, was yet another niche, with stucco embellishments, containing a statue of Bacchus playing with a panther. The order of the temple is Corinthian, with Attic bases, the columns worked in stucco over unfluted tufa cores. The temple walls were finished with stucco on the exterior in imitation of drafted ashlar and trimmed at the back corners with pilasters. Crowning the walls was a deep frieze of acanthus scrolls. Were the side chapels omitted, the temple would be regular enough, but these, combined with the extravagance of the stuccoes with which it is embellished, give it an exotic air.

The peristyle around it is broad and unencumbered. The columns are of brick, half-columns engaged against square pillars to either side of the gap at the centre of the east end, rendered in stucco. The order is Doric in its general lines, but with the addition of a deep band ornamented with rosettes under the echinus. The tufa gutter fits tight against the stylobate and is provided with settling basins at intervals. In half a dozen intercolumniations are remains of bases for dedications following no particular plan. In the open area around the temple, which is paved with slabs of tufa, are a number of features. In front of each side chapel is a square altar of horned form, while that of the temple proper in front of the stair is displaced from the axis to the south. This altar too was of horned form. Two small, plain bases probably for dedications, rather than altars, flank the temple stair. Near the northeast corner of the open area is an enclosed pit for the refuse from sacrifices; the enclosure wall is gabled at its east and west ends.

In the southeast corner of the open area is a high, walled enclosure, roofless but with a shallow triangular pediment crowning the north and south walls and a line of antefixes along the top of the east and west ones. A single door with an arched top breaks into the pediment in the centre of the north side. This contains a narrow stair leading down to the west to a small, tanklike underground chamber of uncertain purpose. Possibly it was to contain the Nile water, which we know was important in the rituals of Isis. The exterior of this enclosure was richly covered with stucco reliefs, many with reference to Egypt and Isis, others seemingly purely conventional and secular. Two Egyptian figures in relief on the front have high tufa altars in front of them.

Behind the temple opens a large rectangular hall accessible from the temenos by five wide, arched doorways. This hall was richly painted with large Egyptianizing landscapes relative to the cult and subject paintings of the story of Io. Against the west wall stood an acrolithic statue somewhat larger than life. It has been conjectured that this room served for ritual meals.

South of this is a space half its size, of irregular shape and uncertain roofing, abutting on the back of the summa cavea of the theatre. This was a sacrarium painted with the major figures of the cult of Isis, very large-scale but crudely executed, after the fashion of lararium paintings. Here were found various vessels, idols, and images, suggesting that this may have served as a sacristy as well as a place of worship. From this space also one had access to other areas behind the theatre.

Off the east end of the south wall of the temenos opens a series of five small rooms, including a kitchen and a stair to a room or rooms in an upper storey. This has been identified as the lodgings for the priests of Isis.

The architecture of this temple is not especially remarkable, although many of the dedications found here were exceptionally fine and testify to the wealth and importance of the cult. For the most part, the building materials were the cheapest and most readily available, and there was heavy reliance throughout on stucco and paint. In its architectural form the temple is not known to be related to temples of Isis elsewhere, such as those at Rome and on Delos.[18] In relation to other Pompeian temples, such as the Temple of Apollo, this seems overdecorated and shoddy, though in the last period there must have been many similarities between the two. But the Temple of Isis was not indicative of a new temple architecture coming into vogue in the last period of Pompeii; for that one must turn to the Temple of Venus Pompeiana. Instead, the taste shown here is that of small houses with cluttered gardens—the Casa dei Vettii, for example, and the Casa di Marco Lucrezio. The temple itself is rather feminine, almost frivolous in its architectural effect, small and elaborately decorated. It is architecture to be seen, not architecture to be experienced. The walls of the colonnade were painted a rich red above a black dado, surmounted by a deep frieze filled with a complicated peopled scroll in polychrome, a grand and dignified scheme against which the little stucco-encrusted temple and the collection of the votive material, most of it less than life-size, must have seemed slightly incongruous and playful. But it was clearly a deliberately chosen effect.

It has been presumed that because N. Popidius Ampliatus, the father of N. Popidius Celsinus, who rebuilt the temple, does not record his paternity on his votive offering, he must have been a freedman.[19] The case is far from proved, since the inscription is brief and he does not record the identity of his patronus either. The cult is supposed to have appealed especially to women of the lower classes, and in pictures the priests are shown as exotic Egyptians with shaved heads, but the importance of the cult in Pompeii was certainly considerable, and it had penetrated the fabric of Pompeian society at the highest levels and become respectable. Isis was worshiped quite publicly in some of the best houses, and as the frieze in the Casa di Marte e Venere (VII ix 47) shows, she had a place in the public feasts and processions, attendant on, if not equal to, that of Venus Pompeiana.[20]

[18] See R. E. Witt, *Isis in the Graeco-Roman World* (Ithaca, N.Y. 1971) figs. 14, 42, 43.
[19] Overbeck and Mau 104; cf. Castrén 207–8, no. 318.
[20] Helbig 1479; Tran Tam Tinh (supra n. 16) 132–33 and pl. 11.

The Terme Centrali

The one conspicuously utilitarian complex that seems to have been entirely a creation of the last period is the Terme Centrali (IX iv 5/18), at the crossing of the Via di Nola and the Strada Stabiana.[21] It was a building still far from completion at the time of the eruption. For it the city planners took one whole block of the heart of the city rather closer to the Thermae Stabianae than one might have expected, but convenient to the heavily residential north-central sector. To give the architects complete freedom, all construction in the block was razed, but along the northern and western fronts of the block, facing on important streets, lines of more or less uniform one-room shops were constructed, with a larger and more elaborate one at the corner, none of which is connected with the bath complex. These have walls in rubble-faced concrete coigned with opus mixtum vittatum, while the bath rooms are of incertum, reticulate, and brick-faced concrete coigned with brick. Throughout the bath rooms, doors and windows have lintels in flat arches of brick with relieving arches above, and drains and heating passages have mouths and relieving arches of brick. This difference may be indicative of different building campaigns, in which case the shops and periphery of the block are presumably older, but no plaster faces either the interiors or the façades, so if the shops were in use, they had not yet been finished.

The bath itself, like the Terme de Foro, was developed in the interior of the block but took all of this. One could enter from the Strada Stabiana (IX iv 5) or the Via di Nola (IX v 18), the latter probably intended to become the principal entrance, the other possibly a late conversion of a shop or intended for conversion into a shop in the finished complex. There is also a little posticumlike entrance to the alleyway on the south (IX iv 10), with a pair of entrances to the service courtyard behind (IX iv 15, 16). All entrances for the public led to a large courtyard, the palaestra, occupying one-third of the area of the whole block. It was evidently intended to be surrounded by colonnades, except on the east side, where the windows of the bath rooms opened and the colonnade was completed as an engaged order. No significant work on this had yet been done. A large rectangular excavation in front of the bath rooms, with a trench leading from it to a large latrine off the southwest corner of the palaestra, is evidence that a swimming pool much larger than that in the Thermae Stabianae was to be installed here. It is interesting that its waste was to be used to flush out the latrine, as that from the pool in the Palestra Grande did. A cistern on the west side of this court that runs over

---

[21] On this complex see Overbeck and Mau 233–38; and Maiuri 1942, 74–77.

the line of the west colonnade is a curious feature; probably this was a builders' installation that would have been removed later. There are surprisingly few dependencies opening off the palaestra. At the north entrance are a pair of small square cubicula, presumably for the balneator and the sale of bath necessities, and at the centre of the north and south colonnades were to be shallow rectangular alcoves to accommodate people who wished to rest or converse, but except for a pair of square rooms of moderate size off the south side and a stair at the northeast corner, there are no annexes. One of the rooms on the south has two windows looking into the palaestra and may have been intended to be a conisterium, a room where the athletes powdered themselves. The other might then conceivably be a coryceum, a room with punching bags, for Vitruvius (5.11.2) said that these should be adjacent to one another in a palaestra. The stair is unusually well built and may have led to a deck for sunbathing.

One entered the baths proper through a lobby off the northeast corner of the palaestra by either of two doors, one to the north colonnade, one to the open area. This lobby may also have served as an apodyterium. Off it was a series of five small dependencies, some of them with windows, probably especially for scraping the athletes down after exercise (destrictarium) and masseurs (aliptae). From this lobby one passed into another apodyterium, a large rectangular room with a rectangular bath basin filling its eastern end. This must have been the frigidarium. It is interesting that here again, as in the Augustan women's suite of the Terme del Foro, the frigidarium appears as a feature of the apodyterium, not a room by itself as it is in the older baths. Water may have been intended to play into this bath basin from the three niches above it. From the apodyterium one proceeded south by either of two doors to the tepidarium, a plain rectangular room, and from this in turn to the caldarium. Possibly the two doors from each of these to the next room were one for entrance and one for exit to govern circulation of the bathers. The floor of the tepidarium was raised on suspensurae, and terracotta pipes for heat were built into its walls. The caldarium is the only elaborate room in this sequence, vaulted, its long walls enlivened with niches, alternately curved and rectangular, presumably for statuary, its short ends filled with rectangular tanks for bathing, while a smaller tank filled a niche at the centre of the south side. Probably the latter was to be a labrum for cold water. Hot water played into the larger tanks from niches above them. East of the tepidarium and entered from it or from the caldarium is the laconicum, a circular room with curved niches opening into the corners of the square in which it is inscribed, very much like the older frigidaria in its architecture but a dry sweat room where the temperature would have been very high. This was covered by a low dome, of which there are only poor remains, and lit by three small round windows just under the dome. This and the caldarium would have had hollow walls, as well as floors raised on suspensurae, and along the exterior to the east runs a trench by which heat would have been brought from the praefurnium. The last was never built, the whole eastern end of the block being now a featureless yard in which it is impossible to discern which part might have been intended for furnaces, which for fuel storage, and which for personnel. The furnaces would almost certainly have been close to the caldarium and the laconicum. Though there is enough space for it, the planning of the men's baths seems to exclude any notion that there was ever to be a women's suite.

Some of the vaults and lunettes had received decorations in stucco; poor remains can be seen along the base of the inner lunette in the apodyterium/frigidarium, and a fallen chunk from the vault of the caldarium showed simple ornaments. But the walls and floors were covered only with a thick coat of signinum, the base for finer pavements and marble revetment. Drains in the various rooms, which are numerous and carefully engineered, had not yet been fitted with pipes and filters. As work progressed, doubtless many modifications and refinements would have been introduced, but at this point we can see only the broader outlines of the architecture.

What is remarkable about this bath is the size of the rooms, the largest of any of the public baths of Pompeii; the inclusion of a laconicum, a new feature the desirability of which is hard to evaluate; and the introduction of three big square windows in the west wall of each of the three principal bath rooms and five somewhat smaller windows in the south wall of the caldarium. Those to the west are so large that it would have been impossible to glaze them; they must have been fitted with shutters that could be adjusted to the weather when it would have made the rooms uncomfortable. But they are a sign of a great advance in thermal engineering, a sign that the Romans had come to understand that when windows faced southwest, the sun would help heat rooms equipped with floors and walls that were radiating heat and would make glazing the windows unnecessary or even undesirable.[22] From now on Roman baths would be oriented to the southwest and have remarkably expansive fenestration. The first of the new public baths in Rome to show understanding of this principle were the baths of Trajan; the last of the old, which may have been influenced by their situation with respect to Nero's Domus Aurea, were the baths of Titus.

The strong emphasis in the Terme Centrali on palaestra and bath rooms, the generally utilitarian quality of the complex with lack of amenities and annexes for those who might wish to converse or otherwise amuse themselves, and the absence of a women's division together suggest that this bath complex was designed especially for the young and vigorous. Might it be that the boys and young men were eventually to be accommodated here, and the Thermae Stabianae given over to the middle-aged and elderly? That seems at least possible.

---

[22]See *MAAR* 24 (1956) 170–261 (E. D. Thatcher) on the Terme del Foro at Ostia.

19 · SEMI-PRIVATE BUILDINGS

Introduction

One of the interesting phenomena of the last years of Pompeii, though its roots probably go further back, is the proliferation of clubhouses. Some of these were relatively simple meeting places, such as the Schola Iuventutis (III iii 6); others were converted houses where the architectural adaptation was minimal and somewhat clumsy, for example, the Casa di Sallustio (VI ii 4). But some, such as the Insula Iuliae Felicis (II iv 2–7), seem to have been planned and built as clubs. In no case is it yet possible to associate any of these with a particular trade or profession, as a guildhall, or with a political or social objective, and except for the Schola Iuventutis, they seem to have been directed more toward eating and bathing, the traditional pursuits of the Romans in leisure time, than anything else. Probably most of them had social overtones; some of them may even have been covertly political, but the fact is that we know no more about them than we can see in their physical remains.

The Schola Iuventutis

One of the oddest buildings of Pompeii, the Schola Iuventutis (III iii 6) is a single large room, a broad rectangle in plan, obviously of military character, at the northwest corner of the meeting of the street leading up from the Porta di Nocera with the Via dell'Abbondanza.[1]

[1] On the Schola Iuventutis see Spinazzola 1953, 1.135–47; and Maiuri 1942, 90. Maiuri's contention that the whole building is postearthquake is worrisome in view of Spinazzola's assertion (p. 142) that there were remains of a Second Style decoration. The building was severely damaged in the bombing of 1943 and was then reconstructed by Maiuri (see Spinazzola 1953, 1.xxviii, figs. xiii–xiv). In the bombing the fabric of the walls was exposed, showing that the west jamb is quite different from the east one. I therefore presume that Spinazzola was right and part of the west wall at least survived from an earlier phase.

It opened to the Via dell'Abbondanza by a very broad door whose lower part was filled with wooden grillwork in three sections, the form of which was recovered from the print the decaying wood left in the ash. This ran in a track, the ends sliding back to give access, but the interior of the building was exposed to the public view at all times. On the exterior to either side of the door was painted a very large trophy composed of arms piled at the foot of a tree trunk surmounted by the usual arrangement of armor in the semblance of a warrior. The arms include naval equipment as well as a British war chariot and seem to allude to Roman conquest of the world. The excavator, Spinazzola, wished to restore the façade with a crowning pediment but admitted that no evidence for this was found.

Inside, the west wall at least was painted in part with architecture in the Second Style above a new dado to shoulder height in Fourth Style. Although practically none of this survived at the time of excavation, it is important in ascertaining the age of the building. Against the other two walls a series of square masonry pillars rising to shoulder height carried a series of high wooden cupboards, and the walls behind these were bare of plaster. The high dado was painted dark red and decorated with Victorias carrying arms. The cupboards were believed to have contained arms, of which only a single fragment, a carved bone mount, was recovered. A small door near the east end of the north wall led back to areas not yet fully excavated, presumably quarters of a custodian.

Della Corte identified this as the Schola Iuventutis, a sort of clubhouse for the Pompeian collegium of the Augustan paramilitary organization in which he took a special interest, but the epigraphical evidence is meager (Della Corte[3] 351–55). Spinazzola wished to see it as the armory of the militia of Pompeii. Its strategic location with respect to three of the city gates might incline us to the latter identification, but the lack of security in the building and the fact that so little in the way of arms was actually found here suggest that any weapons kept in the cupboards would have had to be of perishable material, which must incline us to Della Corte's theory. We may remember that in 49 B.C. Pompeii had a militia of three cohorts (Cicero *ad Att.* 10.16.4). The Second Style decoration of which bits remain can hardly be dated more than twenty years after 49, but this building is too small to have been the headquarters for three cohorts, or indeed, one would think, more than one. In the absence of similar buildings elsewhere in the city, it seems best to accept Della Corte's identification.

To complete the building one must imagine a large gable roof, probably projecting in front to cover the sidewalk and protect the painted façade. Thus the building called attention to itself, and the vastness of the entrance invited inspection, proclaiming that this was neither a house nor a shop. It is odd that electoral programmata advertising the support of the Iuventus for candidates were not numerous, but one can think of various explanations for this—that most of the candidates were past members of the collegium and it would be unseemly to support one against another; or that the youth of the present membership made their political views a matter of small interest. Certainly the trophies of the façade made the general character of the building clear enough and link it to the central exedra on the south side of the Ludus Gladiatorius (VIII vii 16), which was flanked by similar trophies.

We know something of the organization of the Iuventus in Pompeii, though not its size or the necessary qualifications for membership, from the investigations of Della Corte following the discovery of this building. It was evidently a well-entrenched institution whose members liked to advertise their membership, and it was involved in religious matters, especially the cult of Venus Pompeiana, as well as athletic and military training.

The Insula Iuliae Felicis

Those who frequented the Insula Iuliae Felicis (II iv), down the Via dell'Abbondanza from the Schola Iuventutis, had no such high purposes and interests.[2] This establishment, which takes the whole of a double city block—though more than half the area is left simply as a kitchen garden—is divided between bathing and dining. Its parts are listed for us in a dipinto on the exterior in which it was advertised to let:

IN PRAEDIS IVLIAE SP. F. FELICIS

LOCANTVR

BALNEVM VENERIVM ET NONGENTVM TABERNAE PERGVLAE

CENACVLA EX IDIBVS AVG PRIMIS IN IDVS AVG SEXTAS ANNOS

CONTINVOS QVINQVE

S . Q . D . L . E . N . C .

(*CIL* 4.1136)

The question immediately arises, What is a *balneum uenerium et nongentum*? The other parts are clear: shops, mezzanines (presumably shops with mezzanine lofts are meant), and upper-storey apartments. Since there is no mention of the extensive dining facilities,

---

[2] The Insula Iuliae Felicis was excavated in 1755–56 and then reburied after removal of the choicest objects and pictures (*PAH* 1.1.12–41 [30 March 1755–29 May 1756], 1.2.95–102). It was reexcavated in 1951–52, and the marble colonnade restored, but no account of the reexcavation has been published.

these must be included in the balneum, as must also the atrium house at the southwest corner. The intention seems clearly to include the whole complex in the description. Della Corte decided that the reference was to a youth organization, the Iuvenes Venerii et Nongenti Pompeiani, but if this was their clubhouse, they would hardly have put it up to let as such or described it as a balneum. Pliny tells us that the title nongentus was given to those of the equestrian order who were elected keepers of the ballot boxes in the comitia, with the implication that this was a considerable distinction.[3] Among the electoral programmata painted on the street façades of the building were one in which support was offered by veneri (*CIL* 4.1146), one in which the support of the pilicrepi (ball players) was requested (*CIL* 4.1147), and one in which support was given by a fornacator, an anonymous functionary of the baths in charge of the praefurnium (*CIL* 4.1150). There were also programmata of Proculus et Canthus (*CIL* 4.1140), Cantus alone (*CIL* 4.1149), and Papilio (*CIL* 4.1157). Papilio has been identified by J. L. Franklin as a professional scriptor (*CronPomp* 4 [1978] 63–64). At least eight men in Pompeii, including three candidates for municipal office, carried the cognomen Proculus, while Canthus is unattested elsewhere and is very rare outside Pompeii. The pilicrepi must have been frequenters of this establishment accustomed to playing ball here as part of the ritual of bathing.[4] The veneri may then be simply those who frequented this bath, those who managed it, those who gave it its name, or any combination of these elements. But it does not appear that Venus was especially venerated here, since there was an elaborate shrine for Isis and the Egyptian gods in which she does not seem to have appeared (Boyce 471; Helbig 79). Then if the nongenti were an elite, it stands to reason that the appellation *venerium* described the luxurious appointments of this bath in some way—"worthy of Venus" or "as elegant or seductive as Venus."

The bath, in the middle of the block, had its own impressive entrance (II iv 6) framed by columns and seems to have functioned independently of the rest though communicating closely with it. One entered a square courtyard paved with mosaic surrounded by a colonnade. This is too small to have functioned as a palaestra, and around its southwest corner have been built partitions creating cubicles that one imagines might have served for dispensing oil and towels and similar necessities. In the southwest corner itself has been built a tiny laconicum only big enough to hold one or two bathers at a time. It is essentially circular in plan, with little niches opening off

[3] Pliny *NH* 33.31. One should note that in the advertisement for letting the Insula Arriana Polliana, part of the complex was described as cenacula equestria (*CIL* 4.138).

[4] See Seneca *Ep.* 56.1.

the north and east sides. Its location was dictated by the existence of the praefurnium just west of it from a time before it was conceived of, and it has to open slightly awkwardly out of the northwest corner of the tepidarium. This clumsy modification of the originally handsome entrance court of the baths, work in much of which no architect would seem to have had a hand, is all clearly postearthquake and must represent a hasty effort at modernization when proper labor and building materials were not yet available.

The bath proper, though the rooms are small, has an unusually complete sequence. The apodyterium is rectangular, with a small rectangular frigidarium opening out of its south wall. The tank is also rectangular, and there is a rectangular niche in the centre of each wall except the entrance wall. The tepidarium, west of the apodyterium, is a little larger than the apodyterium and has a shallow rectangular niche in the centre of the north wall and another of the same size toward the west end of the south wall. One might imagine that these were for bathing tanks, or a tank and a labrum, but there is no sign of either. According to the excavation reports, in the south niche were found the marble legs of a tripod table with small horned gryphon heads atop lion's paws (*PAH* 1.1.31, 1.2.97 no. 41). Out of the northwest corner of the room opens the laconicum. The caldarium, west of the tepidarium, is a rectangle broken by niches in three walls. A bowed niche for a labrum the stuccoed support for which survived at the time of excavation opens in its south wall, and a large rectangular niche for a bathing tank nearly fills the north wall. The floors of the warm rooms were raised on suspensurae and paved with black-and-white mosaic, in part figured, and their walls were lined with tegulae mammatae under the plaster. The praefurnium was in an L-shaped courtyard north of the caldarium and had its own entrance (II iv 4) on the Via dell'Abbondanza. From the praefurnium an isolating trench ran around the foundations of the warm rooms from the northwest corner of the caldarium to the southeast corner of the tepidarium. This sophisticated refinement, which we find again in the Terme Centrali, must be taken as evidence that the bath is not very old.

From the apodyterium a short corridor led south to a large latrine with a sewer trench along its south and east sides that was flushed by the waste from a large rectangular swimming pool in an open court east of the apodyterium accessible from either the apodyterium or the entrance lobby. A broad walk surrounds the swimming pool, presumably for those who wished to sunbathe on its edge, and south of it, on axis, is a curved niche holding a fountain. Directly accessible from the area of the swimming pool is a thermopolium, and a wine-shop lies across the entrance lobby from this. One gathers that the bathers consumed a good bit of food and drink. To the east the walk area around the swimming pool opens out in a large featureless yard stretching to the eastern limit of the block. This is protected by a high perimeter wall and must have served as a palaestra. A large enclosure against the north wall roofed with a series of light beams suggestive of an arbor seems to have been a combination of an al fresco dining room served by the restaurant facilities with which it communicates and a resting place for those exercising. A small outbuilding in the southeast corner may have been for maintenance and gardening equipment.

The more elegant wing of the complex is entered through a displuviate Tuscanic atrium opening directly on the street by two doors (II iv 2–3), the only such atrium known in Pompeii.[5] It is rectangular, rather handsome, with a marble impluvium that is in effect simply a plate set off by a low rim. The atrium once boasted a continuous frieze of scenes of forum life that was cut up into small sections in the eighteenth century and is now in the Museo Nazionale, an invaluable but puzzling source of knowledge about Pompeian life (Helbig 1482, 1483, 1485, 1489–1500). From this the public passed directly to a broad colonnade, almost as broad as the atrium itself, running north and south along an ornamental garden, while the management of the establishment could go directly to the praefurnium court on the east or to the shop on the west or by a corridor out of the southwest corner to the kitchen and service quarter.

The roof of the colonnade is supported on sixteen fluted marble pillars with Corinthian capitals elaborated with the addition of rosettes. Two just south of the middle are higher than the rest, drawing the eye to an exedral nymphaeum opening behind the colonnade at this point, a triclinium of masonry veneered with marble into which water cascaded down a miniature flight of stairs in an axial niche at the back (*RömMitt* 71 [1964] 182–94 [F. Rakob]). The walls are in part veneered with marble, in part painted, and certain Nilotic landscapes with ducks and crocodiles in the Museo Nazionale are reported to have been found here.[6] In each side wall is another niche, presumably for small-scale sculpture. A channel separates the triclinium from the surrounding walls, and the water collected in this was piped through it to a shallow basin in the middle and from there underground to the euripus in the garden. It is impossible to imagine that people could have dined here with water playing all about them, and there is no table. Conceivably it was for use in drinking parties, but

[5] On displuviate atria see Vitruvius 6.3.2. The problem Vitruvius mentions with displuviate atria would not obtain here, since on the north and east there were no adjacent roofs, and on the west and south the adjacent roofs stood at a much lower level.

[6] Helbig 1538, 1566; M.N. Inv. No. 9732. Cf. *PAH* 1.1.15 (4 May 1755).

it is more likely that this was simply another example of Pompeian playfulness, a fountain room to be viewed especially from the garden and the arbor across the garden from it, framed in the architecture of a dining room but drenched in water.

This water drained off into a euripus that runs nearly the whole length of the garden parallel to the colonnade and gives the garden a dominant axis. It is a broad channel, its margin finished with marble plates, crossed at intervals by bridges and enlivened by a series of niches, both curved and rectangular, that open in responsive pairs along its sides. Its size and depth suggest that this was a breeding tank for fish, as well as an ornamental water and a means of cooling the garden in the summer. It was also embellished with fountains at the middle and with statuary along its whole length. Seven statuettes are listed as having been found along its margin, including the famous group of a heron with a lizard in its beak[7] and a Pan cradling a young kid in the skin fastened around his shoulders.[8] And numerous small herms were found when the garden area was excavated.

Along the south and east sides of the garden ran an arbor supported on masonry posts plastered and painted green. On the east the wall behind this above knee height is broken into ten niches, alternately curved and rectangular, covered with limestone rustication. These arbors may well have served to shelter dining arrangements, al fresco triclinia, in the summer months. Off the southern arbor opens a small room that served as a sacellum of the Egyptian gods. Here were found the magnificent bronze tripod supported by three ithyphallic satyrs and also a statuette of Priapus,[9] as well as pieces of jewelry and household furnishings.

The back wall of the marble colonnade has a series of twelve small niches that held a collection of curiosities and sculptures, for the most part rather salacious, including priapic jugs and a terracotta representation of the Caritas Romana group.[10] Opening off the colonnade to either side of the central nymphaeum are four dining rooms of varying size, all with access as well to a service corridor that runs along the west side of the building and connects them to kitchens at either end, a large one with its own street entrance (II iv 12) at the north end, a small one at the south, each with storage closets in addition to the kitchen proper. An interesting feature is a peephole to the service corridor in each room, evidently to allow waiters to keep a quiet eye on a party's progress and requirements.

At the southern end of this block, directly connected to the colon-

[7] *PAH* 1.2.98 nos. 46, 51, 54, 57, 58, 59, 61; Spinazzola 1928, 62.
[8] Jashemski 49, fig. 83; cf. *PAH* 1.1.34 (2 November 1755), 1.2.98, no. 61.
[9] Grant 9, 84, 123; cf. *PAH* 1.2.98, no. 55.
[10] Grant 130; cf. *PAH* 1.1.16 (11, 18 May 1755), 18–19 (1 June 1755).

FIGURE 44.
The Insula Iuliae
Felicis, Marble Order
of the Peristyle

nade by a wide door but at a level three steps below the colonnade, is a house. This consists of a small Tuscanic atrium surrounded by rooms but without tablinum or alae. A second storey covered at least some of the rooms on the south side. The finely decorated rooms here look west on the kitchen garden behind the building complex; there is only one window to the ornamental garden. While rather small, the house is too fine to be the apartment of a caretaker, and it has all the appointments of a private house, including its own kitchen and dining rooms, one of which was decorated with a series of figures of Apollo and the Muses identified by inscriptions in the Greek alphabet. One thinks of a club secretary or some similar functionary.

The remaining feature of special interest in this complex is a caupona (cookshop) just east of, and connecting with, the entrance lobby of the baths, the thermopolium of which we have already had occasion to mention. The cookshop opened to the street by a wide door (II iv 7) partially filled by the thermopolium counter, and passers-by were evidently courted by the display of food, but they might eat in comfort if they chose. A large room east of the shop is fixed up with a plastered masonry triclinium for reclining and two masonry bench-and-table arrangements where one could sit at one's meal in company with friends. The latter are of special interest, since they show that a good many Pompeians preferred to sit while eating at least some of the time.[11] Since cookshop meals were probably almost always relatively simple affairs, one would not want to exaggerate the significance of this, especially since it also seems to be unique in Pompeii.

As one contemplates the various parts of this complex and various of the furnishings found in it, especially the bronze tripod supported by ithyphallic satyrs and the jugs in the form of large membered dwarves, one is struck by the indications of wealth—the tripod is an extraordinarily fine bronze, and the marble pillars of the colonnade are an uncommon luxury—and the recurrent touches of the salacious. They all suggest a place where men only, especially prosperous men, congregated, and the frieze in the entrance lobby showing a panorama of life in the forum would fit in very well with the notion that this was a bath and eating club. What is surprising is that certain parts were evidently open to the general public, but that is the case in the Casa di Sallustio too.

The Terme del Sarno and Palaestra/Baths

A similar but less high-spirited establishment was the club at VIII ii 17–24, the Terme del Sarno and Palaestra/Baths, at the juncture of the Via delle Scuole and the Vicolo della Regina.[12] This is near the forum but in an essentially residential neighborhood and commands a magnificent view from the brow of the site over the Sarno Valley and the Sorrentine Peninsula. It is developed in multistorey buildings descending the slope of the site in terraces and can be divided into two parts, 17–21 and 22–24, but there is every indication that the parts worked closely together. In making the club three older houses were thrown together, one of them being almost completely rebuilt, one left largely in its original form, and the atrium of the one in-between preserved, while its other parts were sacrificed.

---

[11] One may compare Helbig 1504e, a scene in a caupona where four men, two of them wearing the cucullus (hooded cloak), sit around a round table eating and drinking, a rack loaded with foodstuffs hanging overhead, and a boy brings them a pitcher.

[12] For this complex see Noack and Lehmann 84–110 (with bibliography); and Maiuri 1942, 140–41.

FIGURE 45.
The Palaestra/Baths,
Plan of the Final Phase

Description must begin with the palaestra entered at VIII ii 23 down broad fauces paved with white mosaic in which a pair of wrestlers in black silhouette advertised the character of the establishment. East of the fauces is a caupona (VIII ii 24), opening to the street by a shop door, to the palaestra by an ordinary door, and to the fauces by a window. The window to the fauces suggests that the caupona was run by personnel of the palaestra, serving rather to keep those entering under surveillance than for waiting on customers. The shop has an L-shaped counter in the street doorway veneered with second-hand marble, with a set of step shelves for drinking vessels at one end. There are no pots for keeping food hot in this counter, so presumably it was only for dispensing drink, but a small kitchen east of the shop shows that food was available, and a small room off the shop may have been a dining room or a storeroom. On the street flanking the doors to the palaestra and caupona are two long masonry benches of the sort with which nearly every such establishment is provided. They seem to have been especially for servants waiting for their masters, but here they may have provided customers of the caupona with a place to sit as well. A door west of the entrance to the palaestra led to a stair to an apartment in an upper storey, evidently let out and probably confined to the area over the room west of it. Under the stair was a storage closet.

The palaestra is small for such activity and somewhat irregular in the alignment of its walls, with a deep portico on the west and north that must have been supported on wooden posts. The stylobate, in blocks of white limestone of irregular size, some and perhaps all secondhand, marks its edge, but both portico and open area are paved with white mosaic and at the same level. This suggests that no exercise more vigorous than trigon could have been anticipated here. The walls of the open area are covered with remains of a magnificent scaenae frons decoration in which athletes, judges, and Victorias are shown in various attitudes. Around the northwest corner on the portico of the palaestra open three exedral rooms of varying size all paved with mosaic, and off the smallest of these opens an inner room with a window to the portico. These must have been especially for masseurs. Another small exedra with mosaic pavement on the opposite side was walled off in the last period to make a more private room; the evidence for shelving on its east and south walls indicates that it then was probably used to store towels and bathing necessities. Off the northeast corner of the palaestra opens an L-shaped corridor leading east and then south to the praefurnium of the baths. Only the first leg of this corridor was roofed, but the praefurnium was covered by a vault. Evidently all fuel and service for the praefurnium had to pass through the palaestra, there being no exit to the street. The praefurnium, with heavy installations almost entirely of brickwork, is elaborately equipped with tanks and furnaces, testimony to heavy use of the facilities. Off the corridor leading to it is a large latrine with a sewer trench along the north and east walls, but not so large as that of the Insula Iuliae Felicis, and a stair led to a loft, evidently over the vault of the praefurnium, possibly living quarters for the fornacator.

The bath suite occupies an area between the palaestra and the edge of the city site and is entered at the south end of the west portico of the palaestra. It consists of the usual sequence of rooms, first a squarish apodyterium with a rectangular frigidarium opening out of the west side. The tank fills the whole frigidarium, its margin raised above the sill of the door to the apodyterium, its floor then sunk three steps below this. East of the apodyterium and of about the same size, the tepidarium has a floor raised on suspensurae, and there are large shallow rectangular niches of uncertain purpose in the east and west walls. The caldarium, though its outer half was lost in the collapse of the terrace on which it was supported, seems to have been very large, almost twice the size of the other rooms. A rectangular niche for a bathing tank filled its north wall, and a semicircular niche for a labrum opens in the middle of the east wall. Though the outer half is gone, the general lines of the room can be projected from the remains of terraces below. Beyond the bath suite an open deck overlooking the view ran along the apodyterium and tepidarium and was accessible from the former. Whether this continued to the west or whether there were rooms rather than a deck beyond the apodyterium is unclear.

This is the only part of this complex that was in working order at the time of the eruption. Though it interlocks in plan with the atrium building west of it (VIII ii 21), the only possible communication between them would have been along the terraced edge of the city. Probably doors would have been broken to link them once VIII ii 21 had been remodeled and refurbished. Certainly there is every indication that VIII ii 18–21 was a building of much the same character and complementary to the palaestra/baths. But one must remember also that there is little communication between the baths and the other parts in the Insula Iuliae Felicis.

VIII ii 18 is a large Tuscanic atrium entered by short fauces with a large axial tablinum but no other dependencies. One can imagine that it was to be used as a place of assembly, a semipublic hall. It communicates with a spacious corridor to the south running from a broad street door (VIII ii 20) to a lobby near the edge of the site from which a stair descends to terraced storeys below, at which point it narrows and bends to the south and probably ran to an open terrace along this part of the complex. North of the street door is a small shoplike room open to both the street and the corridor (VIII ii 19), probably the shop of an artisan who doubled as ostiarius. Across the corridor from this opens a large trapezoidal court with the hearth platform and cistern head of a kitchen. Food for a large number of people could have been prepared here. West of this is a triangular light well with a double window to the corridor, its main source of light; followed by a narrow corridor leading east to a separate suite of good-sized rooms, some facing the view, some around a little peristyle; then a triangular space that Noack and Lehmann see as having once been a stairwell with a stair to a second storey, but for this there is no evidence.

The separate suite seems to have been essentially a dwelling accessible only by the little corridor leading off the broad one from VIII ii 20 or along the terraced front. It consists of a small, square interior garden with porticoes on three sides paved with black-and-white mosaic and a roof supported on masonry pillars at the corners, a large oecus dominating this on one side and a small room and a triangular closet on the side opposite. Along the terraced front was probably originally a sequence of five rooms all opening on a common deck, probably uncovered. This suite served to fill the corner between the main blocks of the complex, but it is difficult to see it as public rooms.

VIII ii 21 was clearly in complete confusion at the time of the eruption. Originally it had been a large atrium house of canonical plan, but most of its eastern dependencies had been absorbed into the palaestra, and the atrium itself was undergoing an extensive remodeling. What we see today is the outline of a big Tuscanic atrium with shallow alae and a large tablinum completely open at both ends. Between the street and the atrium, the fauces and the rooms flanking the fauces have been destroyed to make a lobby in continuation of the big trapezoidal kitchen court to the west, out of which a stair descends to a long corridor leading to the lower terraces. Flanking the tablinum are two rather narrow rooms, much of that on the west having collapsed, and beyond these must have run a terrace at least as deep as the tablinum, probably with rooms at either end, to judge from bits of masonry that survive and the thickness of walls in the lower storey. To judge from the comparanda in similar houses here and in Herculaneum, such rooms may have been the most splendid triclinia in the house. How they would have been remodeled there is no way of telling.

There were four storeys built in terraces below the main storey in part of this complex, two in another part, one in yet another. The interconnection of these by ramps and stairs is very complex, clearly the result of repeated rebuilding and modification. Two main blocks can be distinguished: that beyond VIII ii 21 and accessible from the stair just inside that door to the west and one beyond VIII ii 20 and accessible at VIII ii 17. The former was probably once a separate apartment with its own street door. The ramped corridor leading down to it from the foot of the stair is narrow and inconvenient but not more so than many such corridors. At the further end a short flight of three steps brought one into a large lobby. Just west of this stair opened another that in combination with a wooden stair led up steeply to a mezzanine consisting of a low, vaulted exedral room and two narrow storage closets, one an extension of the stair. From the lower lobby one could go east by a corridor along a row of three small, windowless vaulted rooms behind two larger ones provided with windows to a chain of three more small rooms that give into one another, only the last being lit by a slit window. The unwindowed rooms are probably all bedrooms and storerooms, the windowed rooms living rooms. West of the lobby a corridor that connects with the adjacent complex beyond VIII ii 20 runs between a low vaulted room under the mezzanine—to judge from its proportions, a triclinium—and a vast rectangular oecus, one corner of which is blunted by an oblique foundation. Openings in the back wall of this, which is now in ruins, gave light to the corridor and triclinium beyond, so presumably it was originally generously supplied with windows. Remains of the dado show that it was once finely decorated, with figures of anguiped giants and a group of Thetis mounted on a hippocamp. On the whole this suite would have made a very satisfactory small house, though it lacks a kitchen today.

The other complex of terraces was originally a building standing on the floor of the Sarno Valley against the base of the hill of Pompeii connected with the city by a ramped tunnel with a few steps at either end. But then an older lower storey above this originally belonging to the atrium house entered at VIII ii 18 was incorporated into it and enlarged by new rooms built over the vaults of its roofs, probably the finest rooms in the whole building. But the stair from VIII ii 18 seems never to have been walled off, so either the owner of VIII ii 18 built this new block and maintained control of it or it was the intention in the last period to rebuild VIII ii 18/20/21 as an extension of this block. There is so much opus mixtum vittatum in the fabric of this block and so much evidence of work in progress there that one inclines to the latter view.

The complex is best described by beginning with the rooms of the third terrace in descending order, the one into which the tunnel from VIII ii 17 debouches. Beyond a small square lobby this level consists of a bath complex of half a dozen rooms and a low-ceilinged wing of seven rooms off to the east, all but the first, which has to be trapezoidal, of uniform size, opening off a common corridor. The bath complex was not in working order at the time of the eruption; there is clear evidence that workmen were laying pipe and building in every room. Only the frigidarium preserves painted decoration, and this is gouged by construction work, but it is clearly Fourth Style.

From the entrance lobby one could go east to the frigidarium, south to a room that was probably to be the apodyterium, or west to the praefurnium. The frigidarium is windowless, getting its light from a large square window with a small overwindow in an antechamber to the south. The bath basin is against the north wall, filling this end of the room, provided with three rounded steps in the southwest corner for those who did not wish to plunge in. A row of large square windows, with flat-arched lintels and smaller overwindows under the relieving arches over these, lights all the rooms in the southern bank, the principal bath rooms, except for the frigidarium. The caldarium in the southwest corner was still without suspensurae,

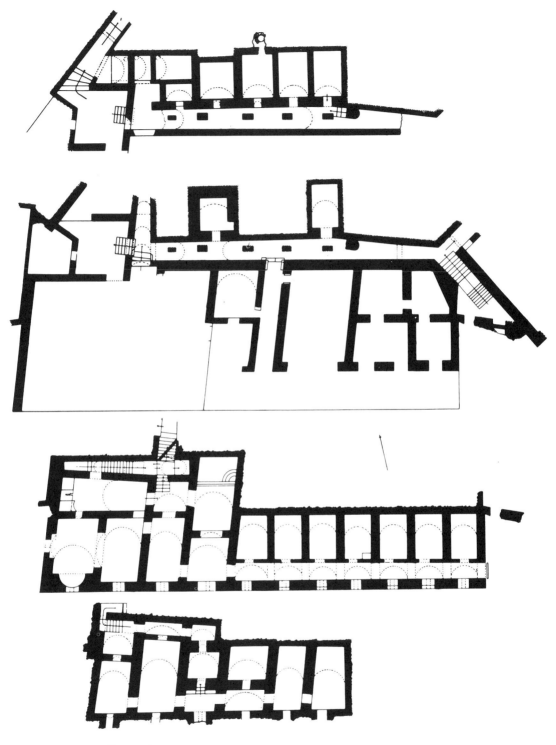

FIGURE 46.
The Terme del Sarno, Plans of the Final Phase

the mere shell of a room with a semicircular niche in the middle of the south wall and a shallow rectangular niche in the middle of the west wall, both with windows opening into them. The door between the tepidarium and the caldarium is unusually large; probably it would have been closed down once construction work here was completed. The praefurnium behind the tepidarium and caldarium had only the remains of old heating installations, for the most part torn out for replacement. Fuel for the praefurnium may have been kept in the storey below this one.

The wing of uniform rooms off to the east cannot be dissociated from the bath, though they seem almost an afterthought. They appear to be rooms for individual use, and it seems at least possible that the explanation for them might be that we are dealing with a mineral-water bath. The ancient Romans thought highly of the therapeutic value of mineral waters,[13] and an inscription on marble found just outside the Porta di Ercolano speaks of the *thermae M. Crassi Frugi aqua marina et baln. aqua dulci* (*CIL* 10.1063), which may have been a bath in the neighborhood. Today the vicinity of Pompeii is rich in mineral springs, there being an abundant spring of hot water impregnated with iron at Pompei Santuario and a great range of springs of different qualities at Castellammare di Stabia. There is every reason to suppose that there may have been a special water available to this thermal establishment and that these rooms were used for individual treatment, such as massage or mud packing.

Below the bath rooms and the first two rooms of the east wing was a basement storey with very thick lateral walls reflecting the plan of the rooms above them. This is accessible by a stair leading off the entrance corridor from VIII ii 17 behind the praefurnium of the bath. Those in the southern bank all had small windows to the exterior, but only one, a small lobbylike room in sequence with two more in series behind it, had a door. But the character of the whole storey as a sequence of storerooms is very clear. Whether these served an industrial establishment, or establishments, in the neighborhood is unknown, but they are too many and too spacious to have served for the baths alone, and the multiplication of doors among them suggests that space was to be let out in various amounts. In view of the likelihood that there were suburban commercial and industrial establishments not far away, it may be that the door that leads back to a corridor to the stair leading up to the bath storey was to be a public entrance.

At the height of the roof of the east wing of the bath storey, consid-

[13] See, e.g., Pliny *NH* 31.1–66, esp. 59–66. For the baths of M. Crassus Frugi see Della Corte[3] 29–30, nos. 1–2; and C. Malandrino, *Oplontis* (Naples 1977) 41–49.

erably below the roof of the bath suite, a corridor leads east from the entrance corridor, gradually narrowing toward the east end, and joins the west corridor of the lower terrace under VIII ii 21 at an obtuse angle. At the point of juncture a broad stair making a wye leads down to a triangular space east of the east wing of the bath storey at that level. Collapse has damaged the evidence here, but it looks as though an entrance to the baths from VIII ii 21 had been planned. The narrowing corridor has a series of five rectangular lights cut through the crown of its vault and the floor of a corridor above; these must have been protected by metal gratings. A sixth opening with a curved end was for a narrow wooden stair connecting the two corridors and must have been closed by a trapdoor. North of the lower corridor, cut into the hill of Pompeii, are two small chambers surviving from the early Augustan construction here. South of it, accessible by a corridor opening midway along its length, was a suite of large rooms with many interconnections, all but one in two rows, all facing south to a terrace probably defended by a parapet rather than roofed. None of these rooms is a perfect rectangle, all being slightly rhomboidal or trapezoidal. Only one, a deep exedra, seems clearly identifiable as a dining room.

West of this, on the other side of the entrance corridor from VIII ii 17, a flight of seven steps leads to a large square lobby at the level of the roof of the bath rooms, accessible also from the broad corridor leading in from entrance VIII ii 20 by the stair broken with ramps at its southwest end. The latter now widens as it descends and makes an awkward elbow, probably the result of remodeling. Remains of masonry and painted decoration show that a suite of rooms similar to those over the east wing, but one of them much larger, was built over the vaults of the bath rooms. Unfortunately the remains are too poor, and there has been too much modern restoration of the roofs, for us to be able to make out the plan.

Five steps above this lies the floor of the corridor over the skylighted corridor, now largely in ruins. It was apparently originally built to support a narrow terrace along the southwest front of the ground storey,[14] and behind it to the north open eight vaulted chambers, some of those at the west end made by remodeling older cisterns, that must have been service quarters in the last period. They are certainly to be regarded as more substructures than rooms in their own right, but the loss of most of the vault of the corridor that gives access to them, together with the east end of its floor, makes understanding the functioning of this level problematic.

---

[14]Noack and Lehmann (99) believe that the thickness of the walls suggests rooms above, rather than a terrace, but the argument is of dubious value.

Despite differences in level in the terracing and the evidence that here we are dealing with a building that was originally three atrium houses that preserved some parts of the original layout down to the last period of the city, it seems clear that during the last phase of Pompeii the owners of this property intended to complete it as a single complex with a focus on bathing and eating. The eastern part (VIII ii 23), had been hurriedly patched up after the earthquake to serve the interim needs of the clientele. The architecture of the baths here is handsome enough to suggest that these rooms would have been kept in the finished product, but the palaestra was makeshift, and the provisions for eating rudimentary. One feels that all the northern part of this wing was slated for reworking. Probably the areas of VIII ii 18–21 at ground level eventually would have been in part converted to accommodations for athletics and exercise and in part, especially the part to the southwest, made into reception rooms and dining rooms, with more of the same atop the baths in the terrace built out from the hill below these. The lower bath complex may have been for special therapy. If this reconstruction is anywhere near correct, it would have been a sumptuous addition to the city.

The Portico dei Triclini of the Agro Murecine

We must add to these examples one of the most remarkable buildings discovered in the environs of Pompeii, the so-called Portico dei Triclini of the Pagus Maritimus, or Agro Murecine, discovered during the construction of the highway from Pompeii to Salerno in May 1959.[15] The building could not be completely excavated. What was uncovered consisted of a peristyle enclosing a garden area with porticoes supported on the north and east on pillars and covered with a flat roof, on the west by arches and vaults. The masonry, faced with reticulate in grey and yellow tufa, is typical of the period A.D. 62–79. Over the north wing at least there were rooms of a rustic character in a second storey. The five rooms giving onto the north and east porticoes in the ground storey were all triclinia, all similar. They opened to the portico their full width but were closed by wooden grilles that could be folded back. The pavements in front were of black-and-white mosaic; the three diners' benches of masonry revetted at their ends with marble filled the rest of the room. The walls behind them were richly decorated with paintings in the Fourth Style.

In the centre of each group of benches stood a circular mensa on a masonry base with a marble leaf pierced in the centre by a jet of

---

[15] On this building see *RendNap* n.s. 35 (1960) 29–33 (O. Elia); and *BdA* 46 (1961) 200–211 (O. Elia). A model has been made of the parts of the building that were excavated.

water. The masonry base was stuccoed and painted with vine tendrils, sprays of leaves, and birds. Along the front of the benches, where one might expect a step on which food could be placed, was a shallow channel revetted with marble into which water played from pipes under the upper margin of the bench, in the way described by Pliny (*Ep.* 5.6.36–37). There were five pipe mouths in each lateral bench, four in that at the end. The overflow fell through holes at the ends of the channel into a basin sunk ten centimeters below pavement level around the foot of the table, and into this must also have dripped the water falling from the central jet on to the mensa.

Identification of the purpose of the building is complicated not only by the incompleteness of the excavation but by the discovery there of a large archive of wax tablets kept in a wicker basket in the upper storey over the central triclinium on the north side. These are records bearing dates of A.D. 37 to A.D. 55, with frequent mention of a certain C. Sulpicius Cinnamus, who did business at Puteoli. It has been supposed, therefore, that the building was the seat of a commercial house or collegium of men engaged in sea trafficking, a sort of clubhouse, like the Insula Iuliae Felicis.

In any case, the evidence of the triclinia seems very clear. The mensa is in every case permanent and too far distant (ca. 0.80 m) from the occupants of the benches to have been within arm's reach, a reach that was made more awkward by the channel full of water in front of the diners. Dishes that one wished to keep cool might have been set in the trough, except for the danger presented by the little jets behind it. If these only welled out water in the fashion described by Pliny, it would be possible. But the arrangements seem especially designed for drinking. They seem to be practical, not ornamental. Only the jet in the centre of the mensa might have been for show; the rest was designed to keep what was served cool. We can conclude that it would not have been food that was consumed here, but wine.

20 · THE HOUSES

Introduction

Following the earthquake of February, A.D. 62, Pompeii had to undertake the rebuilding of at least three-quarters of the city. The destruction of public buildings was everywhere matched by destruction
in private houses. But the workforce must have been limited, even if
it was supplemented by recruits from Naples. Rome can hardly have
sent any help after the terrible fire of 64. And private houses must
have had to wait upon more pressing public works. The water system
had to be overhauled; the public baths had to be improved and enlarged; the markets had to be rebuilt or repaired. Everyone who could
must have made do with what was still usable, and the installation
of workshops in what had been comfortable houses—the fullonica
(fullery) of Vesonius Primus in VI xiv 22, for example, and the industrial and commercial establishments along the Via dell'Abbondanza—is clear enough illustration of the makeshift expedients to
which they resorted. Families must have moved into a room or two—
whatever could be salvaged and shored up—to wait until they could
get the builders and decorators necessary. Often the work proceeded
by fits and starts, a few rooms in an atrium complex one year, a few
the next. Throughout the city we find evidence of construction still
in progress, a heap of chunks of alabaster to be ground to make plaster in the Casa degli Elefanti, a pile of lime in an oecus of the Casa
della Calce, builders' dolia and amphoras, often tools, but most commonly simply naked walls in rooms clearly intended, we can see from
their architecture, to be important reception rooms. Even so sumptuous a house as the Casa dei Vettii had not received its final touches,
and the room beside the red triclinium that was clearly going to be a
ladies' dining room is bare of plaster. Throughout the city we are
reminded that reconstruction was still in full swing and that what we
see as the houses of the Fourth Style is a record of some seventeen

years of hectic activity. There is so much domestic architecture of the Fourth Style that it is hard to classify it at all neatly. Much of it is makeshift and can hardly pretend to be called architecture; it was the fixing up of a place to live and work until better times should come. And with the passage of years and the snail's-pace progress of recovery, more and more of the artisans and small shopkeepers, the freedman class, must have decided to settle for less than they had hoped. Carved out of the fine apartments of venerable houses or squeezed into whatever space they could afford, the small industrial establishments of Pompeii present a sorry, if sometimes almost comical, picture.

Many of the fine houses of the last period are simply older houses repaired and redecorated, sometimes combined with one another, sometimes in part rebuilt, but essentially nothing that could be described as new architecture. The Casa dei Dioscuri may be taken as representative of this class. The Corinthian atrium, tablinum, and pseudoperistyle all received splendid new decorations, but the rooms in this part of the house and their relationships remained basically those of an older period, and older construction is found nearly everywhere in the walls here. The peristyle and the oecus dominating it are new construction but in a space of predetermined dimensions. The oecus, once veneered with marble, which the survivors removed, may be taken to show the size and proportions of the great banquet halls of this period, and it is interesting that there is a ladies' dining room attached to this. But we should be wrong to take the peristyle to show a new aesthetic; it is simply worked out in the space available. And the Domus Caetronii Eutychi was simply annexed, its back parts converted to use as stables and offices for the household, the front essentially a separate dwelling. This was one of the greatest houses in Pompeii, belonging to the Nigidii, a distinguished old family, and can be taken as typical of the taste of the more conservative aristocracy of Pompeii. The owners of the Casa del Fauno seem to have had little intention of changing the First Style character of their house more than might be absolutely necessary. The layout of the Casa di Pansa remains essentially what it was when it was first built. The Casa del Citarista, belonging to the Popidii, a vast mansion of superlative decorations and appointments, is simply a conglomeration of atria and peristyles without a governing architectural pattern.

There are, however, two types of houses that appear to be essentially creations of the time of the Fourth Style; these we may call the peristyle town house and the garden house. Each has its roots in early Pompeian building but comes to full blossom only in the last period; but neither looks forward to the multiple-unit blocks of Ostia. There was still abundant space in Pompeii, and privacy and individuality were still prime concerns of the majority of Pompeians.

The most obvious characteristic of the peristyle town house is the suppression of the tablinum and the bank of rooms between atrium and peristyle, so that the peristyle not only is the focus of all the reception rooms of the house but becomes the focus of the atrium as well. Often there are three doors between atrium and peristyle, so that in fine weather one seemed almost to flow into the other. This feature was already employed in the Second Style Villa dei Misteri and was very likely common in villas, but there the peristyle was a working courtyard, while here it was an ornamental garden. It tended now to be decorated with fountains and sculpture, as well as plants and flowers; commonly there is a marble table, and often there is a fish pool that doubles as ornamental water. The peristyle had now become as much a room in its own right as a communication with, and background for, other rooms; the salutatio, which the continuing prevalence of the tablinum, as well as the literary evidence, indicates persisted, here must have taken place against a background of water playing among foliage and sunlight. No privacy would have been possible unless you withdrew to a closed room, but probably business of a private nature had ceased to be presented at the salutatio, and it had become essentially a ritual occasion.

At least eighteen examples of this house type are known in Pompeii, of which the most familiar are probably the Casa della Venere (II iii 3), the Casa dei Vettii (V xv 1/2), the Casa di Gavio Rufo (VII ii 16), and the Casa della Calce (VIII v 28).

In the garden house the atrium complex seems almost superfluous, though it is usually retained. Usually it is an old atrium simply redecorated in the Fourth Style without significant architectural change. All life and interest is centred on a garden that is as large and handsome as possible, not a peristyle garden, but still a garden in which architecture is important, often with change of level, always with a concern for vista. Water and sculpture are also important. Since gardens, being fragile and impermanent, are hard to recover in Pompeii, there may well have been many more such houses than we know. Three examples, however, will serve to show the type and its range: the Casa dell'Ancora Nera (VI x 7), the Casa di Apollo (VI vii 23), and the Casa di Loreio Tiburtino (II ii 2).

Houses of More or Less Traditional Type

The Casa di Vibio

The Casa di Vibio (VII ii 18) is of special interest because it was built almost entirely in the last period, as the brick- and opus mixtum vittatum–faced masonry visible everywhere that still awaited a plaster finish shows, yet in most features and proportions it conforms to the domestic architecture of the Third Style, rather than that of the Fourth, another example of the conservatism of many Pompeians.[1] The house belonged to C. Vibius C . . . and C. Vibius Italus (Della Corte[3] 153–154, nos. 271–73). The name is Campanian, and the cognomen suggests that the family took a proud part in the Social War. The family was numerous in Pompeii, and a number of its members held magistracies, though not those with whom we are concerned here, so far as we know (Castrén 240–41). That they were rich is attested by the quantity and high quality of the furniture found here.

The façade is rather blank and featureless. The fauces are short, between a winter dining room to the east and a cubiculum to the west. Over these was a second storey let out as a separate apartment accessible by a stair from the exterior (VII ii 19) under which is arranged a closet off the cubiculum. The atrium is Tuscanic, canonical, with alae and a tablinum and two cubicula to either side. On the south side of the impluvium are the limestone legs of a cartibulum carved with winged panthers. In the second cubiculum on the east are preserved remains of a fine Third Style decoration with two large landscapes of the quality of those from the Villa di Agrippa Postumo at Boscotrecase.[2] Clearly it was the intention of the builders to salvage these. In the first cubiculum on the west is a stair leading to a second storey that cannot have extended over more than the two cubicula here.

The tablinum is open across both front and back. According to Fiorelli (1873, 32), it had an east wall of wood or thin masonry in a wooden frame that had completely disappeared by his day. This made the tablinum a very long, narrow room but created an andron beside it. The pavement is of black-and-white mosaic with a broad maeander border and a sill panel on the atrium side. Small doors at the southern end of the tablinum and andron lead to the dining rooms to either side, that on the east being smaller. Both open to the garden by very wide doors. That on the west is paved with white mosaic around a panel of squares and triangles of colored marble. Here were found the remains of three dining couches with magnificent mounts of bronze inlaid with silver (Ruesch 382, nos. 1739–41; Spinazzola 1928, 282); these have been reconstructed and are in the Museo Nazionale in Naples.

[1] On the Casa di Vibio see Fiorelli 1873, 32–33; and Fiorelli 1875, 189–90.
[2] See P. H. von Blanckenhagen, and C. Alexander, *The Paintings from Boscotrecase, RömMitt* supp. 6 (1962).

The peristyle is a long rectangle with seven brick columns on the long sides, four on the short. In the middle of each short side, opposite the tablinum and the great oecus, half-columns engaged against square pillars have been substituted for columns, and the intercolumniations have been broadened. At the southern end of the garden is a rectangular pool with an apsidal addition, no doubt intended to be given a fountain to enliven the view from the oecus. There is also a deep well here, almost certainly a survival from a much earlier period. Down the east side of the peristyle, in the triangular space between this house and the Casa di Gavio Rufo, are arranged three closets and a small cubiculum, all provided with shelving. At the south end of the west wall is a large rectangular niche surmounted by a triangular pediment with a painting of a sword in a red sheath on its back wall. Boyce thought this very unlike a lararium (Boyce 62, no. 252). Perhaps it was for the display of mementoes of the Social War. Beside this is a second, larger recess that was almost certainly for a cupboard.

On the south side of the peristyle is a single huge central oecus, the banquet hall of the house, flanked by yet another cupboard on the east and a cubiculum on the west. The oecus had to be somewhat skewed off the axis of the peristyle but was clearly intended to dominate it. Out of the southwest corner of the peristyle a narrow corridor leads south to the kitchen court and the latrine closet. From the kitchen a wooden stair led down to a large shop (VII ii 42) on the busy Via degli Augustali. This, though essentially an independent unit with a second storey for living quarters, will have been occupied by a dependent of the Vibii.

Overall the house is simple and straightforward in its plan, the house for a small family but a rich one, and one that expected to entertain on a lavish scale. The long, narrow tablinum is surprising, but it is dictated by the shape of the plot and the canonical symmetry of the atrium and the rooms flanking it. In many atria of the Third Style one finds distortion of the normal proportions or diminution that may almost amount to miniaturization (for example, in the Casa dei Calavi [I vi 11]; the Casa di Ceio [I vi 15]; and the Casa di Marco Lucrezio Frontone [V iv a (or 11)]). The object seems always to have been to give space and importance to the garden or peristyle and the rooms giving onto it at the expense of the atrium. The one feature here that seems characteristic of the Fourth Style rather than the Third is the great oecus on the axis of the peristyle. While vast rooms for entertaining guests at dinner had been known since the time of the Second Style, such a room on the axis of the peristyle is a late development.

The Casa degli Amorini Dorati

The Casa degli Amorini Dorati (VI xvi 7/38), excavated between 1903 and 1905, lies across the street from the Casa dei Vettii but has its main entrance on the Strada Stabiana and fills most of the broad southern end of block VI xvi.[3] A fullonica (VI xvi 3/4), a shop (VI xvi 5), and three cauponae (VI xvi 1/2, VI xvi 6, and VI xvi 39/40) cluster around it and take most of the frontage on the Strada Stabiana and the Vicolo di Mercurio, the cauponae, at least, attracted principally by the constant flow of traffic along the Strada Stabiana. The smallest of the cauponae, VI xvi 6, is in communication with the house and must have belonged to a dependent of it, but the largest and best-provided, VI xvi 39/40, seems to have been independent. The house belonged to Cn. Poppaeus Habitus, and numerous epigraphic allusions to the princeps here and in the vicinity suggest that he was a fairly close relation of Nero's second wife, the beautiful Poppaea, whose family was originally Campanian. A large lararium in the peristyle shows that he was an enthusiastic devotee of Isis, and a second large lararium shows that he also adhered to the state religion of Rome. The house was thoroughly ransacked in antiquity after the disaster.

The façade of the house is unimpressive, the door flanked by low benches. The short fauces lead to a small, squarish Tuscanic atrium with a small impluvium stripped of its finish in the centre. There are small square cubicula flanking the fauces but none along the sides of the atrium. Opposite the fauces is an irregular and off-axis tablinum with mosaic pavement. Doors at the west end of the south wall and the south end of the west wall lead to a large square oecus and the peristyle. Two doors in the tablinum communicate with the peristyle. The decoration of fauces, atrium, and tablinum is Third Style, with painted pilasters to trim some of the openings and central subject paintings, for the most part illustrative of the story of Troy. This part of the house must be regarded as a survival from a Third Style house but is probably no older than that, despite remains of First Style decoration in the cubicula flanking the fauces.

The house is focused almost entirely on the peristyle, a broad rectangle of five columns in the east portico by six in the north and south porticoes. The porticoes are generously wide, and the garden is spacious. The west portico is raised above the garden some five steps, and to bring it into conjunction with the others, that on the south slopes steadily, while that on the north slopes perceptibly less and has three steps at its juncture with the west portico. The roof of this

---

[3] On the Casa degli Amorini Dorati see *NSc* 1906, 374–83; 1907, 549–93; 1908, 26–43 (A. Sogliano).

FIGURE 47.
The Casa degli
Amorini Dorati,
Peristyle

west portico consequently has to be raised above that of the others, and the corner columns are divided and carry architraves at two levels. In the centre of the west portico a wider than normal intercolumniation in front of the great oecus of the house is framed by a pair of reeded Corinthian pillars that rise above the architrave to either side and must have carried a pediment, but the design of this is not entirely certain, and what has been restored is rather graceless. Against the pillars to either side are engaged half-columns. All the columns and pillars of the west portico are Corinthian and reeded, left white, while those of the other porticoes are fluted and generally Doric with high, unfluted base drums painted sometimes dark red and sometimes yellow, in symmetry. The resulting emphasis on the centre of the west portico has repeatedly led to speculation that it was a stage for private theatrical performances, but this is unlikely. The garden would have been an awkward place in which to try to arrange seating for an audience. It is more likely that this was meant simply as a dramatic entrance to the oecus beyond.

The walls of the peristyle are given a black-ground decoration that serves to set off the series of reliefs, for the most part of theatrical masks, let into it in the south portico, which is interrupted by only a single doorway. In the southeast corner is a shrine to the Egyptian gods with elaborate paintings, which slots in the plaster show was set off from the portico by a wooden screen or similar architectural feature. In the north portico is an aedicular shrine with two columns and a pediment containing statuettes of the Capitoline Triad, enthroned, a seated Mercury, and two dancing Lares.

In the centre of the garden is a fair-sized pool, rectangular with an apsidal west end, framed with a broad margin of white marble. At the centre of the west end a rectangular base for a statue is pierced by a hole for a pipe, while in the middle of the pool rises a cylindrical masonry column probably for another statue. Numerous ornamental marbles were scattered about the garden, some of them small herms, some reliefs carved on both sides of a plate set on carved pillars, some small-scale animals, a sundial, a statuette of Omphale, and two small-scale male portrait heads of mediocre quality. The only principle that one observes in their disposition is that the smallest are placed toward the centre around the pool, the others toward the outer edge at roughly equal intervals. In addition, five marble masks carved in the round and two disc oscilla were discovered at various points; these must once have hung from the architrave of the peristyle and have now been hung around the west end of it.

The rooms around the peristyle were casually disposed, except for the suite at the west end and the service quarters in the northwest corner. Off the east portico is a large square oecus paved with a beautifully patterned mosaic and decorated in the Third Style, clearly a survival from the house of the atrium and tablinum. Next to this on the south is the base of a stair that must have led to a room over the oecus and then a large recess that once held a great wooden cupboard.

Off the north portico, just west of the tablinum, opens a small ladies' dining room, doubtless for use in conjunction with the oecus off the east portico. This has a window to the peristyle beside the door and places for two settees marked out in its mosaic pavement. The walls are painted in "carpet style," with a repeating geometric pattern of red hexagons framing stars on a yellow ground, while over the couches were attached four medallions of glass with putti etched and framed in gold leaf behind them, from which the house takes its name. Next to this is a long, narrow closet provided with shelving, then a latrine, then a second closet. Just before one mounts the steps leading to the west portico there opens a second square oecus, nearly as large as that off the east portico, with a signinum pavement and restrained Fourth Style decoration of black ground. The ceiling was flat with a large recessed panel in the centre that is bowed. The only room off the south portico is a small square one with simple Fourth Style decoration of yellow ground above a red dado. Its use is indeterminate.

The rooms off the west portico are a suite. That in the centre was to be the banquet hall of the house and has the places for three couches laid out and paved with signinum around the back half of the room. The rest was paved with stone in small square plates that was salvaged in antiquity. The walls had not yet received their plaster finish. A large windowlike opening toward the west end of the south wall that could be closed with a door gave onto a small square garden at the southwest corner of the house raised to room level. A second large window to this garden opened to the room south of the great banquet hall, a rather small, square room given a Fourth Style decoration with figures of the seasons on a white ground above a red dado. This room was covered with a barrel vault decorated with molded and painted stuccowork. The room balancing this on the north side of the banquet hall was of the same size and had a very similar ceiling but had a Fourth Style decoration with a yellow ground and a white upper zone above a red dado. These two rooms we may see as ladies' summer and winter dining rooms in conjunction with the banquet hall.

The service quarters in the northwest corner of the house need not detain us long. The whole area had beaten earth floors and consisted of a central courtyard, from which a short passage runs to the posticum on the Vicolo dei Vettii (VI xvi 38); the kitchen proper, northeast of this, with hearth platform and latrine to either side of a light well; a large workroom southwest of the central court; and a storage room north of the passage to the posticum. A second storey covered the rooms along the west and another part of the kitchen. These were accessible by stairs in the central court, and the latter, at least, was probably only a loft.

The house as a whole is the result of attaching a large colonnaded garden dominated by a suite of large dining rooms to the atrium complex of a Third Style house of modest elegance, a sort of remodeling that one also finds elsewhere in Pompeii. Probably originally the peristyle or garden of the house was proportionate to the atrium, no larger perhaps than that of the Casa del Sacerdote Amando (I vii 7) or the Casa del Frutteto (I ix 5/6). How many houses may have been destroyed to create the Casa degli Amorini Dorati there is no way of telling, but it was probably at least three or four.

The Casa di Meleagro

The Casa di Meleagro (VI ix 2), close to the northern end of the Via di Mercurio,[4] was proably the house of L. Cornelius Primogenes (Della Corte[3] 47–48, nos. 38–39). The Cornelii, who were numerous in Pompeii, probably arrived with the Roman colony and were represented in almost every social class. The house is clearly that of a rich man. Parts of the structure are very old, but the whole has been rebuilt and redecorated so thoroughly that it can be regarded as a house of the Fourth Style.

The façade is stuccoed, and the high dado is painted with panels of zebra striping, a common utilitarian finish, the wall being left white above. The doorway is without special emphasis; apparently a small shed roof over it protected visitors from the weather while they waited. The fauces were decorated with a painting of Meleager and Atalanta, which is responsible for the name the house has been given, and with another of Mercury and Ceres, which Della Corte concluded must indicate the source of the owner's wealth. The Tuscanic atrium is small for the size of the house, with an impluvium veneered with plates of marble and given a raised rim. On the east margin stands a square statue base revetted with fragments of colored marble plates behind which is a splendid marble cartibulum with legs featuring winged gryphons. Beneath the cartibulum, between its legs, is sunk a marble box divided into two equal compartments, the purpose of which is mysterious. The walls were richly painted in the Fourth Style with numerous subject paintings.

The tablinum is in its canonical position, small, being in scale with the atrium, but given a very rich decoration in a combination of stucco relief and painting with extraordinary play on scale and optical effect. The opening is trimmed with pilasters with red, reeded lower shafts and white, fluted upper ones. A small shallow bay in the east end of the north wall probably held a cupboard for business documents, since there is no ala. There are cubicula only on the south side of the atrium, the north wall being breached by a very wide door that gives immediately to the peristyle. The footings sunk in the floor for this show that it had a wooden frame and consisted of four leaves hinged together in pairs so that they could be folded back on one another, each leaf being secured in place when closed by a bolt that dropped into a stone socket.

The room south of the fauces was a storeroom finished with plain plaster and provided with shelving. A flight of steps led up from the

---

[4]See *PAH* 2.224–40 (14 June 1829–30 September 1830); *Museo Borbonico* 7, "Relazione degli scavi" (G. Bechi); and Overbeck and Mau 307–14.

atrium along its north wall to rooms in a second storey that probably covered only the rooms west of the atrium and was chiefly storage space. The three rooms opening off the south side of the atrium all seem to have been cubicula but were all nicely decorated. The middle one, with a green-ground decoration, was especially handsome. Off the southeast corner of the atrium opens a winter triclinium that communicates with the cubiculum west of it by a square window of doubtful purpose.

North of the tablinum a long, straight corridor led through to the back of the house and a door to the alley behind the house (now walled up). Off this corridor opens a large door to the peristyle on the north, opposite which is a ladies' dining room with places for two settees marked in the mosaic pavement, which Pernice (1938, 80) dates to the time of the early Second Style. In the last period it was given a very simple decoration and may have been used as a bedroom. At the eastern end of this corridor is a block of rooms on the south that must have been service quarters. Since some of these are accessible only through others, and since only that at the eastern end was provided with windows to the exterior, they cannot have been very useful. One feels a complete lack of architectural design here. And over all of these extended a second storey reached by a ramp supported on vaults, where a small army of slaves might have found sleeping accommodation.

At the east wall of the house the service corridor seems to have emerged in an open court that ran north and south along the back of the house. Here the hearth platform was built against the east wall of the colonnaded oecus, where a buttress wall for the roof of the oecus supported on arches gave a little shelter. Beside the hearth is a cistern head made from a storage jar (seria). South of the hearth, opening east into the corridorlike extension of the kitchen court is a room with a mosaic floor and walls finished with polished white plaster on which a spirited painting of a prancing horse survives. This is too elegant to have been a service room and may have been a morning room. North of the hearth the corridor continues but was closed by a door and roofed, for five small windows in the east wall have been walled up in modern times. Along this corridor we encounter first a masonry stair leading north, then west, as if to reach a gallery around the oecus or the roof of the oecus; then a latrine closet; then a generous lobby behind the great banquet hall and opening into it, where one must presume food was dressed for serving in the reception rooms. Beyond this, probably closed off by a door, is a series of three small square rooms, each lit by a window opposite its door in the east wall of the house, probably stables for animals that would have been closed by wickets. At its north end the corridor debouched into a large stable yard with a broad door (VI ix 13) to the Vicolo del Fauno on the east. This has buttress spurs along its south and west walls, but not along the others, so these must be to support the walls and roofs adjacent, not a roof or roofs here. There is a cistern head in the northwest corner of this yard.

The glory of the house is the peristyle and the series of reception rooms opening on it. The peristyle is a broad rectangle of eight columns by six with deep porticoes. The order is Fourth Style Doric, with a deep cavetto necking ornamented with acanthus scrolls and narrow egg molding under a circular abacus. The fluting is filleted, and the lower shaft is reeded and painted red above a rather tight Attic base. Small sockets in the bases and rings in the pavement indicate that the intercolumniations could be closed with curtains. The centre of the open area is taken up by a large rectangular tank, its perimeter broken into bays alternately bowed and rectangular, its interior painted blue, its margin revetted with fragments of marble plates. At the middle of the west side is a water stair of six steps, and in the middle of the tank rises a masonry cylinder crowned by a marble fountain that resembles a column base. South of the water stair is a small square tank much shallower than the big one but in communication with it by a pipe, also with a margin revetted with marble, probably, as G. Bechi surmised (*Museo Borbonico* 7, "Relazione degli scavi" 9–10), for obtaining water for the garden without disturbing the water in the large tank excessively; the depth of the large tank suggests that it was used for breeding fish. A similar small tank with marble frame at the east end of the garden is a cistern head that was covered with a trapdoor of wood, of which the excavators found remains; a puteal in the south portico of the peristyle also gave onto this cistern. Another cistern head appears in the first intercolumniation of the west portico from the south. A broad gutter runs along the stylobate on all four sides, with quarter-circle enlargements in the corners. These may have been intended to hold potted trees or shrubs. The area for planting is thus somewhat restricted, a band around the tank. We have no information about how the beds may have been designed, but the gutter is bridged by a travertine block at the middle of the south side, which suggests that this was the beginning of a path across to the tank. The walls of the peristyle porticoes were richly painted with many small subject pictures, for the most part in two- and three-figure groups.

Six rooms give onto the peristyle—four large reception rooms off the east portico, a trapezoidal room off the northeast corner, and a small room off the southwest corner. The last properly belongs to the atrium complex and has a door to the atrium, as well as a door and window to the peristyle. But in the last period it was clearly meant to be a place of privacy, off in a corner away from the bustle and traffic of the household, where one could sit and contemplate the garden porticoes. And it was given a charming decoration with a blue ground. It may have been a study or a small sitting room for only a few people.

The central oecus on the east portico is Corinthian, open across its whole west side but surrounded on the other three by colonnades. The columns are raised on cubical plinths and are fluted full-height with Attic bases and low Fourth Style Corinthian capitals with a single zone of acanthus and reversed volutes that carried an architrave in low segmental arches. Across the front of the room are remains of an engaged order, two half-columns against the end columns of the oecus and two finishing the walls to either side. These have no plinths, reeded lower shafts, and Attic bases. The pavement is of white mosaic with black framing lines and broad panels of geometric ornament as sill and between each pair of columns. The decoration is in yellow monochrome with numerous figures in the style the French call *camaïeu*. Vitruvius (6.3.9) said that Corinthian oeci should have arched ceilings, and there is no reason to doubt that the central area was so roofed here, while the passage around the room will have had a flat ceiling. In that case, the stair leading up behind the east wall of the room, which seems to have no reason for existing, may have led to a door or aperture in the lunette that would have to have existed on the east side, from which flowers and dinner favors could have been made to descend or showered down on the diners after the fashion described in Trimalchio's dinner party (Petronius *Sat.* 60) and in accounts of Nero's Domus Aurea (Suetonius *Nero* 31). An arched ceiling would also help to explain the use of a larger-scale engaged order across the opening. Except for that in the Casa del Labirinto (VI xi 9/10), this is the only Corinthian oecus that has come to light in Pompeii and the only one that can be regarded as an example of the Fourth Style.

The oecus is flanked by other exedras, a smaller one to the south, which had still to be painted at the time of the eruption, although a mosaic pavement had been laid and its walls had been plastered and trimmed with a stucco cornice, and a larger one to the north, of the oblong shape associated with triclinia. The last is richly painted with decoration that includes many large figures against a predominantly black ground. The floor is paved with hexagons of white mosaic framed in black, with a sill panel of peltae. North of this the largest room of all, a true banquet hall, opens to the peristyle only by a generous door and has a north/south axis. It is a magnificent room with a rich black-ground decoration with many figures, an elaborate architectural frame, and large subject pictures. The pavement is of white mosaic with black stripes and sill panel. The fenestration of this room is puzzling, for while it probably rose well above the roofs around it and so could have had windows high up in its walls, no trace of these can be discovered in what survives. The last room, that off the east end of the north portico, is of minor interest. Its long narrow trapezoidal shape suggests that it is a biclinium, a notion that is reinforced by the addition of a vestibule, or procoeton, decorated *en suite* with it. The walls are decorated in a late Fourth Style, while the pavement is older, signinum decorated with lines of little crosses in mosaic. We may think of it as a place for simple dinners with a few guests.

When one considers the house as an architectural whole, one is struck by how much the traditional focus has been changed, while so many traditional features of the atrium house have been retained. The atrium with its axis and tablinum is there, but these have been eclipsed by the cross axis and the almost magnetic attraction of the visitor to the peristyle. The atrium seems a mere appendage to this, the elaborate tablinum a distraction. Quite as much as in the Casa dei Vettii, the peristyle is the heart of the house and draws everything around it, including the atrium. Everything else is service quarters. And the focus of the peristyle is the pool in its centre with its fountains. Views of this from the reception rooms are regularly considered and paramount. It is also remarkable that although this is a house designed especially for summer dinner parties, little special attention is given to ladies. There is only one ladies' dining room, and that seems to be a survival from an earlier period and probably not so used in the last period, while the small exedra at the southeast corner of the peristyle was probably intended to serve as a ladies' dining room. We must conclude that here ladies sometimes reclined in company with the men, as Valerius Maximus (2.1.2) said was becoming customary in Rome in his day, toward the end of the reign of Tiberius. The house is the best example of a type that is fairly common in Pompeii. A close parallel is the Casa dei Dioscuri (VI ix 6/7).

The Casa del Poeta Tragico

The Casa del Poeta Tragico (VI viii 3/5), which derived its name from a mosaic emblema of actors in the tablinum and certain of its subject pictures, captured the imagination of many who saw it in the days soon after it was excavated in 1824–25.[5] It was a small jewel of a house, well proportioned, with uncommonly rich walls and pavements, one of a very small group of houses of more or less canonical plan in which, despite diminutive size, there is a lavish display of

[5] See *PAH* 2.121–35 (4 December 1824–27 June 1825); and Overbeck and Mau 285–89.

wealth. Its nearest parallel in plan and quality may be the Casa dell'Orso (VII ii 45). Today, even though it has been extensively reconstructed and roofed, it is unimpressive and dingy, a faded ghost.

There is no continuous axis. The fauces are very long and oblique in relation to the Tuscanic atrium. The tablinum lies off to the west of the axis of the atrium, while the peristyle is moved back toward the east. Two very large shops flank the fauces and connect with them by small doors just inside the street door. The fauces are paved with mosaic and boasted the famous CAVE CANEM mosaic. The small Tuscanic atrium is also paved with mosaic of black and white around an impluvium revetted with marble. The painted decoration of the atrium was rich, embellished with large subject paintings, an unusual addition. That these were of exceptionally high quality increases their interest. They were long thought to be a set of illustrations of the *Iliad*, but that is now known not to have been the case. There is a single ala in the canonical location on the east paved with a figured black-and white mosaic, but with only architectural motifs in its painting. There is a single good-sized cubiculum on each side of the atrium, and on the west is a room for the atriensis and a storeroom. At the south end of the atrium on either side a wooden stair led to space in a second storey, probably only over the rooms immediately adjacent, but the mosaic pavements of these, which were found by the excavators, show that they were more than lofts.

The tablinum is unusual, raised a low step above the atrium, a rectangular room more closed than most tablina and broader than deep, a fact that is emphasized by the square of patterned mosaic around the emblema at the centre of its floor. Off this to the west opens a small room with simple decoration and a window to the street, presumably a cubiculum. Although the effect of the tablinum is rich, it seems somewhat cluttered and untidy.

The diminutive peristyle has Doric porticoes on three sides, three columns to a portico. At the north end of the east portico was the famous painting of the sacrifice of Iphigeneia. In the garden, tight against the north end of the west portico, is a large aedicular lararium embellished with stuccoes. The wall between was painted with a vast vista of azure sky with a fringe of greenery along its lower edge, a very unusual sort of garden painting, to serve as background for the planting of the open area. Off the west portico open two cubicula and a corridor leading to the posticum. Off the southeast corner opens a tiny courtyard with kitchen and latrine. And off the east, commanding a view of the garden through a broad door, is the one room in the house for entertainments, a large square oecus with rich painting and a black-and-white mosaic pavement.

What one sees here is conservative adherence to the general architectural lines of the past, the normal sequence and complement of rooms, combined with an expanded use of most of these and a tendency to play with architectural and visual effects. The broken axes with a succession of contrasting richnesses at small scale, the disproportionate length of the fauces and surprising garden painting at the two extremities, and the conversion of atrium and tablinum into living rooms are all innovative within the general framework of traditional atrium architecture. Not only has its stateliness been sacrificed but space has been made to crowd upon space in a deliberate confusion.

The Casa dei Vettii

The Casa dei Vettii (VI xv 1/2) is the best-preserved and most interestingly decorated of the houses without tablinum and may serve as the model for these.[6] It also shows evidence of being constructed almost entirely in the last period of Pompeii, though over remains of an older house of which the alae and doorway are a survival in substantially original form (Maiuri 1942, 105–12). But it occupies the whole of the southern end of block VI xv, so the architect enjoyed maximum freedom from limitation of space.

It stands in a good position in the midst of fine houses, a little withdrawn from heavily traveled thoroughfares but readily accessible to these and to the forum. It belonged to A. Vettius Restitutus and A. Vettius Conviva, probably freedmen, since the latter was an Augustalis and they carry the same praenomen. The gens was numerous in Pompeii, and a number of its members attained high position. Della Corte has argued on the basis of representations of Mercury and his attributes in the house that these two men were merchants and probably especially engaged in the trade in wine (Della Corte[3] 67–71, nos. 89–93), but the evidence is not conclusive. They were certainly rich and seem to have been pretentious.

The house is entered from the east through a vestibule and fauces stepped sharply up from the street and from one another. The street door is framed with plain jambs capped with block capitals of tufa. The door arrangement is the traditional one of a great double door facing the street and a small private entrance at right angles to this. The fauces are presided over by a grimly humorous painting of Priapus. The atrium is Tuscanic, very large, nearly thirty-five feet in depth, with a commensurately large, deep impluvium veneered with marble, most of which was removed by survivors (*MonAnt* 8 [1898] col. 238). It had been converted to use as a fountain with a jet in the centre. The rain water was not impounded, but drained off to the

---

[6]See *MonAnt* 8 (1898) cols. 233–388 (A. Sogliano).

street. There are alae in the canonical position, but in the place of the tablinum a set of three doors, a very broad double one at the centre flanked by two smaller ones, opens directly to the peristyle. The atrium gives a general feeling of strong symmetry, though there are several small deviations from absolute symmetry. It is very richly decorated with architectural fantasies of great elaborateness peopled with little figures of children and erotes engaged in various games and occupations painted in a subdued palette against a black ground. All the doors seem to have had wooden frames. The entrance is flanked by a pair of small bedrooms. Another on the north side is balanced by a storeroom on the south. There are remains of two large strongboxes, once sheathed in iron with mounts and studs of bronze, facing one another across the atrium. The alae are given harmonious, rather simple decorations in dull reds and yellows. The southern one is provided with a masonry counter across its opening, once sheathed in wood, and must have served as the archives and office of the owners' clerks; the northern one has a large window to the peristyle and connects by a small door to the exedra at the northeast corner of the peristyle. It might have served as a sitting room. Out of the southeast corner of the atrium opens a winter triclinium, a square room with low ceiling and white-ground decoration lit by a single high window to the street.

Out of the northeast corner opens the service quarter, arranged around a little atrium with an old tufa impluvium, evidently bought secondhand, that served as the basin for a pipe brought in from the aqueduct. This must have been the supply for the washing up, possibly for the laundry. A large but very shallow lararium with a triangular pediment fills the centre of the west wall. Off this atrium on the north and east sides open storage rooms, and a stair in the southeast corner led up to a gallery along the north side giving onto a decorated room that must have been for the women of the house, a sitting room or morning room from which they could supervise the work of the household. From the northwest corner of the service atrium one passed into the little kitchen courtyard, where the high hearth fills most of the south wall. A masonry bin for fuel is arranged under it, and another, probably also for fuel, is to its left. Out of the northwest corner of this courtyard opens a little low *camera d'amore* simply decorated with crudely painted symplegmata.[7] This is an uncommon feature for a private house but is not unknown elsewhere.[8] One might gather from the location of the room and the clumsiness of the paintings that the owners were a bit ashamed of it, though the Pria-

[7] See M. Grant, *Eros in Pompeii* (New York 1975) 52.
[8] Cf., e.g., the Casa del Centenario (IX viii 3/6); Schefold 280 (room 43); and J. Mercadé, *Roma Amor* (Geneva 1965) 7, 79, 126.

pus at the entrance, the priapic fountain figure of the garden, and the hermaphrodite of the red triclinium show that they had no aversion to pornography. Possibly the room was for the entertainment of guests.

From the south side of the atrium a corridor led south to the stables; half of this corridor was occupied by a stair leading up to a large room of uncertain purpose over the winter triclinium. The upper storey might have been no more extensive than this, or there might have been a second room to the west over the yellow exedra of the peristyle. Under the stair were found remains of horse harness with ornaments of bronze (*MonAnt* 8 [1898] cols. 264–65). The main room of the stables was a lobby, roofed today but probably in large part an open court in antiquity, since it has no window, with a street door large enough to admit a cart.[9] Off this is the stall for the animals and a latrine closet, its location explained by the fact that it is here adjacent to the sewer under the Vicolo di Mercurio. A well off the northwest corner was walled off and inaccessible in the last period. It was found full of building debris, presumably dumped there after the earthquake.

The peristyle is a narrow rectangle, seven columns by four, at right angles to the axis of the atrium, the area of the portico proportionately large compared with that of the garden, and since there are rooms on only two sides, it must have been intended as much for strolling and sitting as for communication. The excavators were able to recover the outlines of beds, which have been preserved in the replanting and show a broad walk down the long axis with swelling bays around ornamental features and a narrow crosswalk off-axis between the third and fourth columns from the south. There seem to have been no large shrubs or trees here. There is a collection of numerous small sculptures, especially herms and small-scale fountain figures (one-half to one-third life size), two in bronze, the rest in marble. These threw small jets into marble basins set around the edge of the colonnade, round ones in the corners, rectangular ones on the long axis and opposite the atrium. They were fed by pipes laid in the broad signinum gutter of the peristyle in a convenient, if unsightly, way. Ancient plumbing evidently left much to be desired in both efficiency and aesthetics, but here one might imagine that ivy or other trailing plants could have disguised it. There are more fountains in the open area, as well as puteals and round marble tables. This is one

---

[9]Sogliano (*MonAnt* 8 [1898] col. 385) is of the opinion that there was a second storey over this part of the house. He cites as evidence for this beam holes, all at the same level. But it was not accessible by the known stair off the atrium, nor is there evidence of other access. Lofts for storage might have been accessible only by ladders, but it is hard to imagine that the central lobby was not largely an open court.

of the largest collections of marbles in Pompeii, but a similar taste is shown in the marbles of the gardens of the Casa degli Amorini Dorati, the Casa di Marco Lucrezio, and the Casa di Loreio Tiburtino. While each house shows a particular facet of the taste, only here is the use of jets of water so extensive. Clearly it was fashionable to have small sculptures of indifferent quality as garden ornaments. The peristyle order is hybrid, a sort of simplified Corinthian with Attic bases, rendered in stucco, with an architrave embellished with acanthus scrolls. After the great height of the atrium, as it has been reconstructed, for which there seems to be no real justification, the peristyle seems intimate. Probably there should be a greater harmony here. The painted decoration of the peristyle is rich but restrained, the main panels being black to enhance the brilliance of the garden.

Directly off the peristyle open three brilliantly decorated rooms and two others bare of plaster that were probably intended to receive equally rich decorations sometime in the future. They vary in size; the smallest is the yellow exedra south of the south ala, a low room with a decoration that includes large subject pictures of high quality and extraordinary vistas of architecture but has almost no upper zone, probably a room for intimate parties. North of the north ala is a larger exedra with a richly polychrome decoration against a white ground with panels of red and blue. It is a lofty room with a shallow, vaulted ceiling and contrasts sharply with its yellow neighbor. Its proportions suggest a triclinium. The third and most splendid room is a large banquet hall with a mosaic pavement and a decoration in which panels of red and black predominate. The painting is exceptionally fine and well-peopled with figures in every zone, including the famous predelle of erotes engaged at various trades and occupations. But the large centre pictures, probably on wooden panels let into the walls, have not survived; they must have been the crowning glory of one of the finest decorations in Pompeii.[10] This was a great banquet hall, and adjacent to it and connecting with it was a much narrower room, also open nearly its whole width to the peristyle, that must have been designed as a ladies' dining room and never finished. One regrets not knowing what decoration it might have received to accord with that of the red triclinium.

Just east of the red triclinium on the peristyle opens a door to a tiny garden with a portico on three sides on which faces a suite of triclinium and ladies' dining room. It is the classic arrangement in architecture, although the garden is too small for the development of much in the way of planting. The triclinium has a black-ground dec-

[10] It seems likely that they were retrieved by the survivors. Cf. *MonAnt* 8 (1898) col. 339, where the evidence of nails around the border suggests that they were on wooden panels.

oration, the ladies' dining room a white-ground decoration, and the garden portico a red-ground decoration, but the same painters were responsible for the figure paintings in both dining rooms, and the decorations are harmonious with one another. The whole seems clearly designed so that a fair-sized dinner party could be given without disturbing the rest of the house. Once the food had been prepared and the company had assembled, the door to the peristyle could be shut, and one need hardly have known that anyone was there. This feeling of seclusion is strongly borne in on the visitor today, hence the explanation popular with guides that this was the women's quarter. But it is not clear what would have prompted such an arrangement. We know that the house was inhabited by two businessmen; might it conceivably have been so that they could entertain quite different companies of guests simultaneously?

One's ultimate impression of the architecture of the house is of great economy, convenience, and balance. Light is abundant, and the division of space for business, pleasure, and household necessity is kept architecturally clear in the six courts around which the house is built. Though the parts of the house flow easily into one another, and the atrium is the hub of the plan, one had only to close doors to separate the service quarters from the public rooms, or the atrium from the peristyle. The stateliness and ritual of First Style houses has completely disappeared, and in its place we find a clever tightness, almost intricacy, of plan, engagement and diversity for the eye, and comfortable proportions. No room here overwhelms the visitor; no axis insists on preeminent importance. This is a house designed for life's pleasant interludes rather than its ceremonies.

While the Casa dei Vettii offers the best example of town house architecture of the last period built in large part ex novo, many of its innovations are to be found repeated elsewhere in houses that are hybrid creations of rooms and suites that survived the earthquake unscathed combined with new construction and houses that are largely new but fitted onto highly irregular plots of ground that forced the builders to curious, often awkward, expedients. The suppression of the tablinum with retention of one ala or two, usually with dramatic enlargement of the opening between atrium and peristyle, can be found in the north atrium of the Casa del Citarista (I iv 25), the Casa di Trittolemo (VII vii 5), the Casa di Ganimede (VII xiii 4), the Casa del Banchiere (VII xiv 5), and the Casa della Creta (VIII v 28). Peristyles of similarly elongated proportions and similar importance appear in the Casa del Citarista (I iv 5), the Casa di Meleagro (VI ix 2), the Casa dei Dioscuri (VI ix 6), the Casa del Cinghiale (VIII iii 8), and the Casa di Cornelio Rufo (VIII iv 15). Well organized, self-contained service quarters carefully separated from the rest of the house are numerous; one might cite especially those of the Casa dell'Efebo (I vii 10–12), the Casa di Apollo (VI vii 23), the Casa di Meleagro (VI ix 2), and the Casa dei Dioscuri (VI ix 6). And a selection of handsomely painted dining rooms of various sizes and color schemes seems to have been the rule. But the private suite consisting of small garden, triclinium, and ladies' dining room connecting with this seems to be unique.

Garden Houses

The Casa dell'Ancora Nera

The Casa dell'Ancora Nera (VI x 7) on the elegant Via di Mercurio, [11] belonged, according to Della Corte (Della Corte[3] 56–58, nos. 55, 57), to members of the Melissaei, an old Campanian family whose money derived from the sea traffic, in token whereof the short fauces display a large anchor in the mosaic pavement and pictures allusive to the gods of the sea adorned the walls. Although the atrium complex was repaired and refurbished in the last period, it kept the lines of a small Tuscanic atrium of the First Style, with a shallow, tufa impluvium and fluted pilasters with molded bases framing the opening to the tablinum, which is raised a low step above the atrium. There seem to have been wooden jambs for a door to either side of the inner end of the fauces. To either side of the fauces is a small cubiculum, but there are rooms opening only along the north side of the atrium: a single small ala on the cross axis of the atrium, an oblong triclinium lit by two high windows in the west wall off the northwest corner of the atrium, and a room that was probably a bedroom off the northeast corner. Between the door to this and the ala are remains of a masonry arca base. The door of the ala could be closed in some way, perhaps by a folding lattice like that discovered in Herculaneum in a similar context.[12] The tablinum is relatively small, but it was handsomely finished and opened across its back, except for short jambs, onto a broad gallery above the north side of a large sunken garden. North of the tablinum is a square room with minimal decoration imitating drafted masonry too mean to have been a reception room, possibly a storeroom. And to the south of the tablinum a door opened to a small lobby from which a narrow stair of nine steps led down to the level of the sunken garden. Against the wall to the north of the house door, on the sidewalk of the Via di Mercurio, are two blocks of a tufa cornice and two lower shafts of engaged columns of an upper-storey

---

[11] On the Casa dell'Ancora Nera, which is very poorly published, see *PAH* 2.183–85 (30 January–26 February 1827), 236–39 (April–July 1830); and Fiorelli 1875, 142–43.

[12] Cf. A. Maiuri, *Ercolano: I nuovi scavi (1927–1958)*, 2 vols. (Rome 1958), 1.229–30 (Casa del Bicentenario).

FIGURE 48.
The Casa dell'Ancora
Nera, Sunken Garden

order. The cornice may have been the lintel of the house door, but it is hard to find a place for the columns. They are fluted, without bases, engaged against plain rectangular piers, and stand on plain plinths, typical elements of a loggia or colonnaded cenaculum. It seems likely that they belong properly to VI x 6, the Casa di Pomponio, where we know there was a second storey over the west part of the house with an unusually well-constructed stair of access off the southwest corner of the atrium.

The garden is a long rectangle, more than twice as long as it is wide, surrounded by a cryptoporticus, narrow and vaulted on three sides but flat-roofed and broad on the north. Along it on the west are four rooms and a slotlike closet, as well as a stair leading up to the gallery above at the southwest end. These rooms seem to have had flat ceilings with beams running north and south and to have been bedrooms with simple decorations, while the rooms above them in the second storey were probably reception rooms, but of these practically nothing survives. Originally the garden seems to have been surrounded on three sides—east, west, and north—by arcades, the arches on the east and west framed within rather deep, flat-headed rectangular niches, while that on the north was given a broad, plain pilaster between each pair of arches. Later most of the arches were walled up and provided with high masonry bases, as high as would be suitable for the display of statuary at half or one-third life size, while a window was left under the crown of the arch to light the cryptoporticus. The windows vary in size, being sometimes square, sometimes little more than a horizontal slot or bull's-eye, while sometimes the archway was walled up only partway. Three arches were left open in the west wing, in the second, sixth, and twelfth bays from the north; three in the east wing, in the fourth, ninth, and twelfth bays from the north; and one in the north wing, the westernmost of the five. One feels that the effect would be much improved with the arches open and with a play of depth and shadow in the corridor behind. But wherever the masonry has been exposed, true opus mixtum vittatum occurs only sporadically, and the rest is an older sort of masonry in Sarno limestone in roughly squared blocks and broken chunks, chunks of lava and the irregular addition of pieces of tile. It seems obvious that this garden had existed earlier in a somewhat different form but including the cryptoporticus.

The assertion frequently made that the new niches were for fountains is not borne out by evidence of pipes; indeed, on the contrary, the lack of pipes, holes through which these might have passed, and basins shows that water was not used at all here. The complete lack of statuary is also puzzling, for the collections of garden sculpture found elsewhere in Pompeii indicate that these would not have been of high quality and would not have warranted recovering. One concludes that the bases were not intended for statuary.

The south end of the garden is filled with a nymphaeum of three large niches,[13] symmetrical apsidal niches roofed with half-domes flanking a rectangular niche with a flat roof containing a large aedicular shrine with two columns and a triangular pediment. The apsidal niches are each divided into three bays by stucco pilasters of a generally Doric order decorated with mosaic and with garlands in relief swung between them. The pilasters support a plain, heavy architrave and a simple, strongly projecting cornice around the base of the dome, above which small hemicyclical domed niches open to either side of a central rectangular window through to the cryptoporticus behind. The dome and the niches were covered with rustication in bits of coarse limestone laid down around vegetation framed with lines of shells. It has generally been thought that the central window was for a water source, and the side niches for statuary, but the former, at least, seems dubious. There is no sign of pipes, and such a fountain would be entirely without parallel in Pompeii, where water stairs are regularly provided for water introduced at any considerable height above a basin. A low pedestal in each niche that must have

[13] See Neuerburg 125–26, no. 27 (with bibliography).

carried a small-scale fountain figure seems to have been the only source of water here. The aedicula in the central niche was painted in lively colors, the columns being in imitation of giallo antico, the base black, the architrave dark green, the tympanum pink. The interior contains a curved niche painted blue with a red border. Here two busts are reported to have been found, one a portrait of a man, the other a portrait of a young girl (*PAH* 2.238 [9 July 1830]). A slender palm trunk worked in stucco relief flanks the aedicula on either side.

Behind the opposite end of the garden were the stables. Here the cryptoporticus was enlarged to become a lobby as wide as the tablinum and roofed with a flat roof carried on a series of stout beams. The door from this lobby to the Vicolo del Fauno on the east is wide, but the high sidewalk along the street would have prevented the entrance of carts. Behind this are three large stalls for the animals, while a room carved out of it at the southeast corner may have served as a tack room; this has a window to the Vicolo del Fauno.

In the upper storey around the garden variations in a similar pattern to those in the ground storey appear. In the galleries on the east and west sides rectangular pillars of opus mixtum vittatum alternate with small-scale unfluted Doric columns in tufa. At the south end there is nothing but columns, but these are like those on the sides. At the north end two stout piers projecting in at the ends are finished with fluted tufa columns addorsed against them, not actually engaged. These are on a much larger scale than the rest and must have carried a Rhodian portico, but there is no sign of support except at the ends. The span is wide but by no means impossible, not so great as those in the atria of the Casa delle Nozze d'Argento and the Casa di Obellio Firmo and only a little greater than that at the ends of the peristyle in the Casa dei Dioscuri. This arrangement ensured an uninterrupted view of the garden from the reception rooms behind this gallery. One must presume that some sort of light fence guarded the drop to the garden level, a drop of about 2.80 m, but if it were of open design, it might not have interfered much.

There are three rooms behind this gallery, all apparently dining rooms and all open across their whole south side to the view of the garden. The painted decorations are very poorly preserved, but it is clear that they were fine rooms. The first on the west is a dining room for small parties, the second and third a suite with a connecting door for larger parties. The mosaic pavements in these are dated by Pernice (1938, 78) in the period of the Second Style, but it is abundantly clear that the rooms, like the garden, were rebuilt after the earthquake.

In trying to assess the aesthetic of this garden we are hampered by knowing nothing of the scheme of planting and very little about the scheme of other decoration. A walk around the edge set off from the garden area by a low pluteus is too narrow to permit more than individual strolling. A square base that interrupts the pluteus in front of the aedicular shrine on the south has been interpreted as an altar, but because of its low height it might at least as well be a statue base. Water was used only sparingly in two small jets, decorative sculpture perhaps not at all. Yet it is hard to imagine a more elaborate garden architecture, with its rich play of forms in both the niches of the lower storey and the galleries above, the use of light and rhythmic repetition, and the imposing focus of the southern end. Whatever sort of architectural frame may have preceded this, what we see is very much of the taste and architectural idiom of the last period. It finds its closest relations in the sunken garden of the Villa di Diomede and the south portico of the peristyle of the Casa del Menandro. The fact that it seems to have been conceived simply as a prospect from the reception rooms at the north end and to a lesser degree for those strolling in the galleries in the upper storey must strike us as the more surprising.

The Casa di Apollo

The Casa di Apollo (VI vii 23), near the northern edge of the city on the Via di Mercurio,[14] belonged to A. Herennuleius Communis, whose bronze bread stamp was found in the room south of the fauces (*PAH* 2.235 [March 1830]; Della Corte[3] 45, no. 30). He may have been the only representative of this gens—an offshoot of the Herennii—in Pompeii, but others are known from Salernum and Reate as well as from Rome. Our man served as witness three times in the records of Caecilius Iucundus, so he was probably a prosperous businessman. His house is elegant without being ostentatious, expressive of an individual taste, with interesting secrets and surprises. In general character it resembles the Casa di Loreio Tiburtino, but individual features are very different.

The atrium complex goes back to the early Tufa Period, with a façade in large blocks of Sarno limestone and a number of stands of limestone blocks in "carpentry style" in the interior walls, visible where wall coats have fallen. The fauces are short and relatively broad, giving onto a small Tuscanic atrium with an impluvium revetted with fragments of broken plates of marble. There is no puteal or cistern. Two cubicula flank the fauces, and over these were rooms in a second storey approached by a stair along the south wall of the atrium. There are no rooms off the atrium to the south, and the two

[14]See *PAH* 2.235–36 (February–March 1830), 310–11 (8–30 June 1835), 354 (30 April–1 May 1838), 362–69 (13 November 1838–10 July 1839); and *Museo Borbonico* 13, "Relazione degli scavi" (G. Bechi) and pl. A.B.

to the north are each preceded by two steps, evidence that they were a later addition. The first is essentially exedral in character, and according to Bechi, its opening was closed by curtains; the other is a large cubiculum with simple decoration. The decoration throughout the house is Fourth Style.

Opposite the entrance is a small tablinum open across its whole width, except for jambs, to the atrium and across its whole back wall to a garden beyond. To either side of the opening to the atrium is a high base revetted with marble that must once have held a portrait bust. The tablinum is very richly painted in a fussy miniaturistic style but in conformance with the canonical wall divisions of the Fourth Style; the individual pictures are not of special interest. North of the tablinum is a square room of indeterminate purpose, south of it a narrow andron leading back to the garden.

The little garden was framed on three sides—east, north, and west—by a walk that must have been covered by an overhanging roof, as there is no sign of support; on the fourth side it ran to the house wall. The walks were bordered by a low masonry pluteus broken by a passage in the middle of the north side. Inside this a fountain filled nearly the whole of the open area, leaving only a narrow passage between it and the pluteus, enlarged at the outer corners by oblique cutting. This passage may have been especially to hold potted plants. The exterior of the fountain wall was plain, the interior broken into a series of five little steps in an elaborately baroque alternation of curved and rectilinear bays, concave along the back wall, convex elsewhere, and just inside this was a series of square masonry bases that must have held statuary; one thinks of fountain figures that might have played jets into the central basin. Whether the stepped bays were for trailing plants is not known; there was no sign of water here, and the wall is broken by a passage at the middle of the north side. The central feature is a shallow square pool with a low margin in the middle of which rose a truncated octagonal pyramid crowned with a square, entirely revetted with marble, with four tiny water stairs of nine steps each leading down the principal faces. In the excavation were recovered three marble urns decorated with bas reliefs, as well as an oscillum, some fragments of marble furniture, and fragments of statuary (*PAH* 2.362–65 [13 December 1838–31 January 1839]). The wall behind the fountain was painted with a garden in which there were lattice fences, trees, birds, and a fountain crowned with a figure of Diana as huntress (Helbig no. 240).

North of this garden open a trapezoidal storage cupboard and a large oecus with a pavement including at least a panel of square and triangular plates of colored marble. The walls were elaborately prepared by covering them with terracotta tiles before applying several

FIGURE 49.
The Casa di Apollo,
Sunken Garden

coats of plaster. It must have been splendidly painted, but little survives today. Off the northwest corner of the garden opens a lobby
that served as a stairwell for access to rooms in a second storey that
covered four rooms here, probably essentially storage space. West of
the lobby opens the kitchen court, a long rectangle with hearth platform, latrine closet, and lararium. North of this is a combination
storeroom/workroom with only rustic finish.

From the fountain garden a broad passage leads north to a great
sunken garden. Along the passage open first shallow rooms to either
side, each with a window to the fountain garden. Beyond these the
passage was closed by doors beyond which there was once a portico
with fluted Doric columns of tufa, but this had been broken up into
rooms, three of the columns included in the new walls for these. It
was remodeled to make a lobby in continuation of the passage from
the fountain garden, a bay raised a steep step above this to the east,
and a suite of two rooms in sequence to the west. These were both
paved with marble, and at least the lower walls were revetted with
marble, most of which was removed in antiquity. Each had a window

at least partly framed with marble that looked out on the great garden. These are clearly living rooms and might have been used for small dinner parties.

From the lobby one descended four steps to the sunken garden, approximately equivalent to the rest of the house in area, around the edge of which ran a broad terrace at about waist height that was retained by a stout masonry wall. This must have been planted with shrubbery, and behind it the walls are painted dark red and embellished with sea monsters, statuary, and other garden ornaments. An Egyptianizing landscape on the south wall (Helbig no. 1546b) has entirely disappeared. At the northeast corner two square masonry pillars covered with rustication stand on the retaining wall, evidence that a large arbor filled this space. It does not seem to have been accessible and may have served only as a support for vines. The central feature of the garden was a deep circular pool, not very large, set in a square marble frame with a Corinthian pillar at each corner and a marble water stair in the middle of the south side. The fountain figure was a small seated Bacchus. The pool was surrounded on all four sides by a bed enlivened with marble furniture and small-scale statuary. This must have been planted with flowers and ivy. Against the middle of the north wall was built a squarish pavilion on a platform raised a single step above the garden. This has a marble margin, and the six columns—two engaged against the north wall, two at the outer corners, and two at the middle of the east and west sides— were revetted around the foot with small plates of marble, the shafts covered with a decoration worked in mosaic and shells, of which little remains. These carried a light gable roof, the print of which, with the socket for its rooftree, is plainly visible in the north wall. Within the pavilion there are three large niches in the north wall, symmetrically disposed flat-headed ones flanking a larger round-headed one, that must have been intended for statuary. Within the pavilion this wall seems to have been left rough deliberately but not artificially rusticated, while outside the pavilion it is covered with bits of coarse limestone formed in warm water around aquatic vegetation.

In the northwest corner of the sunken garden is one of the main features of the house, a biclinium in a separate structure. The exterior wall on the south is covered with a large Egyptianizing landscape of romantic character interrupted by a small square window set high (Helbig no. 567; Spinazzola 1953, 1.280, fig. 311). That on the east, facing the pavilion, was covered with rustication in bits of limestone arranged to give the effect of ashlar masonry in large blocks, into which are let a variety of decorative objects, including three subject pictures in glass mosaic of rather coarse tesserae (M.N. Inv. Nos. 10004, 10006; Ruesch 60, nos. 197, 199) bordered with lines of shells, and a number of reliefs, including oscilla. The door is at the north end of this front, and a large window takes up much of this side. One mounted to the interior by four steps. The building is L-shaped; the couches filled alcoves to the west and south that are floored with mosaic finished with a border and a marble edge. Evidently the rest of the floor was covered with opus sectile that was salvaged. The dado was revetted with marble, also salvaged, continued by painting in imitation of marble behind the couches. The main zone is a continuous scaenae frons peopled with Apollo and his associates, notably a group of the divinities of light and the cast of the story of Marsyas. Above the main zone, which finishes on a very even line, there may have been wooden paneling.

The general effect of this house is much like that of the Casa di Loreio Tiburtino. Although the atrium preserves the lines and some of the air of a very old small atrium complex of gracious proportions, both the painting of the tablinum and the design of the fountain garden emphasize the miniature. This is not a large house, but it is a pretty and comfortable one. Like the Casa di Loreio Tiburtino, it seems to have been designed for a small family—five rooms seem to have been bedrooms—but here there is much more opportunity for, and thought given to, entertaining. And here the garden was purely a pleasure garden. It is preeminently a house for summer use but would probably not have been uncomfortable except in the depth of winter.

The Casa di Loreio Tiburtino

The Casa di Loreio Tiburtino (II ii 2)[15] exerts a peculiar charm on most visitors, yet the refurbishing of its gardens and the rerooofing of parts to protect decorations fall tactfully short of attempting to restore the aesthetic of the house or the relation of covered and uncovered parts. The atrium complex, which one enters by long fauces between two large shops, is essentially all of the early Tufa Period, probably of the early second century B.C. The house door is drawn well back down the fauces, a towering affair of two leaves studded in places with bronze and iron bosses on long shanks, its form recovered in a plaster cast, preceded by a masonry bench to either side. Above, to either side, Spinazzola believed a columnar loggia, with four columns on the façade and four running back along the fauces, surmounted each of the shops,[16] but evidence in the form of column elements does not

---

[15] See A. Maiuri and R. Pane, *La Casa di Loreio Tiburtino e la Villa di Diomede in Pompei* (I monumenti italiani ser. 2, fasc. 1, Rome 1947), 3–9 and pls. 1–8; and Spinazzola 1953, 1.369–434.

[16] Spinazzola 1953, 1.372–73. The upper storey proposed by Spinazzola for the rest of the atrium complex is architecturally illogical and unsupported by any evidence.

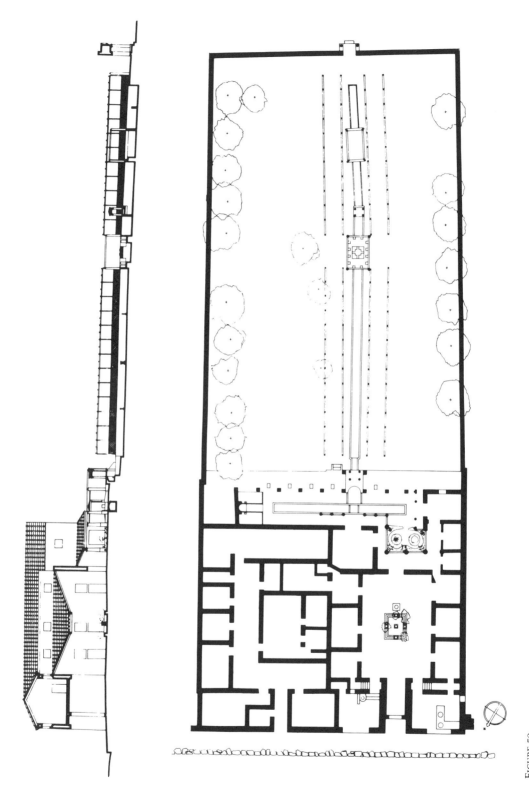

FIGURE 50.
The Casa di Loreio Tiburtino, Plan and Long Section

exist, which makes Spinazzola's idea unlikely to be correct. Closed rooms are more probable. In the last period, and probably always, these belonged not to the house but to the shops and were accessible by a pair of approximately symmetrical stairs rising between shop and house. But the shops communicated with the house and must have been in the hands of freedmen or clientes of the household. That to the west was a modest cookshop, connected to the house by a door to the atrium and another to the first cubiculum on the west. That to the east belonged to a worker in small pottery or terracottas of some sort, for it is connected to the house by a door to the atrium and another to the first cubiculum on the east, where a small kiln is found. Here, too, was found the stamp of the artisan D. Octavius Quartio (Spinazzola 1953, 1.369, 419–20). Since these shops did not have mezzanines, Spinazzola presumed that his loggias served as places of entertainment for patrons of the shops and as vantage points for watching parades down the Via dell'Abbondanza, but they are much more likely to have been living quarters.

The atrium itself is spacious, with soaring doors to the cubicula around it, but not large. Its walls were undecorated in the last period, but the floor had been repaved with signinum ornamented with geometrically shaped plates and chips of marble laid at intervals in lines, and the impluvium had been converted into an elaborate fountain. Two low walls around its edge framed a wooden trough that must have held ornamental plants. This was interrupted at the middle of each of three sides by a square base, while on the fourth, the north or entrance side, there was a square basin completely revetted in marble. The bases were presumably for statuary, possibly fountain figures, since there is evidence of rescue operations here. In the middle of the impluvium stands a somewhat higher and more elaborate base, to which lead pipes still lead.

The alae of the original atrium complex have been converted to other use, that on the west being made into a cubiculum by partly walling up its opening, that on the east into a vestibule leading into a tiny kitchen court and latrine closet arranged in space taken from the house next-door. Since the arrangement of the latrine necessitated cutting one corner of the great oecus south of it, the one splendid reception room in the house, it is hard to imagine why this was permitted. The three cubicula off the atrium, including the converted ala, are pleasantly painted in the Fourth Style but are undistinguished rooms.

There is no tablinum. Instead one passes by a wide axial door directly to a tiny peristyle garden filling what would be the area of the tablinum and part of the area of the oecus that must originally have flanked the tablinum on the west. The oecus to the east of the tablinum, on the other hand, was kept virtually unchanged. The garden is rectangular, with porticoes on three sides, while on the south it opens nearly full-width to the upper terrace of the euripus. The order is a squat, reeded Doric with plain red lower shafts. The garden area was planned with two circular beds, and on a narrow little pluteus that framed it were set at least six Egyptian statuettes of glazed terracotta (Spinazzola 1953, 1.395–96). To the west open two tiny rooms with pleasant Fourth Style decorations, and beyond these, overlooking the hortus and on axis with the upper euripus, is a pavilionlike room preceded on the east by a little portico of two columns and two columns engaged against rectangular piers. The columns are of hybrid order, reeded, essentially Doric but trimmed with a band of acanthus under a plain abacus. The lower drums are black, the shafts white. The room itself has a coffered plaster ceiling and a delicate miniaturistic decoration, mainly in red and black on a white ground. There is a picture of a priest of Isis that was once inscribed with his name, transcribed by Spinazzola as Amulius Faventinus Tiburs (Spinazzola 1953, 1.428–29), by Della Corte as Amplus Alumnus Tiburs (Della Corte[3] 373, no. 801 r). This has led to the supposition that the large rectangular niche in the centre of the west wall held an image of Isis. Although Spinazzola thought of a statuette (Spinazzola 1953, 1.386), the rough plaster covering the back of the niche indicates rather a painting on a wooden panel.

On the east side of the little peristyle is a large square oecus, the one room in the house clearly intended for entertaining. This has a portico six columns long of the same order as that of the diaeta of Isis along its south front, under which the principal door opens wide to a vista down the lower euripus. These columns stand along the margin of the upper euripus. The room is painted with a high socle imitating colored marble and two continuous friezes, a narrow one of subjects illustrating the *Iliad* and a deeper one illustrating the lesser-known exploits of Hercules.

The upper euripus is arranged on a broad terrace running east and west from the diaeta of Isis to a biclinium of masonry flanking an aedicular niche framed by two columns and a low triangular pediment. The columns are of grey-blue bardiglio, the rest white marble; the capitals are an early example of the composite order. The curved back of the niche is covered with rustication, and presumably the base within it, painted in imitation of marble, once held a statue, though none was found. The euripus runs right to the aedicula between the couches of the biclinium, and there is no table, so this must have served only as a place for conversation, reading, or simply lounging and enjoying the cool. The euripus channel is narrow enough to hop across, just about a meter wide but equally deep. It

FIGURE 51.
The Casa di Loreio
Tiburtino, View East
along the Upper
Euripus

has a narrow marble margin and is crossed by two bridges, one in front of the biclinium and one in front of the door to the oecus. The latter led to a remarkable fountain consisting of a semicircle of fine jets that played in toward a central jet on a floor paved with fragments of marble plates, all at ground level. Beyond this is an open pavilion supported on four plain columns that once held a statue. Euripus, fountain, pavilion, entrance porticoes to the oecus and the diaeta, and the biclinium were all covered by a wooden arbor supported by the house wall on the north and by a row of eight square masonry pillars on the south, with two more making a projection on the axis of the oecus to cover the pavilion in front of it. A row of five masonry bases just south of the line of pillars was for small-scale statuary, and a collection of small marbles was scattered at intervals around the edge of the euripus. The collection included two archaistic herm heads and an Egyptian sphinx.

A stair of two steps leads from the terrace of the upper euripus to the hortus, which occupies the whole southern end of this block, several times the area occupied by the house in size. On the line of the axis of the oecus, though with some deviation from an absolutely straight line, the lower euripus runs from a nymphaeum under the little open pavilion with four columns almost as far as a garden door to the street behind the Palestra Grande. The nymphaeum is recessed in a low storey behind two stubby columns under the outer pair of the pavilion columns, a water stair of two steps fed by a fountain statuette of a child with a mask, while another mask that poured water from its mouth is fixed to the wall behind. The euripus is of approximately the same width and depth as its counterpart above and is interrupted in its lower course by three features. First, about halfway along its length a large rectangular basin with twelve bases for fountain figures around its periphery has a central pyramid of four tiny marble water stairs, each of five steps, descending from a square platform pierced for a central pipe.[17] The whole basin was covered by an arbor supported at the corners by plain, stuccoed masonry columns. A little below this is an aedicula the width of the euripus of four stubby columns supporting a flat-roofed superstructure with four segmental arches springing from column to column that is decorated with graceful stucco scrollwork enlivened with erotes and swans against a background of red and blue and trimmed with simple but elegant moldings. Last is a large rectangular basin with a square pillar of opus mixtum vittatum at each corner set obliquely to the axis; this must also have carried an arbor. These interruptions divide the euripus into a series of basins, the water running from one to another through apertures in the upper rim.

Down either side of the euripus ran a walk covered by a light wooden arbor, and along each of the long side walls ran a row of sizable trees, so presumably all the planting emphasized the longitudinal rows and beds familiar from kitchen gardens. Sockets for beams in the east and west walls indicate that shelters for plants were built against these, and toward the middle in the eastern half a row of forty-four storage amphoras were buried up to their necks in earth heaped about them, probably for aging wine. A pair of cartibulum legs of good quality near the root cavity of a large tree southeast of the pyramid of water stairs indicates an area reserved for relaxation and enjoyment of the garden, and at the south end of the euripus the door to the exterior was preceded by a transverse arbor supported on four columns. The door itself was treated ornamentally on the exterior with a frame of two columns (and a triangular pediment?) mounted on a small projecting platform.

Throughout this house one is struck by the combination of the

[17] The statue of a sleeping hermaphrodite placed here in the restoration of the house does not belong. It was found by the south wall of the garden (cf. Spinazzola 1953, 1.413–14).

ornamental and the utilitarian. The house itself preserves the lines of most of the rooms of a very old house, with suppression of the tablinum and remodeling of the alae. The garden combines the practicality of kitchen-garden planning with a central euripus and an upper terrace the main purpose of which was to delight the eye and refresh the senses. If the owner of this house was a rich man, he was not wasteful. It was not a place for entertaining on a lavish scale or with a considerable familia. Rather it is a large garden designed for productivity into which enough in the way of amenity has been introduced to give it the look of a pleasure garden. That these touches are all characteristically Fourth Style in both architecture and decoration also gives it a superficial gloss of high modernity.

Three Small Houses of Unusual Plan

Three small houses of different sorts of plans and architectural foci need at least brief attention, since they are clearly work of professional designers and organized with identifiable principles. They can also be seen as middle-class housing. But the first is a fine specimen of a house type, while the second is a unique solution to a difficult problem.

The Casa di Ifigenia (III iv b [or s.n.]) occupies a square plot on the street leading in from the Porta di Nocera just north of its crossing with the Via dell'Abondanza.[18] It was actually the house of Pinarius Cerialis, a gem cutter; numerous examples of his art found here show him to have been an accomplished artisan. The sidewalk in front of the house was sheltered by a shed roof that continued to the north. One entered directly to a garden framed on two sides by porticoes, that on the north being deeper than that on the east, while the garden area itself is square. The porticoes are supported by a combination of heavily stuccoed Doric columns and plain piers joined by a pluteus that is broken by a passage only near the southeast corner. All the rooms open off the porticoes or off an exedral bay at the east end of the north portico. On the north portico are first a stair to rooms in a second storey, then a small room half under the stair for the atriensis, and last a nearly square room with a large rectangular window to the portico and garden painted with a splendid scaenae frons decoration including an illustration for Euripides' *Iphigeneia in Tauris*, from which the house derives its common name. Here were found remains of a couch that Spinazzola took to be for sleeping, leading him to identify the room as a cubiculum fenestratum. But the window is clearly intended to provide a view from the couch and could do so only if one sat. And the decoration is far too splendid for a bedroom. It is much

---

[18] On the Casa di Ifigenia see Spinazzola 1953, 2.689–709.

more likely that this is a dining room and that Pinarius and his guests were accustomed to sit at table, as the old Romans had (Isidorus *Orig.* 20.11.9).

In the east bank of rooms, beginning from the north, are a triclinium with a vaulted ceiling lit by a bull's-eye window to the garden next-door, then a large, bare workshop, a slotlike closet with a small window in its east wall, and last a good-sized rectangular room with a yellow-ground Fourth Style decoration where Pinarius kept his work and displayed it to clients. This room too had a vaulted ceiling.

The remains of the upper storey are meager, and the house was ransacked after the disaster by survivors who were destructive. The bedrooms must have been upstairs, and Spinazzola took the stout supports of the porticoes around the garden to indicate that the second storey covered all the rooms in the ground storey and more or less reproduced its plan. That is possible, but I am more inclined to believe that the second storey covered only the north wing. The absence of a kitchen and latrine here, as well as the lack of aqueduct water, which means that the cooking had to be done on portable braziers and water had to be hauled by hand from the public fountains, does not suggest a very numerous household.

The decorated rooms in this house are all painted in advanced Fourth Style, and the stucco rendered columns and pluteus are elements characteristic of the last period of the city. But peristyle houses without an atrium are not a new phenomenon. The Casa dei Gladiatori (V v 3) is simply a large peristyle, six columns by eight, with a single bank of rooms around it that includes a triclinium with a fine decoration transitional between the Second and Third styles. And in the later Third Style one finds the Casa di Iasone (IX v 18–21) and the Casa di Sulpicio Rufo (IX ix b/c [or s.n.]).

IX v 6, excavated in 1878, is a very curious house on a long narrow plot running through the middle of a block from street to street.[19] One entered from the Via di Nola by long fauces between independent shops. The Tuscanic atrium with small, unusually deep impluvium has the form of a cross, a squarish cubiculum being built into each corner of the rectangle we expect, making the side arms oversized alae on the cross axis of the impluvium. The axial room that must have served as tablinum is of generous size, with a large window looking out to the south. A cross corridor in front of it takes one to an andron to the east of it leading to the back parts, while a rather broad stair in symmetrical position to the west led up to a second storey. Another corridor across the back of the tablinum isolated it,

[19] On this house see *NSc* 1877, 330–33; 1878, 261–62. Overbeck and Mau 289–90. Boyce 85, no. 422. Schefold 1957, 253–56.

and a broad unroofed throat three steps below this leading south gave a vista of the garden from the tablinum. Two closets and four small rooms along this throat provided storage and service quarters, the kitchen being the last room on the east side, the latrine a closet on the west.

Beyond this the long narrow rectangle of the garden, scarcely a good-sized room in width, stretches back to the south, having at its southern end a large stable next to the posticum of the house (IX v 17). In the east wall of the garden is a lararium niche, and in the northwest corner a masonry basin with a water pipe. Four marble heads found near this basin included an Epicurus and two other philosophers, and on the south wall were remains of a painting of animals. Into the southeast corner of the stable is built a small room with an upper storey, possibly housing for a groom. Remains of harness were found under the stair beside the tablinum.

The width and careful construction of the stair indicate that the upper storey was extensive and in constant use. Beam holes indicate that it may have extended over everything but the atrium and the east "ala," but it is not likely to have covered the service quarters, and the location of the stair suggests that it was probably confined to the area of the tablinum and the corridors around this, together with the two cubicula on the south side of the atrium, since the plan would have to reproduce that of the rooms in the ground storey. Indeed, this seems to provide the explanation of the unusual plan of the tablinum. The rooms over the cubicula could be lit by windows to the atrium, but the rest must have looked out over the roofs of the service quarters.

The house, except for the service quarters, is decorated throughout in a pleasant but unpretentious Fourth Style. Overbeck and Mau date the architecture to the republican period, but while there may be older construction here and there, the design of the house seems to belong with the decoration and is both innovative and ingenious, the work of a clever professional. But it was a good solution to a special problem and a design not used elsewhere, so far as we know.

VI xv 9 is a tiny atrium house the efficient design of which suggests that the type should be much commoner than in fact it is.[20] The atrium is entered by short fauces flanked by cubicula with windows to the street. The atrium is almost square, tetrastyle, with columns of naked brick that supported a second floor, a gallery lit by large rectangular windows into the compluvium well. This was accessible by a small stair against the north wall of the atrium. While it must have made the atrium rather dark, it made living space available over the

[20] On this house see *NSc* 1897, 38–39, 62–64.

atrium, as well as over the cubicula at the front of the house, and this could have been subdivided by wooden partitions. On the far side of the atrium open an ample triclinium and the service area. The service area in the southwest corner of the house was lit by a second light well and had a second storey of its own, probably simply a loft for storage. There is no suggestion that this was anything more than a family house; there is no decoration worth describing and no provision for entertaining more than modestly. But as housing it is convenient and makes maximum use of the space available.

21 · THE VILLAS

Introduction

Although we have abundant evidence about urban domestic architecture of the last period in Pompeii, lack of evidence makes our knowledge of suburban and rural housing rather poor. In the course of time numerous villas have been excavated at Boscotrecase, Boscoreale, Scafati, and Valle di Pompei, but many of these were excavated only in part, and almost all of them have been reburied without an adequate record of the architecture and decorations (when these were of significance), so that we must rely on the evidence of the few still accessible in forming our notion of the direction such architecture was taking at the time of the eruption. Fortunately the suburban Villa di Diomede was extensively remodeled early in the last period, the Villa dei Misteri was in the process of being remodeled, and significant additions were made to the Villa di Oplontis, so we are not too badly off. But the evidence of Stabiae, especially that of the San Marco complex but of elsewhere as well, suggests that dramatic innovations in new villa buildings were numerous at this time and that those we see in the neighborhood of Pompeii are only a rather pale and conservative reflection of a revolution in architecture that began with the Domus Aurea of Nero[1] and was to find full expression in the villa of Hadrian at Tivoli. It entailed the dissolution of a villa into a number of essentially separate complexes and exploitation of the landscape as a garden element, the introduction of rooms of bizarre form and audacious engineering and the creation of vistas in which one looked from a covered space across a bright court into another covered space, sometimes with repetition beyond, and lavish displays of water in every imaginable form and context. None of these finds clear expression in Pompeian villas.

[1] See Tacitus *Ann.* 15.42.1; Suetonius *Nero* 31.1–2; and A. Boethius, *The Golden House of Nero* (Ann Arbor, Mich. 1960).

The Villa di Diomede

The large suburban villa known as the Villa di Diomede lies about two hundred meters northwest of Pompeii, outside the Porta di Ercolano on the Via dei Sepolcri.[2] It was excavated in the years 1771–74, one of the earliest parts of Pompeii to be cleared, and takes its name from the tombstone of a freedman of the gens Arria actually found in a plot on the opposite side of the road from the villa (*PAH* 1.1.279 [24 September 1774]). The name of the real owner of the villa is unknown. The land on which it is built slopes steadily down from east to west along the Via dei Sepolcri and from northeast to southwest along the axis of the house, and the architect took splendid advantage of the slope to create vast panoramas with glorious views of the Bay of Naples, the Sorrentine Peninsula, and the island of Capri.

In front of the door on the Via dei Sepolcri is arranged a little platform to which the sidewalk on either side slopes gently up and from which a stair of seven steps takes one to the house door and the level of the peristyle complex. The stair is flanked by a pair of brick columns on high plinths that carried a little porch to shelter visitors from the weather. Since the axis of the house lies at almost exactly 45° to the line of the façade, the fauces had to be a triangular lobby, and the triangular block of rooms between the peristyle and the façade required ingenuity in arrangement. From the fauces one passed directly to the peristyle, a broad rectangle of five columns by four with deep porticoes. This is the arrangement prescribed by Vitruvius for country houses (Vitruvius 6.5.3.), and the peristyle was very much a hub from which the life of the house radiated. The order is Fourth Style Doric, with reeded white shafts above plain red lower shafts. There is a broad signinum gutter around the viridarium, and the rain was impounded in cisterns served by puteals in the last intercolumniations of the long sides away from the door. A rectangular basin in the centre despoiled of its veneer in antiquity must have been for a fountain (*PAH* 1.1.264 [6 June 1772]).

The rooms of the four wings of the peristyle differ sharply from one another. On the right from the fauces one finds first a triangular lobby with a rather awkward stair leading down to the service quarters and a corridor to the sunken garden. Then comes a biclinium for intimate dinners (?) connecting with a larger room with plain walls, perhaps for heating and dressing the food. At right angles to this in the main block of rooms is first an exedra from which a short corridor

[2]On the Villa di Diomede see *PAH* 1.1.249–80 (9 February 1771–26 November 1774); 1.2.156–60; 1.3. pls. 4–6. See also Overbeck and Mau 369–71; and A. Maiuri and R. Pane, *La Casa di Loreio Tiburtino e la Villa di Diomede in Pompei* (I monumenti italiani ser. 2, fasc. 1, Rome 1947) 10–17 and pls. 9–16.

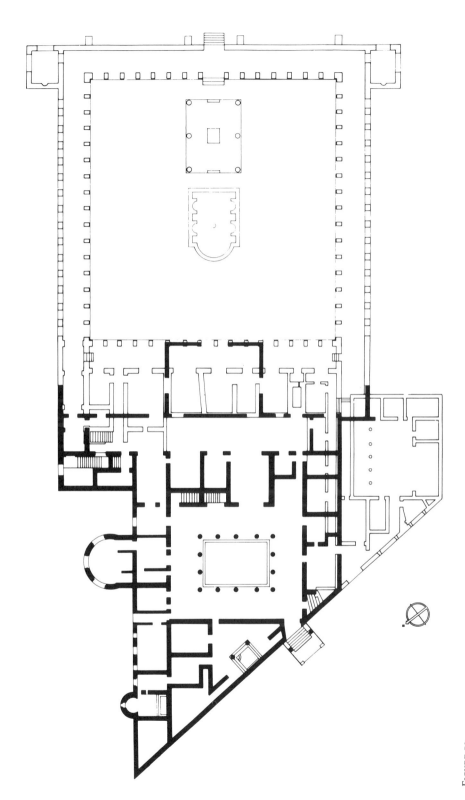

Figure 52.
The Villa di Diomede, Plan of the Final Phase

leads back to a long gallery (described below). Off the corridor open a cubiculum and a small room with a large window opening on the gallery where a number of oscilla and a fountain, presumably from the peristyle, were found.[3] Next come the tablinum, which is not on the axis of the peristyle but open nearly its full width front and back, and then a stair to an upper storey, under the upper reaches of which a large closet has been arranged. Since the stair runs along the peristyle, not away from it, the upper storey might have been of almost any extent, but because of the proximity of the tablinum, it probably was not more than a room or two. Behind the stair at peristyle level are small exedral rooms opening on the gallery, one of which had a decoration that Mau identified as Second Style but is more probably Fourth Style with reminiscence of Second Style.[4] The last room in this bank is a triclinium opening on the gallery and connecting by a small door with the exedral room next to it; these together make a classic dining suite. The long gallery on the far side of this wing is a late creation, made out of what had been a deep columnar portico; when this was walled in, the tufa columns were included in the wall and their bases were once visible.[5] It was still a very light and airy apartment, there being concentrations of windows and doors at either end giving onto the view.

The southwest wing of the peristyle is of special interest, for it is dominated by an apsidal room that is our best evidence of what Pliny meant by his *cubiculum in hapside curuatum* at his Laurentinum (*Ep.* 2.17.8). At the centre of this wing is a suite consisting of an antechamber in which a portion has been walled off, perhaps to make an alcove for a cubicularius, and a bedroom thrust out from the rest and given a great curving apse containing three large windows. The place for the bed is defined by two short, light partitions and could be closed off by a curtain,[6] and a little alcove beside it may have served for washing, as a depression in a masonry base suggests. The excavation reports speak of finding vessels suitable for oil and perfume in this room, along with a great deal of furniture and tableware.[7] The three large windows, and probably a small window over the central one as well, could be closed by shutters. Outside the room there must have been a garden on a parterre at street level accessible by a narrow corridor at the east corner of the peristyle and connected by a broad,

[3] See *PAH* 1.1.250–51 (23 February 1771); 1.2.156. See also *RömMitt* 88 (1981) 276–77 (E. J. Dwyer).

[4] Mau 1882, pl. 7; H. G. Beyen, *Die pompejanische Wanddekoration vom zweiten bis zum vierten Stil*, 2 vols. (The Hague 1938–60), 1, fig. 153.

[5] See Maiuri and Pane (supra n. 2) 12.

[6] See *PAH* 1.1.259 (14 September 1771).

[7] See *PAH* 1.1.259–60 (14 September 1771).

almost monumental stair with a lower parterre along the sunken garden. The other rooms in this wing are a cubiculum with a small window on the garden side and another to the peristyle, an antechamber to the triclinium at the south corner, and a large room off the corridor with three windows, but without decoration, where the excavators found a quantity of household goods and remains of cupboards (*PAH* 1.1.261 [21–28 December 1771]).

The rooms on the northeast side of the peristyle had to be fitted into a triangular space. They consist of kitchen and baths. One enters first a triangular courtyard having a narrow walk paved with mosaic on two sides, the roof supported on seven slender octagonal columns. In the open space against the house wall is a small tank, 1.10 m deep, its sides raised above the ground and capped with marble plates, into which one could descend by a stair of two rounded steps built into one corner. This was covered with a light roof supported on two columns of brickwork at the outer corners. Clearly this served as a frigidarium, and the wall behind it was painted with sea creatures on a blue ground, while the rest of the garden wall was painted with a garden and trees. At the west end of the portico is a small hearth where a kettle and several cups were found; evidently hot drink was prepared here for the bathers. The rest of the bath consists of an apodyterium, a small vaulted tepidarium, and a caldarium with an apse for a labrum and an alveus at the inner end. The tepidarium and caldarium are paved with black-and-white mosaic; they communicated by a small round window, and the tepidarium had a window to the garden closed by four square panes of thick glass set in a wooden frame (*PAH* 1.1.267–68 [14–21 November 1771]). The caldarium apse is half-domed and finished with a shell worked in stucco; it also has a window to the garden. The floor is raised on suspensurae, and the walls are lined with tegulae mammatae. It was heated from the kitchen, a triangular court off the frigidarium court where there is also a tank for hot water to supply the alveus. Against another wall is a hearth platform with a small oven at one end, and against the house walls are supports for a worktable. In one corner is the latrine, and off the kitchen a wooden stair led to a second storey over the apodyterium and two good-sized storerooms next to it; this probably served as sleeping quarters for some of the house staff. A reservoir between the caldarium and the Via dei Sepolcri seems to have been the main water supply of both the house and the bath.

To complete one's tour of this level of the house one must return to the long gallery. Off this to the southwest by doors at the north and west corners opens a great oecus, a broad rectangular banquet hall with a great central opening reaching almost to the floor in each of the three remaining walls, as well as two windows to the view to the southwest. This is not on the axis of the peristyle but on that of the sunken garden below it, which is displaced from that of the peristyle to the southeast. It was to create this room that the gallery was enclosed. It overhangs the garden and opens to either side onto broad decks, so it enjoyed a glorious view. The dining couches must have been set up in the middle of the room, as the placing of the doors also suggests, and there is more than enough space for two triclinia facing one another. At either end of the gallery is a small room that also opens to the deck, possibly a place for small dinner parties. The deck ran over the porticoes on all four sides of the sunken garden but was interrupted by the oecus. It was deep in front of the gallery but otherwise of uniform width. Whether there were rooms over the diaetae at the outer corners is not clear, but it seems logical to presume that there were. This was a place to stroll and converse. Behind the southeast end of the gallery are the stair that must have been the principal access to the lower storey and garden and a couple of small closets.

The complex of service quarters along the northwest side of the house, accessible from the north corner of the peristyle, lies at a lower level and is separated from the house by a narrow corridor that connects it with the garden portico. It was poorly built and discovered in a very ruinous state. It had its own door to the Via dei Sepolcri, and a series of slit windows lit the rather awkwardly planned rooms and corridor filling the triangular space here. The corridor leads to a central courtyard, along the southeast side of which was a portico of five columns. On the southwest and northwest sides open a series of rooms of uncertain purpose, but the discovery here of bottles and glasses, kitchen equipment, and agricultural implements proves that this was the service quarter, were there any doubt. The skeleton of a goat was also found here (*PAH* 1.1.272–74[1–29 May 1773]).

The garden storey of the house and the sunken garden present a rather sorry appearance today, but this was not always the case. This level is reached by a long passage accessible out of the north corner of the peristyle beside the house door, by the stair behind the southeast end of the long gallery, and by the corridor from the service quarter just mentioned. Access is thus at either end of the principal wing. The rooms are in a single bank and of uniform depth except along the access corridor, where a series of closets open, and at the southeast end, where greater depth was possible and the builders could arrange a suite of triclinium and ladies' dining room on either side of a corridor leading from the stair of access to the garden porticus. The garden porticus is composed of stout pillars with flat arches run between them, giving an effect of multiple doorways in this wing. The rooms behind are so nearly of a size and shape that they must have had similar purpose, and three of them are connected to one another by doors. They seem to have been especially places to work in the heat of the summer, not rooms for the entertainment of guests or bedrooms. At the north end of the wing is a small source of water, a niche walled off from the porticus by a pluteus to make a basin that is fed by a pipe in its back wall. The other three porticoes around the garden are raised four steps above this one but are otherwise similar. They are paved with unglazed tile laid in diagonally run panels. They have no rooms opening off them, except at the outer corners, and those along the sides once had windows to the exterior responding to the openings to the garden. Only five on the northwest side now remain. These were all painted with representations of flowers and birds, so that the garden seemed almost continuous. At the outer corners are two small windowed diaetae, rather like those found in the sea-front houses at Herculaneum, places where one might retire to read or work. The southwest front required buttressing, and in its centre opens a door to the exterior at the top of a flight of six steps.

Two architectural features emphasize the axis of the garden. Near the centre of the garden is a large tank suitable for the keeping and breeding of fish. At its centre rose a cylindrical column crowned with a marble disc pierced for a fountain, and around the perimeter were pipes and jets that played into the tank (*PAH* 1.1.257 [17 August 1771]). The end nearer the house is bowed out in an apse, and each side wall is broken into a series of five niches, alternately rectangular and curvilinear. This tank is so similar to that in the Casa di Meleagro that it seems very likely to have been designed by the same architect. Between this and the southwest wing of the porticus is a large rectangular platform raised two steps above the garden paved with white mosaic with a black edging stripe and bordered by a pluteus on which stand six brickwork columns, one at each corner and one in the middle of each long side. These must have been connected by a light wooden frame over which vines were trained to make an arbor for summer dining. The excavation reports mention carbonized trees but do not specify their disposition.[8] Along the southeast side of the garden a broad terrace leads from the diaeta at the south corner back to a broad stair leading to the upper garden along the peristyle.

[8] *PAH* 1.1.257. Jashemski (315–17) proposes that certain broken lines and dots on the plan of La Vega (*PAH* 1.3 pl. 5) should be interpreted as flower beds and trees, but it is odd that the evidence should be so scant, once the excavators had been alerted to its presence. In explanation of this, Jashemski proposes that at least some of the trees were small fruit trees. They seem to have been planted in lines parallel to the axis of the garden, a line on each side of the pool and dining pavilion and perhaps another line down each side of the garden. This might also be paralleled in the planting of the interior of the Porticus Pompei in Rome with lines of plane trees (see Nash 2, fig. 1218; and Propertius 2.31.13).

Along the northwest side a much narrower terrace leads gradually up to the service quarter. Presumably the former was landscaped, the latter not.

The reason for raising three of the porticoes above the garden was to permit lighting a cryptoporticus under these by a series of apertures piercing the shoulder of its vault. The cryptoporticus is plastered but undecorated, accessible only at its north and east ends by rather narrow stairs. The number of amphoras found here shows that this was used for aging wine, which must have been the principal product of the estate (*PAH* 1.1.274–75 [31 July–20 November 1773]). Also found here were the skeletons of eighteen adult victims and two children.

The decoration throughout the house is Fourth Style. Most of the wall schemes are delicate and rather spare, evidence of a well-defined taste. What subject paintings there were, were small. A few decorations have been suggested to be survivals from the time of the Second Style, but this is surely a mistake. Such a decoration as that with colonnading is not Second Style but a Fourth Style scaenae frons,[9] while the scrollwork in the room painted with Nereids would be very unlikely to occur in a Second Style decoration.[10] It is far more likely that these are products of the last period done after the manner of the Second Style. The use of brickwork, opus mixtum vittatum, and reticulate in the tank and garden pavilion, in the diaetae, in the main entrance to the house, in the bath complex, and in the columns and architraves of the peristyle show that the house was thoroughly remodeled after the earthquake and many new features were introduced at that time. The date of the original construction is harder to establish. The tufa columns of the original portico later built into the long gallery might be as early as the middle of the first century B.C., but the porticus of the sunken garden is almost entirely in the masonry of small blocks that is characteristic of Augustan building in Pompeii. Possibly the lower storeys are an Augustan addition to an older building. But it is likely that the whole edifice ought to be regarded as an Augustan creation extensively remodeled and modernized after the earthquake.[11]

When one considers the effect of the modernization and the aesthetic of the house in the last period, one is struck by the similarities to modernizations in the Villa dei Misteri and the Casa dell'Atrio a Mosaico and the Casa dei Cervi in Herculaneum, in particular the

[9] See Beyen (supra n. 4) 1, fig. 26.
[10] See Mau 1882, pl. 7; and Beyen (supra n. 4) 1, fig. 153.
[11] Maiuri (1942, 157–58) distinguishes three main building periods but, as usual, puts the original construction far too early (pre-Roman). No true "carpentry style" construction is to be found in the villa.

arrangement of the banquet hall with relation to the garden and the view and the enclosure of space to make a gallery. Galleries seem to have become very popular in the last period, much as the underground cryptoporticus had become in the late republican period. They were places to stroll and converse well protected from the weather, be it hot or cold, and afforded new opportunities in arranging communication with other rooms. We find them already making a limited and tentative appearance in the Aedificium Eumachiae and the Villa di Oplontis, but in the last period of Pompeii they seem to have proliferated. Perhaps their usefulness in the seaside villas of the Julio-Claudian period was responsible for this. And huge banquet halls that hang poised on the edge of a dramatic sweep are now also a common feature in fine houses. One finds them in the Villa dei Misteri and the Casa di Fabio Rufo in Pompeii, in the Casa dei Cervi and the Casa dell'Albergo in Herculaneum, and in the Villa di San Marco in Stabiae. Probably wherever such a panorama was available the architect was prepared to take advantage of it. What is surprising is that Pompeians of the late period should have wanted rooms on so vast a scale; it amounts to a revolution against Julio-Claudian taste. The apsidal bedroom, despite the probability that its similarity to the one that Pliny describes was not fortuitous, is unique in Pompeii, not symptomatic of a trend.

The Villa dei Misteri

A number of alterations made in the Villa dei Misteri after the earthquake of A.D. 62 indicate the direction in which villa architecture was moving. None of these had been brought to final finish or been given much in the way of redecoration. It seems probable that the owners intended to work out the new form the building was to take a little at a time, dividing rooms or throwing them together as might prove advantageous, adding important rooms and porticoes and then seeing how space around these might be best utilized, at first working not a little by trial and error and only after several years of such experiments intending to carry out a general redecoration, possibly of the whole building, possibly with notable decorations of the Second Style preserved, such as those of rooms 5, 15, and 16. These at least were still in excellent condition when the villa was excavated and showed no sign of having been tampered with in antiquity.

The remodeling extended to all four fronts of the villa. The most important changes were those along the southern front, overlooking the bay.[12] Here, slightly off the axis of the atrium but not perceptibly

---

[12] See Maiuri 1931, 53.

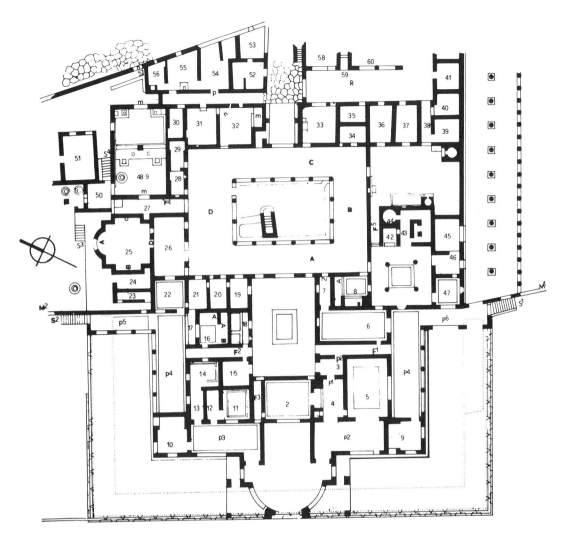

FIGURE 53.
The Villa dei Misteri,
Plan of the Final Phase

so, a great new room was built out from the "tablinum," which, if it ever really was a tablinum, in the time of the Third Style had been converted to serve as a sitting room. The new room ran over the portico along this side of the villa and then swelled out in a great hemicycle that came tangent to the edge of the parterre over the cryptoporticus. It had three vast windows with a dramatic view seaward, others to the gardened parterres to either side, and doors leading back to the porticoes so these could be used in conjunction with it. Marble window sills attest to the sumptuousness with which it would have been finished. A great rough hole torn in the wall between this and the "tablinum" strongly suggests that the wall between them would have been entirely, or almost entirely, torn out, and this would have become the great banquet hall of the house, comparable in size and the splendor of its view to the banquet hall in the Villa di Diomede. How communication with the atrium would have been effected and why a hole should have been torn connecting this with room no. 4, the little room to the southeast, is not clear. Conceivably both are part of the rescue operations of survivors. Around the hemicyclic end columns and pillars faced with brick show that a rectangular arbor covered with vines was to enclose this end.[13]

To either side of this new room the old villa portico was enclosed to make a long narrow gallery with a vast window to the view, and at each corner a generously windowed diaeta with an alcove for a couch or similarly large low piece of furniture was built (Maiuri 1931, 59). The design of the pavements emphasizes that the furniture would not have been moved, and stood well above the floor, while a window in each alcove indicates that these were not to be used for sleeping. Probably they should be thought of as studies or small sitting rooms. That at the west corner communicates with the new gallery southeast of it, that at the south corner with only the old southeast portico. Since the new long galleries made out of the southwest portico would have made the rooms behind them rather dark and had no clear function of their own, we may tend to see them as a measure to adapt the villa to use in midsummer, intended to keep the sun from overheating the rooms along this front, while the openness of the architecture of the new banquet hall will have made this unnecessary for it. This front of the villa, when finished, would have shown many similarities in architecture and function to the sea fronts of the houses along the southwest edge of Herculaneum.

Along the southeast side of the villa a long double portico was built running from the end of the southeast parterre over the cryptoporticus along the bath wing, kitchens, and service quarter as far as excavation has been carried (Maiuri 1931, 82–85). No door connects it with any of these, except for a rough hole torn in the southeast wall of the kitchen court, so the portico turned out to the garden rather than in and probably turned a corner at its northeast end to run to a new wing or building added to the villa relatively late. The depth of the portico is remarkable, and it is well built, an extra thickness of wall having been built at its back to carry the roof. The outer line of columns is simplified Doric, built of opus mixtum vittatum, with drums faced alternately with brick and reticulate to be finished with stucco. The final finish was not yet carried out, although some columns show a roughcast coat. The inner line of columns is higher and has only half as many columns as the outer, located behind al-

[13] This was misunderstood by Maiuri, who concocted an incongruous roof to be carried by these elements. This reconstruction has deceived many people.

ternate columns of the outer line, the cores faced entirely in brick. These too are Doric but of a Tuscanic character, more elaborate than the outer line, with carefully molded capitals and bases. Since they stand on the line of the face of the southeast parterre, it is tempting to see them as a replacement for a utilitarian portico with simple pillars of limestone balancing a similar portico on the opposite side of the villa. This would have been installed at the time of the Third Style alterations and redecorations of the villa and then enlarged by doubling its width after the earthquake. That would account also for the difference in style and refinement between the two orders and the rather stubby proportions of the outer line.

In the triangular space to the northeast between the villa and the road, which once presumably had been farmyard, were built two farm buildings flanking a broad paved throat leading to the villa entrance. That to the northwest was living quarters, divided up into small apartments for families among the servants. That to the southeast consisted of a long rectangular court and a building behind it, not yet excavated, that had a big room with a wide door, so wide that its lintel had to be supported in the middle by a column, in the ground storey. This might possibly have been a stable. Rooms in a second storey above were accessible by at least two stairs. What had once been open space, perhaps surrounded with sheds, was now organized into a well-knit complex. Remains of rooms decorated in the Fourth Style in a second storey over the throat leading to the villa entrance indicate that an apartment for the vilicus (manager) reached by a narrow stair in the entrance throat was distinctly more luxurious than the rest of this wing.

On the northwest front of the villa in space that was earlier part of a utilitarian portico with simple pillars of coarse limestone was built an impressive room in the shape of a Greek cross with an apse containing a window opening at its northwest end (Maiuri 1931, 74–76). This was a mere shell at the time of the eruption, and it is impossible to tell how it would have been finished or how it was ultimately to relate to the large rectangular antechamber that lies between it and the peristyle. Maiuri identified it as a lararium, or household shrine, but that is highly improbable. It is more likely that it is the beginning of a new bath suite, for it has the architectural lines of a caldarium, and the old bath suite off the south corner of the peristyle was cramped and obsolete and no longer in use in the last period of Pompeii. If this identification is correct, then the new bath was to be commodious, and one might imagine that the antechamber would have been divided between a tepidarium and an apodyterium. There is no indication as to the what the owner's intentions for the bath may have been. How the heating of the new bath would have been engineered is also obscure, but an abundance of marble veneer, including moldings and pilaster capitals, in this room shows that it was to be extensively revetted, as one might have expected.

Thus the alterations made in the villa following the earthquake suggest that it was to be larger, grander, and more luxurious than the original house. The alterations made in the time of the Third Style had aimed only at making certain parts more useful or more beautiful. The last lot of alterations indicate a greatly enlarged familia and entertainment on a lavish scale at the same time that the agricultural activities of the villa remained essentially what they had always been. If additional vineyards had been acquired by the owner, we see no sign of that.

Inferences

There are interesting parallels between certain features of the Villa di Diomede and modifications that were being introduced in the Villa dei Misteri in the last years of Pompeii. The windowed gallery onto which the important rooms at the upper level of the Villa di Diomede give, with symmetrically placed diaetae to either end commanding the view, is closely related to the rehandling of the southwest portico of the Villa dei Misteri with its broad windowed galleries on which the main rooms now came to open and its diaetae. The oecus flanked by open decks that dominates everything around it in the Villa di Diomede is not in concept unlike the new apsidal banquet hall of the Villa dei Misteri, thrust forward from the rest and given great windows looking out to the sea. We cannot be sure how far-reaching the remodeling of the Villa dei Misteri would ultimately have been; certainly it would not have extended to a general rebuilding. But its new southwest front had much in common with the Villa di Diomede, and we find the same elements in slightly different form appearing also in the Casa dell'Atrio a Mosaico and the Casa dei Cervi at Herculaneum.

These fall somewhere between the town house and the villa, with features of each. They take some advantage of the view over the bay but are on a single level and have an enclosed garden on which suites of staterooms open, presumably rooms especially for use in the spring and fall. But each has a bank of very fine rooms between the enclosed garden and the prospect toward the sea. On the sea side of these rooms ran a gallery provided with windows and doors so that it could be thrown open to the air and view or closed against intemperate weather, and beyond this was an open walk, but there were also provisions for planting here to relieve and frame the vista. To either side was set a little diaeta, apparently now a regular feature, though it is not clear how often this was intended for sleeping and how often for sitting. One gathers from Pliny (*Ep.* 2.17.20–22) that if there was an architectural difference, it was small.

Some notice seems required at this point of the villas of Stabiae, but these are only imperfectly understood at best, and of the two areas in part excavated in recent years, only that known as the Varano villa seems to have been private houses. These are portico villas in concept, the majority of the living rooms ranged in a line to enjoy the view over the sea and a deep colonnade with widely spaced columns in front of these providing communication. In front of the colonnade is an unroofed walk supported on an arcade framed by plain pilasters. But though much of the architecture here is of the last period and the decoration of most of the rooms is in the Fourth Style, substantial parts are as old as the late Second Style (Augustan), and some rooms with Second Style decorations were kept intact in the last period. So the probability is that these houses were portico villas from the beginning, and the late masonry faced with brick is repair rather than rebuilding. The San Marco villa, east of this, with its spirally fluted columns and multiple porticoes, is certainly a building of the last period, but it does not seem apt to have been a private house. It was a building designed to accommodate people in large numbers, and one thinks most readily of a hotel or sanatorium. But its true nature can only be clarified by further excavation; for the present it remains an enigma.

22 · THE TOMBS

Altar Tombs

In the last period of Pompeii far the most popular form of monumental tomb was the funerary altar, a form persisting from the earliest appearance of monumental tomb architecture, for obvious reasons. Aedicula tombs seem almost to have disappeared in this period, but other forms popular earlier—the schola, the tholos, and the arch—still occurred, as did the simple bustum in a number of variants. But the altar tomb now became the great favorite; it too appears in a number of variations.

The classic form is that of the tomb of C. Calventius Quietus, Via dei Sepolcri south no. 20 (Kockel 90–97). The tomb stands at the centre of a square plot surrounded by a wall punctuated at the corners and the midpoint of each long side by a pillar capped with a little pyramid. The wall on the street side is lower than elsewhere to allow a view of the tomb and access, but there is no door. The back wall is finished with a gable scarcely visible behind the mass of the altar, finished with stucco reliefs and with a framed place for an inscription. Reliefs of mythological subject decorated the pillars. The altar stands on a high stuccoed base surmounted by a crowning molding and three steps leading up to the altar proper, which is covered with reliefs on front and sides and plain behind. On the front, surrounded by richly carved moldings, is the inscription informing us that this is the tomb of C. Calventius Quietus, Augustalis, to whom the decuriones, with the concurrence of the people, awarded the honor of a bisellium. Below is shown the bisellium itself with cushion and footstool. The decoration, though elaborate, seems rather clumsy. On each side of the altar is a corona civica; the allusion must be to the position of Augustalis. A deeply projecting cornice trims the top of the altar below a plain worktable framed by pulvini carved with leaves. There is no tomb chamber; presumably the cinerary urn of Quietus is at the centre of the monument.

As Kockel (96–97) observes, we are clearly dealing with a tomb of two phases, but both of the last period of Pompeii. This was first constructed as a bustum with elaborate decorations in stucco but never finished, as the lack of an inscription on the back wall shows. Then after Quietus's death his heirs, presumably his son Quietus, who stood for the duovirate (*CIL* 4.7604), built a more sumptuous monument in the taste of the last period.

Similar to this in type is the tomb of N. Festius Ampliatus (?), Via dei Sepolcri south no. 17, nearby (Kockel 75–85). The altar stands in the left forward corner of a slightly trapezoidal enclosure, the base on the façade of tufa framed with stringcourses above a brickwork footing but otherwise entirely of brick finished with stucco. The entrance is a low door with tufa frame flanked by a pair of fluted stucco pilasters with Corinthian capitals. The altar stood on three steps, the top one finished with a molding; it was badly ruined when discovered, and its height and character are conjectural, but it is said to have been finished with stucco, not marble reliefs. A large fragment of an inscription on marble seems to belong here. The tomb chamber is approached from the west, just inside the enclosure door, square in plan, vaulted, with a square pillar at its centre. The central pillar is pierced in cruciform fashion to show the urn that must have stood at its centre, and at least three of the openings are reported to have been covered with glass. Around the walls of the tomb chamber open arched loculi, four in every wall but the entrance wall, where one to each side flanks the door.

The tomb was remarkable for the stucco reliefs that decorated the steps below the altar and the façade on the road. The reliefs on the steps showed scenes from a venatio, men and dogs engaged in fighting a variety of animals. The façade wall showed an upper register of gladiators, identified by a painted inscription as the final day of the games of N. Festius Ampliatus, the individual gladiators and their victories identified by smaller dipinti in black. Although now these reliefs have almost completely perished, Mazois made careful drawings of them while they were still fresh, and these are of the highest interest. A lower register showed a venatio scene. Since the reliefs were added late, the large tufa plates of the façade being picked to give the stucco purchase, we may presume that these were games for Ampliatus's funeral, although other evidence shows that he was the owner of a gladiatorial familia (*CIL* 4.1183–4).

A somewhat simpler altar tomb is that of the aedile C. Vestorius Priscus, who died at the age of twenty-two, as the inscription informs us, presumably while in office, for the place for his tomb, just outside the Porta del Vesuvio, was given by decree of the decuriones, while his mother built the monument *pecunia sua*.[1] It stands on a high base within an enclosure. The high enclosure wall is lowered a little on the side toward the road to permit a better view of the altar and finished with merlons capped with pyramids at the corners. The base is not exactly centred within the enclosure but set a little to the north and abuts the enclosure wall on this side. The altar is much smaller than the base, which is finished at the top above an elaborate stucco cornice with four merlonlike bases that hold omphaloi around which serpents coil.[2] The bases are decorated with erotes in stucco relief, and the altar, also of masonry finished with stucco, is decorated with Bacchic figures. Moldings and decoration are all in the taste of the Fourth Style. The enclosure and altar are painted inside and out in the Fourth Style, the outside very simply, the inside with an elaborate program celebrating Vestorius Priscus and his magistracy. The scene on the front of the altar shows him togate, seated on a curule chair on a tribunal under an awning, with groups of people to either side. The back of the altar shows him again, tunicate, standing in the doorway of a room hung with garlands and furnished with couches and tables covered with a book box, scrolls, and tablets, the abode of the blessed. Other paintings show a gladiatorial duel, a banquet, a table set with a large drinking service of silver, a hunt, and a garden. There is no tomb chamber.

Another variation on the altar tomb is offered by the Porta di Nocera necropolis tomb east 2 (2 EN) without enclosure, a low base trimmed with a simple offset at base and crown surmounted by four steps that grow progessively narrower, so that the altar itself is almost a pillar. These steps were originally revetted with marble, and the altar was crowned with a large egg of white limestone that carried a meniscus of bronze. From the back one descended a narrow flight of steps to a tomb chamber half sunk below ground level. This is vaulted and provided with arched loculi, three in each side wall, two in the end wall. Curious paintings decorate the end wall, including a shield, a large bird, and a hunter fighting a boar in the lunette. An amphora sunk in the floor in the back righthand corner served to receive libations.

Very similar to this in form appears to have been tomb north no. 8 on the Via dei Sepolcri (Kockel 152–59), though little remains today of the superstructure. The base was deliberately rusticated, the stepped superstructure revetted with marble. The tomb chamber was

---

[1] G. Spano, "La tomba dell'edile C. Vestorio Prisco in Pompei, "*MemLinc* ser. 7, 3 (1943) 237–315.

[2] Such omphaloi also appear in the tomb of Eumachia in the Porta di Nocera necropolis.

entered from behind from a court entered from the Villa delle Co-
lonne a Mosaico, a small square chamber, vaulted, with a single loculus in each side wall and the end wall. Here was found the large
amphora of blue cameo glass that gives the tomb its name, as well as
two more ash urns, a terracotta mask, and thirteen terracotta statuettes, including divinities, porters, and gladiators. There is no place
for an inscription on either of these tombs, despite the relative richness of the grave goods in both.

Tholos Tombs

Far below the altar tomb in popularity appears to have been the tholos, of which we have two excellent examples. Next to the tomb of N.
Festius Ampliatus on the Via dei Sepolcri, south no. 18 (Kockel 85–
90) is a tholos tomb set well back in a small rhomboidal plot surrounded by a high enclosure wall of brickwork on a base of tufa rubblework trimmed at each corner and the midpoint of each long side
with a square pillar capped with a pyramid. In the front wall of the
enclosure was immured an inscription, probably *CIL* 10.1003, recording that Marcia Aucta built the tomb for herself, her husband C. Fabius Secundus, and her daughters. The pillars of the enclosing wall
were originally embellished with stucco reliefs having a funerary
theme. The door to the interior is at the right end of the façade, and
the interior lies at a higher level. The tomb itself stands on a low
rhomboidal footing following the lines of the plot, a cylindrical tower
of brickwork finished with stucco rendered as orthostats below three
courses of drafted ashlar finished by three projecting courses of brick,
the armature of a molding. Just below this projection on the street
side is the setting for an inscription, which was not found. Above
this nothing was preserved, so the crown of the tomb remains somewhat doubtful. The tomb chamber, entered from the rear, is round,
with three niches for ash urns. It is roofed with a bell-shaped ceiling,
not a true dome, that resembles the caldarium of the bath of the Villa
dei Misteri; the crown of this was missing. A simple Fourth Style
decoration covers the walls.

Another tholos tomb appears in the Porta di Nocera necropolis,
tomb east 17 (17 ES). This has a square base storey faced with brickwork, the main façade framed by engaged Corinthian columns and
architrave, within which an arch surrounds the recessed tomb door.
Bases and capitals of the columns are of tufa, and the doorframe is of
white limestone. Over the door is an inscription on a plate of marble
identifying it as the tomb of C. Cuspius Cyrus, magister of the Pagus
Augustus Felix, and his wife, Vesvia Iucunda, and C. Cuspius Salvius, also magister of the same pagus. The storey is finished with a

modillion cornice. The upper storey consists of a low square base faced with brickwork and a drum faced with reticulate trimmed at the base with a double torus. Less than a meter of the drum is preserved, above which it is impossible to say how the architecture continued. The tomb chamber is rectangular, vaulted, with two rectangular loculi with arched tops in each side wall and a pair of similar loculi flanking an apsidal loculus in the back wall. Although this tomb is older than those that flank it on either side, it is so clearly of the same architectural aesthetic that it must belong in the last period of Pompeii. Moreover, yellow tufa was used extensively in the reticulate facing of the drum. Unlike the tomb of Marcia Aucta, it falls in the tradition of older tholos tombs, a cubical base surmounted by a circular upper storey, which one would like to restore with open architecture, whereas the tomb of Marcia Aucta seems rather to have been a tower and might well have continued blind. Like tomb east 4, east 17 combines the architectural ideas of the arch tomb and the tholos tomb, but more dramatically and authoritatively; the form has now crystallized. It is repeated, with the base storey a true arch, in tomb 1 of the Fondo Pacifico, farther to the east.

Schola Tombs

A third sort of tomb persisting from earlier times was the schola. Two immediately outside the Porta di Nola are believed to be of the last period, though firmly in the Augustan tradition. One, without identification, had not been completed at the time of the eruption.[3] It was fitted into the acute angle between two roads, which gave it a rather odd shape, and tufa was used as a revetment for concrete, rather than as structural stone, but otherwise it resembles earlier scholae, having a classic lion's-paw termination and an altar behind the midpoint carved on the right side with a wicker cista mystica from which a serpent's head emerges and an elaborate torch to either side of this. The front of the altar is damaged; only the right half has survived. It shows the setting for an inscription on another stone, a crown of grain ears and a situla. The allusion is believed to be to the Bacchic mysteries. The freshness of the carving, the lack of a termination on the right side, and the absence of pavement in the area in front of the seat show that this was still under construction at the time of the eruption.

The schola of Aesquillia Polla, across the road from this in the obtuse angle between roads, is one of the prettiest tombs of Pompeii, a

---

[3]Cf. E. Pozzi, "Exedra funeraria pompeiana fuori porta di Nola," *RendNap* 35 (1960) 175–86.

seat of blocks of Nocera tufa finished at one end with a lion's-paw termination. It is interrupted at the middle by a plinth supporting an Ionic column. The plinth carries an inscription on a plate of marble identifying this as the tomb of Aesquillia Polla, who died at the age of twenty-two, wife of N. Herennius Celsus, twice duovir and praefectus fabrorum. The plot for the tomb was granted by decree of the decuriones, so presumably she died while he was in office. The column is given an Attic base and a Pompeian Ionic capital and is reeded the full height of the shaft. It carries a marble urn in the form of an amphora with ovoid body, elongated neck and handles, and a conical cover. At the four corners of the capital are menisci in the form of iron tridents. The general effect is charming, and against suitable planting it would be even more charming. The reeding of the column shaft, the support of the schola with a buttress of mortared masonry, and the marble embellishments are indication of a late date.

On the north side of the Via dei Sepolcri, tomb no. 9 offers a particularly interesting variation of the schola form. It is tucked between the tomb of the blue glass vase and the first of a long series of shops, entirely filling the space. It consists of a schola of tufa lifted a high step above the sidewalk and covered by a high half-dome of masonry faced with brickwork and veneered with painted stucco. The façade is framed by reeded Corinthian pilasters in two storeys without bases. The lower storey reaches to the impost of the half-dome; the upper storey springs directly above and supports a triangular pediment framed with a modillion cornice in which the rectangular marble plate for an inscription, uninscribed, is set. In the spandrels are Nereids mounted on searams. The deep arch of the entrance is decorated with coffering similar to that in the apodyterium of the Thermae Stabianae; the rest of the dome is treated as a great shell. The walls below this are decorated in a severe Fourth Style decoration with big red panels; the taste is entirely that of the very last years of Pompeii. This tomb belongs to the general group of schola tombs but is sharply differentiated from all the others, even those of the last period. The absence of an inscription is also puzzling; it would seem to indicate that though built as a tomb, this was never used.

Arch Tombs

The arch tomb has a similarly long history and continues to appear in the last period. In the Porta di Nocera necropolis, tomb east 28 (28 EN) consists of two stout piers of opus mixtum vittatum on a footing of masonry of broken lava veneered with white stucco. These should certainly be completed with an arch, but in the absence of finds of any sort, it is impossible to say how the superstructure might have developed. A second late arch tomb found farther to the east on the same road, number 1 of the Fondo Pacifico, was an arch surmounted by a tholos (*RömMitt* 3 [1888] 121–23 [A. Mau]). A third, a variation on the classic form, is south 1 on the Via dei Sepolcri, the tomb of M. Cerrinius Restitutus, a deep vaulted niche fitted into the space between the schola of A. Veius and the Porta di Ercolano (Kockel 47–51). From the road it appears to be a more substantial building than in fact it is, faced with reticulate coigned with small blocks and with walls of reticulate extending to either side. Its upper parts are lost, but the architecture suggests a deep attic. At the back of the niche is a small niche that contained a marble frame from which a herm appears to have been removed; the frame is inscribed with the name of M. Cerrinius Restitutus, Augustalis, and the information that the plot was granted by decree of the decuriones, as we might expect. In front of this stood a horned altar of travertine. A masonry bench lined each side wall of the niche, and others flanked the façade. Since M. Cerrinius Restitutus is known from the archive of L. Caecilius Iucundus to have been active in the years 56–62, a date after the earthquake is likely for the tomb. Aesthetically it presented the appearance and proportions of an arch while serving the functions of an aedicula.

Monuments of Unusual Form

Two unusual tombs of the last period are the funerary triclinium of the Via dei Sepolcri and the tetrapylon of the Porta di Nocera necropolis. The former, south 23, the tomb of Cn. Vibrius Saturninus, was erected by his freedman Callistus (Kockel 109–11). It is enclosed by a high wall of reticulate coigned with small blocks, the façade crowned by a low gable into which the marble plate of the inscription was let. On the interior, accessible by an axial door, the walls were painted with decorations in a rather severe Fourth Style. A masonry triclinium fills the inner half of the space, the bench running on three sides of a rectangular masonry table. Mazois shows another round table or base in front of this and on axis with it that has since disappeared (Mazois 1, pl. 20 [Kockel pl. 31b]). The tomb is thus very much the sort of triclinium one might expect to find in any Pompeian garden in a space decorated like a room. The high enclosure wall assured the diners privacy, but originally this may have been planned as a simple bustum, the triclinium added later.

The tetrapylon of the Porta di Nocera necropolis, tomb east 20 (20 EN) is one of the most imposing tombs of Pompeii. The footing is of masonry of broken lava supporting a base course of blocks of white limestone, above which rises a low podium faced with opus incertum coigned with opus mixtum vittatum and covered with white plaster.

In the centre of the main façade is a low arched niche. The podium is crowned with a cornice of stucco over a brickwork armature. The upper storey is composed of four clusters of four engaged columns at the four corners standing on unitary plinths veneered with stucco and finished at base and crown with moldings. The back of the monument was closed by a wall joining the two rear clusters, with suppression of two of the engaged columns, thus making a niche. Column bases and Corinthian capitals, of which nine are preserved, are of white marble. Nothing is preserved above this, and the crowning member may have taken a number of forms—pyramidal, quadrifrontal arch, or rectilinear attic. No inscription was found, and since the columns are bare of plaster today, the tomb may never have been finished. Good parallels for it are hard to find, although tetrapylon gateways, such as that of the sanctuary of Aphrodite at Aphrodisias (Crema 452), show clearly the origins of the form.

Inferences

Thus it appears that as in other things, the Pompeians were essentially traditionalist in their tomb architecture. While Romans in the capital and even so near to Pompeii as Puteoli and Capua were indulging in flights of fancy in the design of their tombs,[4] with rare exceptions the Pompeians clung to a few well-established forms and seldom embellished these pretentiously. They seem to have been more adventurous in the tombs of the first half of the century than they were after the earthquake. Possibly external forces were at work in this—the lack of money and the lack of an adequate work force. In any case, the restraint of these tombs is remarkable and refreshing when compared with the extravagance of other Flavian architecture.

[4]Cf. M. Eisner, *Zur Typologie der Grabbauten im Suburbium Roms* (Mainz 1986), and A. de Franciscis and R. Pane, *Mausolei romani in Campania* (Naples 1957) passim.

APPENDIX I

The Stones and Building Techniques
of Pompeii

Stones

Pappamonte stone (lava tenera). The hill of Pompeii is a mass of black volcanic matter liberally sprinkled with small beads of lime, variously known as pappamonte tufa and lava tenera, overlying strata of hard lava (trachite). It is cindery and friable along the exposed front, scarcely harder than packed earth, and can be readily dug out with a spade. In many places throughout the city it has been pierced with wells driven down to the water table of the Sarno Valley, which show that the stratum of pappamonte stone is relatively thin. It is poorer than the poorest Roman tufas and is unsuitable for building in any form. Maiuri found it scarped, slabs used in places in short stretches in a single footing course of the fortifications along the south side of the city, from which he concluded that there had once been a fortification of this stone (*NSc* 1939, 232–38 [A. Maiuri]). Not only is that conclusion unwarranted but it seems clear from the appearance of the base of the wall near the Porta di Nocera that the use of slabs of this material was never more than a terracing operation in preparation of a bed for blocks of Sarno limestone or Nocera tufa.

Sarno limestone. Sarno limestone is a coarse travertine, a secondary limestone formed in the lower valley of the Sarno River when the streams from the Apennines, heavy with lime, hit the warmer coastal plain of Campania, thickly strewn with volcanic springs, and the lime precipitates in the warm water. From Sarno to Pompeii this travertine, which is constantly forming, is quarried as part of agricultural work; otherwise the ground becomes swampy and sterile. It can be sawn into large blocks, and as such, it is fair building material but too deeply fissured to carve into anything but the simplest forms and of an unattractive, cold grey color. Its use for the capitals of the archaic Doric temple of Pompeii is not surprising, since at Paestum the temple builders used a similar local stone for the columns and evidently repaired its deficiencies with plugs and stucco. After the opening of the quarries of Nocera tufa, Sarno stone was sometimes used for unfluted column drums to be finished with stucco, but not for more delicately shaped members. It is used in large blocks in city buildings for footings and coigning and for façades. It is used extensively in the fortifications and the edging of streets. It is used in broken chunks up to the size of a loaf of bread in rubble masonry and incertum facing.

Much has been written about a so-called Limestone Period or Period of the Limestone Atria in Pompeii, a time when the architecture of the city used nothing but Sarno stone—in blocks for façades, in piled stands of blocks for the framework and coigning of walls, in broken chunks packed with clay for filling.[1] It is variously dated somewhere between the fifth and the third century B.C. and is entirely mythical. Sarno stone was always cheaper and more readily available than Nocera tufa; consequently, whereas Nocera tufa was used for façades, columns, and other carved members, impluvium floors and stylobates, places where it would be exposed to view, it was never used as primary material for the body of a wall. The handsomest tufa façades regularly stand on Sarno stone footings, and behind them the interior walls are framed and coigned with Sarno stone.[2] These all would have been covered with plaster and hidden from view; there was no reason to waste expensive stone in their construction. The local Sarno stone was not only cheaper, it was relatively light and very durable. Whether we should see the time of packing broken Sarno stone in clay as a phase antedating the general use of mortar must also be doubted. In the form of stucco, mortar is as old as the archaic period, and it appears in regular use by the beginning of the third century B.C. It seems unlikely that any house we see in Pompeii is that old; therefore the use of clay must be a matter of convenience or economy rather than a necessity. When a wall was to be covered with plaster, if the wall was framed with large blocks, the packing would not be dangerously weakened by this use of clay. And the façades of limestone blocks were merely a simpler and cheaper version of the façades in Nocera tufa, appearing in houses of the same plan and proportions as these and always with a tufa impluvium in the atrium.[3] Had the owner so wished, he might have had his façade stuccoed to imitate tufa.

[1]Fiorelli 1873, 78–83; Nissen 49–53, 397–457; Overbeck and Mau 500–502; Mau 1908, 36–38.

[2]E.g., the Casa del Fauno, the Casa di Pansa, the Casa della Fontana Grande, and the Casa di Sallustio (cf. Maiuri 1973, 162–63, 169).

[3]See Maiuri 1973, 9–10, where he states that the evidence shows that there was no

Nocera tufa. The warm brown to grey stone sprinkled with black scoriae that is generally known as Nocera tufa is quarried all along the foothills of the Monti Lattari, the spine of the Sorrentine Peninsula opposite Pompeii. It may have been carted to Pompeii from some of these, as well as brought by barge down the river. It seems always to have been a moderately expensive stone and quarried in large rectangular blocks. It is a well-compacted volcanic ash that breaks with a conchoidal fracture and can be carved with greater flamboyance than any stone in regular use in Pompeii, except marble. It is used by the beginning of the second century B.C. for façades and carved members: columns, architraves, and cornices, altars and impluvia, puteals and lintels. It is not really suitable for inscription, because of its color, but is occasionally used. It continues in regular use at least down to the Augustan period, where we find it the commonest stone for fine tombs. It is ultimately displaced in favor only by marble.[4] Besides its nobler uses, one should note that thresholds and edging blocks of this tufa are fairly common and that before the installation of a limestone pavement the forum of Pompeii was paved with cement framed by a double file of slabs of Nocera tufa (Maiuri 1973, 66–70). It seems an unsuitable stone for pavements, but there is a broad walk around the inside of the porticus of the Aedes Apollinis in slabs of this stone, and the stair to the Temple of Jupiter is built of it. Except as broken material in rubblework, it is not used as caementa. In buildings where it is used throughout for finishing members the body of the walls is entirely of other stone, Sarno stone for the most part, sometimes lapis pompeianus.

Lapis pompeianus. Lapis pompeianus is the hard, heavy, grey to blue-black volcanic stone now known to geologists as vicoite, commonly called lava, sometimes trachite. It was used in the manufacture of grain mills, olive pulpers, and similar apparatus and was prized for its quality as early as the time of Cato the Elder, who recommended that all one's mills should be obtained from either Pompeii or Nola (Cato *Agr.* 22.3–4, 135.2). The quarries have never been located; presumably they lie on the slopes of Vesuvius above Pompeii, and the stone was worked at the quarries. It appears in Pompeii in the Tufa Period, first for thresholds, edging, and paving blocks; for pavings it is worked in polygonal shapes, tightly fitted. It can be carved in simple shapes, and we find it used in window frames, cistern heads,

---

impluvium in the Casa del Chirurgo antedating the present tufa basin. Yet it is impossible to imagine an atrium testudinatum of the size and architecture of the atrium of this house.

[4]The tomb of Mamia P. f. sacerdos publica, who built the Temple of the Genius Augusti (*CIL* 10.816), is a schola of tufa (*CIL* 10.998). That of Eumachia is a more elaborate edifice largely of tufa.

drain covers, and stair treads through the first century B.C. Ultimately cores for Doric capitals to be finished with stucco were cut in this stone, and most of the standards of the public fountains of Pompeii are carved in it. In broken chunks it makes excellent building stone, and masonry exclusively of this stone in moderately heavy beds of mortar, often with coigning of brick, is characteristic of the early years of the Roman colony (80–50 B.C.). It is used widely throughout the city in the construction of vaulted cellars, even being roughly shaped into voussoirs, though these are more commonly of Sarno stone.

White limestone (Caserta stone). A fine-grained white limestone with very few veins or flaws is used for thresholds, impluvium rims, cistern heads, strongbox bases, puteals, cartibula, and the like. This is a secondary limestone deposited in thin strata but with the inclusion of very little foreign matter, so it is compact and hard, with little tendency to chip or spall. Its earliest appearance may have been in the large tesserae used to make decorative patterns in signinum pavements and in chips the size of coarse gravel used as a paving surface, a precursor of mosaic. It is used for the mensa ponderaria of the forum, which dates from Samnite times and was recut to the Roman standard after the deduction of the colony (Mau 1908, 88–89; Sogliano 194); it is also used for some of the few important public inscriptions in Oscan that survive.[5] Later it appears for two of the public fountains and for the colonnades of the forum in the course of construction at the time of the eruption and the pavement laid at the north end of the forum sometime earlier, before the earthquake.[6] It is not used at all in the basilica or the Theatrum Tectum, except for the inscriptions commemorating its building (*CIL* 10.844). It is used for the altar of the Aedes Apollinis, which carries a crown of marble and an inscription of the magistrates responsible for its erection (*CIL* 10.800); here the absence of cognomina indicates a republican date, but the letter forms are relatively close to the Augustan alphabet. It is used extensively in the base of the podium of the Temple of Fortuna Augusta, the lowest four steps and the altar platform being faced entirely with this stone. The base of the arch east of the Temple of Jupiter (Arco di Tiberio) is also faced with blocks of this stone, while

---

[5] See E. Vetter, *Handbuch der italische Dialekte* (Heidelberg 1953) 46–54.

[6] On this pavement see A. W. Van Buren, *MAAR* 2 (1918) 70–71 and 5 (1925) 104–5. The complete absence of so much of the whole must lead us to suppose that it was salvaged after the eruption of A.D. 79. One notes that it had already been patched east of the Temple of Jupiter where an arch, destroyed before the earthquake of 62, had stood.

the upper parts, to be covered with plates of marble, are faced with brick. So probably this stone was used only for inscriptions and limestone-chip pavements down to the time of the deduction of the colony and came into use for ornamental work shortly thereafter. It must have been largely displaced by marble for inscriptions after the beginning of the Augustan period, but it continued in use for thresholds and pavements down to the destruction of the city. It is not a local stone and may have been carted all the way from Caserta, where quarries of it are known; but most of the blocks of this stone in Pompeii are large, and some of the threshold blocks are massive.

Cruma. A dark red solidified volcanic foam, rather like slag or a very coarse pumice, cruma is found occasionally used as building material in walls of random rubblework. It is frequently associated with lapis pompeianus, usually appearing in the upper parts of walls. Though it is one of the lightest of volcanic stones, it does not appear to have been employed for lightening vaults. It cannot be cut or carved, except into crude reticulate blocks, and its use is random.

White marble. Fine-grained marble, white or white veined with grey or blue, from the north Italian quarries of Luna appears in Pompeii toward the end of the republican period. It is used for statuary and reliefs of all sizes, from tiny garden figures of animals less than a foot long to the colossal head of the cult statue of Jupiter. In architecture it was used extensively in the Temple of Venus and the Temple of Fortuna Augusta for all carved and molded elements and was used as veneer over the lower parts of walls. In private houses it was used for cartibula, often richly carved, for garden furniture and fountains, rarely for a sundial or jamb capital, and as veneer for impluvium linings, window sills, statue bases, and the like. Its one purely practical use seems to have been for mortars; these are relatively common, sometimes large. On rare occasions it was used as a kickplate around the base of a wall or for revetment of a room. Clearly there were marble workers in Pompeii ready to do work of almost any sort on order.[7]

Large crystalled Greek marble is almost unknown in Pompeii, except for sculpture, but a large fountain basin in the Forum Triangulare facing the statue of Marcellus as patronus coloniae is of Greek marble.

Colored marble. The very common use of fragments of colored marble

[7] Cf. the Casa del Marmorista (VIII vii 24).

in the revetment of counters in cookshops and wineshops has led to the supposition that these were the broken remains of plates damaged in the earthquake of A.D. 62. No real proof that this is the case, however, has been forthcoming. These may be the scraps left over from other work and secondhand material of any sort. The only statue base on the forum of Pompeii that retains its marble veneer is revetted with africano (from Teos); in the Augusteum there is part of an inscribed slab of cipollino (from Euboea); and the pavement of the orchestra of the Theatrum Tectum is of pavonazzetto, cipollino, africano, and giallo antico, marbles that came into general availability about the middle of the first century B.C. Bits of banded alabaster and other marblelike colored stones are used in the pavement of the porticoes of the Villa dei Misteri. Elsewhere we find portasanta and a grey-and-white mottled marble. More exotic stones are virtually unknown.

Beginning in the time of the Second Style colored stones are used in small fragments and plates of various geometric shapes to decorate pavements (Casa del Fauno), and later they are combined with a mosaic ground to give a randomly scattered effect (Casa del Criptoportico, Villa dei Misteri). Colored marbles gradually replace other colored stones and become common in the time of the Third Style (Casa di Lucrezio Frontone). Opus sectile, except in small panels of simple geometric forms, is rare (Casa dell'Efebo, Casa di Fabio Rufo). Public buildings of the last period were sometimes revetted with colored marble, but rooms in private houses so decorated are rare (Casa dei Dioscuri, Casa di Sallustio).

Terracotta and brick. The oldest terracottas in Pompeii are decorative architectural terracottas from the archaic Doric temple and the Aedes Apollinis, belonging to the sixth century. These are well pressed, and their color is fired on, so they appear fresh and strong today. In style they belong with terracottas from Capua and Cumae, and clearly the makers thoroughly understood their art. Thereafter at Pompeii a broken sequence of decorative terracottas runs down to the destruction of the city. For the most part these are simas, especially compluvium simas with rainspouts in the form of animal heads or forequarters, and antefixes. Temple terracottas do not continue beyond the early Hellenistic period, and the few plaques approaching the so-called Campana type that have been found appear to have been merely decorative in purpose.[8] We may presume that together with these there was a sequence of roof tiles, but these have not been collected, classified, or dated.

[8]See H. von Rohden, *Die Terracotten von Pompeji* (Die antiken Terracotten, vol. 1, Stuttgart 1880) 1–39 and pls. 1–24.

The first structural use of terracotta appears to have been in the columns of the nave of the basilica of about 125 B.C. There pieces of heavy plates as thick as modern brick have been carefully molded and chipped into shape and then mortared together to make the cores of great columns. At the centre of each is a relatively small disc, and the shaping of the fragments fitted around this is very expert. Shortly thereafter we find stacks of similar discs used as the cores of the columns of the second peristyle of the Casa del Fauno, and from then on such cores are not uncommon, and for private houses probably the rule. In the so-called Palestra Grande, probably of early Augustan date, all the columns are of stucco over a core of fine brickwork using specially shaped bricks (*NSc* 1939, 177–82 [A. Maiuri]). The Porticus Tulliana on the Via del Foro is of similar construction (Maiuri 1942, 176–77), and in postearthquake repairs masonry column construction is very common.

Terracotta was also used in plates as a base for woodwork. We find it covering the treads of stairs and the frames of doors and windows, where telltale grooves in the wall coats often show that there was once a wooden covering. Very occasionally it is used to line walls as a protection for the wallcoat against damp (Casa del Fauno). It regularly lines the walls and floors of bath rooms and regularly covers the top of hearths. It is used for grilles to fill windows; in sleeved sections for drainpipes and downspouts to convey rain from roofs and gutters; and, in the form of tiles with deep-eaved lanterns attached, to light and ventilate dark corridors and cramped kitchens (Casa del Centenario, Casa di Giulio Polibio).

Its first use as brick appears to have been in the Theatrum Tectum, where it is used for coigning, the coigns toothed in triangles into the body of the wall. This appears still to be broken roof tile, rather than true brick, but it is used throughout the building. In the Augustan period brick coigning is still much less common than coigning in small blocks. Its employment for finishing and for points of stress continues into the last period of Pompeii; one sees it clearly in the three buildings at the south end of the forum.

The building on the east (curia) has brick coigns in the parts surviving from an earlier building and in the last period was given a new front on the forum and an arch separating its apse from the main room faced entirely with brick. The building in the centre, still in construction at the time of the eruption, has a brick-faced façade and a high brick-faced bench along each side wall but rubblework above this. The western building is faced with brick throughout its lower parts. Brick, it would appear, was an expensive material, to be used for strength and for protection against damp. In the Terme Centrali we find it used with great freedom throughout the bath rooms and as dressing and coigning throughout the whole complex (Maiuri 1942, 74–77). It is also used extensively in the bibliotheca, in the honorific arches around the forum, and in the scene building of the Theatrum Maius. The only house in which it is used lavishly is the Casa di Vibio (VII ii 18).[9]

Building Techniques

Tufa Period, 200–80 B.C.[10] House façades through the first part of the Tufa Period are of three readily identifiable types: (*a*) large blocks of Nocera tufa, undrafted in the socle, drafted above, laid dry in regularly staggered courses, often finished with pilasters, especially at jambs and corners; (*b*) large blocks of Sarno limestone, more rarely Nocera tufa, without drafting, laid in courses without special attention to the staggering of joints, occasionally (Casa di Spurio Messore) with limestone and tufa blocks in the same façade; (*c*) blocks of Sarno limestone set in vertical stands to coign corners and doorways and, when necessary, to strengthen wall joints, the interstices filled with smaller material, for the most part chunks of broken Sarno limestone (sometimes called limestone framework masonry, sometimes carpentry style).[11] The range here is very great; in some façades, such as the south façade of block VI xiii, the filling amounts to little more than snecking in the parts that remain, though in the higher parts, especially over the shop doors, one would expect large expanses of filling. In others (e.g., the façades in block V iii) the filling amounts to more than half the wall and is carefully laid, the broken stone skillfully set in tightly packed courses. But (*c*) seems always to have been intended for stuccoing and might have been finished to resemble, or counterfeit, (*a*). The latter occasionally has a thin coat of hard stucco applied to pilasters and jamb capitals but is commonly left plain. The second type, (*b*), often shows a coat of plaster over the lower parts, a high socle not treated decoratively and perhaps never original, but these façades clearly seem not to have been considered of aesthetic interest.

[9]Cf. A. Maiuri 1942, 121–24.

[10]Tufa continues to be used for decorative elements down to A.D. 14, or later.

[11]These three types have been discussed and classified by many students of Pompeii, notably Overbeck and Mau (497–503) and R. C. Carrington (in *JRS* 23 [1933] 125–38). The dates assigned them and the relative chronology are based only on style and will not stand up to close examination. The beginnings of the style are set far too early (cf., e.g., the houses of Priene and Delos), and differences in wealth are seen as differences in date. The Casa del Chirurgo is thus seen as preceding the Casa del Fauno by at least a century, but their plans, proportions, and aesthetic are so close that they cannot really be very far apart in time.

Façades of drafted tufa blocks commonly have doorways trimmed with pilasters and surmounted with ornamental lintels. Main doorways may be very wide and high, sometimes with doors in leaves that folded back on one another. The more elaborate houses have carved capitals to finish the jambs, either of a somewhat simplified Corinthian design (Casa del Fauno, Casa di Pansa) or a Corinthian design in which half-figures or heads fill the area between the volutes (Casa dei Capitelli Colorati, Casa dei Capitelli Figurati). Jamb capitals of other orders are rare, but the doorways of the Terme Stabiane surviving from the Tufa Period all have simplified Doric jambs. All such doorways are regularly surmounted by a deep architrave, often divided into two equal fasciae, and a cornice of which the principal feature is a base line of tightly set dentils capped by a plain overhang of the same depth. In a fairly common variation of this the jamb capitals are replaced by plain rectangular blocks. Maiuri considered these a primitive form of jamb capital that persisted after the introduction of carved orders;[12] but it is evident that they really originated as unfinished members that became popular as a form of rustication. Proof of this is the cenacula of I vi 7, the Fullonica Stephani, and IX xii 1–5, where block capitals are combined with half-columns with Ionic fluting and bases.

In this period interior walls are regularly a version of the third style of façade masonry, limestone framework or carpentry style, and can be found all over the city. Variations show that it was not the product of a small group of builders or a short period but the prevalent building technique throughout more than a century. Admixture of material other than Sarno limestone is rare and may always be due to later repairs. Toward the last quarter of the second century B.C. broken lava (lapis pompeianus) becomes a substitute for Sarno limestone as the popular building material for filling and interior walls. A harder, heavier stone whose smoother fractures did not make it especially suitable for packing, it is soon regularly laid in moderately heavy beds of mortar, eventually without use of coigning or framing, except in somewhat larger chunks of lava. Footings laid in trenches, as well as walls, come to be built of this, and the only parts in cut stone are then columns and moldings, stairs and façades. The basilica, which still has a façade in drafted blocks of classic design, is an early example of this style of building, the towers and Porta Marina of the city walls, rebuilt after the deduction of the Roman colony and entirely of stucco-faced masonry without any coigning in cut stone, being a late example. In its final form this masonry approaches opus

---

[12] A. Maiuri, "Portali con capitelli cubici a Pompei," *RendNap* 33 (1958) 203–18.

incertum, the interior of a wall of any thickness being a concrete of mortar and small fragments of lava, the faces only built up of larger stone, but few walls in Pompeii are so thick, and Pompeian masons seem habitually to have worked with individual stones, mortaring each into place and then bringing the wall to a level at regular intervals to set, work done with lines and plumb bobs rather than with wooden forms. So properly speaking, there is little opus incertum in Pompeii.

Work of the early Roman colony, 80–50 B.C. With the arrival of the Roman colony, we notice some changes in building technique. The masonry continues to be of broken lava in bearing walls of any load, in lava and broken Sarno stone elsewhere. Carved members are of Nocera tufa in the Theatrum Tectum, the amphitheatre, and the Temple of Jupiter. The exterior stairs of the amphitheatre have treads of well-cut blocks of lava. The retaining wall and its buttresses are faced with incertum of broken lava coigned with blocks of tufa and Sarno limestone, and the buttresses are joined to one another by vaults built of unshaped wedges set in mortar on centering and trimmed on the exterior face with cut voussoirs of tufa and Sarno stone. These vaults are barrel vaults, as are all others in the entrance tunnels, while those in the annular corridors are segmental with sharp shoulders. The triangular brick coigning of the Theatrum Tectum seems to be unique.

In houses of this period one notes the continuance of tufa for carved members (atrium of the Casa delle Nozze d'Argento, peristyle of the Villa dei Misteri) and an increase in the use of stuccoed columns of simple form (peristyle and tetrastyle oecus of the Casa delle Nozze d'Argento). The faceting of the lowest third of Doric columns appears a little before the beginning of this period (Casa dei Dioscuri, Ludus Gladiatorius) and apparently grows in popularity until by the end of the period it has become regular in porticoes much in public use. Colonnaded loggias (cenacula) along exterior fronts also seem to be characteristic of this period; they were probably introduced in interior use for summer dining rooms about the middle of the second century.[13]

---

[13]Cf. Varro *Ling.* 5.162. Faceting of the lower shafts of columns seems to appear first in the Stoa of Attalus in Athens in the middle of the second century. It is used only with the Doric order. The tufa shafts of some of the columns of the palaestra of the Terme Stabiane are faceted to their full height. If these belong with the other Tufa Period construction in this complex, as seems likely, they should be dated late in the second half of the second century (see Nissen 155–56; and Eschebach 1979, 68), but they are a type very uncommon in Pompeii.

Julio-Claudian construction, 30 B.C.–A.D. 62. The striking innovation in construction in this period is the use of small, well-cut blocks of Nocera tufa and Sarno limestone. These appear in the facing of the system of standpipes that were erected at the time of the introduction of the aqueduct to maintain pressure in the pipes supplying the individual buildings and houses, all of which appear to be part of a single public program. The aqueduct was possible thanks to Agrippa's work on the Portus Iulius in the thirties and the great Serino aqueduct.[14] The same blocks appear in the circuit wall of the Aedificium Eumachiae and the Temple of the Genius Augusti, where they can be seen in walls that are decorated with shallow panels crowned with low pediments, alternately triangular and segmental. Here we see flat arches with voussoirs cut in the same stones, the whole finished with stucco. In the Palestra Grande we find masonry in such blocks around the doors on the north side and in the pyramidal merlons that crown the east wall, parts of the original construction (*NSc* 1939, 202–14 [A. Maiuri]).

It is impossible to say whether opus reticulatum appeared in Pompeii before the earthquake of 62. In the Theatrum Tectum and the Temple of Jupiter Meilichios the facing is so close to reticulate that it is often described as quasireticulate, and both belong before 50 B.C. Yet there is no reticulate in the public buildings that can with assurance be given an Augustan date, and it is only in some of the undated tombs that reticulate appears that might be pre-earthquake. Clearly, it was not in common use then.

Postearthquake construction, A.D. 62–79.[15] Three styles of masonry are readily identifiable as postearthquake: (*a*) rubblework or concrete faced with reticulate, (*b*) masonry faced with brick and masonry coigned at corners and openings with brickwork in regular square keys, and (*c*) masonry faced or coigned with opus mixtum vittatum (also called opus mixtum listatum), a combination of courses of small blocks alternating with two or more courses of brick or tile, sometimes with bands of brick that make leveling courses. But since the Pompeians had the debris of the earthquake to dispose of and commonly got rid of as much of this as possible by reusing it as stone and caementa in rubblework and concrete masonry, we can go further and say that any wall containing significant amounts of broken

---

[14] *NSc* 1938, 75–97 (I. Sgobbo); O. Elia, "Un tratto dell'acquedotto detto 'Claudio' in territorio di Sarno," *Campania romana, Studi e materiali* 1 (Naples 1938) 101–11; I. Sgobbo, "L'acquedotto romano della Campania: 'Fontis Augustei Aquaeductus,'" *NSc* 1928, 75–97.

[15] On postearthquake construction in general see Maiuri 1942.

marble or fine limestone, the stones used earlier for finishing and ornamental work, or any wall containing a significant amount of terracotta as rubble will be postearthquake. And the yellow tufa of Naples, quarried from Pizzofalcone to Puteoli, came to Pompeii in quantity only after the earthquake, so a wall containing a significant amount of this must belong to the last period of the city.

Reticulate blocks are cut of yellow tufa, Nocera tufa, and red cruma, much more rarely of Sarno limestone. The walls of the Temple of Venus are faced almost entirely with yellow tufa reticulate coigned with small blocks of the same stone. The relieving arches over the shop doors along the forum front of the macellum are filled with masonry faced with yellow tufa reticulate, while they themselves have voussoirs of Nocera tufa above piers that are faced with brick, a common combination. Except in the Temple of Venus, reticulate is not common in Pompeii and tends to be used ornamentally. One notes façades along the Strada Consolare, the Via di Nola, and the Strada Stabiana where stripes, checkerboards, and chevron patterns have been made in reticulate of two contrasting sorts of stone, a phenomenon not uncommon in reticulate elsewhere in Italy.[16] These would hardly have been introduced were the wall to be immediately stuccoed over. In the necropolis outside the Porta di Nocera the tomb of C. Cuspius Cyrus has a base faced with brick surmounted by a drum faced with patterned reticulate (Jashemski 149, fig. 234), and in the Via dei Sepolcri necropolis a number of tombs and walls of reticulate seem to have been left exposed to view at least temporarily.

Brick (fashioned from roof tile) having been in use since the time of the deduction of the Roman colony, it is not always possible to decide immediately whether a brick-faced wall is pre- or postearthquake. In the easternmost hall on the south side of the forum the front of the building is a postearthquake modification faced with brick, while the back with brick coigning is presumably preearthquake. The Terme Centrali, still unfinished at the time of the eruption, are clearly postearthquake. The bibliotheca, which has only coigning in brick, must be substantially, if not entirely, postearthquake, and the market building and latrine in the northwest corner of the forum, which seem still to lack the finish they would have been given, are of similar construction.

On the other hand, opus mixtum vittatum, the combination of courses of small blocks alternating with two or more courses of brick,

---

[16] See G. Lugli, *La tecnica edilizia romana* (Rome 1957) 489–91.

is readily identifiable, and nowhere that it occurs does it appear to be pre-earthquake. In public buildings we find it in the Porta di Ercolano and the superstructure of the amphitheatre.[17] In private buildings it seems almost ubiquitous and is used not only for walls but for piers and columns as well. Some very intricate use of it also appears in tombs.

[17] Maiuri (1942, 83–84) holds that the superstructure of the amphitheatre must be part of the original design even if actually constructed some time after the lower parts. In this he follows M. Girosi, "L'anfiteatro di Pompei," *MemNap* 5 (1936) 27–57, esp. 48–50. But in the absence of good examples of opus mixtum vittatum datable to a time before the earthquake, it seems best to see the brick-faced buttresses introduced to reinforce opus mixtum vittatum sectors as modifications necessary to the rigging of the velaria rather than repair of earthquake damage and to date the whole superstructure of the complex to the last period of Pompeii.

APPENDIX II

The Development of the Pompeian House

The history of the atrium house before the Hellenistic period is a matter of speculation. If it derives ultimately from the Italic hut that we see in the hut urns of Latium and southern Etruria, as seems most likely, it is essentially the result of dividing the space under a unitary roof by introducing nonbearing walls to make rooms for sleeping and storage around a large central area. The centre will have served as a lobby on which these opened, and its names, *atrium* and *cavum aedium*, suggest that it was originally covered over, what Vitruvius calls testudinatum, and dark. Since if it was covered, the only source of light readily available to it would have been the main door, it is likely that exedral wings reaching from the central lobby to the outer wall, forerunners of the alae of the Pompeian atrium, were left so that windows could be introduced here, but this would have to have been in a time when the house normally stood free of any adjacent building, surrounded by its farmyard and garden, a time before the building of anything we see in Pompeii.

The alternative to this is to suppose that the atrium grew from the coalition of rooms around a courtyard. This development has been suggested by the evidence of the early houses of Cosa, a Latin colony founded in 273 B.C. Here one entered the house down a narrow axial corridor between small rooms and emerged in a large central lobby beyond which lay the principal rooms for living arranged in a block. Beyond these, in turn, was a spacious open area roughly as deep as the rest of the house, the hortus. Rain water was collected along the street front and garden front of the house and piped back into a cistern under the central lobby.[1] The excavator, F. E. Brown, proposes to roof such a house with simple shed roofs front and back, leaving

---

[1] F. E. Brown, *Cosa: The Making of a Roman Town* (Ann Arbor, Mich. 1980) 63–66 and figs. 81–83.

the central lobby roofless. It seems simpler and more logical to cover the whole with a roof of two slopes so that the central lobby becomes in effect a simple atrium testudinatum, which would better agree with the evidence of the water collection and at the same time make a more habitable dwelling. Windows for lighting the central lobby could be arranged in the side walls, or skylights could be lifted in the roof. Moreover, the new evidence from Marzabotto seems to show conclusively that a compluviate atrium plan, complete with tablinum and alae, had already been developed there by the fourth century.[2] If this was the case, the Cosan houses, as a type, seem hopelessly primitive.

In a series of excavations carried out in the 1930s and 1940s, A. Maiuri demonstrated that the great houses of Pompeii are relatively late in date. Contrary to what had been believed earlier, in house after house near the forum the great limestone atria were found to be no older than the second century B.C., and in one house, the Casa del Gallo (VIII v 2/5), certain mason's marks seemingly in the Latin alphabet led Maiuri to conclude that the house could not antedate the foundation of the Roman colony. One may doubt the precise value of this last bit of evidence, since Pompeii had been exposed to strong Roman influence at least since the Second Punic War, and the date of the change of mason's marks is hardly likely to have depended on the arrival of the Roman colony. But the general conclusion drawn from these excavations not only is unassailable but now is supported by the results of a number of excavations at other sites in the Mediterranean: great private houses with luxurious rooms for the entertainment of guests were a phenomenon of the later Hellenistic age, not the earlier. Despite glaring differences in construction technique, there is little, if any, difference in date among houses of the same plan and architectural aesthetic.

The oldest house plan surviving in use in Pompeii in A.D. 79 seems to be that of a group of houses generally neglected as poor and of small interest and usually so much rebuilt in later times that the original house plan is hardly recognizable. Two excellent examples, however, side by side, VI xi 12 and 13, permit recognition of the type, and its occurrence elsewhere in the city confirms its antiquity and importance. In essence it consists of a rectangular unit, deeper than broad, that presents a lofty façade along the street but does not fill its plot. The façade is broken by an imposing axial doorway out of scale with the rest giving onto a corridor (fauces) leading back to a central lobby on which open the minor apartments. The lobby is rectangular in plan and extends the full width of the rectangular unit, rooms open-

---

[2]G. A. Mansuelli, "La casa etrusca a Marzabotto," *RömMitt* 70 (1963) 44–62.

ing off it front and back. In the side walls windows could be arranged but are not in the surviving examples, thanks probably only to the proximity of other buildings. There is no impluvium. To either side of the fauces are rooms lit by windows to the street that might have served any of a variety of purposes but are more apt to have been bedrooms than anything else. Opposite the entrance on the far side of the central lobby seems to have opened an arrangement of two rooms with a passage between, similar to that in front, though the passage was sometimes, perhaps regularly, off-axis, so one of the flanking rooms was much larger than the other, and usually these rooms were deeper than those flanking the fauces. These rooms were lit by windows to a courtyard or garden behind the house, to which the passage led. In the best-preserved examples, VI xi 12 and I xiv 6/7, the larger room appears to have been a dining room.

This rectangular unit must have been covered with a simple roof of two slopes, front and back, from a peak over the cross axis of the central lobby, and the evidence of drainage and water collection suggests that this was the rule. In early houses at Cosa the water was piped from the front façade to a cistern under the lobby, and that may have been the case at Pompeii—at least it would suit the evidence of I xiv 6/7. In other examples it seems to have been only the water from the rear slope that was collected, and this was impounded in a cistern in the rear court. Such is the case of I xiv 3.

The important characteristics of this house plan as an architectural form are its simplicity and organic unity and its obvious relation to an atrium complex. This house does not provide for any of the humbler and more necessary functions of life. The central lobby, which we may be justified in calling an atrium testudinatum, despite its rudimentary plan, was the common room of the house. Here presumably most of the activities that required shelter were performed. The rooms flanking the house door were bedrooms or storerooms, and there were other such rooms, sometimes in a second storey above these accessible by a stairway in the atrium. When there was a large room at the back, it seems to have been a dining room. And in at least one case the room on the opposite side of the back corridor was divided, the back part used for the latrine. By and large, however, the latrine, like the kitchen and stables, had no place in the atrium complex. Since even in the last period of the city the kitchen of a Pompeian house was regularly a courtyard off which the latrine might open, this should excite no wonder. But if this is the original atrium plan, the atrium is difficult to derive from the capanna of hut-urn type, since a change in the axis of the roof, a radical reorientation, is involved.

But the plan is not only one that is being found with increasing frequency in Italy in the third and second centuries B.C., it is a plan that was remarkably persistent at Pompeii, continuing in use and being built with variations at least through the end of the republican period. In the southeastern quarter of the city, among the dwellings of the poorer sort, it is astonishingly common, considering its short-comings. Yet these houses show none of the hallmarks of high antiquity and are finished in a utilitarian fashion or very simply decorated. The basic unit can be best seen in I ix 8; I xi 12,13, and 14; I xii 16, and I xiv 3 and 6/7, in addition to the genuinely old examples, VI xi 12 and 13. Variations in the pattern are not uncommon; in some the central lobby is made square, or deeper than broad (as in I iii 24), or is reduced to a corridor (as in I xiii 11), while in others it seems itself to have become an unroofed or partially roofed courtyard (as in II viii 6).

The steps between this original unit and the atria of Vitruvius are easy to see but not easy to set in their proper sequence. One is the change in the roofing, the creation of a light over the centre of the atrium toward which the surrounding roofs converged so the rain from these could be caught in a basin beneath and kept much cleaner than that brought from a street façade. Another is the addition of further rooms at the sides of the central lobby, so that it grew larger and gradually changed axis to become the complex familiar to us from the great houses of Pompeii. The former is apt to have taken place in an urban context, where land was expensive and the houses were built against one another. The latter is more apt to have been invented where space was abundant and the wish of the owner was for more rooms in the house unit without having to resort to the expedient of a second storey. Probably the two developments were not far apart in time, and independent of one another; in cities like Pompeii, which had densely built-up areas around the forum and along the main streets and yet included big gardens and vineyards within the circuit of the walls, there would have been the conditions requisite for both. And since in Pompeii old tetrastyle atria most often had two storeys of rooms around them, while Tuscanic atria of the older period regularly had only one, it is tempting to see the tetra-style atrium as somewhat older and invented precisely for the congested heart of the city.

The type of the earliest impluviate atrium may then be seen in the Casa di Ceio (I vi 15), [3] which preserves all the characteristics of early testudinate atria: axial fauces flanked by small rooms and somewhat deeper rooms beyond the atrium, with the corridor to the garden off-axis, so that one of these becomes a large room for entertaining, while

[3] See Spinazzola 1953, 1.257–74.

the atrium itself is approximately square, and rooms in a second storey both front and back accessible by separate stairways.

Another example of an early tetrastyle atrium house, perhaps slightly later than the Casa di Ceio, is the Casa della Grata Metallica (I ii 28), of which the original parts are the atrium and the rooms opening off this front and back. The façade and most of the east wall were subsequently rebuilt, but coigns and stands of limestone blocks prove that the rebuilding followed the original lines of the walls, while all the back parts of the house are accretions and additions of various later dates. Here one has the simple scheme of the traverse atrium house with the atrium enlarged and turned to continue the axis of the fauces, and the rooms beyond the atrium are now developed as a central exedra, or tablinum, and a pair of cubicula flanking it. There were rooms in an upper storey probably from the beginning, given the proportions of the cubicula and the organization of the house unit. One is struck by the strong resemblance of this house to the Casa Sannitica of Herculaneum in everything but scale and the form of the atrium, which there is Tuscanic.

The atrium houses of Pompeii are by and large impluviate, which is to say that the atrium is lit by a rectangular opening in the centre of the roof, the compluvium, over a basin sunk in the floor, the impluvium, in which the rain was collected. This development obviated the need for windows in the side walls and meant that buildings could now abut on one another for maximum utilization of space along thoroughfares, but it brought problems of its own. Foremost among these was the problem of roof design, the change from a single transverse rooftree from which the slopes of the roof descended to either side, with subsidiary roofs front and back, to a roof supported on a pair of beams bounding parallel ends of the compluvium between which others at right angles to these could be hung. Beyond this there was the problem of disposing of the rain that was collected.

Vitruvius (6.3.1–2) distinguished four sorts of impluviate atria: Tuscanic, tetrastyle, Corinthian, and displuviate. In the first three the roof is pitched inward to throw a maximum of rain through the compluvium, generally provided for this purpose with a sima with ornamental spouts, and thence into the impluvium. In the displuviate the roof is pitched the other way, toward the perimeter, to throw off as much rain as possible. Since Italy is dry in the summer and water is therefore precious, we may presume that the displuviate atrium was the oldest of these and goes back to a stage only one remove from the testudinate, when the house stood free and the rain was collected in gutters around the eaves and stored in tanks and cisterns nearby. For by the time houses abutted on one another the problem of how and where to store rain collected in a trough between two roofs at the top of the wall and the likelihood of damage to the wall from water standing in this trough must have made this the least popular of the types. It would have admitted the most light but also would have allowed rain the widest splash.

In Pompeii far the commonest type of atrium is the Tuscanic, columnless, while the tetrastyle and the Corinthian, in which the compluvium is supported, respectively, by columns at the corners and multiple columns, are variants used only sparingly, often in conjunction with a Tuscanic atrium. It seems never to have been a question of size, for while the largest atrium in Pompeii is the tetrastyle atrium of the Casa delle Nozze d'Argento, in two-atrium houses the smaller atrium is likely to be the columnar one, while it is hard to find any grander architecture than the Tuscanic atria of the Casa del Fauno and the Casa di Sallustio.

As we see it in its classic form in Pompeii, the Tuscanic atrium was approached down a short axial corridor from the main door. The doorway is impressive for its height and breadth, often trimmed at its jambs with pilasters, which are sometimes given richly carved, occasionally figured, capitals and are regularly surmounted by a projecting lintel that drew attention to and defined the house as belonging to nobility. Though the rest of the façade might be harmoniously handsome in fine drafted ashlar, nothing was allowed to detract from the preeminence of the door; it drew the eye and by its amplitude invited entrance. Its sumptuousness of material and fittings were designed to impress the visitor, but it was also on ceremonial occasions to stand fully open and then to afford an unimpeded view of the interior. The door was usually of two main leaves, rarely of four hinged together in pairs. Usually there was a smaller door cut in one of the leaves or set to one side for use when the house was closed to the general public. The great doors have never been recovered, though their fittings of bronze rings and bosses are familiar, but in the Casa di Loreio Tiburtino one can see a plaster cast that shows what such a door was like, studded with rows of large ornamental nails. From representations of doors in wall decorations and other evidence it appears that ordinarily the doors did not fill the full height of the opening but were surmounted by a blind panel or grillwork.

From the door one passed up the fauces, a passage a little wider than the door, to the atrium. The fauces almost always have a distinct, sometimes steep, slope up from the entrance and might be provided with another door at the atrium end or somewhere along their length. Their length depends on the rooms or shops that flank them; they are sometimes very short but usually long enough to give the feeling of a distinct architectural unit. Occasionally they are very long. They seem ordinarily to have been finished as sumptuously as the atrium to which they led and generally in a style consonant with it. In the Casa del Fauno, however, stuccowork decorations of a richness that has no equal in Pompeii were lavished on the fauces, and the pavement was also exceptionally fine.

At the atrium end of the fauces the full splendor of the atrium complex opened upon the visitor. To left and right, great doors, proportioned not to what they might open to but to the atrium itself, marched in uniform dimensions and symmetrical alignment down either side, while in the centre, forcing one to pause and then interrupt further progress along the axis, lay the basin of the impluvium. The doors were probably always more for show than for use; probably they were provided with grillwork overdoors for light and ventilation. For the rooms behind them were bedrooms, storerooms, and triclinia stripped to the couch frames, an unprepossessing assortment of utilitarian spaces. The atrium, on the other hand, and the tablinum, developed on the longitudinal axis of the atrium as its culmination, were closely connected as a single architectural progression, the tablinum open across its whole width to the atrium and the focus of the atrium. Its decoration is, as a rule, the most elaborate in the house; it is usually framed at the entrance by pilasters of plaster or wood, and curtains or a folding wooden partition might give it just enough separation from the atrium to suggest privacy. The name of this room is puzzling, since it seems obviously related to *tabula*, yet there is no evidence of either documents or woodwork in what we can see today. Perhaps this is a name that goes back to the customs of earlier days, for certainly this was especially the place where the dominus of the house stood when receiving the salutatio of his clientes in that first ritual of the Roman morning.

The funeral masks of his ancestors, blackened with age but provided with identifying tickets listing their honors, were displayed, according to Vitruvius (6.3.6) on a cornice around the atrium at a height equal to the width of the opening to the tablinum. Here they would contribute to the tablinum and enhance the dignity of the patronus dressed in his toga, ready for a morning in the forum. To either side of the tablinum entrance might be herms of his immediate forebears, possibly also himself, as Pompeii has taught us. And in very old-fashioned houses there might have been a lectus adversus, that very Roman institution, a wedding bed set in the atrium between impluvium and tablinum where his marriage had been consummated and where his wife sat when receiving guests. The institution had generally disappeared by the time of Pompeii's destruction; the last to mention it are Propertius (4.11.85–86) and Asconius (*in Milon.* 38 [Clark 43]); and in Pompeii this place is regularly occupied by a cartibulum or a fountain. But in the paintings of the great triclinium of the Villa dei Misteri we see a domina seated on such a couch, and there are other representations of it in Pompeian decoration. So it was not a custom that had been forgotten.[4]

The architectural unity of the atrium plan is of the highest importance; there is a single overriding axis, an almost inexorable progress from the house door to the tablinum. The whole is designed with a single idea in mind: the presentation of the patronus to his clientes. To this now must be added the alae, those exedral wings whose existence became superfluous with the opening of the roof, yet whose survival, in a position that seems a trifle incongruous in a scheme that is otherwise insistently logical, is constant down to the destruction of the ancient city. In the Casa dei Vettii, for example, the owners could dispense with the tablinum, but they could not dispense with the alae.

The alae came to be the place of the clerks and secretaries of the dominus. Sometimes, as in the Casa dei Vettii, an ala is provided with a counter across its front. Sometimes, as in the Casa dei Dioscuri, there is evidence that wooden cabinets lined its walls. In the alae the business staff of the dominus would be out of the way of the crowd bringing its greetings, business affairs, and troubles to the dominus. But at the same time they could be available. The cliens who needed a recommendation to this or that person of influence, the cliens whose lawsuit was making small progress because of the machinations of the opposition, the cliens whose investments needed looking into, and so on, all required secretarial help. When the dominus wanted this or that clerk, this or that document, such and such a sum of money, all these would be at hand, having only to be summoned by a peremptory finger, but the staff would also be out of the way if the conversation needed to be relatively private. The clerks' coming and going would not interfere with the normal flow of traffic in the atrium, and they could get on with other business. I believe that for these reasons the Tuscanic atrium drove out its competitors in popularity and the location of the alae at the far end of the atrium became canonical (as it did not in other forms of atrium).

This will explain all the parts of the atrium plan except the four corners. If the house fronted on a busy street, the spaces along the front, except for the doorway, were usually used for shops, either in the hands of the household or let out. These usually had a second storey, often no more than a loft, however, and were independent units, the shopkeeper's family living as well as working in the shop.

[4]See, e.g., Kraus and von Matt figs. 119, 265.

If this space was not used for shops, that to one side of the door might well be a winter triclinium, a dining room without windows, or with only small windows, that could be heated easily by braziers. The space to the other side might be broken into smaller spaces for sleeping, storage, the cell of the ostiarius, and so on. At the far end of the atrium the two great rectangles flanking the tablinum were regularly triclinia, one for use in winter, if there was not a winter triclinium elsewhere, one for use in summer. One Roman author after another tells us of the need for a variety of dining rooms of different exposures, different architecture, and different decoration to suit the various seasons and the size of the company (Vitruvius 6.4.2; Petronius 73, 77). And when one considers that the evening meal was the crowning event of the Roman day, the focus of all social activity and a pleasure on which one spent as much as a quarter of the day, this is understandable. From a very early period every good house must have had at least two large dining rooms, and as wealth and luxury became commoner, dining rooms multiplied. One could never use more than one tablinum, but the possibilities for triclinia were almost infinite.[5]

The atrium plan as described fits perfectly the evidence we receive from Pompeii and the archaeological probabilities and alternatives. We have no early testudinate atria; we cannot find any certainly early displuviate atria, though perhaps there might be a rare example or two. Presumably the only criterion would be the shallowness of the impluvium, as we see it in the Insula Iuliae Felicis. The evidence from Pompeii begins with the second century B.C. and with impluviate atria, the house façades in blocks of either Sarno limestone or Nocera tufa, their carved members, including their impluvia, always of Nocera tufa, their walls of a wide variety of masonries, including limestone framework and lava rubblework in good mortar. The unit consists of an atrium and the rooms around it, fitting neatly into a rectangle, a plan of maximum economy designed to accommodate and enhance the two great events of the Roman gentleman's day, the salutatio and the cena.

But as proposed in outline and concept this unit makes no provision for the meaner necessities of life. There is in the atrium plan no place for cooking or washing up, no laundry, no latrine, no bath, and no stables. All these functions must have been served elsewhere. Bathing might well have been left to the public baths, which came to function like a gentlemen's club; and in a world of abundant slave labor, laundry might have been sent down to public laundry facili-

[5]See L. Richardson, Jr., "Contribution to the Study of Pompeian Dining Rooms," *Pompeii Herculaneum Stabiae* 1 (1983) 61–71.

ties. But the other things needed their places around the house. So from the beginning some part of the house plot must have been given over to hortus and these functions arranged in more or less independent sheds out in the garden, away from the house proper, where they would be available without impinging on the dignity of life. The form of an early hortus cannot, of course, be recovered in Pompeii, but early ones were in all probability like later ones, kitchen gardens laid out in long, relatively narrow beds.[6]

A number of houses in Pompeii preserve a substantial part of an atrium complex of the sort described. These must be divided into two groups: those without a cistern under the floor of the atrium and those with one. The diffusion of the atrium plan did not, as one might have supposed, depend on the discovery of the principle of the vault, which allowed the rain water collected to be impounded in cisterns under the house for use in the dry season. Instead, in the oldest houses in Pompeii either rain was not stored at all, but let run off in drains to the streets nearby, or it was conveyed through a channel to a tank in the hortus that could be covered with a roof that needed to carry no extra weight. An example of the former is the atrium of the Casa di Cecilio Giocondo (V i 26), which, although it has been redecorated, is quite without a cistern. An example of the latter is the Casa di Sallustio (VI ii 4), where the channel that took the water to the garden is marked by a slot to receive a lid cut diagonally through the eastern rim of the impluvium. This can be followed back beyond the atrium complex to the cistern still in use in the last period along the eastern side of the property, the drawshaft for which, capped by a lava head, is very conspicuous and stands at a level much higher than the atrium and even the pavement of the garden portico. Later, when the garden portico was added, a modification that could be carried out only by excavating part of the garden to accommodate it and raising the level of the pavement of the triclinium now turned to open on it, the rain collected from the roof of the portico was turned into this cistern, and that from the impluvium was then diverted to the south to a cistern in the south peristyle, but the original system is still easily traced.

Other ancient atria of the general scale, proportion, and style of those we have been discussing seem to have had from the beginning a cistern under the atrium into which the water from the impluvium could pass more or less directly. Some of these, such as that of the Casa del Chirurgo, with its façade of Sarno limestone cut in big blocks and interior walls of limestone framework, look at first to be of high antiquity. It is impossible, however, to imagine a house of this plan

[6] See Jashemski 233–50.

without an impluvium or to dissociate the tufa impluvium still in place today from the atrium cistern.

The date of the invention of the vaulted cistern thus becomes crucial to the history of the Pompeian house. And if houses such as the Casa di Sallustio, with its façade of Nocera tufa, fine capitals, and First Style decorations, are without an atrium cistern, it becomes apparent that such cisterns must appear only sometime after the Second Punic War. The Pompeian evidence is confirmed by discoveries at Cosa in Etruria, whose fortifications were provided with gates with arches of cut stone, while the cisterns around the forum were not vaulted.[7] In the basilica of Cosa, on the other hand, built ca. 140 B.C., the fieldstone vault is so well understood that a line of columns is footed on the crest of the one roofing its larger cistern. Fieldstone vaults on a small scale were probably tried as early as the time of the building of the Atrium Publicum of Cosa, ca. 190 B.C.; it has one that seems to be part of the original construction. But only with the advance of understanding of building technique did the grandiose architecture of the Pompeian Tufa Period become possible, and this is as early as any housing that survives at Pompeii. If we date the Casa di Sallustio and its congeners to the first quarter of the second century, that is certainly as early as the style of its architectural members will permit.

The first change and enlargement of the atrium complex was not the addition of a peristyle but the addition of a second atrium. Since this was built alongside the main atrium, it will not have raised any complicated roofing problems, but it brought problems in the proportioning and utilization of space. The atrium was designed especially to enhance the ceremony of the salutatio. At such times the wife and children of the dominus and the household slaves were superfluous and must have stayed behind closed doors or left the house; no provision was made for them. The second atrium was designed to accommodate them and their life, while the main atrium was now given over exclusively to the world of the master's affairs. Consequently the second atrium might be much smaller than its neighbor, with more that was comfortable and graceful in its appointments. It needed no tablinum, and its scale did not have to agree with an imposing architectural concept and unity. By and large, in the grander houses the secondary atrium is columnar, but smaller than the main atrium, and has only small rooms around it. There is no tablinum, and if there are alae, they function as reception rooms, set

[7]Brown (supra n. 1) 11, 22, 27–28. The cistern in the pronaos of the Capitolium, built in the second quarter of the second century, was roofed with an elaborate gable of specially cut stone slabs brought from the quarries of Vulci (Brown [supra n. 1] 53–54).

on a secondary axis through the middle of the impluvium at right angles to the axis from the house door. Good examples of this sort of house are the original portions of the Casa del Fauno, the Casa della Fontana Grande, and the Casa dell'Argenteria. The first two, at least, were originally built without cisterns under the atria and must be dated to the first quarter of the second century.

Whether the addition of a portico along the back of the atrium unit facing on the hortus came with the second atrium or was an independent development, possibly older, seems a matter for debate. In the grandest of the early Tuscanic atria there is no corridor from atrium to garden, and while we may assume that the garden was always accessible by a door in the summer triclinium, if nothing else, development of a vista of the garden through large windows and doors seems always to show clear signs of being a late innovation. In the Casa del Fauno, passage through from the tetrastyle atrium to the garden is provided, but the main dining rooms still turned in upon themselves, and only a single small room shows any sign of having been a garden room. On the other hand, in the Casa di Pansa a portico on the south side of the rear garden was provided, even though no room took much advantage of the view of the garden, so perhaps in view of the necessity of access to the service quarters and the convenience such a walkway would afford, we should think of this as a relatively early feature. In the case of the Casa di Sallustio the portico is clearly not part of the original house, but in the double-atrium houses it might have been, though still probably architecturally very simple, since it appears always to have been rebuilt later.

Even the invention of the peristyle does not seem to have awakened in Pompeians an enthusiasm for ornamental gardening, though from its inception the Pompeian peristyle garden was ornamental. But early peristyle gardens are small and cramped, more a light well than a garden plot. Perhaps the custom had grown up of keeping potted plants in the impluvium in the minor atrium of double-atrium houses and it occurred to someone that if one had a somewhat larger space and did not floor it, many of the plants could be put in permanently. Early peristyles tend to emphasize their porticoes at the expense of their gardens, and many have blocks sunk in the corners of the gardens (Casa dei Capitelli Colorati, Casa del Fauno), clearly to carry potted trees or shrubs, though no pot seems to have been found in place, so perhaps this was a custom that went out of fashion (Jashemski 238–41).

Among the earliest peristyles still preserving much of their original architecture are those of the Casa dei Capitelli Colorati, the Casa del Centauro, the Casa di Pansa, and the first peristyle of the Casa del Fauno, the last perhaps a bit later than the others in view of its size and certain building techniques that have been introduced. In every one we observe that axial planning does not seem to have been a major consideration and that the original rooms are arranged around the garden rather casually, with consideration for convenience rather than to complement the garden or be complemented by it. In the Casa di Pansa and the Casa dei Capitelli Colorati peristyles, exedral alcoves opened to either side at one end, rather like a *pastas*, enlarging this wing and providing place for possible activity but without close or considered relationship to the garden area, and rooms that might have taken best advantage of the garden do not. That must await a later phase of Pompeian architecture. And while the great columnar Alexander exedra of the first peristyle of the Casa del Fauno opens its whole width to the garden, the axis of the exedra is not the same as that of the garden. The peristyle was evidently considered a separate and discrete unit, and we have no way of knowing what the planting of the garden may have been like in so early a period. There can have been no fountains, and the restricted size of the plot in early peristyles can have given would-be gardeners little scope; perhaps we should think of these gardens as simply a cluster of ornamental plants, an oasis of green decked with an occasional blossom on which the eye could rest, a distraction between the portico one sat or walked in and that opposite.[8]

The interesting thing to note here is that at the time the first peristyle of the Casa del Fauno was built the service quarters of the house were gathered together in a line along the east side of the garden. They are not architecturally well designed, simply a line of spaces allotted to the various humbler functions of the house opening in sequence off a service corridor: stable, latrine, bath, and kitchen courtyard. One might have expected the stable to have ready access to a street, and perhaps originally and usually it did. And in general these rooms in the Casa del Fauno are much the same size and larger than the functions assigned to them require, so we are dealing with an early and tentative solution to the problem, and they were subsequently in large part rebuilt and modernized. But it is interesting to note that the idea of putting the bath next to the kitchen so the fires could be stoked from a single fuel supply, and presumably by a single slave, was probably an early one, and the planning of the kitchen as a small separate courtyard with a hearth platform and cistern came relatively early.

---

[8]Jashemski believes that in the absence of a constant and assured water supply, early ornamental gardens must have consisted largely of trees, but rain collection is at least as old as the invention of the peristyle garden. In fact, the value of portico roofs as rain collectors seems to have been an important factor in the spread of peristyles in Pompeii in the second century.

Once the peristyle had been invented, the possibilities for variation that it offered seem to have been almost immediately appreciated; and we have peristyles of many shapes and proportions, depending, one gathers, on the land available, the importance of the house, and the functions the peristyle was called on to fill. For it early replaced the second atrium, which it made largely superfluous, and gathered around it as a centre bedrooms, workrooms, service quarters, and ultimately dining rooms, the last, however, not before the time of the Sullan colony and perhaps not before the middle of the first century B.C. Some of the more interesting peristyles of the late Tufa Period are those with one line of columns engaged or rendered illusionistically to make a pseudoperistyle. Among these we may cite the Casa dei Capitelli Figurati, six columns by six, the Casa della Parete Nera, six by four, the Casa di Marte e Venere, six by seven, and the Officina Uboni, four by five. The proportion preferred was evidently a broad rectangle, slightly longer than wide.

With the appearance of the peristyle and its possibilities for variation the Pompeian house has all the members necessary to produce the houses of the First Style that we know, except for an upper storey. A great many tufa column elements at reduced scale have come to light, most of them at present left lying about the houses in which they were found without clear context, but in the Casa del Cenacolo, the Casa del Centenario, the Fullonica Stephani, IX xii 1/2, and elsewhere, enough has been found in significant contexts to show that the upper storeys of houses of the late Tufa Period abounded in loggias, apartments with a columnar front giving onto an atrium, a peristyle, or both, or onto the street. These were usually a single unit accessible by a steep stair at one end, and a location over the tablinum and adjacent rooms, between atrium and peristyle, was preferred, perhaps because of the increased privacy this afforded at the same time that it allowed opening opposite walls to a variety of prospects and to permit air to circulate. The columns of these loggias are almost all half-columns engaged against a plain pillar, and wooden shutters set between them must have permitted shutting off a chill wind or too strong a light. For these second-storey rooms were called cenacula and were invented for dining in the summer (Varro *Ling.* 5.162), perhaps about the same time that the peristyle was invented.

But throughout the history of Pompeian architecture upper storeys in houses were limited in extent and, except for the cenacula, inconvenient and unprepossessing. Even the cenacula, with their rather stubby columns, are not as light and graceful as the aesthetic of Tufa Period architecture might seem to demand, yet the size and proportion of these elements are remarkably consistent throughout the city. Perhaps this was out of concern for statics, but it is more likely that it was a question of taste. The majority of the columns are of the Ionic order, and the progression from Doric to Ionic in superimposed orders seems to have been regularly observed by Tufa Period architects. So this must have seemed to them a correct proportion, and we should accept it as such.

In First Style houses after the invention of the peristyle we can observe a certain elasticity of plan afforded by the choice between atrium and peristyle for the location of individual rooms, and with the introduction of a passage between the two, the andron, the flow of traffic among the rooms need no longer seriously interfere with any activity. Since the atrium had to be immediately accessible from the street and the principal entrance, the peristyle tended to find its place beyond the atrium, and the andron ran alongside the tablinum, but occasionally, as in the Casa del Centauro, the peristyle was located to one side of the atrium, and then no andron was necessary. In older houses either there is no andron or it has clearly been produced by remodeling, but it is an integral part of the plan of houses of the Second Style.

With the coming of the Second Style to Pompeii—an event generally associated with the arrival of the Roman colony in the time of Sulla, ca. 80 B.C.—one notes a change in domestic architecture, not so much in the patterns of the house as in the shapes of individual rooms. In houses of the First Style rooms tended to be simply convenient rectangles, whatever the dominant scale of the atrium permitted, so that with a large atrium like that of the Casa di Sallustio or the main atrium of the Casa del Fauno even the cubicula are of generous size, while the dining rooms tend to seem vast. In the Second Style, however, the rooms are proportioned to their functions and shaped for these. We do not have many houses clearly of Second Style build in Pompeii, though we have a good many rooms, some of very high quality. And while we can sometimes determine that an atrium must have been built in the Second Style, that of the Casa dei Dioscuri, for example, subsequent alterations will have obscured many of its features. We do have two houses in almost complete state—the Casa delle Nozze d'Argento and the Casa dei Capitelli Figurati—and extensive parts of two others—the Casa del Labirinto and the Casa del Criptoportico (with rooms later incorporated in the Casa degli Elefanti). Moreover, three villas built in this style are well known: the Villa dei Misteri, the Villa of Fannius Synistor at Boscoreale, and the Villa di Oplontis at Torre Annunziata. Coastal pleasure villas were made safe when Pompey cleared the sea of pirates in 66 B.C., and probably this led to intensive building activity all around the Bay of Naples within the next decade.

In this period atria continue to be large and usually of rigid symmetry, very much the same as in the early Tufa Period, larger than is necessary, especially imposing in their height. In the Villa dei Misteri the doors around the atrium were disposed symmetrically on all walls, four on each long wall and three, a broad centre door flanked by narrower ones, on each short wall, yet of these, four were false doors, simply functionless wooden dummies, and two more were in part false. In the Casa dei Capitelli Figurati the doors around the atrium are similarly symmetrically arranged, three doors on each side, two flanking the tablinum and two flanking the fauces, but here they all function, while in the peristyle the fondness for symmetry has led to the introduction of an engaged order.

Other changes were to prove more important and influential. The tablinum of the Casa delle Nozze d'Argento is considerably wider than deep, the full width of the atrium except for a very narrow andron along the west side and a symmetrical amount to balance on the east, a proportion we find again in the Villa dei Misteri. And the back wall of the tablinum disappears entirely, broken open to an uninterrupted view of the peristyle beyond. The garden now became a focus, not merely a convenience and a pleasure. Rooms opened their whole width to it whenever possible, and while axial planning was seldom attempted, nearly maximum use was made of it.

In the Casa delle Nozze d'Argento the portico of the peristyle looking south, that along the tablinum, is higher than the others, of larger columns more widely spaced, a Rhodian portico, and this makes the transition from the grandeur of the atrium to the intimacy of the peristyle easy and graceful. From the atrium one sees the peristyle as larger than in fact it is, while once one is in the peristyle the comparatively intimate rooms that open onto it seem designed to go with it. There is now only one triclinium of the squarish proportions of the early Tufa Period, that east of the tablinum; the other three—the winter triclinium off the west ala and those at the southern corners of the peristyle—are all long rectangles,[9] with a space at the far end for the dining couches and a squarish area left in front of these for service and entertainment. The divisions are clearly marked in the mosaic pavements of both peristyle triclinia and in that which preserves its Second Style decoration emphasized by the architecture and decoration as well. The room is a tetrastyle oecus, the ceiling over the couch area being a false vault carried by four columns set in from the walls, while the ceiling over the service area was flat and stood at the level of the crown of the vault (Vitruvius 6.3.9).

In conjunction with the two great triclinia of this house are two

[9] Vitruvius (6.3.8) recommended that triclinia be twice as long as wide and that their height be equal to half the sum of their breadth and width.

smaller rooms that have much the appearance of bedrooms, including even the setting off of a couch area at the back of the room in the pattern of the pavement. But these can hardly be bedrooms, because of the richness of the decorations and the excessively wide doorways, clearly intended to afford a panoramic view of the garden. These must be the dining rooms of the ladies, who will have eaten by themselves while the men ate in the great triclinia. For we know that while it was considered shocking for a Roman matron to recline at dinner, they were regularly invited in after the meal was over to take part in the conversation and enjoy the entertainment, and at such times they sat on the edge of the dining couches.[10] Here, then, is provision for them, a suitably decorated room adjacent to, but not in view of, the men's triclinium where seated on a couch (and perhaps also chairs, if necessary), they could eat the same food as the men and then move to the triclinium after dinner.

This pattern now becomes standard for great banquet halls and continues down to the destruction of the city. In the Villa dei Misteri there are no fewer than three pairs of these banquet rooms,[11] while in the Casa dei Vettii, the Casa di Marco Lucrezio, and the Casa dei Dioscuri, all sumptuous houses of the last period, they still appear as a regular feature. In the Villa dei Misteri one notes an experimentation with the form of these banquet halls. At the west corner of the house was originally a vast L-shaped room, the largest dining room in the house, almost half again as big as the triclinium of the Dionysiac frieze, decorated with an architectural perspective of extraordinary quality. This was a double triclinium, each of the arms capable of accommodating its complement of three couches, while the service area was in the square joining these (Maiuri 1931, 59–61). To go with this was a similar double ladies' dining room, room 16, having folding doors along its north front that gave onto the view toward Vesuvius and a shelved cupboard for tableware fitted into the corner between the two couch areas. The double triclinium can hardly have been a success, because of the way it divides the company, and the experiment seems not to have been repeated, but the double ladies' dining room appears twice more in the Villa dei Misteri, once in conjunction with the south triclinium, room 8, and once in conjunction with the triclinium of the Dionysiac frieze, room 4, and in each case the cupboard for tableware appears. And the shape appears again in modified form at the northeast corner of the peristyle of the Casa del

[10]See, e.g., Valerius Maximus 2.1.2; and Petronius 67.

[11]These are Maiuri's rooms 6 and 8 (spring), 5 and 4 (fall), and 11–14 and 16 (summer). But since the pairs vary in size as well as in aspect, one must suppose that it was rather the size of the dinner party than the exposure that determined which was to be used.

Labirinto, but perhaps it too was not a great success, as experiments with other shapes soon replaced it, and in the last period of Pompeii the suite seems to have crystallized as a pair of rooms next to one another and usually communicating, the larger a long rectangle, the smaller of similar proportions but much smaller, both open, usually their whole width, to the garden and having the same exposure.[12] The two are similarly richly decorated but not identical; the decorations of the Villa dei Misteri already illustrate this difference. No house of pretentions to style is without such a banquet suite.

Another experiment with the form of dining rooms can be seen in the Corinthian oecus of the Casa del Labirinto, where an exedra facing south onto the garden was ringed on the three remaining sides by a colonnade brought forward from the walls that created a screen between the company and a particularly rich decoration in architectural vistas and left a passage behind the couches. Here again one feels that the result is not altogether a happy invention, but the wish to introduce novelty into the architecture of these staterooms, as well as into the decoration, is very striking and nowhere better studied than in the series of rooms, all evidently dining rooms, on the north side of the peristyle of the Casa del Labirinto. The Corinthian oecus is flanked by charming ladies' dining rooms, the western one of more bizarre decoration than the eastern, painted with great telamons of sea gods mounted on ships' prows in the foreground. And at the western end of the series are two huge rooms, one with a vault over the couch area, one without.

Other innovations that belong to the period of the Second Style are an increase in variety and luxury in the appointments of private baths and in the use of the cryptoporticus. Private baths became much commoner, and it became regular to have a variety of rooms. The Villa dei Misteri has a laconicum, for example, while the late Second Style baths of the Casa del Menandro were entered through a little Corinthian atrium that probably served also as a frigidarium. Baths of this period seem regularly to have been floored with mosaic and handsomely painted, and while the hot rooms are small and cramped, some effort was made to make them attractive.

The cryptoporticus was probably invented as an engineering expedient to lift part of a house above the slope of terrain commanding an important view, the use to which we see it put in the Villa dei Misteri, where a cryptoporticus with a façade of essentially blind arches supports the outer part of a gardened terrace in front of the

[12] Good examples of this are the pair of rooms north of the peristyle in the Casa di Pansa (VI vi 1), the pair east of the peristyle in the Casa dei Dioscuri (VI ix 6/7), the pair on the little pseudoperistyle in the Casa dei Vettii (VI xv 1/2), and the pair south of the peristyle in the Casa di Obellio Firmo (IX [xiv] 2/4).

porticus that looked out over the Bay of Naples. The cryptoporticus is itself undecorated, though it is plastered and provided with a small window for ventilation in each bay, and it was accessible only by a narrow stair at one end. It cannot have played any large part in the life of the house and must have served more for storage than as a retreat in summer (Maiuri 1931, 86–89). In the Casa del Criptoportico, on the other hand, the cryptoporticus, on which a peristyle was once raised, was itself a major feature of the house, magnificently decorated with painting and a richly stuccoed vault, and off it opened not only an exedral room for those who might like to sit and converse in its cool twilight but also elaborately decorated rooms, including a grand winter triclinium (Spinazzola 1953, 1.451–542).

Yet another development of Second Style architecture was the use of illusion. One observes that this was the original basis of the decorative style, a wish to make rooms seem more spacious by the introduction of architectural perspectives that made the walls seem to recede from their actual lines, though later painters lost sight of this intention with the introduction of architectural fantasies and figures. And in the Casa delle Nozze d'Argento the peristyle is given a Rhodian portico that makes its proportions, when it is seen from the atrium, seem to harmonize with the grand scale of the atrium. In the Casa dei Capitelli Figurati we find still a further architectural illusion. Here the plot did not permit the laying out of a peristyle of proportions approaching a generous square, evidently the preferred shape of the period, so the architect laid out a rectangle, spacing his columns on the short sides closer than on the long and making the west colonnade an engaged order with stuccowork in the bays that shows a Tuscan porticus some distance beyond. The illusion is not really deceptive but rather decorative, but it is interesting as a continuation of First Style uses of plasterwork into the period of the Second Style to achieve a Second Style aesthetic effect.

APPENDIX III

Ground Plans Covering the Excavations of Pompeii down to 1969

Taken from the Plan of H. Eschebach 1970 (scale 1:1000)

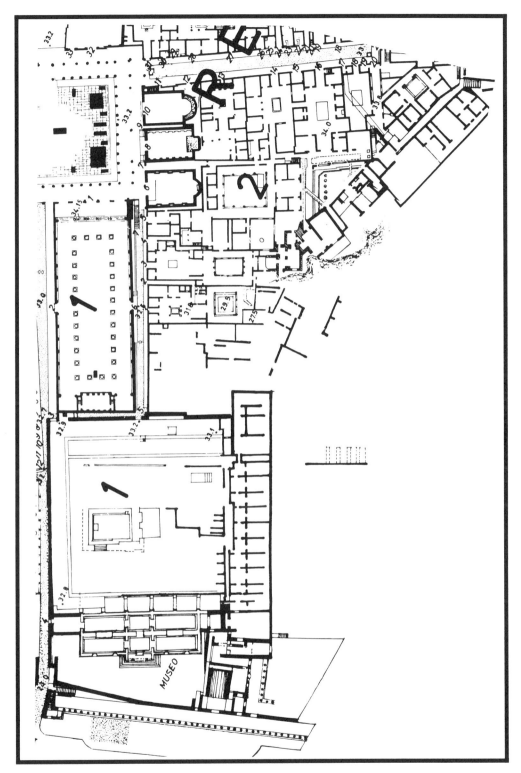

1

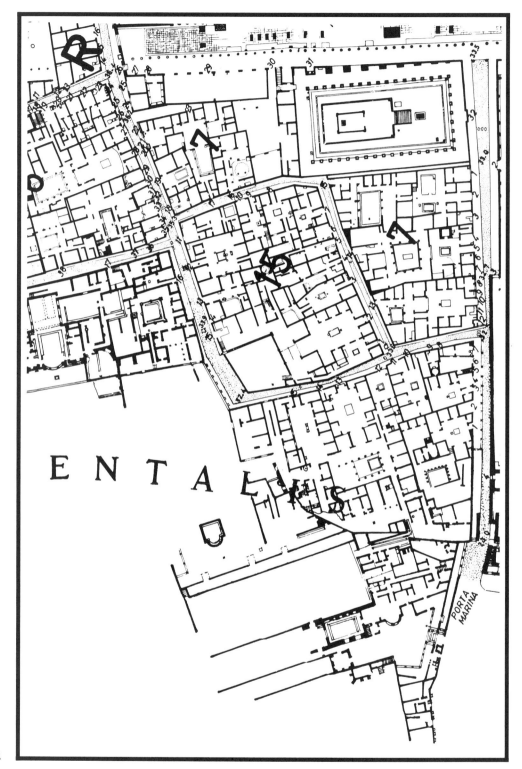

ENTALIS

PORTA
MARINA

2

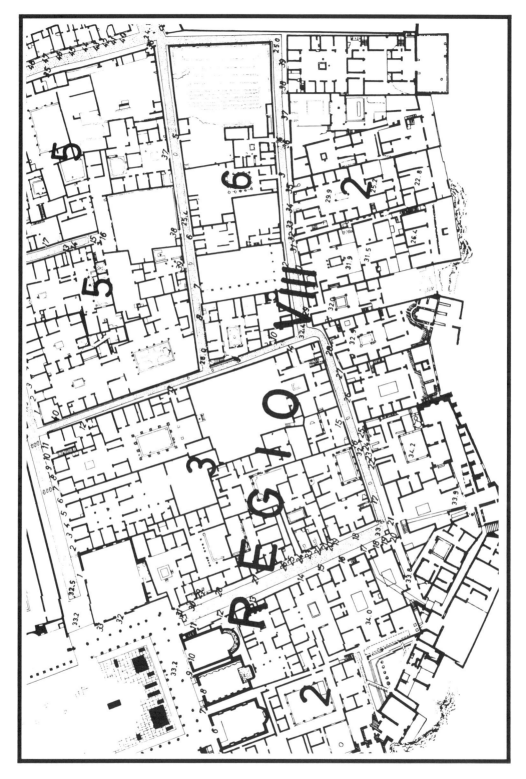

3

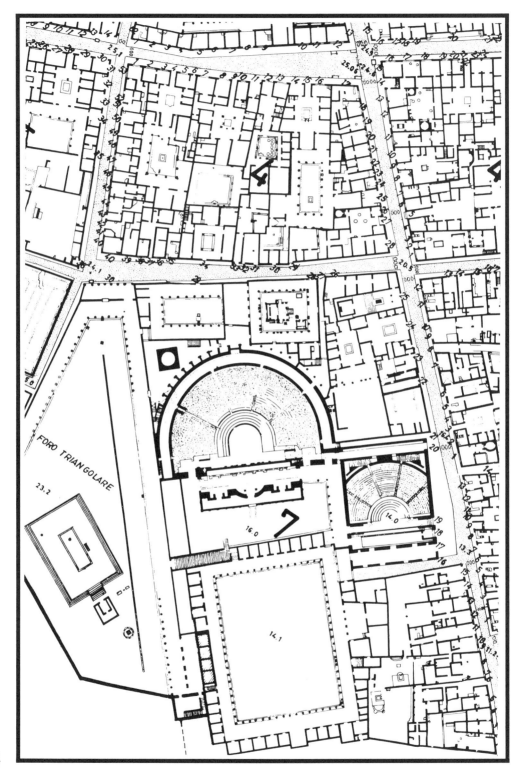

FORO TRIANGOLARE

4

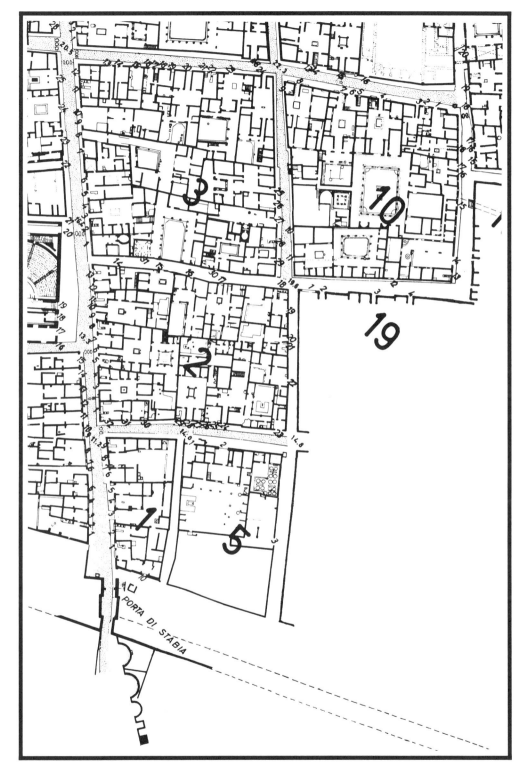

PORTA DI STABIA

5

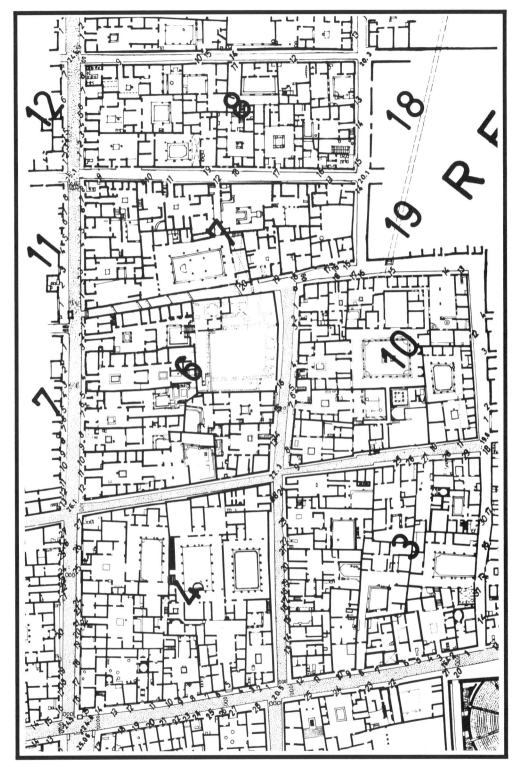

6

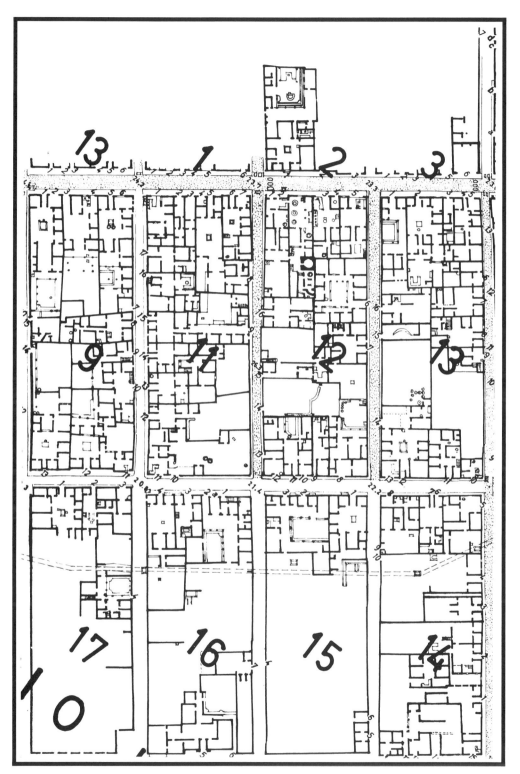

7

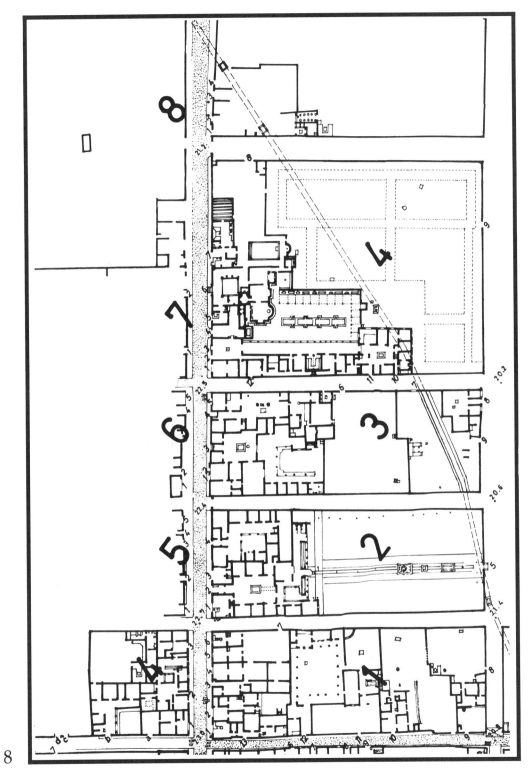

8

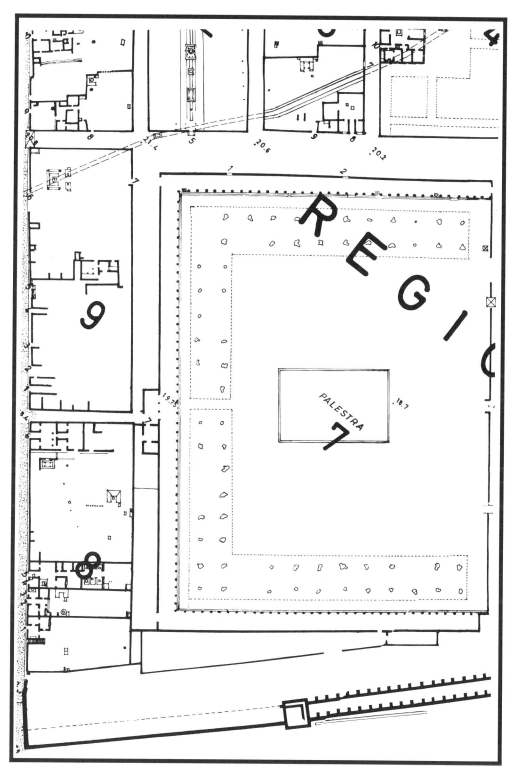

PALESTRA

REGIO

9

9

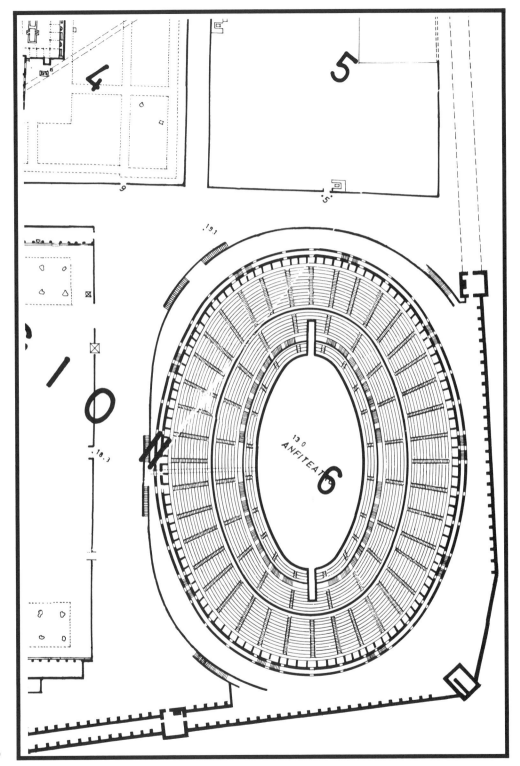

10

412 • APPENDIX III

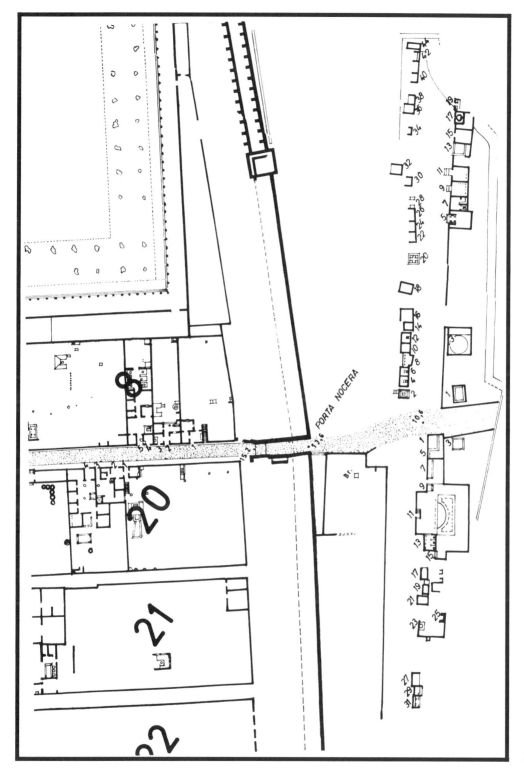

PORTA NOCERA

11

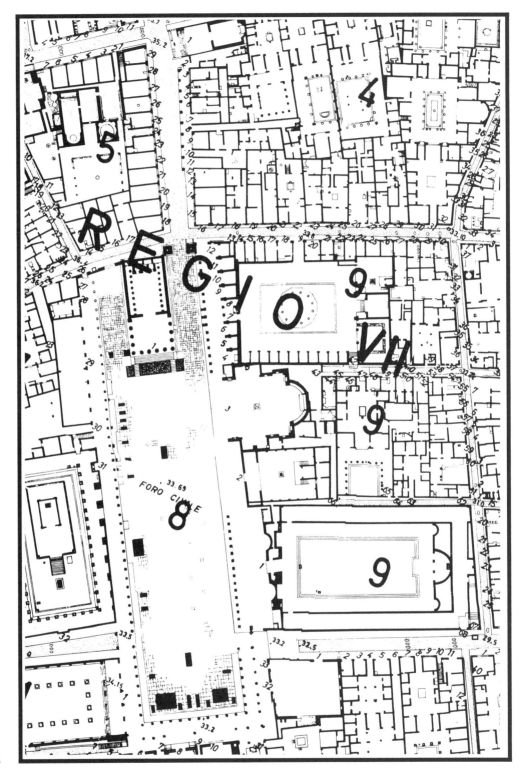

12

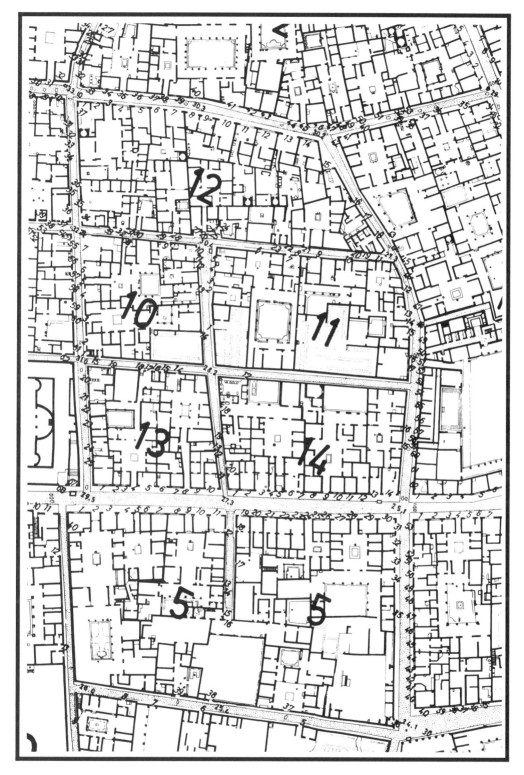

13

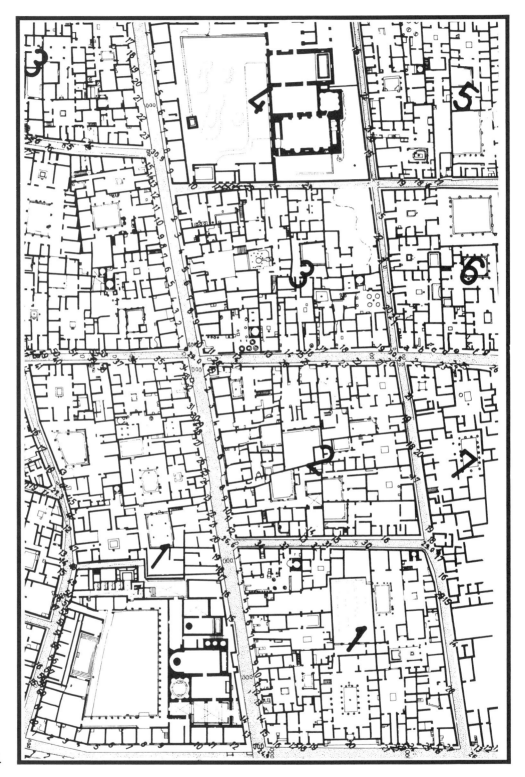

14

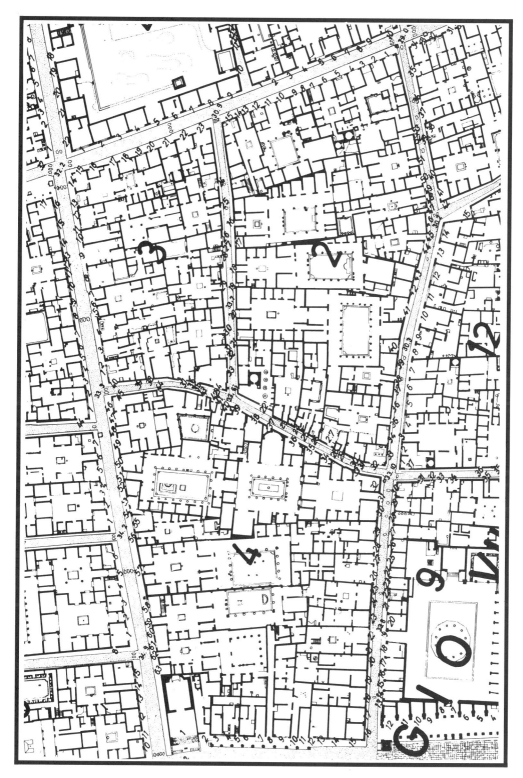

15

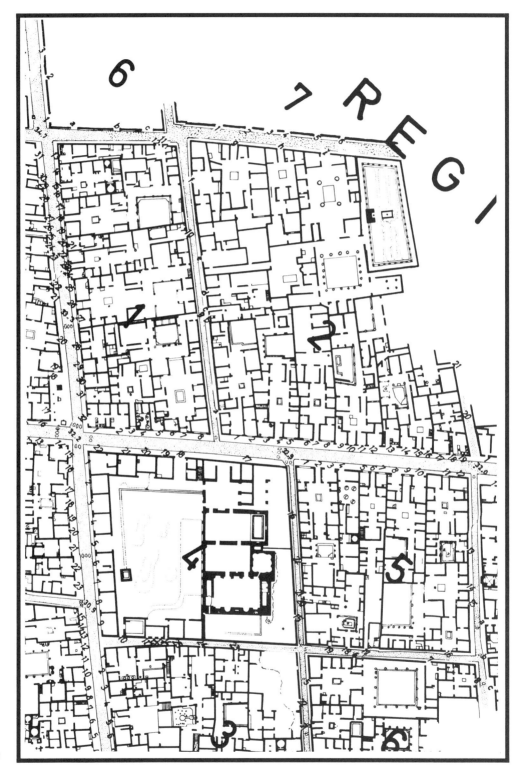

16

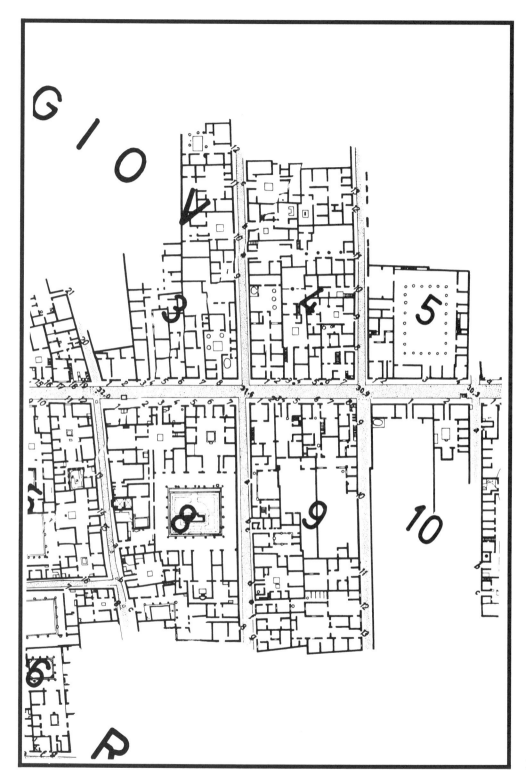

17

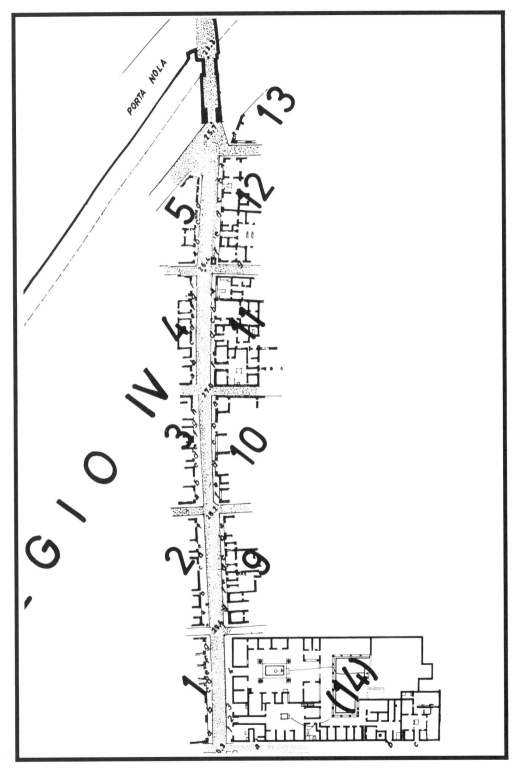

18

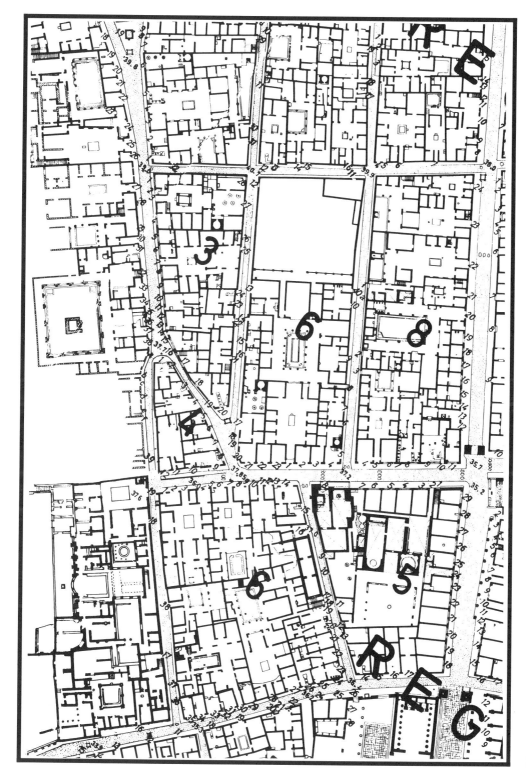

19

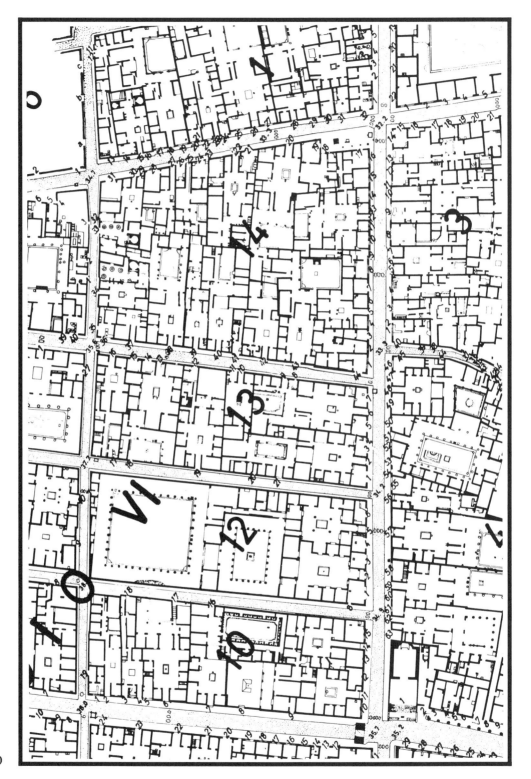

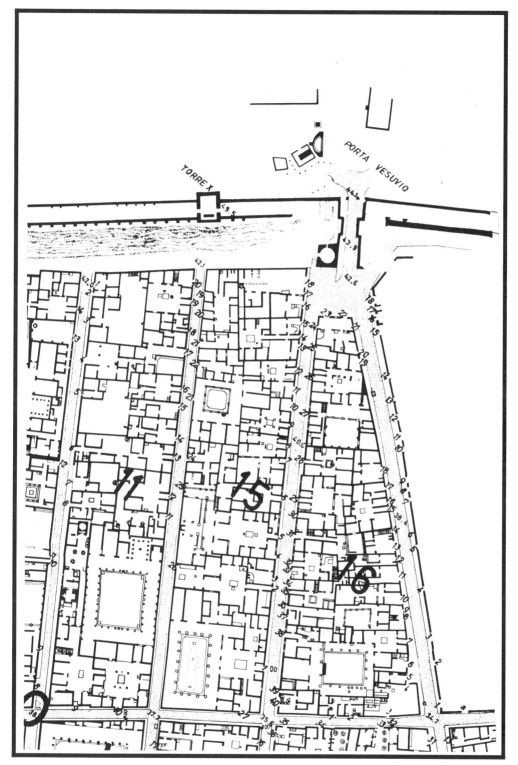

TORRE X

PORTA VESUVIO

11

15

16

21

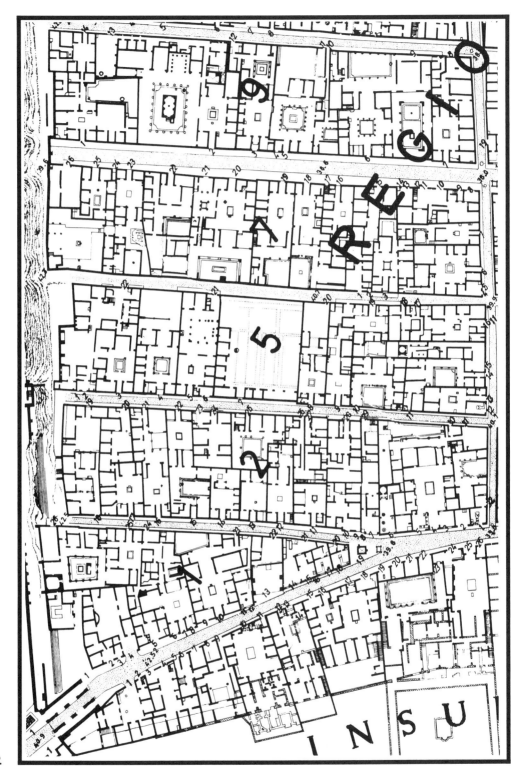

22

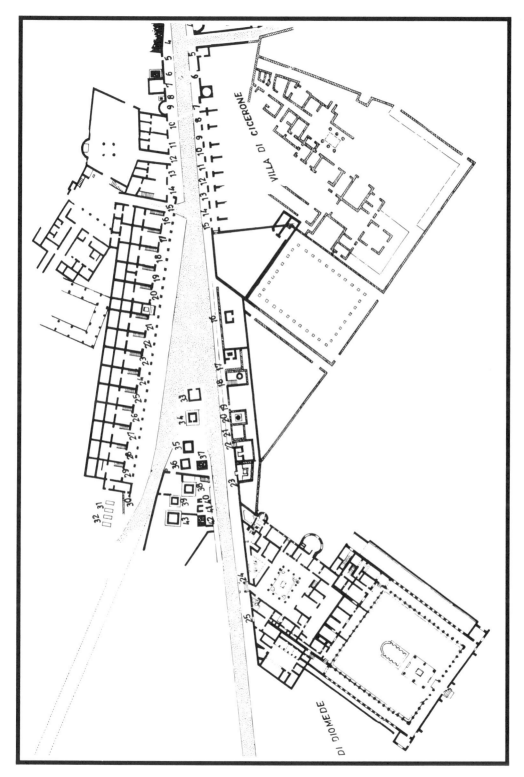

VILLA DI CICERONE

DI DIOMEDE

23

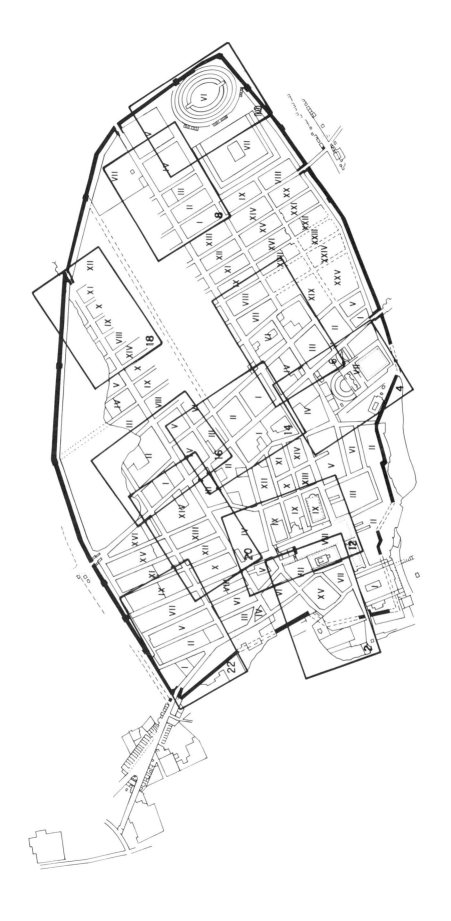

GLOSSARY

ABACUS. The crowning element of a column capital, square in the Doric and Ionic orders, with concave sides in the Corinthian.

AFRICANO. A colored marble, also called marmo luculleo, quarried at Teos in Asia Minor, purplish black and grey in color, profusely veined and splotched with bright red and white.

ALVEUS. A relatively deep bath basin in which one could sit or recline largely submerged, chiefly used for the hot basins in caldaria.

AMORINO. A male child divinity with small bird's wings, a cupid or eros, a very common figure in Pompeian decorations, often shown in pairs or groups. *See also* PSYCHE.

ANDRON. A corridor connecting an atrium and a peristyle or two peristyles.

ANGIPORTUS. A narrow lane or alleyway, essentially public but often a cul-de-sac.

ANGUIPED. Having legs that develop into serpents, a characteristic of the earthborn giants

APOPHYGE. The concave passage finishing the shaft of a column under the capital or above the base.

ARCA. A strongbox, usually rectangular and very large, heavily bound with metal and bolted to the floor.

ARCOSOLIO. A large, low niche, usually with a bowed ceiling, let into a tomb wall to receive a body or sarcophagus.

ASHLAR. Masonry of rectangular blocks laid in regular horizontal courses with fine joints, usually staggered so that the joints between blocks in successive courses fall over the midpoints of the blocks above and below them.

ASTRAGAL. The regular decorative treatment of a small bead molding, often called bead-and-reel.

ATRIENSIS. A slave in charge of the atrium of a house who acted as usher, a majordomo.

BALTEUS. A relatively broad passage around the cavea of a theatre or amphitheatre to divide one zone of seating from another and facilitate the movement of spectators, in Greek called diazoma.

BARDIGLIO. A handsome blue-grey marble quarried at Luna in Italy.

BICLINIUM. An arrangement of two couches, either facing one another or at right angles, for dining in small groups or conversation.

BISELLIUM. A straight-legged backless seat for one person, handsomely decorated, awarded as an honor to public benefactors.

BUSTUM. A walled enclosure in a cemetery where a family burned its dead and interred the ashes. Inscriptions might be immured in the circuit wall, but there was no other funerary monument. Regular in the republican period, busta become increasingly rare under the empire.

CAMAÏEU. A form of grisaille in which ochres replace grey, giving the effect of cameo relief.

CARTIBULUM. A large rectangular table of stone, occasionally with only one leg but regularly with two or four, often richly carved, that stands in an atrium or peristyle. Sometimes spelled *gartibulum.*

CAVAEDIUM. *See* CAVUM AEDIUM.

CAVEA. The part of a theatre or amphitheatre for the spectators, regularly provided with seating.

CAVETTO. A concave quarter-round molding. When large, it is usually decorated with either a tongue pattern or strigillation.

CAVUM AEDIUM. The central lobby of an atrium complex, an atrium.

CIPOLLINO. Carystian stone from Euboea, a pale green resembling onion skin in its veining.

CIPPUS. A stone stele or block, usually small, that serves as a marker of any sort, often inscribed on at least one face to indicate its purpose.

CISTA MYSTICA. A covered basket or other cylindrical container, often large, in which were kept sacred or ritual objects of any religious cult to conceal them from the gaze of the profane.

COMPLUVIUM. The rectangular opening in an atrium roof, regularly framed with spouted gutters of terracotta or metal, through which rain fell into the impluvium basin.

CUBICULARIUS. A slave acting as a personal attendant, a *valet de chambre.*

CYMA RECTA. A molding of S-shaped profile, the lower half convex, the upper concave, regularly given a leaf pattern when decorated.

CYMA REVERSA. A molding of S-shaped profile, the lower half concave, the upper convex.

DECURIONES. The senate of Pompeii as a Roman colony, probably limited to one hundred members.

DIAETA. A small chamber for use in the daytime for lounging or study, more or less isolated and of relatively open architecture, regularly provided with a couch; a summerhouse.

DISTYLE. Having two columns.

DRAFTING. A narrow margin set off from the rest along the edge of a squared block or plate of stone or panel of stucco.

ECHINUS. The swelling or flaring cushion-like member under the abacus of a Doric capital and under the volutes of an Ionic capital, the latter usually decorated with an egg molding.

EITUNS INSCRIPTION. One of several inscriptions in the Oscan alphabet painted in red found in conspicuous locations along the main streets of Pompeii. These all include the word *eituns* near their beginning and seem to give directions for troop movements during the siege of Sulla in the Social War. They must have been preserved as memorials of that defense and have been repainted at intervals in antiquity.

EMBLEMA. A subject picture, usually small and in fine polychrome tesserae, set into the middle of a mosaic pavement. These were often made in a special terracotta tray, evidence that they could be bought separately.

ENTASIS. The slight but perceptible curved swelling of the shaft of a column.

EPISTYLE. The member of an order resting immediately on the column capitals, the architrave or architrave and frieze in combination.

EROS. An amorino; in the plural, *erotes,* amorini and psyches. *See also* AMORINO; PSYCHE.

EURIPUS. An ornamental watercourse in a garden, usually at least a meter deep and ornamented with fountains and sculptures along its length. Euripi were sometimes used for breeding fish.

EXEDRA. A room or alcove open across the whole of one side.

FASCIA. A flat band or strip, broader than a fillet.

FAUCES. An entrance passage leading into a building, usually a house, from the street. It may be of any length but is usually only slightly wider than the street door itself.

FIRST STYLE. The style of Pompeian decoration that imitates masonry, the plaster wallcoat being worked in relief to simulate blocks, columns, cornices, and so on, and painted various colors. In Pompeii it dates from the Hannibalic War or earlier to the early years of the Roman colony.

FOURTH STYLE. The style of Pompeian decoration characterized by a return to the illusion of plastic reality that marks the Second Style, but a reality in which the architecture is flamboyant and heavily embellished, patently theatrical. Mythological subject pictures, often large, floating groups and figures, and staffage of every sort are lavishly added. The taste runs to polychromy. This was the prevalent style in the last seventeen years of Pompeii's existence.

GIALLO ANTICO. A deep yellow stone with veining and mottling in red from quarries in modern Tunisia.

GUTTAE. The pendant pegs, usually flaring, found under the triglyphs of a Doric frieze and in rows adorning the mutules of a Doric cornice.

HORTUS. An open area behind and/or to the side of a house in which a kitchen garden, stables for animals, and offices for the house could be arranged.

IMPLUVIUM. The basin in an atrium for catching the rain falling through the compluvium, usually the centre of the plan.

IMPOST. The surface or point from which an arch or vault springs.

KOINE. A lingua franca, or common language, of any sort.

LABRUM. In the caldarium of a bath, a waist-high circular basin with a jet of cold water at its centre where bathers who became overheated could stand and sluice themselves down.

LESBIAN LEAF. A decorative pattern usually used to embellish a cyma, hence often called cymatium, composed of leaves alternating with darts. It varies greatly in design.

LESCHE. A broad and proportionately shallow building open across its whole front to a colonnaded porch but closed behind.

LOCULUS. A small niche for depositing an urn in a tomb or valuables for safekeeping in the base of a temple.

LUNATE. Used to describe a pediment that is bowed rather than triangular.

MANTELE. A cloth with a thick nap and a fringed edge used by Roman priests when sacrificing.

MEDIANUM. A large lobby in a flat dwelling of the sort best known from Ostia from which other rooms radiate. It seems to have replaced the atrium as the central focus of the dwelling unit.

MEGALOGRAPHY. Painting in which figures and objects appear life-size or near life-size.

MENISCUS. A pronged metal fitting, often a trident in form, set in the top of an ornament or cresting, evidently as a deterrent to birds.

MENSA. A table leaf.

MENSA PONDERARIA. A counter in which are cut bowls of standard capacities, sometimes together with inscribed linear measures, usually set up in a public place, often a market, for the protection of the public against fraudulent merchants.

MERLON. A small projection atop a wall or battlement, either ornamental or to afford protection to defenders crouching behind it.

META. A domed shape into which ivy was trained, a common feature in Pompeian viridaria and frequently shown in wall paintings.

MONOPTEROS. A ring of columns standing free, not enclosing a cella.

MUTULE. A beam end of a major roof rafter. In Doric architecture the mutules are the rafters that carry the cornices on both the ends and the sides.

NYMPHAEUM. A fountain house. It may be as simple as a single rusticated niche in a garden or as elaborate as an artificial grotto embellished with a program of statuary and multiple jets and pools.

OECUS. A large reception room often used chiefly for dining, but without the characteristic shape of a triclinium. Vitruvius (6.3.8–10) distinguished several sorts of oeci according to the architecture.

OMPHALOS. A large domed stone, shaped like half an egg, supposed to be the tomb, or the egg, of the Python at Delphi and regarded as the navel of the world. It became a symbol of Apollo and is sometimes shown enclosed in the base of his tripod.

OPUS INCERTUM. Concrete facing of stone broken into irregular shapes a little larger than a man's fist, and carefully fitted together in thin beds of mortar. It is the first facing used for Roman concrete, appearing in the last quarter of the second century B.C. and continuing down to the mid first century or later.

OPUS MIXTUM VITTATUM. Concrete facing of courses of small rectangular blocks alternating with two or more courses of brick or broken tile, characteristic of the last period of Pompeian building and much used for coigning.

OPUS QUASI-RETICULATUM. Concrete facing of small stone roughly cut to the square shape of reticulate blocks but irregular enough that the joint lines do not run straight. It is characteristic of the mid first century B.C.

OPUS RETICULATUM. Concrete facing of small blocks of stone carefully cut to the shape of a truncated pyramid of four sides and to nearly uniform size. These are fitted together, often with great precision, so the joints make a regular network pattern, hence the name. In Rome opus reticulatum appears in the time of the second triumvirate, but in Pompeii it is especially characteristic of the last period, A.D. 62–79.

OPUS SECTILE. Plates of colored marble and glass cut into elaborate shapes and figures, mosaicked into panels, and used for walls and table tops or inlaid ornamentally in floors. It is rare in Pompeii except

in panels of squares and triangles in the middle of triclinium floors.

OPUS SIGNINUM. *See* SIGNINUM.

OSCILLUM. A marble disc or peltate plate carved with low reliefs and hung from the architrave between columns in a peristyle as an ornament. Marble masks are used in the same way. The subjects are usually Bacchic, theatrical, or rustic, and the work is seldom of high quality.

OSTIARIUS. A doorkeeper, especially one who is provided with a cell adjacent to a house door.

PASTAS. A deep portico in a Greek house, usually longer than the courtyard on which it gives, so that the ends have something of the character of exedras. Behind this open the principal rooms. Vitruvius (6.7.1) made *pastas* synonymous with *prostas,* but there are two clear types of porticoes, one with exedral extension, one without.

PAVONAZZETTO. A white stone veined with purple shading to violet quarried in western Asia Minor.

PELTA. The shape of the shield associated especially with the Amazons, a half-moon shape in which the inner edge is developed as two semicircles half the diameter of the whole.

PLUTEUS. A wall, usually a little more than waist-high, run between columns in a portico or around a tank or basin.

POMPEIAN IONIC. Ionic capitals in which all four faces are identical, there being four volutes at the four corners set diagonally, and all sides presenting an echinus carved with an egg molding.

POSTICUM. A minor entrance to the side or rear of a house.

PREDELLA. A narrow panel between socle and main zone in a decoration, often decorated with figures at a reduced scale, with the effect of miniature. Predelle are especially prevalent in Third Style decorations.

PSEUDOPERISTYLE. A peristyle in which the colonnades do not run completely around the garden area. Sometimes one or more wings appear as an engaged order along the garden wall. But peristyles of only one, two, or three wings are very common in domestic architecture, and anything less than a full peristyle may be called a pseudoperistyle.

PSYCHE. A female child divinity with butterfly or bat wings, the female counterpart of an amorino. They appear together in Pompeian decorations in many contexts, especially in Fourth Style painting. *See also* AMORINO.

PUDICITIA POSE. The pose of a heavily draped woman with her left forearm laid horizontally across her waist and wrapped in veils to conceal the hand, while the right, raised to the chin, seems just now to have pulled the head veil back from the face. It is especially used for funerary portraits in Pompeii.

PULVINUS. The rounded bolster at the end of the working platform of an altar, often decorated with rosettes or volutes at the ends.

PUTTO. A child divinity, an amorino or psyche. *See also* AMORINO; PSYCHE.

REEDING. The filling of the flutes of an Ionic or Corinthian column shaft so that it becomes in effect a cylinder scored with shallow relief instead of fluting. Reeding appears in Pompeii only after the end of the republican period.

RETICULATE. *See* OPUS RETICULATUM.

REVETTED. Covered with a veneer of another material, usually more costly, sometimes for protection.

RHODIAN PORTICO. A portico in a peristyle with columns that are taller than the others (Vitruvius 6.7.3) and usually of greater diameter as well.

RUSTICATION. The deliberate omission of finish or roughening of a surface for aesthetic effect. In Pompeii bits of coarse limestone formed in warm water around aquatic plants were pressed onto walls, column shafts, and especially fountain niches, sometimes in patterns, sometimes in combination with shells and colored glass mosaic tesserae, to produce a rather garish rustication that was prob-

ably somewhat mitigated by the vegetation. Rustication is especially characteristic of the last period of Pompeii.

SALUTATIO. The ceremony in which clientes called upon their patroni at, or shortly after, dawn on specified days when the patronus announced he would be at home. At this time the cliens presented any business he needed his patronus's help in expediting.

SCHOLA. A curved, usually semicircular, stone bench with a back, occasionally roofed with a half-dome. Scholae were erected in conjunction with temples and were a popular tomb form at Pompeii beginning in the time of Augustus.

SECOND STYLE. The style of Pompeian decoration that gives architectural illusion of various sorts, but all more or less realistic. Vistas of architecture come in time to open to landscape and to include figures. The effect is always rich and richly colored and tends to be somewhat heavy. It appears in Pompeii through most of the first century B.C.

SEGMENTAL. Used to describe an arch or vault in which the curve is less than a full half-circle.

SIGNINUM. Lime mortar to which crushed terracotta, usually potsherd, has been added as an aggregate. When the terracotta is finely crushed, it is used as a lining for gutters, cisterns, and the like; when coarsely crushed, it is used for pavements. A variety in which lava crushed to the consistency of gravel is substituted for terracotta, used for pavements, is sometimes called lava signinum.

SINUS. The looping overfold of an imperial toga that hangs deep in front. In this fold small objects were commonly carried.

SNECK. To fill the interstices between large blocks on a wall face with smaller stones of the same sort.

SPALL. To chip or flake, as in the working of blocks or the deterioration of masonry; also used as a noun for a chip so produced.

SPECUS. The enclosed channel of an aqueduct in which the water flows.

STANDARD. The upright stele or bollard of a fountain carved with a device from which the feed pipe issues.

SUGGESTUS. A raised platform, usually small, for a magistrate or one from which a speaker may address a crowd; a tribunal.

SUSPENSURAE. Short columns or pillars used under the floors of hot rooms in Roman baths to create a low cellar in which air heated by a nearby fire could circulate.

SYMPLEGMA. A couple in sexual embrace.

SYZYGIUM. Two isolated columns joined by an epistyle or entablature. This was a common architectural feature in rustic sanctuaries, often spanning a sacred tree. It may be mounted on plinths, or a continuous plinth, and carry dedications on its crown or tied to the column shafts.

TABLINUM. The focal room of the atrium plan, at the end of the axis starting at the street door. It was the main reception room, open its full width to the atrium and in early times raised a low step above it. Vitruvius (6.3.5–6) said that it should be in proportion with the atrium. It is almost always as handsome a room as possible. The origin of the word is debated.

TEGULA MAMMATA. A flat, rectangular tile provided on one face with small breastlike protuberances near the four corners. These were used to line the walls of the hot rooms of Roman baths, the space between them and the wall serving as a flue through which the hot air and smoke could rise from the hypocaust system below, warming the walls and escaping through vents at the top.

TEMENOS. The court, or precinct, of a temple, usually carefully delimited and consecrated.

TESTUDINATE. Used to describe an atrium having no opening in its roof.

TETRAPYLON. Essentially a monumental gateway, a structure of four piers, usually in a square, surmounted by a superstructure that might take any one of several forms. It was usually either honorary or funerary and embellished with statuary.

THIRD STYLE. The style of Pompeian wall decoration characterized by large panels of flat color and delicate miniaturistic figures and ornaments in bright polychromy. The architectural framework is always excessively attenuated. The style belonged to the Julio-Claudian period and was short-lived.

THOLOS. A round, templelike building with a ring of columns and a conical or domed roof. There may, or may not, be a cella.

TOGA EXIGUA. The small toga of the republican period without sinus.

TOGATUS. A portrait statue of a man wearing the toga.

TORUS. A large molding of half-round profile. When decorated, it regularly carries a guilloche.

TRIGON. A ball game played by those who preferred only light exercise, probably a sort of three-cornered toss.

TYMPANUM. The triangular field of a pediment, sometimes filled with statuary or reliefs.

UMBO. A boss of any sort, especially the second short overfold of the imperial toga, pulled up from inside the sinus at the waist.

VENATIO. A hunt, especially the show of wild and exotic animals given in the amphitheatre as part of public games. After they were shown, the animals were hunted and killed by both professionals and amateurs.

VIRIDARIUM. The planted area in a peristyle or other interior garden, regularly primarily a green garden planted with ivy and hedges.

VOUSSOIR. A tapered block cut to the radius of a circle for use in constructing an arch or vault.

XENIUM. A present of choice food, the provisions for a first dinner, regularly offered a guest (hospes) on arrival in a foreign city; hence a type of still-life picture showing such food.

CONCORDANCE
Building Names and Excavation Codes

Concordance by Excavation Code Numbers

I ii 28, Casa della Grata Metallica

I iii 25, Casa dei Guerrieri

I iv 5/25, Casa del Citarista

I vi 2/4, Casa del Criptoportico

I vi 4, Casa degli Elefanti

I vi 7, Fullonica Stephani

I vi 11, Casa dei Calavi

I vi 15, Casa di Ceio

I vii 7, Casa del Sacerdote Amando

I vii 10–12, Casa dell'Efebo

I ix 5/6, Casa del Frutteto

I x 4, Casa del Menandro

I x 11, Casa degli Amanti

I xv 3, Casa della Nave Europa

II ii 2, Casa di Loreio Tiburtino

II iii 3, Casa della Venere in Conchiglia

II iv, Insula Iuliae Felicis (Praedia Iuliae Felicis)

II vi, Amphitheatre

II vii, Palestra Grande

III ii 1, Casa di Trebio Valente

III iii 6, Schola Iuventutis

III iv b (or s.n.), Casa di Ifigenia, Casa di Pinario Ceriale

V i 7, Casa del Torello di Bronzo

V i 18, Casa degli Epigrammi

V i 26, Casa di Cecilio Giocondo

V ii h (or s.n.), Casa del Cenacolo

V ii i (or s.n.), Casa delle Nozze d'Argento

V iv a (or 11), Casa di Marco Lucrezio Frontone

V v 3, Casa dei Gladiatori

VI i 10, Casa del Chirurgo

VI ii 4, Casa di Sallustio

VI vi 1, Casa di Pansa, Insula Arriana Polliana

VI vii 20–22, Casa dell'Argenteria

VI vii 23, Casa di Apollo

VI viii 3/5, Casa del Poeta Tragico

VI viii 21/22, Casa della Fontana Grande

VI viii 23/24, Casa della Fontana Piccola

VI ix 2, Casa di Meleagro

VI ix 3/5, Casa del Centauro

VI ix 6/7, Casa dei Dioscuri, Casa di Castore e Polluce

VI x 6, Casa di Pomponio

VI x 7, Casa dell'Ancora Nera

VI x 11, Casa del Naviglio

VI xi 9/10, Casa del Labirinto

VI xii 2/5, Casa del Fauno

VI xiii 2, Casa del Gruppo dei Vasi di Vetro

VI xiii 6, Casa del Forno di Ferro

VI xiii 19, Domus Sex. Pompeii Axiochi

VI xiv 20, Casa di Orfeo

VI xiv 21/22, Fullonica M. Vesonii Primi

VI xv 1/2, Casa dei Vettii

VI xvi 7/38, Casa degli Amorini Dorati

VI Ins. Occ. 23–26, Casa di Polibio

VII i 8/48/50, Thermae Stabianae

VII i 25/47, Casa di Sirico

VII i 40, Casa di Cesio Blando

VII ii 11, Officina Tinctoria Ubonii

VII ii 16, Casa di Gavio Rufo

VII ii 18, Casa di Vibio

VII ii 23, Casa di Amore Punito

VII ii 45, Casa dell'Orso

VII iii 29, Casa di Spurio Messore

VII iv 1, Aedes Fortunae Augustae

VII iv 3–11, Porticus Tulliana

VII iv 31/51, Casa dei Capitelli Colorati

VII iv 48, Casa della Caccia Antica

VII iv 56, Casa del Granduca di Toscana

VII iv 57, Casa dei Capitelli Figurati

VII iv 59, Casa della Parete Nera

VII v 2/8/24, Terme del Foro, Thermae Minores

VII vii 2/5, Casa di Trittolemo

VII vii 10, Casa di Romolo e Remo

VII vii 32, Aedes Apollinis

VII viii, Forum

VII viii 1, Aedes Iovis, Capitolium

VII ix 1, Aedificium Eumachiae

VII ix 2, Templum Genii Augusti, Templum Vespasiani

VII ix 3, Bibliotheca, Sacellum Larum Publicorum

VII ix 7/8, Macellum

VII ix 47, Casa delle Nozze di Ercole, Casa di Marte e Venere

VII xv 1/2, Casa del Marinaio

VII Ins. Occ. 15, Casa del Principe di Montenegro, Scavo del Principe di Montenegro

VII Ins. Occ. 16–19, Casa di Fabio Rufo

VIII i s.n., Aedes Veneris Pompeianae

VIII i 1, Basilica

VIII ii 1, Casa di Championnet

VIII ii 6/8/10, Curiae

VIII ii 6, Augusteum

VIII ii 8, Tabularium

VIII ii 10, Curia

VIII ii 17, Terme del Sarno

VIII ii 21–25, Palaestra/Baths

VIII ii 26, Casa del Cinghiale

VIII ii 39, Casa di Giuseppe II

VIII iii 1/32/33, "Comitium"

VIII iii 8, Casa del Cinghiale

VIII iv 15, Casa di Cornelio Rufo, Domus Cornelia

VIII v 2/5, Casa del Gallo

VIII v 24, Casa del Medico

VIII v 28, Casa della Calce

VIII vii 16, Ludus Gladiatorius

VIII vii 17–19, Theatrum Minus, Theatrum Tectum

VIII vii 20/21, Theatrum Maius

VIII vii 24, Casa del Marmorista

VIII vii 25, Templum Iovis Meilichii (Temple of Jupiter Meilichios)

VIII vii 28, Templum Isidis

VIII vii 29, Palaestra (Palestra Sannitica)

VIII vii 30, Forum Triangulare (Foro Triangolare)

IX i 20, Casa di Epidio Rufo

IX i 22, Casa di Epidio Sabino

IX iii 5/24, Casa di Marco Lucrezio

IX iv 5/18, Terme Centrali

IX v 18–21, Casa di Iasone

IX vii 20, Casa della Fortuna

IX viii 3/6, Casa del Centenario

IX ix b/c (or s.n.), Casa del Porco, Casa di Sulpicio Rufo

IX x 2/4, *See* IX (xiv) 2/4

IX xii 1/2, Casa del Primo Cenacolo

IX xii 3–5, Casa del Secondo Cenacolo

IX xiii 1–3, Casa di Giulio Polibio

IX (xiv) 2/4, Casa di Obellio Firmo

Environs of Pompeii

Agro Murecine, Portico dei Triclini

Boscoreale, Villa of Fannius Synistor

Boscotrecase, Villa di Agrippa Postumo

Sant'Abbondio, Templum Bacchi

Torre dell'Annunziata, Villa di Oplontis

Via dei Sepolcri 24/25, Villa di Diomede

Via dei Sepolcri s.n., Villa di Cicerone

Via dei Sepolcri s.n., Villa dei Misteri

Concordance by Familiar Building Names

Aedes Apollinis, VII vii 32

Aedes Fortunae Augustae, VII iv 1

Aedes Iovis, VII viii 1

Aedes Veneris Pompeianae, VIII i s.n.

Aedificium Eumachiae, VII ix 1

Amphitheatre, II vi

Augusteum, VIII ii 6

Basilica, VIII i 1

Bibliotheca, VII ix 3

Capitolium, VII viii 1

Casa degli Amanti, I x 11

Casa degli Amorini Dorati, VI xvi 7/38

Casa degli Elefanti, I vi 4

Casa degli Epigrammi, V i 18

Casa dei Calavi, I vi 11

Casa dei Capitelli Colorati, VII iv 31/51

Casa dei Capitelli Figurati, VII iv 57

Casa dei Dioscuri, VI ix 6/7

Casa dei Gladiatori, V v 3

Casa dei Guerrieri, I iii 25

Casa dei Vettii, VI xv 1/2

Casa del Cenacolo, V ii h (or s.n.)

Casa del Centauro, VI ix 3/5

Casa del Centenario, IX viii 3/6

Casa del Chirurgo, VI i 10

Casa del Cinghiale, VIII ii 26

Casa del Cinghiale, VIII iii 8

Casa del Citarista, I iv 5/25

Casa del Criptoportico, I vi 2/4

Casa del Fauno, VI xii 2/5

Casa del Forno di Ferro, VI xiii 6

Casa del Frutteto, I ix 5/6

Casa del Gallo, VIII v 2/5

Casa del Granduca di Toscana, VII iv 56

Casa del Gruppo dei Vasi di Vetro, VI xiii 2

Casa del Labirinto, VI xi 9/10

Casa del Marinaio, VII xv 1/2

Casa del Marmorista, VIII vii 24

Casa del Medico, VIII v 24

Casa del Menandro, I x 4

Casa del Naviglio, VI x 11

Casa del Poeta Tragico, VI viii 3/5

Casa del Porco, IX ix b/c (or s.n.)

Casa del Primo Cenacolo, IX xii 1/2

Casa del Principe di Montenegro, VII Ins. Occ. 15

Casa del Sacerdote Amando, I vii 7

Casa del Secondo Cenacolo, IX xii 3–5

Casa del Torello di Bronzo, V i 7

Casa dell'Ancora Nera, VI x 7

Casa dell'Argenteria, VI vii 20–22

Casa dell'Efebo, I vii 10–12

Casa dell'Orso, VII ii 45

Casa della Caccia Antica, VII iv 48

Casa della Calce, VIII v 28

Casa della Fontana Grande, VI viii 21/22

Casa della Fontana Piccola, VI viii 23/24

Casa della Fortuna, IX vii 20

Casa della Grata Metallica, I ii 28

Casa della Nave Europa, I xv 3

Casa della Parete Nera, VII iv 59

Casa della Venere in Conchiglia, II iii 3

Casa delle Nozze d'Argento, V ii i (or s.n.)

Casa delle Nozze di Ercole, VII ix 47

Casa di Amore Punito, VII ii 23

Casa di Apollo, VI vii 23

Casa di Castore e Polluce, VI ix 6/7

Casa di Cecilio Giocondo, V i 26

Casa di Ceio, I vi 15

Casa di Cesio Blando, VII i 40

Casa di Championnet, VIII ii 1

Casa di Cornelio Rufo, VIII iv 15

Casa di Epidio Rufo, IX i 20

Casa di Epidio Sabino, IX i 22

Casa di Fabio Rufo, VII Ins. Occ. 16–19

Casa di Gavio Rufo, VII ii 16

Casa di Giulio Polibio, IX xiii 1–3

Casa di Giuseppe II, VIII ii 39

Casa di Iasone, IX v 18–21

Casa di Ifigenia, III iv b (or s.n.)

Casa di Loreio Tiburtino, II ii 2

Casa di Marco Lucrezio, IX iii 5/24

Casa di Marco Lucrezio Frontone, V iv a (or 11)

Casa di Marte e Venere, VII ix 47
Casa di Meleagro, VI ix 2
Casa di Obellio Firmo, IX (xiv) 2/4, or IX x 2/4
Casa di Orfeo, VI xiv 20
Casa di Pansa, VI vi 1
Casa di Pinario Ceriale, III iv b (or s.n.)
Casa di Polibio, VI Ins. Occ. 23–26
Casa di Pomponio, VI x 6
Casa di Romolo e Remo, VII vii 10
Casa di Sallustio, VI ii 4
Casa di Sirico, VII i 25/47
Casa di Spurio Messore, VII iii 29
Casa di Sulpicio Rufo, IX ix b/c (or s.n.)
Casa di Trebio Valente, III ii 1
Casa di Trittolemo, VII vii 2/5
Casa di Vibio, VII ii 18
Castellum Aquarum, Porta del Vesuvio
"Comitium", VIII iii 1/32/33
Curia, VIII ii 10
Curiae, VIII ii 6/8/10
Domus Cornelia, VIII iv 15
Domus Sex. Pompeii Axiochi, VI xiii 19
Forum, VII viii
Forum Triangulare, VIII vii 30
Fullonica Stephani, I vi 7
Fullonica M. Vesonii Primi, VI xiv 21/22
Insula Arriana Polliana, VI vi
Insula Iuliae Felicis, II iv
Ludus Gladiatorius, VIII vii 16
Macellum, VII ix 7/8
Officina Tinctoria Ubonii, VII ii 11

Palaestra (Palestra Sannitica), VIII vii 29
Palaestra/Baths, VIII ii 21–25
Palestra Grande, II vii
Portico dei Triclini, Agro Murecine
Porticus Tulliana, VII iv 3–11
Praedia Iuliae Felicis, II iv
Sacellum Larum Publicorum, VII ix 3
Scavo del Principe di Montenegro, VII Ins. Occ. 15
Schola Iuventutis, III iii 6
Tabularium, VIII ii 8
Templum Bacchi, Sant'Abbondio
Templum Genii Augusti, VII ix 2
Templum Iovis Meilichii, VIII vii 25
Templum Isidis, VIII vii 28
Templum Vespasiani, VII ix 2
Terme Centrali, IX iv 5/18
Terme del Foro, VII v 2/8/24
Terme del Sarno, VIII ii 17
Theatrum Maius, VIII vii 20/21
Theatrum Minus, VIII vii 17–19
Theatrum Tectum, VIII vii 17–19
Thermae Minores, VII v 2/8/24
Thermae Stabianae, VII i 8/48/50
Villa dei Misteri, Via dei Sepolcri s.n.
Villa di Cicerone, Via dei Sepolcri s.n.
Villa di Diomede, Via dei Sepolcri 24/25
Villa Imperiale, Porta Marina
Villa di Agrippa Postumo, Boscotrecase
Villa of Fannius Synistor, Boscoreale
Villa di Oplontis, Torre dell'Annunziata

INDEX I

Architectural and Topographical Features for Pompeii and Its Immediate Environs

Note: Italic page numbers refer to illustrations. Buildings cited only by their excavation code numbers appear in the General Index under Buildings.

Sacraria, 284, 293, 296, 340. *See also* Lararia

San Marzano sul Sarno, 4

Sant'Abbondio. *See* Temples, Bacchus

San Valentino, 4

Scholae, 72, 116, 133, 191, 254–56, 365–66

Schola Iuventutis, 270, 290–92

Second storey apartments, 114, 115, 117, 118, 119, 123–24, 126, 127, 155, 159, 172, 206, 222, 225, 226–28, 231, 233, 235, 237, 238, 284, 292, 300, 307, 312, 313, 316, 317, 318–19, 323, 325, 326, 329–32, 333, 335, 337–38, 343–46, 350, 351, 358, 385–86, 395–96

Sepulcra. *For tombs of known individuals, see under the name of the person in the General Index*

Sewer system: surface drainage, 59–61; underground sewers, 61–62, 152–53

Signinum. *See* Opus signinum

Standpipes. *See* Water system, standpipes

Stuccowork, figurative, 94, 104, 148–49, 168, 248–49, 250, 283–84, 318, 342, 361, 362, 363, 364, 366

Suggestus. *See* Tribunals

Sundials, 72, 91, 316, 373

Swimming pools, 104, 211, 213–14, 286, 294–95

Tabularium, 270, 375

Telamons, 133, 149, 165

Temples: Apollo, 3, 5, 9, 38, 40–43, 53, 67, 69, 88–95, *90, 93,* 261, 371, 372, 374; Bacchus (Sant'Abbondio), 105–6; Doric

temple of Forum Triangulare, 3, 4 n. 5, 5, 67, 72–73, 369, 374; Fortuna Augusta, 14, 202–6, *203,* 255, 261, 372, 373; Genius Augusti, 14, 81, 191–94, *192,* 197, 254, 261, 266–67, 379; Hercules (?), 75; Isis, 73, 281–85, *281, 283;* Jupiter, 19, 26, 67, 81, 138–45, *139,* 261, 371, 378; Jupiter Meilichios, 9, 26, 80–82, 145, 379; Venus Fisica Pompeiana, 19, 40, 219–20, 277–81, *278,* 285, 373, 380

Templum Isidis. *See* Temples, Isis

Templum Vespasiani. *See* Temples, Genius Augusti

Terme Centrali, 19, 286–89, *287,* 375–76, 380

Terme del Foro, 25, 52, 147–53, *149,* 161 n. 4, 186

Terme del Sarno, 303–7, *304*

Terme Repubblicane, 52

Tetrapylon of the Holconii, 41 n. 5, 215–16

Theatre colonnade, 82–83

Theatrum Maius, 26, 75–80, *76,* 376

Theatrum Tectum, 12, 26, 80, 131–34, *132,* 372, 374, 375, 378, 379

Thermae Stabianae, 25, 52, 100–105, *101,* 152, 161 n. 4, 289, 366, 377, 378 n. 13

Tholoi, 70–72, 165, 179, 200–202, 251–54, 364–65, 367

Towers. *See* Fortifications, towers

Torre dell'Annunziata, Villa di Oplontis, 40, 180–83, *181,* 347, 355, 396

Tribunals, 78, 97, 133, 146–47, 193, 194, 268, 270, 272, 363

Vaulting, 47, 48, 55, 78, 97, 101–2, 114, 135–36, 140, 142, 144, 149–51, 156–57, 166, 168, 172, 187, 197, 204, 219, 223, 228, 232, 233, 237, 238, 239, 246, 247, 248, 249, 277, 282, 288, 300, 302, 306, 307, 321, 327, 330, 344, 351, 362, 363, 364, 365, 367, 372, 378, 397

Veneer: marble, 25–26, 131, 146, 150, 159, 176, 191, 193, 194–96, 201, 204, 206, 207, 208, 213, 231, 232, 247, 248, 266, 268, 270, 271–72, 274, 280, 288, 295, 299, 307–8, 310, 318, 320, 323, 324, 333, 334, 335, 336, 339, 351, 359, 363, 373, 374; tufa, 188, 246, 247, 252, 362

Villa dei Misteri, 26, 38, 43 n. 8, 171–76, *172,* 179, 180, 347, 354–59, *356,* 374, 378, 389, 396–400

Villa di Cicerone, 38, 242, 244–45

Villa di Diomede, 25, 38, 43 n. 8, 333, 347–55, *349,* 357, 359

Villa Imperiale (di Porta Marina), 47, 218–20, 231, 277

Water system, 19, 25, 51–63, *52;* aqueduct, 54–55, 74 n. 3, 100, 104, 379, and passim; standpipes, 55–57, 152, 208. *See also* Castellum aquae; Reservoirs

Wells, 51–53, 70–72, 98, 102, 111, 113, 150, 313, 326

INDEX II
General

Acerrae, 10

Aediles. *See* Municipal administration

Aesquillia Polla, 72, 365–66 (tomb)

Agrestinus Equitius Pulcher, N., 253 (tomb)

Agriculture in the neighborhood of Pompeii, 30, 32–34

Alba Fucens: Temple of Hercules, 75 n. 4; comitium, 145–46

Alleius Minius, M., 255 (tomb)

Alleius Nigidius Maius, Cn., 15, 16

Amplus Alumnus Tiburs, 340

Amulius Faventinus Tiburs, 340

Aphrodisias, tetrapylon, 368

Aquileia, mausoleum, 187, 252

Arellia Tertulla, 255–56 (tomb)

Arpinum, 247

Arrius Diomedes, M., 250 (tomb)

Artorius, M., Architectus, 79, 216

Athens: monument of Lysicrates, 187; monument of Philopappus, 257; Stoa of Atticus, 378 n. 13

Augustales, 15, 247–48, 249, 250, 258, 361, 367

Augustus, 7, 13–15

Ausonians. *See* Oscans at Pompeii

Baiae, 7, 29, 35

Belevi, mausoleum, 187

Benevento, Arch of Trajan, 209

Bisellium, 77, 248, 361

Buildings cited only by their excavation code numbers: I iii 23, 137; I vii 19, 229; I ix 8, 385; I xi 12, 13, and 14, 385; I xii 16, 385; I xiii 11, 385; I xiv 3, 384–85; I xiv 6/7, 384, 385; II viii 6, 385; V i 4/5, 21; VI i 19, 51–52; VI viii 7/8 (cookshop), 152; VI viii 9/10 (wineshop), 152; VI xi 12, 383–84; VI xi 13, 383–84; VI xv 9, 345–46; VII Ins. Occ. 13, 159; IX v 6, 344–45; IX xii 1–5, 21, 377, 395; IX xiii 5, 194

Bulla Regia, 234

Caecilius Iucundus, L., 15, 97, 258, 333, 367

Caesius, L., 186 (tomb)

Caligula, 15, 200

Calventius Quietus, C., 361–62 (tomb)

Campani, 17

Campi Phlegraei, 29

Capri, 30, 244

Capua, 3, 5, 6, 8, 30–31, 368, 374

Ceius Labeo, L., 249 (tomb)

Ceius Sarapio, L., 187 (tomb)

Cerrinnius Restitutus, M., 367 (tomb)

Cicero, M. Tullius, 13

Claudius (princeps), 15, 16, 200

Climate of Pompeii, 34

Colonia Cornelia Veneria Pompeianorum. *See* Colony, Roman, at Pompeii

Colony, Roman, at Pompeii, 11–13, 129–88

Communications of Pompeii by road, 4, 30–31, 34–35

Concordia Augusta, 14, 58, 194, 196–98

Cosa: basilica, 142; cisterns, 392; comitium, 145–46; houses, 382–83

Crassus Frugi, M., baths of, 305

Cumae, 3, 5, 8, 35, 374

Cuspius Cyrus, C., 364 (tomb), 380

Cuspius Salvius, C., 364 (tomb)

Decuriones. *See* Municipal administration

Delos: houses, 376 n. 11; Maison de la Colline, 122 n. 9; temple of Isis, 285

Drusus (son of Claudius), 16

Duoviri. *See* Municipal administration

Duoviri quinquennales. *See* Municipal administration

Earthquake of A.D. 62, 18–22 and passim

Eituns inscriptions, 11

Elea. *See* Velia

Ephesus, Library of Celsus, 275

Eruption of Vesuvius in A.D. 79, 22–27 and passim

Etruscans at Pompeii, 4

Eumachia, sacerdos publica, 14, 16 n. 17, 58, 191, 194, 256–57 (tomb), 371 n. 4

Fabius Secundus, C., 364 (tomb)

Festius Ampliatus, N., 362 (tomb)